July 22

THE TEACHING OF JESUS

PRINTED BY

MORRISON AND GIBB LIMITED,

FOR

T. & T. CLARK, EDINBURGH.

LONDON: SIMPKIN, MARSHALL, HAMILTON, KENT, AND CO. LIMITED.

NEW YORK: CHARLES SCRIBNER'S SONS.

TORONTO: THE WILLARD TRACT DEPOSITORY.

THE

TEACHING OF JESUS.

BY

HANS HINRICH WENDT, D.D.,

ORD. PROFESSOR OF THEOLOGY, HEIDELBERG.

Translated by

REV. JOHN WILSON, M.A.,

MONTREUX, SWITZERLAND.

IN TWO VOLUMES.

VOL. I.

EDINBURGH:

T. & T. CLARK, 38 GEORGE STREET.

1898.

12030

NOTE.—This translation, which has been carefully corrected by Professor Wendt, may be called to some extent a new and revised edition of the work. Some alterations have been made, and the interesting note, p. 70, Vol. II., is new.

AUTHOR'S PREFACE TO THE ENGLISH EDITION.

IT affords me great pleasure to see my work on the teaching of Jesus thus appearing in an English translation; and I have to tender my warmest thanks to the publishers and the translator for the care and pains they have bestowed upon this edition of my work. At the same time, I wish briefly to indicate, for the English reader, the interest which prompted me in the prosecution of my task, and which, I hope, this work may awaken, and in some measure satisfy, in the minds of others.

My interest in the historical treatment of the teaching of Jesus arises from the conviction that the historical Jesus Christ, in His annunciation, by word and deed, of the kingdom of God, was the perfect revelation of God for men; and from the desire that this conviction may, more than ever heretofore, have practical sway in the scientific study and the popular dissemination of Christian truth. The teaching of the Founder of the Christian religion must, with entire consistency, be employed as the standard for testing all Church doctrine and tradition; the highest authority must be accorded to it in regulating our own practical Christian life as well as Christian doctrine.

I am firmly persuaded that a resolute return to the teaching of Jesus Himself will be the most powerful and efficient means of promoting and strengthening the Christian religion in our time, and making it clear and intelligible.

The view that the historical teaching of Jesus Christ was the perfect revelation of God for men, has been always *theoretically* recognised in the Christian Church, and has had its place assigned it in dogmatic teaching in regard to the prophetic office of Christ. The necessary *practical* application of this view, however, has been cramped on the part of Catholicism by the theory of the infallible authority of Church teaching, and of Protestantism by the theory of the normative authority of the Holy Scriptures for Christian doctrine. Where the Holy Scriptures, as a whole, are regarded as expressing the immediate revelation of God, the sayings and discourses of Jesus are indeed viewed as part of the contents of Scripture; but there is no definite reason for emphasising their specific pre-eminence over the other contents of Scripture. Even Paul has in reality had a much greater influence in moulding the form of Christian doctrine in Protestantism than Jesus Himself. I will not here speak of the difficulties with which the old orthodox theory of the mechanical inspiration of Holy Scriptures is attended. Every one who really knows Scripture, will recognise that historical human factors were concerned in the production of its particular parts, and that there are gradations of religious value in the different parts. Such a one will, accordingly, judge that, in setting up Holy Scripture as the standard for Christian doctrine, a *distinction* must be made between the different parts or sides of the contents of Scripture.   But where shall we find the sure principle for making such a distinction ?   If, passing from particulars, we sought to distinguish between the essential and non-essential, the "spirit" and the "letter," an open door would be offered for subjective caprice.   Also, no ecclesiastical formula of doctrine, of greater or less extent, and of older or more modern date, could furnish us with a sure principle of distinction, since the question, whether such a *regula fidei* represented in a full and authentic way the contents of Christian doctrine, would require to be ever anew tested by an independent examination of Scripture. The one sure authorised principle of such a distinction is furnished by Jesus Christ Himself, if we recognise in His teaching concerning the kingdom of God the highest and perfect revelation of God.   The question, how much of the component elements of the Old Testament revelation has permanent value for the Christian Church, must ever be decided by the agreement or disagreement of the Old Testament ideas with the teaching of Jesus.   But even the judgment, that the ideas of Paul and James or any other New Testament writer are of standard authority for Christian doctrine, must, in the last instance, be justified by indicating their agreement with the teaching of Jesus. So far as it may be found opposed to this teaching, the authority of Paul must yield to the higher of Jesus Christ, whose servant and apostle he was.

By such a mode of view, the evangelical recognition of the unique significance of Holy Scripture will not be impaired, but rather, firmly established. For Scripture, both in the Old and New Testament, contains a collection of documents from which alone we learn to recognise as authentic, and historically to understand, the revelation given in Jesus Christ. But the Holy Scriptures are not directly and indiscriminately the highest standard for our Christian doctrine; but the real touchstone is the teaching of Jesus which is borne witness to in the Holy Scriptures. This norm really combines in itself the excellences which traditional evangelical dogmatics ascribe to the Scriptures, but which cannot be shown to belong to the whole contents of Scripture indiscriminately. The teaching of Jesus is a unity, definite and complete, giving incomparable instruction in all that pertains to our saving intercourse with God; it is of transparent simplicity even for an unlettered and childlike intelligence; and it attests its own Divine truth and value immediately to our consciousness without needing to be accredited by an external authority.

If we are in earnest, however, in taking the teaching of Jesus as the highest standard for our own Christianity and our own Christian preaching, we have the highest interest in learning it with historical accuracy. We must endeavour to attain a knowledge of its *authentic* contents, not according to later tradition, but according to the oldest and best sources. We must seek to know its *complete* contents, not merely in its main outlines, but also in its organic connection and its particular details. We must seek to know its *pure* form, not only as unmixed with the dogmatic and ethical teaching of later Christian times, but even with the apostolic system of doctrine. This is what the present work aims at giving : an authentic, complete, unmixed knowledge of the historical elements of the teaching of Jesus.

I beg the reader to approach my work with the inclination to believe that I have honestly striven to my utmost to present the teaching of Jesus just as it was historically formed, and that I have neither set aside nor intentionally obscured anything that might be inconvenient to myself, nor have added anything in order to favour my own opinions. I know well that one who has deeply settled convictions of Christian truth, and who holds a certain form of systematic treatment and defence of Christian doctrine as the right one, finds it difficult to keep himself quite free from prejudice in regard to the historical treatment of the mode of view of Jesus. I also may have fallen short in my task in many ways. But I have not failed at least in the honest attempt at a historical understanding of the subject.

But I must beg the reader on his side to place himself from the outset at the purely historical standpoint, and not merely seek, with traditional dogmatic formulas, to answer the problems laid down by the development of later ecclesiastical dogmas. This request I make expressly with reference to the section in which I give an account of the Messianic self-consciousness of Jesus. It might be shown with little trouble that many selected expressions of Jesus, especially in the Johannine discourses, if considered apart by themselves, can, according to the tenor of the words, be accommodated to the positions of dogmatic Christology. But if we are in earnest in taking the teaching of Jesus as our authoritative standard for dogmatics, we must not deal so lightly with the task. We must seek to understand the particular sayings of Jesus according to the connection in which they occur, and according to His whole mode of view. We must resolve, after having in this way attained the true sense in which Jesus estimated Himself as Messiah, to make this the touchstone of the traditional dogmatic Christology. Therefore we must set out with the assurance that, at all events, Jesus thought in the truest, worthiest and highest way of Himself, and that we cannot estimate Him too low if we adopt the mode of view which He Himself sought to impart to His disciples. I am convinced that whoever will consider in an attentive, unbiassed way the statements of Jesus concerning Himself as I have set them forth, and will ponder them in an unprejudiced way, will perceive that the estimate of the truly Divine character and unique significance for salvation of Jesus Christ which the Church strives to maintain, will not in this way be subverted, but the better and more deeply established.

Whoever will deal historically with the teaching of Jesus must first answer the preliminary question, if our Gospels are without distinction of equal value as sources for that teaching, or if a discrimination must be made among their component parts between what is of earlier and later tradition, of which only the former can be made the groundwork of the historical treatment. As I could, in answering this question, not simply appeal to the results of Gospel Criticism arrived at by others, I have given in the first part of my work an independent critical investigation of the sources of the Gospel narratives, in order to present to the reader the precise grounds of my use of the Gospels. I greatly regret that this independent critical part of my work has not been included in the English translation. Certainly for many readers the brief summary of the results of my critical examination, which I have given in the introductory section of this book, will be sufficient. But I would very urgently press upon theologians, who would arrive at and pronounce an independent judgment upon my treatment of the contents of the teaching of Jesus, not to fail to consider the first part of my German work. Only there will they find explained why, in regard to sayings of Jesus recorded in the parallel Gospel narratives, I have used the form of words or the connection of one account rather than another, and why I have left out of account certain sayings of Jesus recorded in the Gospels, and especially why I have used the fourth Gospel to the extent I have done. Much that may appear arbitrary would, I hope, appear well founded to one who knows my critical views in their connection.

May the loving enthusiasm for this incomparably great and beautiful subject, which has animated me throughout the whole course of my work, be experienced by the reader, and may this book help to contribute somewhat to further on English soil the understanding of the teaching of Jesus.

HANS WENDT.

HEIDELBERG, 1892.

TRANSLATOR'S PREFACE.

———◆———

THIS book, which a competent German scholar has pronounced "an important and permanent contribution to the
study of the life of Christ and to biblical theology," is the
second part of Dr. Wendt's work on the teaching of Jesus,
and, in the German original, it bears the more special title
of "The Contents of the Teaching of Jesus." The first
part, which is as yet untranslated, is occupied with an independent critical examination of the Gospel sources, a brief
summary of its results being given on pp. 20–28 of this
book.

Dr. Wendt's name is already known to English scholars ;
but, at this first appearance of his work in an English dress,
it has been deemed well to give an outline of the facts of his
life. Born in Hamburg in 1853, the son of an Evangelical
pastor, he was at first taught in the Gymnasium of his native
city. In 1872 he began his university course, studying first
at Leipzig, then at Göttingen and Tübingen. At Tübingen
he took his degree of Doctor of Philosophy in 1875. There-
after, returning to Göttingen, he took a further course under
the celebrated professors, Lotze in philosophy and Ritschl
in theology, and there in 1877 attained the grade of Licentiate
in Theology. After exercising the office of "privat-docent"
for New Testament exegesis, he was appointed professor
extraordinarius in 1881. Two years afterwards he was called
as ordinary professor to the Northern University of Kiel.
In November of that year he received the degree of Doctor
of Theology *honoris causâ* from the University of Göttingen.
After a sojourn of two years at Kiel, he accepted, in the
autumn of 1885, a call to Heidelberg as Professor of System-

atic Theology, and at that beautiful university town on the Neckar he at present exercises his functions, lecturing partly in theology and partly in New Testament exegesis.

Still a comparatively young man, Professor Wendt is well known to the German theological world by his published writings, of which the most important is *The Teaching of Jesus*, of which the first part was published in 1886 and the second in 1890. From the perennial interest of the subject, the fundamental character of its design, and the freshness of its mode of treatment, which even a glance over the table of contents will suffice to indicate, this work is fitted to command the attention of British scholars. Appearing at a moment when the controversy in regard to the results of Biblical Criticism has reached an acute stage with us, a few remarks on the general bearing of this work may not be out of place.

The historical method followed by the author is one which will be universally admitted as being not only warranted, but indispensable, in the case of the secular historian. No competent modern historian can dispense with the critical examination of facts and documents, unless his work is to take rank as mere legend. Christianity, as a religion of facts and documents, demands and welcomes legitimate research ; and in this sense Biblical Criticism is not a wayward phase of modern thought, but a weighty task which has been, in a peculiar sense, committed to our age. Thus far intelligent Christians are agreed, however doubtful some may be as to many of the results put forth in the name of criticism. Certainly the time has not yet come for claiming finality for the results of criticism, or for taking a final consensus of critics. For example, Dr. Wendt's original hypothesis of a "third main source" underlying the Gospel of John, which may prove an important *point de depart* in the critical study of the fourth Gospel, shows that the last word has not been said on that important department of New Testament criticism. The hopefulness of criticism lies, not so much in individual results, as in the progressive unity of a process of which the present generation will not see the termination—a process wherein the results of one inquirer are being checked and modified by those of another, and wherein even individual mistakes contribute in the end to the clearer knowledge of details.

It will be seen that, throughout the construction of the present work, our author stands on the scaffolding of his earlier work, in which he has devoted patient and independent study to the examination of the Gospel sources. Here we have, not a process of destructive criticism, but a process of positive reconstruction on the basis of criticism. Many are inclined to ask, in regard to a criticism which seems only to achieve greater confusion and unsettlement of the grounds of Christian faith, "What, then, shall we have left after this devastating flood has passed?" In the present work we have Dr. Wendt's answer to that question, so far as the teaching of Jesus is concerned. Here, he might say, is so much *terra firma*, more or less perfectly reclaimed by historical research from the chaos into which the *Zeitgeist* of modern criticism had thrown the whole territory. Briefly, it may be said that, so far as criticism, apart from exegesis, is concerned, all fundamental Christian doctrine remains ; for though some will take exception to the author's soteriology as being too subjective, in accordance with the theology of Ritschl, this too arises, not from the critical elimination of essential elements of the Gospel reports, but mainly from the fact that it is the teaching of Jesus, not also that of Paul, that is under discussion. In connection with this, the reader will not fail to bestow attention upon the highly-suggestive preface which the author has written for this translation.

It is almost inevitable, in applying the method of historical criticism to this great subject, that many readers should at first be unpleasantly impressed with a certain naturalistic tone and tendency. The Christian scientific historian proceeds on the presupposition that there is a higher and supernatural explanation of the facts ; but his task would be impossible and unwarranted, if God, in bringing His supernatural ends to pass, had not largely carried them onwards through the centuries by long processes of natural sequence. Instead of usually revealing Himself in historically isolated ways which admit of no intelligible explanation, He has generally worked in ways which have a psychological and historical intelligibility. We may instance the growth of the Messianic idea in relation to the national experiences of Israel. When, however we come into the domain of Gospel history, however frankly we admit the idea of the *kenosis*, we are yet face to face with a Divine mystery which appeared phenomenally in the sphere of humanity, and is, no doubt, to a large extent humanly intelligible and conformable to the laws of nature and human life. Yet it is an important question, how far we can take as a safe guide the scientific maxim that, in the investigation of what belongs to a different age and order of things, only those causes must be taken into account of which we have present experience. The scientific investigator, in the sphere alike of geology and history, must sometimes question if certain phenomena are not unique and unaccountable on the ground of modern experience. Jesus Christ was such a historical phenomenon—unique as to His blissful unbroken fellowship with His Father, in the character of His consciousness of Sonship, in the clearness of His intuition and firmness of tread in a high region where others only grope. In regard to those suggestive portions of his work which treat of the development of religious ideas in the mind of Jesus, Dr. Wendt will be the first to admit their necessary incompleteness. He must carry the torch of historical inquiry as far as the historical method will permit him to go; but there is a region beyond, into which historical science cannot pass, and where historical processes fail.

The author has not treated the branches of the teaching of Jesus merely in separate detail, but in their organic connection; and his full, sympathetic treatment of the ethical side of his subject—take, for example, the great theme of universal love as taught by Christ—proves that the historical method, though it may not expressly, can yet really and powerfully, conduce to the setting forth of the practical value of the subject. Not the least important and interesting department of the work will be found to be, the continuous comparative examination of the teaching of the fourth Gospel along with that of the synoptical Gospels, from which the conclusion is drawn that the substance of the former was given by "a disciple of Jesus who was more deeply penetrated than the rest with the original spirit and the inward form of the teaching of his Master."

Something may yet remain for discussion in regard to the amount of significance to be accorded to other departments of the work of Christ as distinguished from the teaching ; but the translator gladly concurs with the author in the hope that, also among British readers, the publication of the work may contribute towards a better knowledge of this great theme, and the furtherance of New Testament scholarship generally.

The present translation has had the benefit of Professor Wendt's careful revision.

The numerous references in the footnotes to *Lehre Jesu*, vol. i., will be understood as applying to the first and as yet untranslated part of the work

J. W.

Montreux. 1892.

CONTENTS.

———◆———

INTRODUCTION.

THE PROBLEM.

FIRST SECTION.

THE HISTORICAL FOUNDATION OF THE TEACHING OF JESUS.

SECOND SECTION.

EXTERNAL ASPECTS OF THE TEACHING OF JESUS.

THIRD SECTION.

ANNOUNCEMENT OF THE KINGDOM OF GOD IN GENERAL.

INTRODUCTION.

———◆———

THE PROBLEM.

1. THE task of giving an historical account of the teaching of Jesus requires a special word of explanation. From the unique significance in regard to revelation which the Christian Church recognises in the person of Jesus Christ, His teaching has been made a subject of special systematic treatment as a part of Christian theology. But, from that systematic method, our purely historical mode of treatment must be distinguished. No doubt the systematic method can be prosecuted with a full view to keeping in as strict conformity as possible to the historical signification of His teaching; and thereby the systematised doctrine will have its character all the more established as authentic Christian truth. But, at the same time, the systematic theologian must keep expressly in view the practical and scientific value of Christian doctrine for the present age. Hence arises for him the special task of conceiving, under the intellectual forms and ideas of the present, that whole religious view of things which was historically introduced by Jesus, and of showing its relation to the scientific ideas and practical circumstances of the time. He

must also develop, in symmetrical completeness, its presuppositions and consequences; and, finally, he must strive to present the evidence of the truth of this systematised teaching as a whole.

On the other hand, our historical method of treating the subject aims at presenting the teaching of Jesus in the form given to it by Himself during His lifetime. It has only to convey, in a reliable and orderly way, the material which must form the groundwork of the systematic treatment; and it will conserve its peculiar value all the more certainly, just by confining itself strictly to its historical purpose, and by allowing no consideration of its present value for Christian instruction to modify the historical exposition. No doubt, even in our historical method, the teaching of Jesus must be elucidated by the help of ideas and modes of view current at present. For that range of ideas which originated at an epoch long bygone, and under conditions so very different from those of our day, requires to be made intelligible to us moderns; and this cannot be done merely by conveying the words. But any intentional explication of our subject, by means of contemporary theological and scientific ideas and modes of view, beyond what is needed for the purpose of intelligibility, falls outside the scope of our historical method. Likewise we must forego any attempt to prove the truth and perennial value of the teaching either as a whole or in detail. We shall aim at making the teaching intelligible through just such explication by means of other ideas and modes of view, along with such application to practical circumstances, and such assertion and vindication of its

truth, as Jesus Himself used and intended. And I
shall seek to estimate its historical significance only in
relation to that religious teaching which lies historically nearest it, I mean the Old Testament Jewish
doctrine.

But though we thus emphatically distinguish our
purely historical treatment of the teaching of Jesus
from the systematic method, this does not prevent
our seeking to set forth the historical contents of that
teaching in systematic order as an organic unity.
Our task is not to arrange the sayings of Jesus in
strict chronological sequence. Apart from the fact
that our sources do not furnish the means for it, such
a chronological order does not correspond to the idea
of our historical method. We have rather to aim at
constructing, from the recorded words and acts of
Jesus, the general religious conception which He held,
which underlay all His self-manifestations in word
and deed, and which, in the course of His instructions, He sought to impart to His disciples. Since
there has come down to us from His own lips no
systematic exposition, not even a brief one, of His
general religious view, our proposed construction of
that view, like the attempt of the historian to com-
pose, out of the separate facts reported in his sources,
a complete picture of pragmatical development, must
be regarded as a hypothesis. But it is necessary to
advance such a hypothesis, since a knowledge of the
character of the whole helps us to know the original
significance of the particular parts. We may certainly regard this hypothesis (as to the central conceptions underlying the teaching of Jesus) as being

historically confirmed, if it not only supplies a framework in which all the various sayings of Jesus find
appropriate setting, but also if it exhibits those particular utterances as members of a uniform organic
structure, such that even the degree of prominence,
greater in some cases and in others less, which Jesus
has given to particular parts of His teaching, is
accounted for by their position as members of that
organic whole. Also the methodical progress which
Jesus has observed in the impartation of His teaching
to the common people, as well as to His immediate
followers, must be seen to be founded on the essential
relation of the different parts of His teaching to one
another. Moreover, by setting up this ideal for our
historical examination of the subject, we do not pre-
judge the question as to whether the teaching of
Jesus does not comprise some heterogeneous and
mutually contradictory elements, and if there is not an
internal development and transformation of His teaching advancing step by step with its external progress.
In a historical exposition, such shades of difference, if
they exist, must, of course, be clearly exhibited ; for
the organic unity of the teaching must not be artistic-
ally presented in greater completeness than we find
historically warranted by our sources.

2. In the first part of the work, I have taken in
hand a critical examination of the evangelical records
which form our main sources, and on the results of
that inquiry our use of the Gospels must be
founded. I here give a very brief summary of those
results.

Our first chief source is the Gospel of Mark.

Certain of its features indicate that the composition of this Gospel has been based on some series of earlier narratives, which were not originally constructed in strict chronological sequence, and which, even by Mark, have been put together in pretty loose connection. Such a series of older narratives we find in the account of the replies of Jesus to objections and questions, given in the two groups, Mark ii. 1–iii. 6 and xii. 13–37. These plainly present the appearance of originally independent fragments amid the surrounding context, even as, from the way in which xii. 13 fits in with iii. 6, they betray their original relationship. Just in so far as we are able to recognise this groundwork of an older series of narratives in Mark, can we regard the accounts given in that Gospel as valuable apostolic tradition.[1] Moreover, our first and third Gospels have both drawn from that of Mark. Therefore, wherever we find passages in Matthew and Luke, or in one of these two, which are parallel to the accounts given by Mark, we must always, in our historical examination, regard the narrative in Mark as the original one.

We have a second main source in the Logia of Matthew, that is, the apostolic collection of sayings and acts of Jesus, which, along with the narratives in Mark, has furnished material for both the first and third Gospels. The composer of our third Gospel was no doubt acquainted with the Gospel of Matthew, in which the compiler had endeavoured to insert those Logia in the historical framework of the Gospel of Mark. But the former had manifestly an independent know-

[1] Cf. *Lehre Jesu*, i. p. 9 ff.

ledge of the Logia of Matthew ; and, on principles of his own, sought, like the first evangelist, to work them into the setting of the Mark narratives. Thus the original connection and word-tenor of those apostolic collections of the sayings of Jesus have in part, if not wholly, remained in better preservation in our Gospel of Luke than in that of Matthew. These parallel constructions of the Logia-sources in our first and third Gospels hold out the possibility, the prosecution of which must be regarded as one of the most attractive and important tasks of Biblical Criticism, of restoring, with approximate certainty, to their original condition and connection, the fragments which furnish the material of both those Gospels. In my more extended examination of those sources, given in the first part of this work, I have started with the endeavour to reconstruct the Logia.[1]

Finally, a third main source is furnished in the groundwork of the sayings of Jesus in the fourth Gospel. I have sought to show that this Gospel by no means bears such a stamp of internal unity as is generally supposed. The form of this Gospel presents undeniable features, remarkable alike in their presence and in their mutual connection, which constrain us to

---

[1] Cf. *L. J.* i. p. 50 ff. Whenever it appears to me of importance for the right understanding of a passage from the Logia, that it should be taken according to the wording and connection which, in my reconstruction on the basis of a comparative examination of the text of Matthew and Luke, I have sought to indicate as the original ones, I shall give express references in footnotes to the paragraph and subsection of my harmony of the Logia-fragments in the first volume. These I shall omit in cases of less importance. Where Matthew and Luke present parallel quotations from the Logia, if those parallels are not mutually supplementary, I will quote only one, and, of course, that one which appears best to represent the form of words and connection of the original.

believe that its author, both in the prologue and the longer discourses recorded by him, has made use of a written source. This source must have come from the same hand as the First Epistle of John. For, *firstly*, it is to be observed that, in very many cases, the members of a uniform series of thoughts or discourses are severed from each other by longer or shorter parentheses. This, indeed, occurs in a way so disturbing to the connection and the mutual external relation of the members, that it cannot have formed part of the original design, but must be the work of a later editor. The following, among other examples, may be given, viz. the interpolation of John i. 15 interrupting the connection of vers. 14 and 16; the interpolation of xiii. 18 f. interrupting the connection of xiii. 12–17 and xiii. 20; the separation of the portion vii. 15–24 from its connection with chap. v.; of the portion viii. 12 ff. from its connection with the words vii. 26 f., 33 f., 37 f.; of the portion xii. 44 ff. from its connection with xii. 35 and 36a.[1]

It is to be observed, *secondly*, that there is a strikingly different cast of ideas manifest in the discourses of the fourth Gospel from that of their historical framework. This difference comes out emphatically, for example, in the fact that the historical parts lay stress upon the miraculous "signs" wrought by Jesus, and base the proof of His Messiahship on them; whilst in the discourses the appeal of Jesus to His "signs" is wholly absent, and only His "works," or His "works and words," or His words alone, are spoken of as valid proofs of His Messiahship (cf. v. 36, vi. 63, 68 f., viii.

[1] Cf. *L. J.* i. p. 219 ff.

26, x. 25, 32, 37 f., xii. 47 ff., xiv. 10 f., xv. 24, xvii. 8.[1] This different cast of thought is further shown in a characteristic way in the explanatory remarks appended to particular sayings of Jesus. Those remarks, judging from the tenor and connection of the words, are manifestly not in harmony with the original sense of these sayings; whilst they clearly show affinity with the mode of view prevailing in the historical parts of the (fourth) Gospel (cf. ii. 19 and 21, vii. 37–39, xii. 32 f., xvii. 12, and xviii. 8 f.[2]). The accounts given in the historical passages in regard to the ministry of the Baptist, as well as of Jesus Himself, disagree in several respects with what is recorded in our other oldest sources, viz. the Logia of Matthew and the Gospel of Mark. At the same time, there are certain clear traces indicating that the author of the fourth Gospel already knew our three synoptical Gospels.[3] Yet the larger discourses in the fourth Gospel exhibit no trace of literary dependence on the other Gospels known to us; albeit, in spite of formal differences, there exist, as will specially be shown in this volume, a wonderful agreement between the thoughts expressed in these Johannine sayings of Jesus and the cast of thought evident in the Logia of Matthew and the Gospel of Mark.

One remarkable fact about the discourses of the fourth Gospel is the clear evidence they show of having originally related specially to the closing period of the public ministry of Jesus, although now, through the elaboration of the evangelist, it appears

---

[1] Cf. *L. J.* i. p. 238 ff.   [2] Cf. *L. J.* i. p. 251 ff.
[3] Cf. *L. J.* i. pp. 311 ff. and 323 ff.

to belong to the whole of His public life. Thus we find that the incident of the cleansing of the temple occupies a place near the beginning of the fourth Gospel (ii. 13 ff.); whilst, according to Mark xi. 15 ff., it took place during the last visit of Jesus to Jerusalem. Thus, too, several expressions of Jesus in the earlier Johannine discourses refer to His ministry as virtually closed, and to His departure as imminent (iii. 11, 19, iv. 32-38, vii. 33 f., viii. 14, 21). Finally, we find in the same discourses a clear avowal of His Messianic claim, which, according to the other sources, Jesus did not openly make at the commencement of His ministry, but only at its close.[1]

If our opinion, that the author of the Gospel of John has drawn from a valuable older source, has a good exegetical foundation, there arises the task of collecting and establishing the traces of those Johannine Logia, so far as they are now ascertainable; just as we have to try to reconstruct, as far as possible, the Logia of Matthew out of the first and third Gospels. But, in the former case, that process cannot be carried out in precise detail. It is more difficult and uncertain than the reconstruction of the Logia of Matthew; for, instead of two parallel ones which can be compared together, we possess only a single Gospel account based on these Johannine Logia. But just as, in the case of the second part of the Acts of the Apostles, we can conclude with certainty that an earlier written source has been used, which, on account of various characteristic marks, can be clearly separated into several large portions, whilst, in relation to the intervening

[1] Cf. *L. J.* i. p. 284 f.

parts, we cannot strictly define the points of junction, though it is clearly apparent that such an older source has been used ; so, in regard to many large portions of the discourses in the fourth Gospel, we can indicate with certainty, though as to others only with probability, that the Johannine Logia have been used. It would be quite illogical to conclude that this hypothesis of the Johannine Logia is entirely uncertain, because its establishment is involved in uncertainty in many particular passages; for, in many others, it can be shown to be necessary and valid.[1]

As a practical result of our critical examination of the fourth Gospel, however, we cannot, in our account of the teaching of Jesus, which we seek to found upon the original sources, simply mix up the material derived from the fragments of the Johannine discourses with that obtained from the Gospel of Mark and the Logia of Matthew. A twofold consideration prevents this. In the *first* place, the form, at all events, is essentially different in the fourth Gospel from that indicated by our other sources. There is no doubt it does not exactly correspond to the mode of speech actually used by Jesus, but is rather stamped with the impress of the thought and expression of the writer. In spite, however, of this generally recognised fact, there is no reason to doubt that the substance and spirit of what Jesus actually said are essentially preserved. Yet, in any case, a simple co-ordinate use of the Johannine discourses, along with those of the synoptical Gospels, is rendered difficult.

[1] Cf. my endeavour to separate the portions derived from the sources, *L. J.* i. p. 258 ff.

In the *second* place, if we overlook their peculiar form, and interpret them by themselves, and not according to the signification and elucidation given by the evangelist, the Johannine discourses furnish a subject-matter quite in harmony with the contents of Jesus' teaching as attested by the other sources. This fact certainly affords a weighty and decisive argument for our contention that these Johannine fragments contain valuable apostolic tradition. This argument would fall to the ground, however, if, in the prosecution of our task, we were simply putting the Johannine discourses on the same level with the synoptical accounts. We would thus incur the risk of taking expressions in a different sense from that warranted by the connection and by the general mode of view of the particular source whence they were derived, and, in an unjustifiable way, interpreting by each other expressions derived from different sources. And even if we could in this way attain a general idea of Jesus' teaching which would be uniform and consistent, the question would still remain, if this general idea were not a factitious one, corresponding in its character neither to the synoptical sources nor those of the Johannine accounts. Therefore it is necessary that we consider the subject-matter of the Johannine discourses separately, in order rightly to compare it with the subject-matter yielded by the other sources. We have first of all to arrange and complete the general picture of the teaching of Jesus on the basis of the Gospel of Mark and the Logia of Matthew. But, in reference to all the main groups composing this picture, we must ask the question of how the contents of the

Johannine discourses are related to them? Such a comparison can be made without difficulty or over-subtlety. It is rendered possible by the fact that the Johannine discourses and those of the synoptical Gospels alike refer to the general subject of the realisation, through Jesus as the Messiah, of the promised salvation of the latter days. In both cases alike, the details of the teaching are occupied with similar main problems. In this comparison we must certainly not leave out of view the question, if the thoughts in those Johannine discourses which, apart from their peculiar stamp, are analogous to the leading features of the synoptical representation, do not bear another interpretation when viewed in relation to the whole system of thought in John? Else how comes it that the general view of the teaching of Jesus presented in the Johannine discourses exhibits a character so unlike the general view presented by the synoptical sources?

3. But the sources for our knowledge of the actual teaching of Jesus do not lie merely in the Gospel accounts, but also in the literature of the apostolic age, especially in the Epistles of Paul. We have here to consider, not merely the various citations of sayings of Jesus outside of the Gospels,[1] but rather the fact that the whole apostolic doctrine gives indirect testimony to the teaching of Jesus. The doctrine of the apostles, even that of Paul, though he did not become a disciple in the lifetime of Jesus, was a product of the mighty influence of the ministry of Jesus. Other

---

[1] Cf. the brief summary, i. p. 343 ff.; and A. Resch, "*Agrapha*," 1889, in Gebhardt and Harnack's *Texte und Untersuchungen*, v. 4.

factors have manifestly conspired to shape this product, and even to alter it, in the case both of Paul and
the early apostles.   Yet the apostles themselves, Paul
included, had certainly no purpose of altering, but only
of communicating, the teaching of Jesus.   Their proclamation of the Messiahship of Jesus was, in their
consciousness, no new doctrine, but only a continuation
and carrying out of the Messianic claim of Jesus Himself.   Therefore, even had no direct accounts about
Jesus been handed down to us, we should still possess,
in the apostolic literature, a perfectly valid testimony
to the historical existence and epoch-making significance of Jesus as a teacher.   It would also be
thoroughly justifiable if, in seeking the deepest basis
for a critical examination of the historical trustworthi-
ness of the Gospel accounts, we took for that purpose
the Pauline Epistles, as being the oldest and most
reliable parts of the apostolic literature.   For from
those Epistles alone could be determined what was,
essentially and in substance, the general views and
teaching of Jesus ; and by the result we could test
the contents of the Gospel accounts.   Yet it would
not be warrantable to apply this method, valid as it
is in itself, where the object is to give a comprehensive
account of the teaching of Jesus on the basis of a
critical examination of the original sources.   For, in
comparison with the rich detailed information as to
the teaching of Jesus yielded by the Gospel accounts
based on the original sources, the knowledge indirectly
derivable from the Pauline Epistles is much too general
in character to form a suitable foundation for the
arrangement and exposition of the whole material

handed down through the Gospels. It is only, therefore, in the way of regarding the apostolic doctrine as
the historical result of the teaching of Jesus, and as
bearing witness to the mighty influence of that teaching, that we can make use of those indirect sources
for the purposes of this work.

4. But we have to consider the connection of the
teaching of Jesus, not with the doctrine of the apostles
only, but also with the religious ideas of the Jewish
people among whom He grew up and exercised His
ministry. The historical character of our task requires
this, on the one hand, in so far as Jesus directed His
teaching in opposition to the ideas of the Jews; and,
on the other, in so far as He founded upon the views
of His countrymen, in expressly accepting some of
their ideas and taking others for granted. It would
tally neither with our historical method nor with the
view of Jesus Himself, did we seek to estimate His
teaching merely in the light of a new and independent
phenomenon, or, judging from the religious standpoint, merely as a new revelation of God, overlooking,
or but slightly taking account of, the degree in which
He adopted the Jewish ideas. It quite accords with
the peculiar greatness of Jesus, to find that He did not
aim at presenting His teaching in as original a form
as possible. He rather placed Himself, with conscious
purpose, in the direct line of the historical development of His people. He set the revelation, of which
He was the conscious medium, in a relation, not of
opposition, but of continuation, to that earlier revelation of which the Jews boasted themselves the
custodians. It is quite true that Jesus, in opposition

to the debasement of the Old Testament religion on the part of His contemporaries, went back to the more original form of the Old Testament religion in the prophetic period. It would be more exact, however, to say that He based His teaching on the religious ideas of the prophetic period, in so far as they had become parts of the religious tradition recognised by the Jews of His time. Moreover, we cannot regard His teaching as being only a continuation of the prophetic type of the Old Testament religion, as expressly opposed to the form in which later Judaism professed that religion. In regard, for example, to such a weighty point of doctrine as the resurrection and eternal life of individual saints, Jesus has decidedly taken part with the teaching of later Judaism as it had been developed in opposition to that of the older prophets.

Rightly to understand the teaching of Jesus in its historical bearings, and to gain a clear idea of its peculiarly new elements, and of the advance it has made beyond the positions of the Old Testament religion, we must regard the religious ideas of contemporary Judaism as its foundation. But, in relation to our special task, to give a full account of those contemporary Jewish ideas would carry us too far afield. Indeed, considering the excellent treatises we possess on this subject,[1] to give such an account is unnecessary. All that is needed for our purpose is to give a brief summary of the main characteristics

---

[1] Cf. especially : E. Schürer, *Geschichte des jüdischen Volkes im Zeitalter Jesu*, Leipzig 1886, ii. § 25 ff. p. 248 ff. Transl. (Clark, Edinburgh), Div. II. vol. i. p. 306 ff.

of the religious ideas of the Jews in the time of Jesus. Specially we shall note those of them which explain for us the development of Jesus on the basis of Judaism, and His acceptance of certain of its essential elements ; and, on the other hand, His conscious energetic opposition to other of its ideas and tendencies. Farther on we shall ever and anon glance, in course of our study of the teaching of Jesus, at its relation to the contemporary Jewish modes of thought.

FIRST SECTION.

THE HISTORICAL FOUNDATION OF THE TEACHING OF JESUS.

———+———

CHAP. I. RELIGIOUS CONCEPTIONS OF THE JEWS IN THE TIME OF JESUS.

1. IF we sought to characterise the religious life of the Jews in the time of Jesus, we should adduce, as its most general and salient feature, the uncompromising zeal with which they clung to the ancient religion of Israel, as delivered to their forefathers by Divine revelation. Almost everything in Judaism that appears great and significant, or conducive to the establishment and foundation of the Christian religion; but, at the same time, everything in it that strikes us as repellent and paltry, or that led to its bitter opposition to, and rejection of Christianity, had its root in their tenacious zeal for the maintenance of the old religion. It is truly magnificent, the way in which the Jewish people, during those centuries of domination by that Hellenism which threatened to level all national and religious differences, were able to preserve their ancestral religion. Although it lost political independence, and was subjected to

all possible influences from the Hellenistic culture; and although there dwelt within itself a tendency towards a world-wide extension, as well as a peculiar adaptability to foreign circumstances; yet nevertheless Judaism did not surrender its ancestral religious heritage by one hair - breadth. Even the Roman power had to make concessions in order not to awaken or hurt the religious susceptibilities of the Jews. Only by paying incessant attention to, and setting store by, little points; only by constant strife against opposition of all kinds, and by ever-recurring acts of self-renunciation, was the maintenance of their ancient religion possible to the Jews. Even when the people in Palestine were externally at peace with Rome, and when the Jews of the Dispersion enjoyed legal permission and protection for their religion, a continual struggle went on in order to maintain in its purity, in difficult circumstances, the practice of the Jewish religion. We must have regard to this in order to estimate aright the power arising from their proud consciousness of truth and of spiritual superiority, which was in those times manifested in their religious self-preservation; and to attain a historical understanding of the harsh, repellent features which the religious life of Judaism at that period shows.

This energetic and stubborn adherence of the Jews to their ancient religion had its clearest expression in the *formation and continuous recognition of the Canon of the Old Testament*. What was handed down out of their sacred past, or, at least, what bore the credit of belonging to the old tradition, was invested with the authority of Holy Scripture, resting purely on Divine revelation, and raised above all association and comparison with ordinary human literature. This collection of sacred writings—"the Scriptures" in a special sense—formed the centre of all their religious as well as their intellectual interests in general. To these all their studies had reference, and all the labours of their scholars, "the scribes," whether in the way of explanation or transmission; upon these all school instruction was built, and all edification in the synagogues; and on these were based all the inquiries of the devout, who were assured that in them they possessed the directions as to attaining everlasting life (cf. John v. 39).

We are now too much inclined to regard this ascription of fixedness and sacredness to the Old Testament Canon merely as a sign of torpor in the free religious life of Judaism, and of the cramping of its proper productive power; we are inclined to lay stress only upon the dead letter-worship that followed as the consequence of their idea of the supernatural origin and peculiarly sacred character of those older writings. But if some truth undoubtedly lies in this mode of view, it yet touches only one side of the matter. To be just, we must realise the priceless importance of the preservation, the laboriously faithful transmission of, and the high estimate set, at least theoretically, upon the collective contents of that religious literature handed down from Israel's past; and we must ask if it were at all possible, under the circumstances of those times, to preserve that treasure inviolate except in the rigid form of canonisation.   Certainly, if we think of the difference of spirit in later Judaism from the spirit which possessed the prophets, we will be sensible of the high importance of the fact, that the products of that prophetic period were guarded as far as possible, not, indeed, from an obscuration of their meaning, but from a tampering with their letter, which is the abiding vehicle of the original meaning.   The question is not merely what the scribes specially sought and prized in the Old Testament, or what meaning they imported into or added to it with their comments and traditions; but we have also to consider what moral and religious truth, what treasures of edification, consolation, and admonition were really locked up in the Old Testament, and what could be derived from it by every one who, with pious zeal, sought to be imbued with an understanding of the Holy Scriptures. Certainly in regard to the origin of Christianity, we have every reason to consider the formation of the Old Testament Canon as the most important historical fact of post-exilian Judaism.   For in the Old Testament lay the chief sources whence Jesus derived His own religious education, and the chief means whereby He could establish the Divine right of His teaching in the view of His Jewish contemporaries.   The sacredness of the Old Testament Canon in the estimation of the Jews rendered it possible, historically speaking, for the teaching of Jesus, and the early Christian society, to develop themselves on the foundation of Judaism.

No doubt, after having laid due stress upon this point, we must consider the reverse side of this exaltation of the traditional writings of the earlier period. By this recognition of the Canon, the current of the religious life in theory was set in a definite direction and kept within narrow limits. The contents of the Holy Scriptures were held as true and authoritative throughout. They had to be explained and observed with the utmost strictness. Any divergence from the text was absolutely prohibited. In point of fact, however, the Canon of the Old included very heterogeneous elements, alike of religious idea and precept and of historical information, which could not simultaneously be held as true and authoritative. In reality, also, the activity of the religious life of the Jews did not allow itself to be regulated and limited by the Old Testament Canon. Their religious views did not really remain stationary in their original forms, but were retained under manifold change and development. And thus, whilst the actual state of things clashed with the theoretical principle based on their canonical estimation of Holy Scripture, the practical result was a certain systematic falsehood by which they beguiled themselves and others in regard to this contradiction. All sorts of sophistical subtleties were employed by the scribes to represent as reconcilable what, in Scripture, could not be reconciled. Allegory was the convenient means used for arbitrarily importing ideas foreign to the text, and causing them to appear as if founded upon it. The scribal mode of interpreting the law, which was adopted in order professedly to draw a hedge round the law and to safeguard its smallest minutiæ, led in reality to an enormous extension of the law. Hence, by a one-

sided method of treatment, one part of the system
of Divine precepts in the Old Testament was emphasised, specialised, and made more difficult, whereas
another part was neglected and rendered void. Whilst
seeking to conform with the utmost strictness to the
letter of the law, they did not hesitate flagrantly to
violate the spirit and purpose of the command. If
the innovations could but be made to appear in the
guise of "traditions," — Mosaic, if possible, — they
commanded respect, and might displace what was
really ancient. Here also we must take note of the
common practice at that period of publishing, under
the borrowed names of great and holy men of old, as
Enoch, the patriarchs and Moses, and with the pretension of resting on wonderful revelations, didactic
and hortatory writings, which aimed at influencing
contemporary society. As the theory prevailed that
the inspired writings of antiquity were of decisive
authority, there was an inducement for new writers
to try to secure consideration for their own works,
by making them appear almost, if not quite, on an
equality with the sacred writings of the Canon. The
authority and influence of those pseudo-epigraphic
apocalypses became in fact, as we know, very great
among the Jews. All these phenomena have this
point in common, that the Jews arranged them in a
fictitious way with the acknowledged authority of the
Sacred Scriptures. If we cannot attach great moral
blame to the single person who followed this disin-
genuous course, since the force of prevalent custom
tended to blind the individual to what was wrong in
that method, still we must regard that prevalent usage

itself as vicious, and as the indication of something unsound in the religious life.

2. As our object in this rapid survey is purely introductory, it does not fall within our scope to give a complete exhibition of the essential harmony in which the Jewish ideas of the time of Jesus, in accordance with the generally recognised authority of Scripture, stood to the religion of Israel of an earlier period. We will only seek to bring out those points which show a development and transformation of the earlier religious ideas, and those, therefore, which were specially characteristic of later Judaism. But in regard to all those points, it is only a matter of relative difference of conception between later and earlier Judaism, and only a question of one - sided expansion of certain principles which, as material for development, existed in Scripture, though not in the same preponderance as in later Judaism.

A clear instance of this we find in the idea, so important for Judaism in the time of Jesus, that *the religious relation between God and His people was a legal one*, upheld by God as righteous Judge, in the way of service and counterservice, reward and punishment. For the origin of this view we must go back to the prophetic period. Especially we find it in the conception, formed by the Deuteronomist and Jeremiah, of the covenant between Jehovah and His people, and in the appeal, continually recurring in the Psalms, to the judicial power and retribution of God. But here the idea of the covenant between God and His people, and of His judicial authority over them, does not so much represent the religious relation as

one of unbending justice as distinct from grace : it is
rather conceived as a moral one, with reciprocal moral
obligations, in opposition to a relation founded on
mere arbitrary power on the part of God.   Therefore
it is thoroughly compatible with that view to find
grace and long-suffering proclaimed as attributes of
God (*e.g.* Ex. xxxiv. 6 f.), to find also references to
free grace on the part of God as the foundation of
the covenant-relation to His people (*e.g.* Deut. vii.
7 f., viii. 17 f., ix. 4 f., x. 14 f. ; Isa. xliii., lxiii. 7 ff. ;
Ps. c. 3), and references to His readiness to forgive
the sins of the people and of individuals (*e.g.* Micah
vii. 18 ff. ; Jer. iii. 12, xxxi. 1 ff., xxxiii. 7 f. ; Ps. xxv.
6 ff., ciii. 8 ff.), and to find the mercies bestowed by
God and the salvation to be hoped for from Him
as infinitely surpassing the merit of the godly
(*e.g.* Gen. xxxii. 10).

Certainly these latter views of the Divine character
were not wholly wanting to later Judaism.   Pious
Jews had always those declarations of the Old Testament before them to remind them that free grace,
long-suffering, and forgiveness were parts of the character of Jehovah, who in His mercy had founded the
covenant-relation with Israel.   They knew that upright obedience to the law formed no equivalent for
the saving good promised by God.   But, in reality,
with most Jews this mode of view was overshadowed
by the legalistic conception, whereby every act of
obedience was regarded as having an exact recompense, and every blessing to be obtained as requiring
previous service.   The incessant vigorous conflict
waged by the Jews of the post-exilian period in order

to maintain their religion, tended greatly to enhance
that legalistic conception and attitude. Their zeal
for preserving intact the smallest point of the traditional knowledge and worship of God, caused their
religion to appear as a commanded duty, which must
be kept and observed with the utmost strictness.
Certainly there is no necessary connection between
zeal for the law of God and the idea that fulfilment
of the law justly entitles a man to the saving grace
of God. Such a zeal for the law, however, was
attended with a great risk of degenerating into
legalism; and indeed, in the post-exilian period,
Judaism came almost entirely under the influence
of this spirit. By the Pharisees, those characteristic
representatives of the religious tendency which had
passed over Judaism in the time of Jesus, the legal
mode of view was regarded as self-evidently valid,
and was in all directions carried into practical effect.
Even in Paul's Christian teaching, the influence of his
early Pharisaism is traceable in his view of the Old
Testament religion, which, while he regarded it as of
Divine authority up to the period of the inauguration
of the economy of grace through the mission of the
Son of God, was yet regarded by him only as an
economy of law and works. As a Christian, however,
he knew that this system of law and works was
incapable of bringing salvation; and that it was neither
the original nor the final ordinance of God, but was
appointed for a temporary educational purpose. But,
for that end, he maintained its validity from the period
of Moses until Christ, as a strictly legal economy in
contrast to an economy of grace and faith: "Moses

writes of the righteousness that is from the law :
The man who doeth these things shall live by them ''
(Rom. x. 5) ; '' Now to him that worketh, the work
is not reckoned as of grace, but as of debt'' (Rom.
iv. 4) ; '' For as many as are of the works of the law
are under a curse : for it is written, Cursed is every
one that continueth not in all things written in the
book of the law to do them '' (Gal. iii. 10).

We must not think, however, that the only effect
of this Jewish legal conception of the religious relation
to God was to produce and foster a legalism which
was manifested by mere outward service. The
example of Paul shows that the Pharisaic zeal for
law could be a profoundly inward thing. It was still
a matter of general religious knowledge to the Jews
that God is the Searcher of hearts, and that obedience
to Him must not be of the lip and the hand merely,
but must come from a pure heart. With a certain
class of Jews—those, namely, who were imbued with
a love of truth, with ardent moral aspirations, and
sincere piety, and such there were within as well as
without the Pharisaic circle, if they were not even
externally the most numerous and influential class—
this legal idea of the covenant of works, through
which men were to earn salvation, produced an unrestful zeal. In seeking to become righteous and
worthy of grace, so as to win the Divine approval,
they not only aimed at the strictest obedience to
all external forms and requirements of the law, but
they sought inner conformity of heart to the law
of God. But we can easily understand that it was
just those sincere, deeply earnest souls who found

the least real satisfaction in their endeavours after righteousness. For the more sincerely they sought righteousness, the more conscious of shortcoming they became, and their efforts after righteousness and salvation were ever attended with anxious doubt as to attaining their end. This tendency, in the Judaism of that time, towards an inward zeal for law that never led to inward peace, must be carefully noted. For it was just those who were going on this line who were most directly met by the teaching of Jesus. Even in the case of Paul, when a persecutor of Christianity, the struggles after a legal righteousness, and the consciousness of want of peace with God arising from a comparison of his actual deeds with the generally accepted ideal of the Divine law (Rom. vii. 7–25), constituted a real, though, on his part, unconscious predisposition to Christianity. And what he afterwards wrote (Gal. iii. 21–25, iv. 1–3) of the significance of the legal economy as a tutor to bring us unto Christ, was truly applicable to those influences which the legalistic idea of the relations between God and men produced upon the morally earnest and sincerely pious Jews.

But with the great mass of the Jews, the idea that one can and must acquire a title to the Divine favour through fulfilment of the law, necessarily caused a terrible obliquity of moral perception and conduct. Desiring to earn a Divine reward, and as great reward as possible, they sought to practise a strict legal righteousness, and, wherever possible, to exceed what the law demanded. But yet again, anxious to attain that reward on the easiest possible terms, they wished to do no more than was absolutely necessary for attaining their purpose. The result was, that while they tried with painful exactness to follow the letter of the law, they were satisfied with the *literal* fulfilment. All the stress was laid on the formal accuracy of the acts of obedience prescribed by the law. The smallest deviation from this was culpable, and a cause of offence. Thus they came to disregard the inner meaning and purpose of the commandment, and the participation of a pure heart in this legal obedience. The Pharisaic scribes, the recognised teachers and patterns of Jewish righteousness, set the worst example to the people of this abuse of the law. They expounded the law with all manner of casuistical subtleties, settling and distinguishing all its possible external circumstances and applications. By their enlargements and additions they sought to insure correct obedience to the law, and they aggravated it by prescribing all possible punctilios. At the same time, they devised subtle quirks for evading an inconvenient command, so as to keep it externally, and find it no longer troublesome.[1] It was a shocking caricature of true zeal for the Divine law. As quibbling sophistry, trifling with the law, it is ludicrous; but it is revolting when we regard it as the teaching of a religion which had the highest pretensions, and as directing men how to win the Divine favour and eternal life. And what evil qualities sheltered under that cloak of zeal for the righteousness of the law—ambitious vanity, which vaunted its superiority in good works; haughty

---

[1] Cf. the details and examples given by Schürer, *Gesch. d. jüd. Volkes*, ii. p. 393 (trans. Div. II. vol. ii. p. 97).

self-complacency, arrogantly comparing and contrast-
ing itself with others; uncharitable and harsh judgment with which they spurned those of less righteous
repute; and hypocritical zeal, which, under pretext of
reforming others, sought but to enhance their own
reputation for righteousness! The reproofs levelled
by Jesus against the Pharisees show us plainly what
vicious consequences resulted from this external zeal
for the law.

3. But the characteristic distinction between the
religious views of the Jews of the time of Jesus and
those of the prophetic period, did not merely consist
in their legalistic conception of man's relation to God,
and in the legal austerity which thence resulted. The
difference also came out in their idea of what points in
the law were weightiest and most essential, and what
were of less moment; and in the different degree of
interest with which they accordingly strove to expound
and fulfil the various sorts of commandments. From
the prophetic writings and the Psalms there comes
ever and anon the call to obedience to the moral commands of God—to just and righteous dealing with
others, to fidelity, and truth, especially in the case of
widows, orphans, and strangers (*e.g.* Ps. xv.; Isa.
i. 16 f.; Micah vi. 8; Jer. vii. 3 ff., xxii. 3; Deut. x.
18 f.). On the other hand, we find the stern repudiation of the idea that Jehovah can be served with
offerings and ceremonies, with festivals and fastings:
"For I desire mercy and not sacrifice; and the
knowledge of God more than burnt-offerings" (Hos.
vi. 6; cf. Amos v. 21 ff.; Isa. i. 10 ff.; Micah vi. 6 ff.;
Jer. vi. 20, vii. 21 ff.; Isa. lviii. 1 ff., lxvi. 1 ff.; Ps. l,

8 ff., li. 18 f.).   This key-note of the great men of
God of Israel's past died out in post-exilian Judaism.
The mode of view which manifestly prevailed among
the majority of the people in the prophetic period, but
which was opposed by the prophets, viz. that the
weightiest and most essential matters which God
commanded, and which made men well-pleasing to
Him, were ceremonies and acts of external worship,
had become, after the exile, not merely the popular
view, but was defended and promoted in every way
by the teachers and authorities among the people.
Their legal zeal was concentrated on acts of worship
and ceremonial ordinances, whilst the moral precepts
of God were relegated to the background.   The
collection of precepts in the middle books of the
Pentateuch are themselves, at least in the form in
which they are presented to us, a clear product of this
post-exilian legal tendency.   No doubt the knowledge
remained, that the moral commands in regard to truth,
faithfulness, equity, mercy, and chastity were true
Divine commands, and that to fulfil them in relation
to their neighbours was a form of piety.   Alms-giving
to the poor played a great part among the works of
righteousness among the Jews.   But the moral duties
of neighbourly love, and the laws of worship and ceremonial observances, were incessantly coming into
conflict, because those laws referred to certain appointed acts and forms of abstinence, and to appointed
days and hours and places which admitted of no
change or postponement; and where the two things
clashed, the moral duties were summarily set aside
for the ceremonial performances.   These latter were

absolutely inviolable ; and, in order to their punctilious fulfilment, neighbourly duties had to give place, even where the nature of the case admitted of no delay, and the omission could not be supplied at another time.

The performance of sacrificial offices in the temple at Jerusalem was a tribal prerogative of the priests and Levites. All other Jews had to show their allegiance to the ceremonial law by taking part in the temple worship, especially at the great feasts, by there presenting their offerings, and by paying taxes and tithes for the support of the temple service and the priesthood. They had to use the appointed prayers at the appointed seasons, and to celebrate the Sabbath and the feast-days by strict abstinence from all work, and by participation in the worship of God in the synagogue. They had to observe the fast-days, and to keep themselves from all defilement, so as to fulfil the laws of Levitical purity. This last point was certainly the most important in the practical everyday life. The Jew found himself continually surrounded with dangers which threatened his defilement, that is, his being in a profane state which deprived him of fellowship with God. He might be defiled by unclean food, by unclean persons and things, and by certain natural or morbid processes in his own body. His whole attention had to be directed towards guarding himself against these varied dangers, as well as carefully performing his ablutions, and bringing the offerings which could remove the defilement where it was incurred. With a profane, immoral disposition of mind,—with what we are accustomed to call sin,

—those cases of defilement had nothing to do. They could be incurred without knowledge or volition, and therefore also without the slightest consciousness of guilt. When it was a question with the Jews in the time of Jesus as to what was, or rendered one, holy or unholy, and what could bring him into, or deprive him of, fellowship with God, he thought primarily, not of the inner disposition, nor of the state of the heart towards God, nor of the moral behaviour towards his fellow-men, but of the means of Levitical defilement and purification.

4. We must seek the ultimate ground of the direction which Jewish legalism had taken in the particular form which their conception of God had assumed, since the mode of reverence shown to God is always relative to the ideas of the Divine character.[1]   For the Jewish consciousness, the first and most important attribute of God was His holiness, that is, His separation from the world, His exaltation above the world. The grand heritage which the Jews had received from the prophetic period was the knowledge of Jehovah, the One, the Incorporeal and Invisible, who could not be conceived or represented in the form or likeness of any finite creature of flesh and blood. The Jews were aware how immensely this knowledge of God differed from and excelled the sensuous polytheistic ideas of deity held by the heathen ; and they took zealous pains to keep safe and sacred their peculiar heritage. No doubt their ideas of the ethical attributes of Jehovah, on which were based His covenant

---

[1] Cf. W. Baldensperger, *The Self-Consciousness of Jesus in relation to the Messianic Hopes of His Time*, Strasburg 1888, p. 38 ff.

relations with His people, as well as His promises of redemption and His gracious dealings with Israel, were not obliterated.   But just as those attributes were regarded as subordinate to the justice and the judicial dealings of God, they were also conceived as limited by the absolute transcendence of God above the world, through His separation from everything transient and mundane.   In strict analogy with this, in conceiving of the righteous conduct whereby men were to fulfil the will of God in order to earn His grace, they set the more purely ethical acts in sub-ordination to those actions whose object was the recognition and safeguard of the exalted glory of God as distinct from the world of sense, and separate from all that is transient and earthly.   The practical result of the stress thus laid upon the holiness, or the super-mundane character of God, was shown in the rigid abstinence from secular work on Sabbaths and feast-days, in the increased usage of fasting on the part of the Pharisees, and in those ascetic acts which had an independent value in themselves, as answering to the will and pleasure of God, and not as conducing to the concentration and elevation of religious feeling, and tending to the moral strength of those who practised them.   Other results of the same tendency consisted in those rites of purification whose foundation and necessity lay in the idea that certain physical effects and processes—everything that was associated with corruption—were incompatible with the character and the near presence of God.   We can now take up the position that the transcendental aspect of God, when thus set in a relation of contrast to the sensible world,

and in particular to certain natural matter and occurrences, was only imperfectly conceived, since this
relation of contrast presupposed that the two could
be compared and subsumed under a common category. But the Jews at that period were not aware
of these limits of their idea of the transcendental
character of God. They were confident that the
necessary condition of man's being raised up to
fellowship with the Most High God was his severance from the natural, sensible world, at least in
certain relations.

We find two further points in which the increased
zeal of the Jews for maintaining the holiness of God,
in the sense we have indicated, was manifested.
First, they removed the names of God from common
use, avoiding entirely the name of *Jehovah*, and
also, as far as possible, the general name of God, in
common speech as well as in oaths, and employing
the circumlocution of such terms as *heaven;* secondly,
they imagined an unlimited number of angels as
media of the will and working of God on the world
and mankind. In proportion as God appeared remote
from the world, and as they shrank from the idea of
His immediate connection with it, and of His active
sympathy with human affairs and human feelings
—in order not to bring Him down from His position of absolute transcendence to the level of the
world and of men—the religious instinct sought in
angelic agency a means of filling the void. They
imagined a series of intermediary beings between
God and the world, who were instruments of the
power and the revelation of God, agents of the forces

of nature, guardians and attendants of men, and avengers of human wrongs. The devout and trustful consciousness of the immediate nearness of God, which is expressed in so many beautiful utterances of the Psalmist, appears to be supplanted in later Judaism by a belief in angels, which is closely analogous to the superstitious belief in the saints on the part of the Romish Church. It is very significant that the Jews in the time of Jesus could no longer conceive even of that promulgation of the law on Sinai, which was to them the foundation of their whole religion, as an immediate revelation of Jehovah to Moses, except as instituted through the mediation of angels (cf. Acts vii. 38, 53; Gal. iii. 19; Heb. ii. 2; Joseph. *Ant.* xv. 5. 3).

5. By the free development of this particular tendency of Judaism in reference to the supposed supermundane character of God, and by the practical results of that tendency, we can almost wholly explain the two forms of specific divergence from the orthodox Pharisaic Judaism of the time of Jesus. Those two forms were *Essenism* and *Philo's philosophy of religion.*

In their exaggerated ideas of defilement and of necessary purifications; in the painful strictness with which they abstained from the smallest acts of work on the Sabbath, and from all that appeared to them defiling; in their renunciation of marriage, which, in their view, could not be carried out without defilement; and in their prohibition of all oaths, the Essenes represent the tendency of Pharisaic legalism, so far as the latter was influenced by the idea of the transcendental character of God. But they exhibit that tendency in a more intense degree.[1]   Their rejection of animal sacrifices and consequent abstaining from the temple worship, which seems out of harmony with the rest of their legal obedience, is most simply explained as the consequence of their idea that to bring to God a bloody animal offering was derogatory to His transcendental character.   Therefore they deemed it incumbent upon them to interpret the Old Testament command in reference to these offerings in an allegorising way.   The monastic life they had in common, along with the community of goods thereby occasioned, and their preference for a life of natural simplicity in certain relations, was certainly less owing to those ethical principles which they held along with, yet independently of, their ceremonial ideas, than to the general endeavour to guard as much as possible against the manifold risks to their purity which were held out by their intercourse with the rest of the world and by participation in its goods.   Finally, the high regard paid to angels by the Essenes must be looked upon as a consequence of the same idea of the transcendental character of God, from which their tendency to legalism proceeded ; and it might be a question worth considering, whether, in their peculiar sun-worship, we have not simply an expression of their reverence for the angels, as the great " powers " through whose mediation, also according to the common Jewish idea, God works on nature, specially in the celestial phenomena of nature.[1]

This tendency of the religious ideas of the Jews

---

[1] Cf. Schürer, *Gesch. d. jüd. Volkes*, ii. p. 484 ff. (trans. Div. II. vol. ii. p. 208).

was also regulative for the system of Philo. Here the thought of the absolute transcendence of God, whereby His nature is set in opposition to that of the sensible world, is carried out to its logical conclusions. The popular Jewish idea of the angels, who are the media of the intercourse of the holy God of heaven with the world and its frail, short-lived inhabitants, is philosophically expanded by Philo in his doctrine of the Logos, and the other agencies who form the links of connection between the abstract, infinite, and remote God and the concrete and finite world of sense. And the Pharisaic mode of manifesting zeal for holiness by rigid abstinence from work on Sabbath, by guarding against contact with certain forms of matter, supposed to be specially opposed to the nature of God, and by occasional fasting, is expanded in Philo's system into the general principle of the ascetic mortification of sense in order to approach nearer to the Divine nature. As the Rabbins were wont in the Haggada to attach a deeper meaning to the text of the Scripture than the literal one, and to bring out weighty spiritual thoughts from the simple historical narratives, it was but a step farther for Philo to interpret the Mosaic law in an allegorising way, and to find in the precepts of external ritual a higher meaning, which appeared more in harmony with the pure idea of the transcendental character of God. The vast difference between the religious philosophy of Philo and the religious ideas of the Old Testament, is plainly shown in his amalgamation of foreign Hellenistic elements with the purely Old Testament conceptions. And, judging from an external point of view, equally marked is the divergence of Philo's system from the orthodox teaching of the scribes and Pharisees of Palestine in the time of Jesus. But we can quite understand that Philo, just because he followed the general direction of the religious tendency which prevailed in orthodox Judaism of his time, regarded his divergence from that orthodox teaching, not as a departure from Judaism, but only as a logical prosecution of its principles. He saw in his interpretation of the Old Testament, not an intrusion of strictly foreign ideas, but only an exposition of its most essential and deepest thoughts.

Jesus Himself, so far as we know, came in close contact, neither with Essenism, nor with the Alexandrian religious philosophy. Nevertheless, in an introductory account of the Jewish religious views, in order to define the historical arena of the development of Jesus, it appears by no means superfluous briefly to sketch those two forms of the religious life of Judaism at that time. For, by considering these, we are able indirectly to estimate the peculiar character and significance of the teaching of Jesus. They show us, in a specially clear way, the direction taken by the religious and speculative tendency of Judaism in the time of Jesus, and the results to which it led, when it kept itself free in regard to Pharisaic traditions, and yielded, in greater or less measure, to enlightening influence. And the fact that Essenism showed at least the possibility of receiving influences from philosophic and Hellenic sources, whilst the Alexandrian philosophy quite openly exhibited a blending of the Jewish religious mode of view with the Hellenic philosophy, affords a clear proof of the affinity existing between the religious conceptions of Judaism of that period—so far as it had developed in the line of a clear recognition in thought and conduct of the abstract transcendental character of God—and the religious philosophic mode of view of the enlightened and cultured Greeks of that epoch. In the ratio in which Jewish orthodoxy diverged from vulgar heathen polytheism, did a cultured Judaism approach the cultured philosophical heathenism of that time.

The prevailing currents of Judaism tended to enhance the idea of God's transcendence of the world, and the deep-rooted idea that man must acquire a right to the Divine mercy by fulfilling the law, tended more and more to the expansion of legalism, especially in regard to ceremonial and ascetic performances, which appeared to be called for by the supermundane character of God. Jesus was not affected by this prevailing tendency as Philo certainly was. Philo is to be regarded as the Reformer of Judaism. In accordance with the spirit of his time, he sought to give a consistent exposition of the conception of God which had become the prevailing one among his countrymen, whilst divesting Judaism of its narrow national prejudices and customs. At the same time, by recognising and accepting the best elements of Hellenic thought, he sought to adapt himself to the intelligence and requirements of the whole world of culture of his time. That this view is correct, is proved in the case of the Christian apologists of the second century, who adopted the Alexandrian philosophy in order to bring Christianity home to their contemporaries. Those apologists, following Philo's example of allegorising the Old Testament, represented Christianity as a spiritualised Judaism; and they so unfolded the idea of the pure supersensuous nature of God, and the necessity of an abstemious and righteous course of life in order to attain salvation, as brought them into harmony with the Greek Idealism.   But, in considering this subject, the question forces itself upon us, whether a religious philosophical system, dominated, like that of Philo, by the idea of the transcendental character of God, could have furnished the inspiring motive to such missionary labours as those of Paul, or to such joyful confession as that of the Christian martyrs.   Would it have been able, not merely to satisfy the intellectual requirements of the cultured of that period, but to give new life and a new ideal to the mass of the common people? And would it have possessed an innate force of truth, sufficient not only for its acceptance as the highest wisdom by the cultured world in that declining period of antiquity, but for proving a perennial revelation for the whole human race, outlasting all the changes of history and all the forms of civilisation?

CHAP. II. THE RELIGIOUS HOPES OF THE JEWS IN
THE TIME OF JESUS.

1. The religious hopes formed an essential part of the system of Jewish ideas in the age of Jesus.   I here devote a separate section to this subject, on

account of the special importance of those hopes as points for the historical foundation of the teaching of Jesus. Whilst Jesus came claiming to bring the fulfilment of His people's hopes, He had nevertheless to explain the distinction between that fulfilment as He understood it and as the Jews expected it. The rejection of His teaching on the part of the great mass of the people, was primarily owing to the fact that the salvation whose realisation He proclaimed did not correspond to the people's hopes, and to the ideal which they cherished.

Wherein, then, consisted the relation of the religious hopes of the Jews to the rest of their system of religious thought? The Jews sought to build the structure of their hopes as a whole on the foundation of the Old Testament. Hopes of a great Divine manifestation of grace in the future, formed a strong element in the prophetic teaching of an earlier period; and the zeal of a later Judaism to maintain the integrity of the religion of that earlier period, was shown in a special manner in their cherishing of those ideal hopes of the future. And we must regard it as a special proof of the energy and confidence with which the Jews clung to the ancient beliefs of their people, that they would abate nothing of the great ideal hoped for in the early time. In the case of the ancient prophets, an incomparably grand expression was afforded of their unshaken conviction of the substantiality of their beliefs, in their taking all hardships of the present, all contradictions between the actual state of things and their religious ideas, only as incentives to the expectation

and prediction of a perfect solution of all such difficulties and contradictions through the future intervention of God. In like manner, we have to note
with admiration how the post-exilian Jews, through
all that long period of fruitless waiting for the fulfilment of the prophetic promises, and despite the contrast presented by the hard realities and the natural
outlook of their present to the brilliant pictures of
their hopes, never for a moment faltered in their
confidence in the validity of those hopes. Certainly
in many respects those hopes underwent a process of
transformation in post-exilian Judaism; yet, on the
whole, the early prophetic ideals were not impaired,
but rather enhanced.

The intensity of these hopes formed a counter-
poise to the tendency of the Jewish theology to
accentuate the supermundane idea of God beyond
His other attributes, and thus served to secure the
specially religious character of their idea of God.[1]
The religious interest is always directed, not to a
mere knowledge of the Godhead, but to a reception of blessings from God as worshipped by men,
whether the blessings they seek are spiritual or
external. The religious interest, therefore, demands
such a knowledge of God as promises the certainty of obtaining from Him certain valuable
blessings. But the bare idea of the absolute exaltation of God above the world, of His essential
opposition to the world as sensible and transient,
and of His supremacy as First Cause of all things,
though it may be sufficient from a philosophic point

---

[1] Cf Baldensperger, *d. Selbstbewusstsein Jesu*, p. 53.

of view, cannot satisfy the religious requirements. These latter demand the supposition of such Divine qualities as will insure the communication of blessings to the world,—a demand which must somehow be reconciled with the other interests which uphold the transcendence belonging to the idea of God, and imparting a special and incomparable value to the blessings He bestows. With Philo, whose philosophic interests so greatly overshadowed the religious, the idea of God's transcendental abstraction, which he set forth with special emphasis, caused a proportionate abatement of the redemptive hopes; yet, because those hopes were an ever-present element in his system, they imparted to it a certain religious character. Conversely, however, in the case of orthodox Judaism, we find, in the lively hope of God's redemptive interposition, a saving salt which, in spite of the strong emphasis laid upon the holy transcendence of God at the expense of His more ethical attributes, maintained the definitely religious character of the idea of God, and preserved it from philosophical petrifaction.

Hence we can explain the relation which these religious hopes of the Jews bore to their legalistic view of the religious relation to God. We must not suppose that this legalistic view and those hopes had no inner harmony, and that they in a measure counteracted each other. Instead of this, they found, in the ordering of the religious relationship between God and His people on the footing of law and justice, the reconciliation of the holy transcendence of God and His gracious dealings. The judicial attitude and acts of God did not appear derogatory to His absolute holiness, whilst it contained a motive, even though it was a conditional one, for the bestowal of blessings on men.   Accordingly, the strictly legal deportment of men appeared a fitting means for obtaining the Divine blessing — I do not mean the Messianic salvation specially, but the blessings of grace in general as conceived by the Jews.   Even the most zealous legalist, as, for example, a Paul before his conversion, could cherish the most intense hope of the Divine favour. But through the legal conception of the religious relation, the Divine blessing, at least in its essential elements, was regarded as something hoped for in the future, and as a reward to be won by righteous living.

The subject - matter of the religious hopes of the Jews in the time of Jesus formed neither a systematic unity nor even something which all were agreed upon, but rather showed manifold vacillations and differences, sometimes in spite of, sometimes also just on account of, the fact of its being based upon the prophetic promises of the Old Testament.   Of those points wherein that uncertainty and disagreement was shown, I may now briefly consider those which were of most importance for the foundations of the teaching of Jesus.

2. The first point of this kind has regard to the relation in which the special expectation of the Messianic king stood to the general expectation of the future promised kingdom.[1]   It need not be exactly shown here, that, in the Old Testament

[1] Cf. especially, Schürer, *Gesch. d. jüd. Volkes*, p. 426 ff. (trans. Div. II. vol. ii. p. 137).

prophets, the general hope that, through a great manifestation of judgment by which the powers hostile to Him would be destroyed, God would introduce a wonderful dispensation of grace for the people of Israel, was not wholly, but only partially, bound up with the expectation of one ideal Davidic king, who should be the means of establishing a blessed condition of peace for the people of Israel. Among the older prophets, the author of Zech. ix.-xi., Isaiah, Micah, Jeremiah, and Ezekiel point to such an ideal Son of David, who should be endowed, not only with the gifts and the virtues of the people of the latter days (Zech. ix. 9 f.; Isa. xi. 2 ff.; Jer. xxiii. 6, cf. xxxiii. 16), but in particular with the qualities of a good, peace-giving, prosperous ruler (Zech. ix. 9 f.; Isa. ix. 5; xi. 2 ff.; Micah v. 3-5; Jer. xxiii. 5 f.; xxxiii. 15 f.; xxxiv. 23 f.; xxxvii. 24). But Amos (ix. 11), Hosea (iii. 5), and the author of Zech. xii.-xiv. (xii. 10; xiii. 1) only indicate the idea that the Davidic dynasty would again be raised to great power and importance; whilst Zephaniah, in his picture of the latter-day blessings (iii. 9 ff.), makes no mention of a Davidic king. In the post-exilian period the conception of the ideal Davidic king had hardly any place among the hopes still firmly cherished of a glorious time coming in the latter days. The idea of a future king is wanting to the author of Isa. xxiv.-xxvii. and to Haggai and Joel, as well as to Deutero-Isaiah; for the expression "servant of Jehovah," as used by him, cannot be interpreted as referring to one particular future king. Malachi (iii. 23 f.) only speaks of the approaching

mission of the prophet Elias to prepare for the Lord's
coming to judgment.   Zechariah (iii. 8 ; vi. 12 f.)
only refers to the coming of the "branch" which he
adopts from Jeremiah (xxiii. 5 f.), and which certainly
has reference to the son of David and descendant of
Zerubbabel.   The book of Daniel and the so-called
apocryphal books are silent in regard to the ideal
king, and only express the general expectation of an
everlasting kingdom to be established by God for the
people of Israel (Dan. ii. 44 ; vii. 13 f., 27 ; Bar. iv.
21 ff. ; v. 1 ff. ; Tob. xiii. 10 ff. ; xiv. 5 ff.).   For the
vision in Dan. vii. 13 f. of one coming in the clouds
of heaven in the form of the Son of man, to whom
God would grant everlasting power and dominion, is,
according to the original meaning of the writer, as
appears from the explanation in ver. 27, to be understood, not of a particular person in the future, but of
the people of the saints of the Most High ; that is, of
the people of Israel, in contrast to the kingdoms of
the world as represented under the figure of the four
beasts.   And in the saying of the son of Sirach, that
God had exalted the horn of David for ever, and had
given him a covenant of kings and a throne of glory
in Israel, as well as in that saying in First Maccabees
(ii. 57), that David had received a royal throne for
ever (even if we do not, in view of the expression
"for ever" as employed in 2 Sam. vii. 13, refer this
to the past glorious kingdom of David and his
successors), we can only see the expression of the
idea of a future and enduring restoration of the
Davidic dynasty, but not the hope of a particular
ideal Davidic king, the mediator of the Divine bless-

ings in the latter - day period. The son of Sirach
(xlviii. 10 f.), founding on the prophecy of Malachi,
refers rather to the expected second coming of Elias;
and similarly in 1 Macc. xiv. 41, cf. iv. 46, the expectation is intimated of the future advent of a true
prophet. This expectation of Elias or of some other
prophet, however, by no means presupposes the
expectation of an ideal king such as was proclaimed
by the early prophets. It rather stands in relation,
as in Malachi, to the idea that God Himself would
come for judgment and for the consummation of
salvation.

But in the scribal period, when the sacred writings
of ancient times were regarded as the authoritative
standard for all religious knowledge, as a matter of
necessity, the authority of the greatest of the early
prophets brought about a reawakening of the expectation—temporarily dormant through the unpropitious
circumstances of the times—of an ideal Davidic king
of the latter-day period, that is, the Messianic hope
in the special sense. That this had already taken
place before the advent of Jesus, is shown by the
prophecies of the oldest portions of the Jewish Sibyl
and of the book of Enoch. These writings point
clearly forward to the mission of the Messiah, but
they imply no close essential connection between the
Messiah's advent and ministry and the Divine
agency which, simultaneously with those events, yet
independently of them, carries on the work of Divine
judgment and salvation (Sibyl. iii. 652–794; En. xc.
16–38). Here the Messianic idea is found to have
regained a place in the conception of the future,

though not the commanding influence in moulding
that conception, which it possessed in earlier times ;
but, in the Psalter of Solomon, dating from the
middle of the first century B.C., the significance of the
expected king, the son of David, the anointed of the
Lord, the consecrated of the Lord, is apprehended in
the same way as in the ancient prophecies.   The
general assertion that God is the Eternal King of
the people, and that it is His sovereignty and glory
which in the latter day shall be fully manifested, was
still maintained (Ps. xvii. 1).   But the special manner
in which the blessings of the new dispensation were
to be brought in, was involved in their idea of the
Messiah.   The Davidic king was to be the mediator
of those blessings.   He should accomplish the Divine
judgment by destroying the heathen who had trodden
down Jerusalem, and by driving sinners out of his
heritage (Ps. xvii. 23–27).   He should establish the
Divine kingdom of grace by ruling the people of
Israel and all nations on earth in righteousness and
peace, by establishing holiness and uprightness among
the people of God, and by creating due reverence
for God among other nations (Ps. xvii. 28 ff., xviii.
6 ff.).   But, further, our Gospel records attest the fact
that in the time of Jesus the same Messianic conception, and even titles, as those employed in the
Psalter of Solomon, were current at least among a
wide circle of the Jewish people.   The Messiah
was known by both as the *Son of David, the King
of Israel, the Anointed One, the Consecrated of God.*
Even where Jesus intentionally abstained from applying to Himself the title of Messiah, His attendants,

by using that title, spontaneously expressed their recognition of His unique pre-eminence in the kingdom of God (Mark viii. 29 ; x. 47 f. ; xi. 10; John vi. 69 ; cf. vii. 26 f., 41 f.; xii. 34). And when Jesus had openly laid claim to Messiahship, His foes associated the claim with the ideas which they had been wont to connect with the title, and impeached and derided Him for the blasphemy of that claim (Mark xiv. 61–64 ; xv. 2 and 32). On one occasion (Mark xii. 35 ff.), Jesus very characteristically, and in direct terms, referred in His teaching to the idea of the scribes concerning the Messiah : " How say the scribes that the Messiah is the Son of David ? . . . David himself calls Him Lord ; how is He then his son ? " We see from this question, not only that the expectation of the Messiah was expressly upheld by the scribes as exponents of the authoritative teaching of the Pharisaic party, but also that the main stress was laid by them on the Davidic descent which they regarded as the fundamental Messianic principle. That the Pharisaic scribes should set great store by the Messianic idea, was quite in accordance with the tendency of their other modes of thought. Thus their theological tendency was opposed to the idea of a direct operation of the holy God upon the world. Politically, also, through their hostility to the Herodian princes, as well as to the Roman domination, their tendency was specially to welcome the idea of a national Davidic king who was to appear in the future as the mediator of the Divine purpose.

We find, however, certain other indications that the idea of the Messiah, widespread and dear as it was

generally among the Jews of that period, had nevertheless no steadfast and essential place among their
national hopes of the future. A consideration of those
indications is, moreover, of no small importance in
order to understand the nature and mode in which
Jesus announced the kingdom of God. It is in the
highest degree remarkable that the "Assumption of
Moses" and the "Book of the Jubilees," writings
which probably date from the beginning and middle
of the first Christian century, make no mention in
their detailed account of the future redemption, of a
coming king through whom as mediator that blessing
was to be realised. They speak of God Himself as
about to interpose in order to punish the heathen, and
raise Israel to a wonderful position of blessing (Ass.
Mos. chap. x. ; Jubil. chap. xxiii.[1]). If we consider
the earlier history of the Messianic idea, we cannot
entertain the view that this idea was omitted by mere
accident on the part of those writers, whilst the defect
was supplied by the understanding in their own minds.
Rather, we must suppose that the writers had appropriated with full consciousness, from the old traditions,
that type of the ideal picture of the future which did
not include the idea of a Messiah. No doubt the
Messianic idea, so widely diffused among their countrymen, was familiar enough to those writers ; and no
doubt party bias, whether directed against the Pharisees or the Christians, supplied the motive which led
to their omission of that idea. But this does not
lessen the significance of the fact that they held it as

---

[1] According to Dillmann's translation in Ewald's *Jahrbücher der
Biblischen Wissenschaft Jahrg.* iii. (1851) p. 24.

quite possible to leave the Messiah out of account in a delineation of the future redemptive period. Had the expectation of the Messianic king really possessed universal and self-evident acceptance among the Jews at that period, Jewish writers would not have passed it over in silence, even had they found in it certain difficulties and stumbling-blocks.

In addition to this, we find it recorded in the Gospel narratives that the popular expectation was aroused, at one time in the case of the Baptist, at another in that of Jesus, that this might be Elias or the coming prophet (Mark vi. 15; viii. 28; John i. 21; vi. 14; vii. 40). The expectation of Elias was founded on the idea expressed by Malachi and the son of Sirach; that of the prophet, on the idea expressed in the First Book of Maccabees. In the Christian Church from the first, a consistent tradition existed as to the relation in which the Messianic idea stood to that of the returning Elias and the prophet who was to be raised up (according to Deut. xviii. 15). As Jesus, in conformity with the consciousness of His Messiahship, declared that the Baptist was Elias, who was sent to prepare the way before Him, and as He regarded the special form of His own Messianic work as primarily that of a prophet and teacher (cf. *e.g.* Luke iv. 18 ff.), the idea continued to prevail in the Christian Church that the Baptist was Elias the forerunner (cf. Mark i. 2), whilst "the prophet" was identified with the Messiah Himself (cf. Acts iii. 22 ff.). Nevertheless this combination of ideas is not borne out by their original meaning. For nowhere in the earlier literature does the expectation of the Messiah occur in

connection with the idea of a forerunner; and wherever, since Malachi, the idea of the return of Elias, or
more generally that of the future prophet, is expressed,
no mention is made of the Messiah.[1]

Originally, it was not two great human personages,
but only one, who was expected to appear in the latter
days. It was either a king who should be the medium of
carrying into effect the Divine judgment and salvation,
or a prophet as the forerunner of Jehovah Himself,
who was coming to accomplish judgment and mercy.
The combination of those ideas by the Christians shows
only how it was possible for the Jews in the time of
Jesus, as it was certainly customary among many
Jewish circles, especially that of the scribes, to combine
ideas which were originally independent and different.[2]

But this combination of ideas was by no means
a self-evident and generally prevalent one. The
passages John i. 20 f.; vii. 40 f. (cf. Mark vi. 15; viii.
28) imply that the promised prophet was not so completely identified with the Messiah in the Jewish ideas
as in the later Christian view. John Baptist's negative
reply to the question whether he were the Messiah,

---

[1] The inversion which the idea of the return of Elias as the forerunner of Jehovah underwent, when it was applied by the Christians to
the Baptist as the forerunner of the Messiah, is indicated in the modi-
fication with which Mark (i. 2) and, following him, Matthew (xi. 10) and
Luke (vii. 27) render the words of Malachi. They write: ἰδοὺ ἐγὼ
ἀποστέλλω τὸν ἄγγελόν μου πρὸ προσώπου σου, ὃς κατασκευάσει τὴν ὁδόν σου,
while the original text and the Septuagint give μου (or its equivalent).

[2] Cf. Mark ix. 11, where the disciples of Jesus asked why the Pharisees
and scribes taught that Elias must first come. From the line of connection in which this conversation occurs, as well as from what we
know otherwise of the general use of the Messianic idea by the Pharisees
and scribes, we must conclude that the Pharisaic teaching in question
referred to a coming of Elias in preparation for the Messiah, not in
anticipation of the coming of God Himself.

did not preclude the further question whether he were the prophet or not. But though, in their surmisings as to the significance of the Baptist and of Jesus, the Jews regarded the question as to the one or other being the Messiah as distinct from the question whether either were "the prophet," it would be wrong to infer from this that both a Messiah and a prophet were expected. The expectation of the prophet rather stood, so to speak, in a concurrent relation to the expectation of the Messiah. Those who said, "This is truly the Prophet," and the others who said, "This is the Messiah" (John vii. 40 f.), had not the same view of the character of the coming dispensation which Jesus, according to their hopes, was to introduce.[1] But though the scribes in the time of Jesus were wont to combine those originally distinct ideas, we must assume that those distinct ideas lay alongside of each other in various ways in the minds of the people themselves.

In brief, the expectation of the Messiah was without doubt widely prevalent among the Jews in the time of Jesus, but it was not quite universal and free from all doubt. There was an unwavering expectation of a divinely-purposed future dispensation of blessing. But the more special ideas in regard to the mediation which was believed to be essentially required at that coming period, through the mission of one or more human personages, were subject to vacillations.

[1] In the passage John vi. 14 f., where it is related that, after the miraculous feeding of the multitude, they said of Jesus, "This is truly the Prophet that should come into the world," and sought to make Him a king, the title of the coming Prophet appears as if it were equivalent to that of the Messiah. Quite certainly, however, the two are not here identified.

3. The second noteworthy point in regard to the form taken by the religious hopes of the Jews of that period, concerns the relation between the personal hope of salvation on the part of individual Jews and the national hope of salvation. No special question in regard to that relation had risen in the consciousness of pious Israelites of the early times. For, on the one hand, the religious hope of individual Israelites did not reach beyond the limits of the present earthly life; and, on the other hand, the national hope, nourished by prophetic intimations, of a time of marvellous exaltation for Israel, did not refer to a vague and distant future, but to a period quite near at hand. The special blessings which pious individuals expected from God consisted in earthly welfare, in the peaceful enjoyment of their possessions, of a long life insured against a violent termination, and the continuance of a powerful and divinely-favoured line of posterity. But this state of blessedness expected for individuals was fully included in that period of national greatness whose imminence was announced by the prophets—a period when all the wicked among the people should be destroyed by the judgment of God, when all external foes and oppressors of the people should be overcome, and when prosperity and happiness should flourish unclouded, under the peaceful rule of the Davidic prince as the vicegerent of Jehovah's power (cf. *e.g.* Amos ix. 12 ff.; Hos. ii. 21 ff.; xiv. 6 ff.; Zech. x. 6 ff.; Isa. xi. 6 ff.; xxxv. 5 ff.; Micah iv. 3 ff.; Jer. xxxi. 10 ff.; xxxvii. 7 ff.; Ezek. xxviii. 25 f.; xxxiv. 11 ff.). But the more the pious Israelites became aware of the disproportion so frequently exist-

ing between the personal piety and the earthly prosperity of individuals, and the less it became possible,
under the limitation of their hopes to the present
earthly life, for seers and poets to find a quite satisfactory solution of the problem of undeserved suffering
on the part of the righteous; the more, also, they
pondered the long delay from generation to generation
in the realisation of the national hopes; and the more
that living faith in the speedy advent of the new
dispensation gave place to doubt as to its nearness,
and to a stress laid upon the signs that should precede
the inauguration of the new era, the greater grew the
religious need of severing the individual hopes of
salvation from connection with the present earthly
life.   Certainly the greatest progress exhibited by the
religious consciousness of post-exilian Judaism lay in
the fact that, instead of their founding the hope of
blessedness upon the continuance of the earthly life,
and instead of the apprehensive dread which the
pious Israelites had of the shadowy existence in
Scheol away from blissful intercourse with God, they
attained the prospect of reward after earthly death,
and of a resurrection of the just out of Scheol to
"eternal life" (Dan. xii. 2; Enoch xc. 33; xci. 10;
xcii. 3; c. 5; ciii. 1 ff.; Psal. Sol. iii. 13 ff.; xiii. 9 f.; xiv.
2 ff.; xv. 13 ff.).   The opposition maintained by the
Sadducees to the Pharisees' doctrine of the resurrection proves that, in the time of Jesus, part at least of
the Jewish people still regarded that doctrine as an
innovation.   But the majority of the people at that
time had certainly, along with the Pharisees, adopted
a belief in the resurrection.

This resurrection hope was assuredly not something quite apart from the national hope of the Messianic kingdom, but was rather included in it : the just would reawake to a blessed life on earth in order to participate in the Messianic dispensation.[1] And an important effect, in elevating the character of the Messianic hope, was produced by thus founding upon it the hope of the resurrection of the just. It was not conceivable, however, that the just who had once risen from Scheol would finally lose their beatific estate and fall anew under the power of death. Hence that hope could now be fully understood and exercised to which the author of Isa. xxiv.–xxvii. had already given such sublime, and, at that early period, unique expression —the hope, namely, that, in the future dispensation of blessing, death itself would be for ever annihilated and all suffering would come to an end (Isa. xxv. 8 ; xxvi. 19). Not only the Messianic kingdom as a whole could now be regarded as eternal, but the participation in it of its individual members could be conceived as the fruition of everlasting life. In this sense of the hope of blessedness for the individual saints, so far as it had reference to a resurrection-life after death being included in the national Messianic hope, the eschatological expectation is represented in the Psalter of Solomon (cf. Ps. xiv. 2 ff. with xvii. 1 ff.; Enoch li.).

But, no doubt, there were other ways in which the hope of resurrection-life on the part of individuals could be combined with the national expectation of

[1] Cf. Schürer, *Gesch. d. jüd. Volkes*, ii. p. 457, note 65 (trans. Div. II, vol. ii. p. 175).

blessedness. On the one hand, the traditionary idea of the Messianic kingdom did not admit of such an extension as would *quite* meet the aspirations of the individual. For that kingdom was still always represented as an essentially earthly one : even though regarded as being established by miraculous power and miraculously continued, it was never conceived as being absolutely without earthly limitations. Even its traditional attribute of eternity was only understood in the sense of an inconceivably long duration, not in the sense in which God is eternal. On the other hand, the idea of a reward after death, and of resurrection from Scheol, tended towards something further than was implied in the participation of the just in the Messianic kingdom. After the thought had been laid hold of that the pious Israelites did not find in the present earthly life the full reward of their righteousness, but that one day, at the dawn of a new era, God would reawaken the slumbering saints to the enjoyment of everlasting bliss, it was an extremely small step beyond this to suppose a universal resurrection of mankind out of Scheol to appear together at God's tribunal to give account of their deeds, and to be individually sentenced to endless life or to endless destruction.

But did this idea of a general awakening from death, and a judgment of mankind in general, fit in with the national expectation of the establishment of the Messianic kingdom on earth ? It is easily understood that, so far as the consideration just mentioned obtained authority, a divergence would set in between the individual and the national

expectations of blessedness. The hope of a realisation of the Messianic kingdom, and of a marvellous
prosperity to be thereby attained by the nation of
Israel, remained intact. That kingdom, it was still
believed, would endure throughout a whole world-
period; but yet it would at length come to an end.
And when, after the closing acts of the general
resurrection and judgment of mankind, the curtain
should fall upon the drama of the world's history,
the personal hopes of bliss on the part of individuals
would begin to be realised, and eternal life would
be entered upon. The fulfilment of the hope of
future blessing in this twofold way is represented in
the Revelation of Baruch (chaps. xxix., xxx., xxxix.,
xl., l., li., lxxii.–lxxiv.), and in the Fourth Book of
Esdras (*esp.* chap. vii. 26 ff.), two works which, though
dating from the close of the first century A.D., certainly
serve to attest the current ideas among the Jews in
the time of Jesus. It was certainly possible so to
combine this mode of view with the other, according
to which the individual hope of blessedness was
merged in that of the Messianic kingdom; that a
first resurrection of the just to a participation in
the Messianic kingdom on earth was supposed, and
then, after the close of this Messianic period, another
and general resurrection of the dead to the world-
judgment. This combination, on which the view
given in the New Testament Apocalypse is founded
(chap. xx.), may have become current among the
Jews of that period. But, nevertheless, the fact
remains that the personal hope of salvation and the
national Messianic hope were mainly independent

of each other. For the personal hope reached
beyond the blessedness of the Messianic period;
the latter appearing only as the vestibule of the
former. According to this mode of view, the
Messianic hope in general necessarily lost its
religious significance, since it no longer corresponded to the original purpose of representing the
ideal after whose full realisation in the future the
godly aspired. Hence also the significance of the
Messianic king in particular would become essentially lowered. For he appeared no longer as the
mediator of God in regard to those offices whereby
the peculiar and final possession of bliss on the
part of the godly was carried out. The judgment
which he should accomplish, and the kingdom of
blessedness he was to establish, were regarded as
distinct from the last judgment and the final blessedness of the saints in heaven. If, with many of the
Jews in the time of Jesus, the Messianic hope had
certainly still retained its original religious character,
so far as this national hope was viewed as including
the highest hope of individual bliss, yet there was
also such a development in the mode of viewing it
that the Messianic hope was in danger of losing,
not entirely its currency, but at least its ancient
religious character, since it no longer appeared to
satisfy individual aspirations after a blessedness
beyond this earth, and freed from earthly limitations.

4. We must turn our attention to yet another
variety in form among the religious hopes of the
Jews, which, though perhaps bulking less largely in
dogmatic tradition, was of special importance for the

possible foundation of the teaching of Jesus. We
refer to the different meaning and stress laid upon
the moral and religious conditions and constitution
of the future state of salvation. With the prophets
of the early period the state of blessing in the latter
day was always so represented that the religious
relationship between Jehovah and His people
appears therein to be realised in ideal perfection.
The descriptions of that period have this as their
constant refrain, that Israel shall then be the people
of God, and Jehovah will be the God of Israel (Hos.
ii. 25; Jer. xxiv. 7; xxx. 22, 25; xxxi. 32; xxxii. 38;
Ezek. xi. 20; xxxiv. 30 f.; xxxvi. 28; Zech. viii. 8).
As the ideal relationship between God and the
people would be upheld, on the one hand, by the
fact of God bestowing upon the people the richest
blessings—restoration of their fallen power, gathering together of their scattered members, sure peace
and unclouded welfare; so it would be upheld, on
the other hand, by the people maintaining perfect
fidelity to God, in contrast to that faithlessness and
impurity of their relation towards God so often
denounced by the prophets, by their obeying His
will with true zeal, and becoming a means of
enlightening other nations in the knowledge and
fear of God. The descriptions of this marvellous
political and social prosperity of the future are
always connected with the exaltation of holiness, and
of moral and religious purity on the part of those
who shall share that future prosperity (cf. Hos. iii.
5; Zech. x. 12; Isa. xi. 9; Micah iv. 5; v. 11 ff.;
Zeph. iii. 12 f.; Jer. iii. 19; xxxi. 22; Isa. xlv. 23 ff.;

liv. 14; lx. 21; xxvi. 2; Zech. viii. 3). The store which was set upon this moral-religious character of the latter-day bliss is specially observable in two points. In the first place, true righteousness based on sincere repentance was emphatically set forth as the condition of participating in that state of blessing. And the Divine judgment which would bring the hitherto imperfect dispensation to an end, and lay the foundation of a new and more blessed state, would not be displayed only against the heathen and the enemies of Israel. Primarily, it would be directed against the Israelites themselves, so far as they might be unfaithful and disobedient to God (Amos ii. 4 ff.; v. 16 ff.; viii. 1 ff.; ix. 1; Hos. v. and viii.; Isa. ii. 6 ff.; iii. 1 ff.; v. 1 ff.; Micah i. 3 ff.; Zeph. i.; Jer. iv. ff.; xxv. 29; Ezek. iv. ff.; Isa. lxv. 1 ff.; lxvi. 15 ff.; Mal. ii. 12; iii. 5, 19). Secondly, however, the moral and religious integrity of the people in the latter day was itself to be included among the Divine gifts then to be bestowed. It was to be inwrought and sustained by the purifying and renewing influence of God's Spirit. Thus Isaiah writes that all the inhabitants of Jerusalem would be holy, because the Lord would wash away their impurity by the Spirit of judgment and the Spirit of abolition (iv. 3 f.), and that the Spirit would be poured out from on high, and judgment and righteousness would dwell in the land (xxxii. 15 f.). The author of Zechariah xii.–xiv. foretold that Jehovah would then pour out the Spirit of grace and supplication upon the inhabitants of Jerusalem (xii. 10); and that all sin and uncleanness would

be washed away, and all idolatry and false prophesy-
ing would be abolished (xiii. 1 ff.).   According to
Jeremiah, God would write His law in the hearts
and minds of the people, so that they would no
more teach one another to know Jehovah, but all
would know Him from the least to the greatest
(xxxi. 32 f.); He would give them one heart and
one way, that they might fear Him for ever (xxxii.
39 f.).   According to Ezekiel, Jehovah would cleanse
them from all their filthiness, and would give them
a right mind and a new spirit; He would take
away their stony heart, and give them a heart of
flesh, whereby they should walk in His ordinances,
and keep His statutes, and do them (xi. 18 ff.; xxxvi.
25 ff.).   Also in the post-exilian prophets we find
once more this promise of the gracious influence
of the Divine Spirit in the latter days.   Deutero-
Isaiah predicts that Jehovah would pour out His
Spirit upon all the Israelites (xliv. 3), and that all
the inhabitants of Jerusalem would be taught of
Jehovah in order to their welfare and righteousness
(liv. 13 f.); Joel promises that in those days the
Spirit of God would be poured out upon all flesh,
old and young, even upon man-servants and maid-
servants, so that they should be prophets and seers
(iii. 1 f.).

How, then, in the time of Jesus, do we find the
eschatological hopes of the Jews standing in this
respect?   Certainly the state of blessedness in that
new era was always represented, in its conditions and
character, as a moral and religious state.   For it was
a fixed underlying principle here that the future state

of blessing was to be a work of God, and would perfect the covenant-relation between God and His people. Therefore that state was necessarily thought of as implying righteousness in the people, so that only the God-fearing Israelites could expect to participate in it; and even alien peoples, upon whom the influence of that blissful time would extend, would be led to worship the God of Israel. Yet the idea of this righteousness might be conceived with various degrees of moral depth; and, for the character of the whole idea of that future dispensation, this difference of moral depth was much more important than any difference produced by representing the future blessings as more or less natural or supernatural, of earthly or of heavenly origin, of sensuous or supersensuous nature.

Among some, at least, of the Jews in the time of Jesus, the hopes for the future were still entertained with the same moral earnestness which pervaded the ideas of the early prophets. A beautiful testimony to this is contained in the Psalter of Solomon, in that description of the latter day which most plainly shows its author's maintenance, not only of the idea of the Messianic king as the vice-gerent of the agency of God, but also of the significance of the Messianic redemption as inclusive of the highest personal hope of blessing for the individual. In Ps. xvii. [1] the misery that has hitherto prevailed is dwelt upon: " Very vile were the children of the covenant among the mixed

---

[1] Cf. Wellhausen's translation, *The Pharisees and Sadducees*, Greifs-wald, 1874, p. 160 ff,

multitude of the heathen; no one among them
practised what was just and right" (ver. 17). The
judgment to come was viewed in harmony with
this declaration. Prayer was offered that God
would raise up the Son of David as King of Israel,
and would gird Him with power, "that He would
overthrow the unrighteous ruler; that He would
purge Jerusalem of the heathen who trample it;
and that, by His annihilating power, His wisdom
and justice, He would drive sinners out of the
earth, and break their pride like a potter's vessel,
and shatter their high estate with His iron sceptre;
that the heathen might flee before His anger, being
destroyed by the word of His mouth, and that
sinners might be punished on account of the
thoughts of their heart" (vers. 23–27). By the term
"sinners," who, along with the heathen, are here
named as objects of Divine judgment, we must, in
harmony with the foregoing accusations, understand
the ungodly in Israel. Immediately after this
follows the description of the state of felicity which
the Messiah should introduce; and here the main
stress is laid upon its moral and religious aspect.
"Then He (the Messiah) shall gather together a
holy people, whom He shall rule in righteousness;
and shall sanctify the tribes of the people to the Lord
His God. He will suffer no iniquity in the midst
of them, nor shall any wicked worker tarry among
them. For He searches out all who are not sons
of God. And He divides them the land according
to their tribes, and neither foe nor stranger shall
dwell thenceforward among them. He directs the

people and their tribes in wisdom, and has the
nations of the heathen under His yoke, that they
may serve Him. And He shall cause the Lord to
be honoured in the chief place of the whole earth ;
and He shall make Jerusalem clean and holy as at
the beginning. The nations shall come from the
ends of the earth to behold her glory, — bringing
Zion's weary sons as gifts,—and to look upon the
glory of God wherewith He shall glorify her. He
shall reign righteously over them as a King instructed
by God ; and no iniquity shall be found among them
in His days : for they shall all be holy, and their
King the anointed one of God. . . . In His life
He shall never stumble in the ways of His God ;
for God will make Him strong in the Holy Spirit,
and teach Him wise counsel, full of power and
righteousness. And the blessing of the Lord shall
be with Him in power, so that He will not stumble.
His hope shall be steadfast in the Lord ; who shall
be able to do aught against Him ? Mighty in His
deeds, and strong in the fear of God, He shall
guard the flock of the Lord in fidelity and righteousness, and under His care none of them shall
stumble on the pasture-ground. In meekness He
shall guide them all, and no haughtiness arises in
Him, nor shall any violence be committed among
them. Thus it shall become the King of Israel to
set Him, the anointed of God, over the house of
Israel to direct it " (vers. 28–36, 42–47). Doubtless
this psalmist has conceived of the righteousness and
holiness of the people in the latter-day quite in the
Judæo-Pharisaical sense, and as essentially different

from the righteousness of the kingdom of God taught by Jesus. But the important thing is that he lays such special and earnest emphasis upon the ethical conditions of participation in the Messianic blessings, and so strongly accentuates the ideal character of the righteousness in the Messianic period. In this respect his description of the coming kingdom of God approaches nearer the idea of the kingdom of God announced by Jesus, than does any other description of the future in the Jewish literature of the age in which Jesus lived. It is also noteworthy that the idea of the earlier prophets as to the more perfect righteousness of the people in the latter days being the effect of the Divine Spirit's agency, has, on the part of the psalmist just quoted, found expression, at least to this extent, that the Messiah is represented as filled with power and wisdom by the Holy Spirit, who thus qualifies Him for the establishment and maintenance of righteousness among the people.

But the Jewish Messianic hope at that period did not universally possess this earnest religious character. The legal righteousness recognised as the condition of acceptance with God, and of obtaining the Divine reward, was viewed by many individuals in a profoundly ethical way, and with regard to purity of heart; but by the great mass of the Pharisaic scribes, as well as of the people, it was regarded and practised in the form of external observances which aimed at conformity to the mere letter of the law. Hence also the righteousness, which was admittedly the condition of sharing in the fulfilment of Israel's hope

as a nation, as a marked feature of the latter-day, was
viewed by most of the Jews in a thoroughly external
manner. What they held as essential in this righteousness was circumcision—the mark of national and
religious connection with the covenant people—and
the correct observance of the external form of worship
and ceremonial laws. The judgment which was to
introduce and establish the latter-day blessedness was
therefore supposed as intended only for the heathen,
without any reference to its purifying effect on the
people themselves. In describing the latter-day glory
they only laid stress on Israel's earthly greatness, her
political power and dominion, the happiness and prosperity of the people, without setting store by the
moral and religious revival and elevation of Israel.
As an example of this form of the idea, we may cite
the description of that blissful period given in the
Assumptio Mosis (chap. x.), where it is just what is
not said that is most characteristic : " Then His
kingdom shall be manifested among all creatures ; and
the devil shall have an end, and with him all sorrow
shall pass away. Then the heavenly One shall arise
from the seat of His power, and shall issue from His
holy dwelling-place with fury and anger on behalf of
His children. And the earth shall quake to its ends,
and the high mountains shall be brought down, and
the hills shall fall. The sun shall no more give light,
and the moon shall be turned to blood, and the stars
shall fall from their courses. The sea shall sink into
the abyss, and the water-springs shall fail, and the
flood be dried up. Then God will exalt Himself in
the highest, the alone Eternal, and will chastise the

heathen, and destroy all their idols.   Then shalt thou
be blessed, O Israel, and shalt mount on the necks
and wings of eagles.   God shall exalt thee, and rear
thee up to the starry heavens ; and thou shalt look
down from on high upon thine earthly foes, and shalt
see them and rejoice, with thanks and praise to thy
Creator."[1]   In quite similar style we find the Jewish
hope depicted in the older part of the Jewish Sibyl
(iii. 652–794) and in the Book of Jubilees (chap. xxiii.).
The whole stress is here laid first on the great Judgment upon the heathen, and next on the power and
prosperity of Israel in that coming dispensation.

5. This lax external idea of the righteousness required in man in order to the manifestation of Divine
grace in the Messianic time, was specially opposed by
John Baptist, the man whom Jesus Himself declared
to be the immediate forerunner of His Messianic
work.   Certainly the Baptist's idea of the nature of the
righteousness demanded by God was in general harmony with the teaching of the Pharisees.   He was himself ascetic in regard to food and clothing (Mark i. 6 ;
Matt. xi. 18), and his disciples conformed to the Pharisaic practice of fasting.   Jesus regarded the Baptist as
indeed the greatest of those born of women, and yet
as only the last representative of those who belonged
to the prophetic period of expectancy.   He was not
already a member of the newly-inaugurated kingdom
of God (Matt. xi. 11–14).   In accordance with this,
Jesus declared the forms of righteousness practised
by John's disciples to be antiquated and out of keep-

---

[1] According to the translation of Schürer, *Gesch. d. jüd. Volkes*, ii.
p. 431 f. (trans. Div. II. vol. ii. p. 144).

ing with the new righteousness which He taught as belonging to the kingdom of God (Mark ii. 21 f.).

Yet Jesus characterised the general tendency of John's work by saying that he came "in the way of righteousness" (Matt. xxi. 32); that is, he made a stand for righteousness, and bore high testimony to the duty of right moral conduct (ἀλήθεια, John v. 33).[1] The grand distinction of the Baptist's teaching lay manifestly in the fact that, besides proclaiming the immediate coming of the Messiah, he conceived, in an inward way and with a moral earnestness which was foreign to his contemporaries, the character of the righteousness which he declared essential to all who would have a share in the Messianic kingdom. Against the proud self-righteousness of the Jews he raised his voice in stern proclamation of the need of repentance.

In the Logia of Matthew it is recorded that John addressed the multitude who went out to him (Luke iii. 7) as a generation of vipers, in reference to their being, in spite of specious outward appearances, full of the poison of sin. He repudiated the idea that their Abrahamic descent furnished security for them in view of the judgment of the approaching dispensation. The essential condition of their sharing in the promised redemption consisted in their bringing forth fruits meet for repentance; in other words, in their giving practical proof of the turning of their hearts from sin to the righteousness required by God. The last opportunity for fulfilling this condition was now held out to them. Already the Messiah was at hand,

---

[1] Cf. *L. J.* i. p. 315.

bringing with Him the searching fire of Divine judgment. He would carry out a sifting process upon
His threshing-floor (that is, according to the tenor
of the discourse, among the Jewish nation), gathering His wheat into the garner, but consuming the
chaff for ever. According to the account of Mark
(i. 4–8), John preached a baptism of repentance for
the forgiveness of sins, and announced a Mightier
who would come after him and bring a baptism of
the Holy Ghost. The immersion under water was
called a baptism to repentance, because the external
ablution performed in acknowledgment of sin symbolic-
ally expressed the resolve after a moral purification
of heart. This baptism of repentance had reference
to the forgiveness of sins; because, along with the
resolution to repentance, whose main object was
the turning from former sin to new obedience, a
gracious remission of past sins was expected from
God. Then, if God thus graciously put away
the former sins of those Israelites who evinced a
resolution towards new obedience to His will, He
would also doubtless regard and treat them as true
members of His covenant people, for whom He
had decreed His blessings so soon to be realised by
the Messiah. It is characteristic that the Baptist
speaks of the salvation brought in with the coming
dispensation as a baptism of the Holy Ghost; that
is, he indicated as the most essential part of the
Messianic salvation, that full endowment of Divine
spiritual power promised by the early prophets as the
means of establishing and maintaining the righteousness of the Messianic King and people. The stress

laid by him upon the moral conditions required for obtaining the Messianic blessing corresponds with the prominence he gave to the moral religious side of the expected salvation. From the fact that special prominence was also given, at a somewhat later date, by the Christians of the apostolic age to the Old Testament promises of the Holy Ghost for the Messianic time, we are strongly inclined to suppose that the impartation of the Holy Spirit was in general regarded by the Jews in the time of Jesus as the chief mark of the Messianic state of salvation. But according to the testimony of the extant Jewish literature of that period, this was by no means the case. The idea of a Divine spiritual energy exercised for the awakening and renewal of man's inner life, as prominently held up by the prophets, was overshadowed in the later Jewish mind by the expectation of a wonderful outward glory and prosperity under the Messiah's reign. But in regard to this point, as well as to his warning of Messianic judgment, even for the covenant people themselves, the Baptist followed the more profound religious views of the older prophets, in opposition to the materialised hopes of his contemporaries.

The reception which the Baptist's preaching met with among the Jewish people, shows how little the earnest emphasis laid by him on the moral and religious conditions and character of the coming salvation corresponded to the ideas and tastes of the majority of his countrymen. Mark certainly relates (i. 5) that the inhabitants of the whole country of Judea and all the dwellers in Jerusalem went out to John, and were baptized by him, confessing their sins. But this declaration as to the Baptist's universal popularity finds a limitation, not only in that later account of Mark (xi. 30–33), according to which, whilst the great mass of the people regarded John as a true prophet, their spiritual leaders—the chief priests, the scribes, and sanhedrists (ver. 27)—disclaimed this idea, but especially in the recorded utterances of Jesus Himself in regard to the reception which the Baptist met with among his countrymen. In the opinion expressed concerning the Baptist on the occasion when John sent a message from prison, Jesus refers, indeed, to the crowds who streamed out of Judea into the wilderness to see John (Matt. xi. 7 ff.; Luke vii. 24 ff.); but He immediately directs a reproach against the Jews, because they had not given personal effect to the will of God declared to them in John's preaching of righteousness. They had not allowed themselves to be baptized by him, whilst the publicans and harlots had received his baptism (Matt. xxi. 32; Luke vii. 29 f.). Towards the Baptist they had acted like children in the market-place, who would not dance to their comrades' piping. They had spoken of John as being possessed with a devil, on account of his ascetic earnestness (Matt. xi. 16 ff.; Luke vii. 31 f.). According to the saying of Jesus, recorded by Mark (ix. 13), the Elias, who was first to come and restore all things to a right footing, had really come, but men had done to him whatsoever they listed. Instead of submitting to the new dispensation which was being set up in preparation for the Messiah, and which it was the Baptist's peculiar mission to set up, they had sought rather to make him submissive to their will. Instead of hearkening to his instruction, they had treated him with caprice. And this accords with the reproach of Jesus in John v., that instead of practically exhibiting the moral conditions demanded by the Baptist, they had only wished to enjoy themselves for a while in his light (vers. 33–35). Only among a small circle of his countrymen had the Baptist gained a genuine success. The great mass, and especially the religious leaders, regarded him as one who did not correctly understand the ideas and wants of his time. This reception of the preaching of the Baptist was of typical significance for the result of the teaching of Jesus among the Jews (Matt. xi. 18 f. ; Mark ix. 12 f.).

Our glance at the state of the religious hopes among the Jews in the time of Jesus, shows that one simple fulfilment of those hopes, in a way that should realise all the existing forms of the ideal of redemption, was impossible. Motives of different origin and value were at work to stamp the Jewish hopes with a variety of forms. And these diversified hopes in their turn laid the basis for different lines of further development. Were we to proceed from any one of those starting-points, and follow the line of its tendency, we should thereby arrive at a position directly opposed to certain other forms of the redemptive ideal, founded on tradition and highly regarded by many in Israel.

CHAP. III. THE DEVELOPMENT OF THE RELIGIOUS VIEWS
OF JESUS.

1. We shall afterwards consider how Jesus presented
His teaching for His disciples and His countrymen in
general, sometimes in agreement with, sometimes in
opposition to, the ideas and hopes of contemporary
Judaism. Here we shall only inquire how, on the
basis of Judaism, Jesus personally attained His
religious views. The Gospel narratives give but few
hints of the development of Jesus before the commencement of His public ministry ; and we will not
seek to use the scanty data they supply in order to
give a detailed account of the history of Jesus. In
relation to our task of expounding the contents of His
teaching, we only require to give a brief outline of the
main points which were of special significance for the
formation of His religious and Messianic convictions.

We must, in the first place, emphasise the fact that
Jesus did not receive His education as a disciple of
the Pharisees and the Pharisaic scribes, those special
representatives and teachers of the Jewish legalism
and mode of interpreting Scripture. He was not
afterwards regarded as a deserter from the Pharisaic-
scribal ranks, but as a self-taught teacher, who, as
such, could have merely a lay acquaintance with the
Holy Scriptures (John vii. 15). Certainly He proved
an acute critic of the doctrine and practice of the
Pharisees, and of the traditions and interpretations of
the scribes (cf. Mark vii. 8 ff., xii. 38 ff. ; Matt. xxiii.),[1]

[1] See *Logia*, §§ 13 and 52, *L. J.* i. pp. 104 ff. and 185 f.

but still on the basis of a knowledge derived from external intercourse with them, or from His acquaintance with their public teaching in the synagogues. His own mode of view remained unaffected by the peculiar religious form in which the Pharisees apprehended and moulded the Old Testament religion; and His mode of teaching was distinct from the method which they employed in their inquiries and teaching. We can also say with certainty that Jesus did not develop His views under Essene influences. The opinion that He had held close relations with the Essenes is only possible alongside of very defective ideas in regard to the peculiar tendencies of that sect. The doctrine and mode of life of Jesus show just as little affinity with the tendencies of the Essenes as with those of the Pharisees. The renunciation of the world which He taught was of quite a different character, and had quite a different motive from that of the Essenes.

Over against these negative elements we have to set the positive fact, that the main source from which Jesus derived the material for the formation and enrichment of His views lay directly in the Holy Scriptures. From the attitude which He subsequently assumed towards the " Scriptures," from His thorough knowledge of them, and His quite original mode of using them; from His defence of their Divine authority, in spite of His knowledge of the imperfection of their contents, and from His assurance that they furnished decisive testimony to His Messiahship, we can draw a certain conclusion in regard to the importance they had for the foundation and development of His religious persuasions. In what particular way He found opportunity, impulse, and guidance for the study, and indeed the independent study, of the Holy Scriptures, we know not. The fact, however, that during His early formative period He lived and moved in an element of Holy Scripture, can admit of no doubt. That the gathering of those ancient Scriptures, with their religious treasures and moral instruction, into a sacred Canon, recognised as having the highest authority as the documents of Divine revelation, was a blessing for Israel, received its highest proof from the influence of those Holy Scriptures on Jesus.

He found in the Scripture something other and higher than the Jews were wont to find. From its pages there spake to Him, not a God who, as the most high and mighty King and Judge, was only interested in the retribution of men's works, and was specially pleased with the amount and exactitude of their performance of ceremonies and acts of worship; but He who was revealed to Jesus in the Scriptures was the Father in heaven, full of grace and mercy, ready to give His gracious gifts to all, even to sinners, but who at the same time, with holy earnestness, required from men such love as He Himself bears, and for whom all merely external human acts, words, and appearances had no value. The elements of this conception of God were indeed contained in the Old Testament Scriptures, especially in the Psalms and the prophets, but not as a collective unity, and not in consecutive detail; they were mingled with heterogeneous elements, in which even the system of external legalism, prevalent in the time of Jesus, found some basis on which to build.   How came it, then, that Jesus found and understood in the Scriptures the revelation of the fatherly love of God, so as to enable Him to collect and unify its various elements into a living whole?   How came it that, in spite of the contemporary religious traditions, different in tendency, and deep-rooted in the whole customs and modes of thought of the people — traditions whose influences and attractions must have reached Him in numberless cases and forms—and in spite of the comprehensive and direct scriptural foundation for these prevalent religious modes of view, He was enabled to reach and firmly to grasp the unique truth of this conception of God?   Great, doubtless, was the influence of parental piety in directing and fostering the religious development of His boyhood and youth.   There is reason to believe that, beside the Sadducean aristocrats, and the Pharisaic scribes, and the extensive classes of people whom they spiritually influenced, and besides the world-renouncing Essenes, there was at that time another circle among the Jewish people whose hearts were the abode of pious gratitude and trust, and of sincere obedience to the duties of faithfulness and love, nourished by a simple and upright searching of the Scriptures.   Joseph and Mary were doubtless among this number; and the revulsion naturally produced in the son, trained in their ideas and by their example, when He came in contact with the spirit of Pharisaic righteousness, must have been great.   Yet the key to a full understanding of the certainty, clearness, and perfection with which Jesus grasped the Scripture revelation of the fatherly love of God, is not found in the mere influence of the piety of His parents. That key must be sought in the peculiar spiritual power which belonged to Himself, and which He felt to be a miraculous Divine endowment, a blessed pledge of the fatherly love of God bestowed upon Himself, and a lively constraining impulse to childlike obedience to the will of God. The testimony of this Divine endowment of which He was inwardly conscious, and the testimony of the Scriptures, conspired to shed light upon each other, and mutually confirmed their Divine significance.

On the ground of the religious self-consciousness which prompted the later words and acts of Jesus, we can affirm that, so far back as that religious consciousness extended, He had always felt Himself in a relation of Sonship to God. Certainly this feeling had grown within Him gradually, and had widened and deepened. Along with the general development of His spiritual and moral life, the true and full significance of His loving fellowship with God, His endowment of Divine life and grace, and His sense of filial duty towards God, had unfolded. But in order to attain that conscious standing in grace, and that position of filial freedom, Jesus had not to work His way out of servile legalism. From first to last He was conscious of His filial relation to God. In this respect His development before the commencement of His ministry shows the greatest difference from the early experience of the man who afterwards became the inspired apostle of the gospel of grace and sonship. This difference was of essential moment, not only in regard to the way in which Jesus and Paul respectively regarded themselves, but in regard to their whole mode of stating and confirming the Christian gospel for others.

All these important elements of the religious development of Jesus, which can be indirectly inferred from the style of His teaching and His later statements concerning Himself, are clearly mirrored in that delightful narrative of the first visit of Jesus at the age of twelve to the temple at Jerusalem (Luke ii. 41 f.). All the features of that account bear the stamp of inward truth; the ardent insatiable thirst for instruction out of the Holy Scriptures, of which such rich promise seemed held out by seeking the society of the doctors in the temple; the originality of His answers, which struck His hearers with amazement, and which already showed the independence of His mental attitude towards the traditional mode of view and of interpretation of the scribes; the calm assurance with which He spoke to His parents of God as His Father, and of His sojourn in His Father's house, as if it were a matter of course; and the childlike *naïveté* and simplicity of judgment with which He conceived it a necessary duty to tarry in His heavenly Father's house in spite of His parents' departure and their anxious quest of Him. We know not from what source Luke derived this narrative; but we can say that it gives us a

thoroughly true and natural picture of the spiritual
life of Jesus as it existed at the dawn of His early
development.

2. Jesus then, even from childhood, was clearly
sensible of the fatherly love of God, and of His
filial relationship to God, and He remained faithful
to that early assurance; and, as will be more fully
shown afterwards, this conception of God as a loving
Father furnished the unifying principle whence
grew in organic connection the later teaching of
Jesus in regard to the saving blessings which God
will bestow on man, and the nature of the righteous
conduct required by God from man.   When we
duly weigh these considerations, we can well conceive how Jesus, when He ripened into manhood,
perhaps even long before He began His public
ministry, possessed a clearly thought-out general
view of the normal relation of man to God — a
general view which was in harmony with His later
ideas and teaching concerning the nature of the
realised kingdom of God.   But at that earlier time
He was not yet fully aware of the relation of His
religious conception to the setting up of the long-
expected kingdom of God; in other words, He
did not as yet know that, in His perfect knowledge
of the fatherly love of God, and in His own perfect
embodiment of the filial relation to God, the
principles of the fulfilment of the Divine promises
in the Old Testament in regard to salvation were
in the highest sense contained.   He certainly shared
in the national hopes based on the Holy Scriptures;
and, from His own special way of reading and

understanding them, as well as from His own experience of what constituted the highest and best blessedness, He formed, in contrast to the ideals prevalent among His countrymen, His own ideas of what would be the chief and most essential elements of the blessedness of the latter-day dispensation. But the knowledge that He was called of God to be the Messiah of the new kingdom did not lie ready to hand for Him long before He entered on His Messianic work; it did not develop itself in Him by a gradual process of reflection; but, even as in Paul's case when called to be a Christian and an apostle, it came to him suddenly and unexpectedly through a miraculous revelation. The difference in the case of Paul lay in the fact that the miraculous revelation caused him to break entirely with his past, and with his whole previous modes of view and course of life; whilst for Jesus the revelation rather disclosed the goal which formed the terminus of the direct line in which He was going.

Jesus received this revelation which awakened His Messianic consciousness, when He was responding to the call of John the Baptist to the Jewish people to prepare for the near approach of the kingdom of God by sincere repentance, and, in token of their earnest purpose of repenting, to submit to be baptized by him in Jordan. In His later estimate of the Baptist, whom He did not hesitate to call the highest of the prophets, the promised Elias, the greatest of those born of women outside of the kingdom of God (Matt. xi. 9, 11, 14; Mark ix. 13), we see what a powerful impression the Baptist made upon Jesus. The features of the Baptist's ministry by which Jesus was attracted and impressed, were the moral earnestness of his preaching, born of a steadfast, world - renouncing personality (Matt. xi. 7 f.) ; his repudiation of the external forms of righteousness and hopes of blessing current among the Jews ; his call to them to shelter themselves, by sincere repentance and good works, from the impending judgments of God ; and the emphasis he laid upon the baptism of the Spirit as the greatest gift which the Messiah would bring them. All these elements of the Baptist's preaching were confirmed as true and scriptural by the religious judgment of Jesus. He viewed them as genuine credentials of the prophetic mission of John, and also, though indirectly, of the truth of his proclamation of the immediate nearness of the Messiah. Whilst the great mass of the people, and notably their spiritual rulers and teachers, turned away in self - righteous contempt from the Baptist's preaching (Matt. xi. 16 ff.; xxi. 32), Jesus attached Himself to those who, even though they had hitherto been open sinners, "publicans and harlots," submitted to the Divine message proclaimed by the Baptist (Matt. xxi. 32 ; Luke vii. 29),[1] and, with moral earnestness, prepared themselves for the approaching Messianic kingdom. Had the main purpose of John's preaching and baptism of repentance lain in confession of sins and penitence, the coming of Jesus to be baptized would appear strange, and might be regarded as an argument against the stainless purity of His religious consciousness, or as the expression of a false humility.

---

[1] Cf. *Log.* § 4*c*, *L. J.* i. p. 77 f.

We must consider, however, that the main element in the idea of repentance lies in the positive bent of the spirit towards conformity with the Divine will ; and that turning from sin, so far as it has existed, forms only the preparation for, or the reverse side of, that process.   We must remember, also, that the final and essential purpose of the Baptist's preaching was to create the positive endeavour after a righteousness conformable to God's will, and to the establishment of the Messianic kingdom.   Hence it appears intelligible and truly fitting that Jesus should, not merely in spite of, but just on account of, His consciousness of integrity and filial obedience to God, feel impelled to submit to John's baptism.   He thereby sealed His resolve to yield His will wholly to the will of God, abjuring all sin, and thereby He gave that resolve a definite reference to the kingdom of God, whose nearness the Baptist proclaimed, and of which He desired to be a member.

At the moment when Jesus underwent the baptism of John, He received—and He alone, according to the clear account in Mark, which is corroborated in the further course of the history—the revelation which imparted to Him His Messianic consciousness.   He became conscious that the Spirit of God, which was to be possessed and given by the Messiah, had been imparted to Him, and that the titles of Son of God and Beloved or Well-pleasing to the Father, which, according to the Old Testament promises, belonged to the Messiah (cf. Ps. ii. 7 ; Isa. xlii. 1),[1]

---

[1] The heavenly voice, " This is My beloved Son, in whom I am well pleased," which, according to Mark i. 11, Jesus heard, does not refer

were then consciously and expressly sealed to Him by the judgment of God. No doubt Jesus was previously conscious that He was the Son of God, and an object of the Divine complacency; but through this revelation was awakened the conciousness of a unique pre-eminence of sonship in relation to God, and of the unique significance which, in virtue of this pre-eminence, He should have for the establishment of the kingdom of God and the Messianic dispensation. Whilst, hitherto, Jesus had been conscious of no peculiar excellence which exalted Him above others in respect to His religious views, experiences, and acts, and that just because they appeared to Him so simple, normal, and self-evident, now, all at once, He recognised the import of those personal qualities. He saw in them not merely a specific advance beyond the religious standpoint of His countrymen, but also the first and supreme realisation of that ideal relationship between God and men foretold in Scripture as characteristic of the Messianic time. The consciousness, however, of His special endowment by God, and His pre-eminent position among men, must, for Him, have involved a recognition of His special duty in regard

merely to Ps. ii. 7, or merely to Isa. xlii. 1, but to both these passages (cf. Beyschlag, *Leben Jesu*, ii. p. 112). The expression, "Thou art my Son," taken from the psalm, serves characteristically as the substitute for the conception, *servant of Jehovah*, of the prophetic passage; whilst, conversely, the conception, *object of the Divine complacency*, taken from the latter passage, serves as a significant expansion and confirmation of the title of Son. We must not suppose that the reference of the words thus revealed to Jesus, to the words of those Old Testament passages, was unimportant. For that very reference was the reason why Jesus could regard the words of that revelation as not only a recognition of His personal religious relation to God, but as an express designation of His Messianic character and vocation.

to God, and of His special vocation. As the Son of God, who for the first time and in perfect measure embodied the promised ideal relationship between God and mankind, He must be the Messiah who was to impart to other men the knowledge and the reality of this relationship; and therefore, also, He was to be the founder of the promised kingdom of God.

3. It is perfectly conceivable that Jesus, after this sudden and miraculous impartation of the knowledge of His Messiahship, was assailed with conflicting doubts, and that He felt it an urgent duty, founded on His Messianic endowments, to bring this conflict to an immediate and decisive issue. Mark intimates this progress by relating that Jesus, immediately after His baptism, was driven by the Spirit, that is, the Spirit of God whom He had seen descending upon Himself at baptism, into the wilderness, where, severed from all human intercourse, He was for forty days tempted of the devil (Mark i. 12 f.). Had Jesus, previous to His baptism, already passed through a process of development, and had that baptism only meant for Himself the confirmation of this process, and, for others, the public acknowledgment of His Messiahship, the inner conflicts through which He would thus have attained His Messianic consciousness would have fallen within the period preceding His baptism. That the temptation followed upon the baptism is a strong confirmation of the view that Jesus for the first time suddenly received at baptism the consciousness of His Messiahship, which then required to be confirmed through an inner conflict. The source of such conflict as even threatened to obliterate His

Messianic assurance lay in certain aspects of the
Messianic idea as conceived by the pious Jews, *e.g.*
the Baptist, and hitherto even by Jesus Himself.
That form of the Messianic idea, He saw, could not
be realised if He proceeded on the Messianic career
in the form, and under the spiritual power, which had
been revealed to Him at baptism.   It was no conflict
against images and ideals arising out of a wicked,
selfish, and ungodly disposition and inclination in
Jesus Himself.   The Christian Church has ever justly
repudiated this idea of the temptation originating in
the state of Jesus' own heart.   But there were Messianic conceptions and ideals which hitherto approached
Him from without, that is, from among the prevailing
views and traditions of His countrymen, and which He
now inwardly possessed, in the sense of their being
known to Him and being imaged in His mind, without
needing any external means of presentation.   They
presented themselves to Him with a plausible appearance of being true and scriptural, and, through such
plausibility, they became veritable temptations which
it cost Him a struggle to overcome.   When He tried
them He perceived the impious principles on which
they were based, and, to that extent, regarded and
treated them as temptations of Satan.

The accounts given by our first and third evangelists (Matt. iv. 1 ff. ; Luke iv. 1 ff.) concerning the
three temptations with which Jesus was assailed by
the devil, bring so vividly and characteristically before
us this inner conflict of Jesus, that we have every
reason to regard this narrative, even in its significant
figurative dress, as having been communicated at a

later period by Jesus to His disciples.[1] Certainly we
should misunderstand the meaning of the narrative,
were we to suppose that, taking for granted the certainty that Jesus was the Messiah, the question only
related to His decision as to the special character and
mode of His Messianic mission, and how His miraculous Messianic powers were to be used. It was
rather His Sonship itself, in a special, that is, a
Messianic sense, that was in question, since He had
not the powers and could not attain the ends which
were traditionally supposed to be essential to Messiahship. Did not the Messiah require to have earthly
means at His disposal, not only in order to live, but
to step forth with a power and a glory corresponding
to His merit? If Jesus did not possess such means,
and could not supply Himself with them in a magical
way, if He were unable to produce even so much of
earthly good things as to shield Himself from earthly
want, how could He be the Messiah? Jesus met and
overcame this temptation by an appeal to Scripture,
which declares the life-giving and preserving will and
word of God, rather than earthly goods, to be the
true source of sustenance : "Man liveth not by bread
alone, but by every word that proceedeth out of the
mouth of God." Even in the lack of all earthly
means, God could, by His creative word, protect
and support the Messiah. But if Jesus wished to
trust in Divine power for support, might He not trust
in it alone to act as a charm for Him against all
earthly dangers and wants? And if He could not
trust so steadfastly in the miraculous help of God as

[1] Cf. *L. J.* i. p. 210 f.

even to let Himself fall down from the pinnacle of the temple, and hope to escape unhurt because of angelic support, how could He go forth as the Messiah ? This incitement to make the assurance of His Messiahship depend on proving the miraculous assistance of God, was repelled by Jesus, on the ground that man must not arbitrarily tempt God : trust in God must be accompanied by humble submission to His will, and is incompatible with the trial to bring the power of God into the service of one's own caprice. As the Messiah, He could trust in God for power and protection only in the line of His high vocation. He could not lay claim to miraculous power to carry out selfish ends or to shield Him from wantonly incurred danger. But would He then be able, if unsupplied with earthly means and without insurance against earthly dangers, to undertake His work in humble confidence in God alone, and be able really to establish the Messianic dominion ? Certainly not a dominion of earthly splendour and power, and not a supremacy over worldly subjects, such as was supposed by the traditional Messianic ideas. But Jesus was now clearly conscious that every aspiration after a dominion of an earthly kind had a self-seeking tendency in entire opposition to the true homage to God. What the fatherly will of God demanded was not to rule over others, but to render loving services (cf. Mark x. 42–45). The establishment of an earthly sovereignty did not befit the nature of the Messianic kingdom, but would rather serve the purposes of sin and Satan. And now when Jesus conceived the possibility of winning all the kingdoms of the world if He would give up His faithful homage to God alone, that possibility had no allurement for Him. The temptations which tended to rob Him of the assurance of His Messiahship had come to an end when He saw that the final goal to which the alluring thoughts pointed, viz. the idea of the necessity of earthly power, glory, and sovereignty for the Messiah, was not really in harmony with the will of God, and could not be reached on the pathway of loyal obedience to Him.

The benefit derived by Jesus from thus fighting out the battle against those temptations which assailed Him immediately after baptism, was, that the consciousness of His Messianic vocation, which had so suddenly come to Him, He now obtained as an abiding personal possession. Henceforth He was no longer subject to a ferment of inner perplexity and doubt; whilst, in the prosecution of His Messianic calling, He was at every step beset by external conflict and hindrances connected with Jewish worldly ideals of the Messiahship, on the part of His disciples and His enemies. Having dealt in no short perfunctory way with this early temptation, but having, after weeks of inner conflict, reached calm and thorough victory, He could now undertake His public teaching and ministry with unshaken conviction of His Messiahship, and with a marvellous clearness and consistency of view in regard to the kingdom of God.

SECOND SECTION.

EXTERNAL ASPECTS OF THE TEACHING OF JESUS.

···—》—·

CHAP. I. THE EXTERNAL FORM OF HIS TEACHING.

1. BEFORE considering the contents of the teaching of Jesus in regard to the kingdom of God, as proclaimed by Him on the ground of His Messianic consciousness, we must cast a glance at its external form. By endeavouring to take exact note of the characteristic features of that form, we lay a necessary basis for ascertaining the contents of His teaching; for in many instances, if we examine the recorded words of Jesus in an isolated way, we find more than one meaning apparently possible, and are able to decide with certainty for one of those meanings by virtue of our knowledge of His mode of teaching acquired by extensive observation in other cases. Our study of the external form, however, is important from another point of view. So far as we have reason to assume that the characteristic features of the external method of Jesus' teaching were no product of chance or of external influence, but were expressly chosen with a view to the subject-matter and the effect proposed, we must look upon this form of

teaching as an indirect but significant expression of the consciousness which Jesus had of the general character and design of His teaching.

For a knowledge of the peculiar method of Jesus, we must only draw upon the Gospel of Mark and the Logia of Matthew. That the discourses of Jesus in the fourth Gospel bear a formal stamp which differs essentially from that of the discourses in the chief synoptical sources, and which must in any case be regarded, in comparison with that of the latter, as less authentic, is an opinion we can quite frankly avow, if we presuppose that the substance of the thoughts in the Johannine discourses is of genuine apostolic authority. A precise study of the form of teaching which is observable in the chief synoptical sources, will render it possible to form a conclusion much more definite and reliable than the first vague general impression, as to the difference of form in the discourses of the fourth Gospel. We can thus ascertain and establish the special points in regard to which that difference exists, and can indicate in what degree certain marks may be found here also of the same form of teaching which we find elsewhere recorded.

2. In the first place, it is of importance to note that Jesus, so far as we can conclude from our sources, has never aimed, in any single discourse or any group of connected discourses, at laying down His doctrine in systematic form. He never presents it in such order as to embrace all the particular parts, and exhibit them as branches of an organic whole. He gives no exhaustive exposition of all the parts in their due

proportion; nor has He symmetrically evolved its antecedents and consequences. Certainly He did not proceed without a plan. A progressive deliverance of His doctrine is observable; for certain parts of it were not presented from the beginning, but He gradually prepared the way for these through other doctrines subsidiary to their establishment and explanation. Yet this methodical progress in His teaching is not identical with a systematic arrangement. On the one hand, that progress is only observable in the course of the development of the teaching of Jesus as a whole and in regard to certain main subjects. On the other hand, Jesus did not absolutely omit the formerly explained problems of His teaching when proceeding to further ones. Instead of a systematic form such as essentially characterises all scientific presentation, Jesus has given His teaching the form of impromptu discourses and utterances. He used the circumstances of the time to enforce points in His doctrine that could be illustrated by them, or from His point of view, and in longer or shorter form as seemed called for in the circumstances. Along with most of His sayings and discourses the special circumstances which prompted them are also given. But even where occasion was only presented for general teaching, instead of instruction for a particular purpose, for example, in the passage Luke vi. 20 (Matt. v. 1) or Mark iv. 1 f., we still find that He did not extend His teaching over a wide field which He reviewed scientifically in all its bearings. He preferred to limit Himself to the discussion of a certain point, for example, in that great discourse recorded at the beginning of the Logia, in exposition of the idea that in the kingdom of God righteousness is estimated according to the purity of the motive whence the act proceeds ; or in the parable-discourse in Mark iv., describing the results of the preaching of the kingdom of God. We must certainly suppose that Jesus did not, in these instances, select the subject with a view to systematic order and completeness in imparting His instruction, but only with regard to the practical need of His hearers at the time.

By this method of meeting the want of the occasion, Jesus has been able to impart two weighty qualities to His utterances and His instruction, viz. *popular intelligibility and impressive pregnancy*. The importance lies in the union of these two qualities. A mode of teaching which aims at popular intelligibility is exposed to the risk of degenerating into platitude and triviality ; and one which aims at pregnant brevity easily becomes stilted and obscure. But Jesus perfectly combined the two qualities, and by this very means attained a peculiar and classic beauty of style. All the characteristic qualities and methods observable in His style can be classed under the head of means for obtaining those two special excellences.[1]

[1] Our view, that the style of Jesus is governed by the aim at intelligibility, is not belied by the fact that in some utterances Jesus expresses the intention to veil His meaning for those who are unsusceptible, or who are unripe for fuller knowledge (Mark iv. 11 f. ; John xvi. 25, cf. x. 6). It would be just as wrong, in view of such utterances of Jesus, to restrict the general application of the characteristic of aiming at intelligibility, as it would be over-hasty,

It was a popular intelligibility that was aimed at by Jesus. Exposition of a scientific kind was never intended by Him. Even in the case of conceptions which were of fundamental importance for His teaching, and which differed materially from those formed from the traditional Jewish point of view, such, for example, as the conception of the kingdom of God, He gives no express explanation, far less a formal

in judging from His manifest general aim at intelligibility, to pronounce those particular utterances impossible and unhistorical in which a contrary aim appears to be expressed. When we observe in the parable-discourses given in Mark iv., several clear traces which indicate that the evangelist has restored, with light touches of his own, the sayings of Jesus already handed down by tradition in a formal stamp (cf. *L. J.* i. p. 30 ff.), we have every reason to distinguish the general conclusions drawn by the evangelist as a historian (ver. 33 f.) from the saying handed down by him (ver. 11 f.), which, however, stand related in thought to the sayings in the context, namely, to the parable of the unfruitfulness of the seed that fell into bad soil (ver. 3 ff.), and to the saying in regard to the mutual relation between what is given and what is received (ver. 24 f.). I cannot here go into an exposition of the meaning and ground of that saying of Jesus (Mark iv. 11 f.) ; the right place will be found for it later, when treating of the nature and conditions of the kingdom of God. Here I might only remark that Jesus makes the veiling of His teaching for " those who were without " the reverse side of its designed revelation for the circle of His disciples. We can also quite well understand how He could judge that His parables, just because of their aim at making plain to the people His doctrine of the kingdom of God, tended, in the unsusceptible, though not in the earnest inquirer, to divert the thought from the peculiar object of His teaching, and to a certain veiling of the doctrine of the kingdom of God. Similarly it is conceivable that, in the Johannine passage recording His farewell address, He clothed His ideas in figurative language (John xvi. 25), where He knew that the literal expression of His thoughts would remain unintelligible to them. For here also the final object is certainly not concealment, but intelligible communication. Where the disciples were as yet unable to understand the thought which occupied Him, He did not, in spite of that, impart this as unintelligible truth ; nevertheless, through the figurative form of the expression, He sought to suggest at least as much as lay within the compass of their capacity, and at the same time furnish a link for their memory to take hold of, whereby at a later period they might penetrate to a fuller understanding of His meaning (ver. 25 and previous verses, cf. xiv. 26).

definition. On the other hand, He possessed a masterly skill of concise portrayal of the subject in hand, and of bringing it home to those of humble, uncultured intelligence. The means He specially employed for this purpose were either concrete individualisation by example, or comparison.

3. General rules and statements which He sought to impress on His hearers, He usually makes clear at a glance by special *examples*. An instance of this is found in the discourse on the true nature of righteousness at the beginning of the Logia. Here the principle is laid down that the perfect righteousness of the kingdom of God, as distinguished from the inferior standard hitherto enjoined, demands the entire supremacy of righteousness in the inner man, and a corresponding absence of the manifestations of an impure spirit, even such as might appear from an external point of view to be trifling and harmless. But Jesus Himself does not at all put it in this general way. We deduce this principle from a series of particular precepts, which He contrasts as His new commandments with earlier rules enjoined upon "them of old time" (Matt. v. 21 ff.). He does not thereby indicate the mode of conduct which He enjoins, and, conversely, that which He forbids, in the general, as occurring in many particular cases, but specially, as occurring in one particular case. After declaring the culpability of anger against a brother, He does not merely emphasise the guilt of using words of hatred in general, but specially of such low terms of reproach as "fool" (Raca), and the till more damnatory term of "godless" (Moreh).

Then, after laying down the rule that one should use the enmity of another, not as an occasion for retaliative hatred, but as a means offered in order to reconciliation, He illustrates this by an example showing how one should act if, in bringing an offering to the altar, he remembers the enmity of his brother (Matt. v. 22–24). Similarly, after giving the exhortation not to resist one that is evil, He subjoins the example of how to act if struck by another on the right cheek, or if robbed by him of a coat through a form of legal process, or if asked to accompany him a mile (vers. 39–41). After giving the general rule, " Take heed that ye do not your righteousness before men to be seen of them," He immediately shows how to apply this rule in particular instances of good works, as alms-giving, praying, and fasting (Matt. vi. 1–18). When He sends His disciples on a preaching tour, and gives them the general exhortation to lay aside thought about their own comfort, and only to be careful about fulfilling their mission, He makes it more definite by enumerating the articles they should take for the journey, as well as what to do and to leave undone on arriving at a new place. Certainly He laid down no exhaustive and unalterable programme for their conduct in every particular case and relation. What He regarded as essential was simply that they should be completely self-forgetful, and should strain every nerve in devotedly applying themselves to the mission they had undertaken. This general principle, however, and the manner of specially applying it, would impress itself more emphatically and enduringly upon their minds by His showing its direct application in particular cases. Again, when encouraging His disciples to trust in God's providing care, by pointing out the Divine interest in all creatures on earth, even those which are little regarded, as well as God's rich bounty and protecting power, He takes examples from the ravens and the lilies of the field (Luke xii. 24, 27), or from the sparrows (Luke xii. 6 f.). When He declares that, at His second coming, the final sentences will be determined for men independently of their outward position on earth, and that those who were nearest each other outwardly may be severed far asunder in destiny, He takes the example of two servants working together in the field, and of two maids grinding at the mill, of whom one should be taken and the other left (Matt. xxiv. 40 f.).

To this department of illustrative examples belong also the narratives of the Good Samaritan (Luke x. 30 ff.), of the Rich Man whose ground had brought forth plentifully (Luke xii. 16 ff.), of the Pharisee and Publican in the temple (Luke xviii. 10 ff.) ; also the account, in Mark's Gospel, of the Widow's Offering (xii. 41 ff.).[1] These narratives have this in common with the parables of Jesus of which we have afterwards to speak, that they describe a certain supposed case which happened under definite circumstances. They are, however, distinguishable from the parable in this, that they do not present a *comparison* whereby from the validity of one fact we can argue the validity of another analogous fact in a different sphere. Again, in the

---

[1] That this story of the Widow's Mite, in the original tradition, was apparently an example used by Jesus in connection with His declaration, Mark xii. 40, cf. *L. J.* i. p. 41.

argument from example, by citing a particular case one can found upon it a general rule, which holds good for all other particular cases belonging to the same class.[1]

Exemplification by word is nearly related to exemplification by action. We can say that the whole active work of Jesus was an exposition of His teaching through His own example. In certain cases, indeed, He has employed certain acts for the sole purpose of illustrating His teaching. Mark (ix. 33–37) relates how, when His disciples were disputing about precedence, He gave them the general reproof, "If any man desire to be first, the same shall be last of all and servant of all," and how He then illustrated the character of this humility and service which gave a foremost place in the kingdom of God, by taking a child in His arms and declaring that such kindly reception of a child was of the highest value. Similarly in those sayings of Jesus at the last supper, recorded in the Logia, whose original connection we can recognise in Luke xxii. 14–35, after taking away the words of vers. 18–25 and 33 (which, according to Mark, have been inserted),[2] it is related how Jesus waited upon His disciples in giving them the cup (ver. 17). He thus showed that He was among them as one that served (ver. 27), and that the greatest among them should become, that is, should comport himself as if he were, the younger, and the leader as if he were the servant (ver. 26).

Analogous to these two cases in which Jesus illustrated precept by example, we have the case, handed

---

[1] Cf. Jülicher, *die Gleichnissreden Jesu*, 1886, i. p. 117.
[2] Cf. *Log.* § 39, *L. J.* i. p. 171 ff.

down from the Johannine sources, of His washing the disciples' feet. Jesus thus sought to picture for them how they ought to wash one another's feet (xiii. 12–15). Elsewhere, however, in John we certainly miss that mode of specialising and exemplifying so abundantly used by Jesus according to our other sources, whereby He passed quickly from the general rule to its application in concrete particular cases. And this want goes largely to the formation of the peculiar character of John's Gospel in contrast to the Synoptists. One can justly say, however, that the theme of those Johannine discourses, being the Divine and saving value of His work and person, did not afford such occasion for particularising cases as the pre-eminently practical admonitions in the synoptical discourses. But even the repeated exhortations to the right exercise of love, and to fearless trust in God, in the farewell discourse in John, have only a general stamp, without receiving point from examples taken from definite cases and circumstances.

4. Next to examples, the chief means used by Jesus to make Himself popularly intelligible were *comparisons*. Facts, events, and modes of conduct, specially in reference to certain characteristic features to be singled out, could be strikingly illustrated by setting them in comparison with some other thing wherein the same characteristic features came out with special clearness. The following are illustrative similes of this sort : " Whoso shall not receive the kingdom of God as a little child, shall in no wise enter therein" (Mark x. 15) ; "Behold, I send you as sheep among wolves : be ye wise as serpents

and harmless as doves" (Matt. x. 16); "I saw Satan as lightning fall from heaven" (Luke x. 18); "O Jerusalem, Jerusalem, . . . how often would I have gathered thy children as a hen gathereth her brood under her wings!" (Luke xiii. 34); "As the lightning issuing from the east and shining to the west, so also shall the coming of the Son of man be" (Matt. xxiv. 27); "Take heed to yourselves, lest . . . that day come suddenly upon you as a snare" (Luke xxi. 34); "Behold, Satan has desired to have you, that he may sift you as wheat" (Luke xxii. 31); "All nations shall be assembled before the Son of man, and He shall separate them one from another, as a shepherd divideth the sheep from the goats; and He will set the sheep on His right hand, but the goats He will set on His left" (Matt. xxv. 32 f.). Also to this class belong the comparisons, of the men of His generation to children sitting in the market-place and calling to their fellows (Matt. xi. 16 f.), of the scribe who has been made a disciple to the kingdom of heaven, to a householder who brings out of his treasure things new and old (Matt. xiii. 52), and of the Pharisees to whited sepulchres (Matt. xxiii. 27).

A higher *rôle*, however, than that of comparisons used for simple illustration is played in the teaching of Jesus by those used by Him in establishing the authority of His judgments and precepts. By pointing to the analogy of facts of more or less familiar experience, or to current views and customs, declarations and precepts may be so illustrated as to make them appear no longer strange, but rather credible and trustworthy, as corresponding with a more general and otherwise valid rule. Religious judgments and precepts, also, which Jesus expresses in conformity with His general view of the kingdom of God, are elucidated and confirmed, by bringing them into comparison with familiar phenomena and effects from the domain of nature and from ordinary human life. Comparisons of this kind, which, from their argumentative purpose, required to be given, not as illustrative additions to particular statements, but as independent themes or narratives, we term parables.[1]

We can distinguish two classes of these *parables*.

The first class refers to some natural event, or some fact of human intercourse or conduct, not as a separate concrete case, but as giving a rule in frequently recurring cases. In Mark's Gospel we find the following parables of this sort: " The whole have no need of the physician, but the sick " (ii. 17). " Can the children of the bride-chamber fast while the bridegroom is with them," etc. (ii. 19). " No man seweth a piece of new cloth on an old garment, etc. ; and no man putteth new wine into old bottles," etc. (ii. 21 f.). " If a kingdom be divided against itself, that kingdom cannot stand; and if a house be divided against itself, that house cannot stand " (iii. 24 f.). " No man can enter into a strong man's house, and spoil his goods, except he will first bind the strong man; and then he will spoil his house " (iii. 27). " Is a candle brought to be put under the bushel, or under the bed ? and not

---

[1] Cf. on the idea and character of the parables of Jesus, Jülicher, *die Gleichnissreden Jesu*, p. 24 ff.

to be set on the stand?" (iv. 21). "It is not meet to take the children's bread and to cast it to the dogs" (vii. 27). "Salt is good; but if the salt have lost its saltness, wherewith will ye season it?" (ix. 50; cf. from the Logia, Luke xiv. 34 f.). "From the fig-tree learn her parable; When her branch is now become tender, and putteth forth its leaves, ye know that the summer is nigh" (xiii. 28). Also those two parables—of the seed "which springs up and grows, the man knows not how" (iv. 26–29); and of the mustard-seed which, when it is sown, is smaller than all other seeds, but when it has grown up, is greater than all garden herbs (iv. 31 f.) — belong to this category, since they do not point to a definite occurrence which happens only once, but to a process always recurring afresh in the cases of wheat and mustard-seed. From the Logia I adduce the following examples: "Do men gather grapes of thorns, or figs of thistles? Even so every good tree bringeth forth good fruit; but the corrupt tree bringeth forth evil fruit. A good tree cannot bring forth evil fruit, neither can a corrupt tree bring forth good fruit" (Matt. vii. 16 ff., cf. xii. 33). "What man is there of you, who, if his son ask him for a loaf, will give him a stone? Or if he shall ask for a fish, shall give him a serpent?" (Matt. vii. 9 f.). "The disciple is not above his master, nor a servant above his lord: it is enough for the disciple to be as his master, and the servant as his lord" (Matt. x. 24 f.) "If the blind lead the blind, both shall fall into a pit" (Matt. xv. 14). "No servant can serve two masters: for either he will hate the one, and love the other; or else he will hold to the one, and despise the other" (Luke xvi. 13).   "Where the carcase is, thither will the eagles be gathered together" (Luke xvii. 31).[1]

Also in the Johannine sources we find numerous parabolic sayings of this kind: "The wind bloweth where it listeth, and thou hearest the sound thereof, but knowest not whence it cometh, and whither it goeth" (iii. 8).   "Are there not twelve hours in the day? If a man walk in the day he stumbleth not, because he seeth the light of this world; but if he walk in the night he stumbleth, because the light is not in him" (xi. 10).   "Except a grain of wheat fall into the ground and die, it abideth alone; but if it die, it beareth much fruit" (xii. 24).   "He that walketh in darkness knoweth not whither he goeth" (xii. 35).   "He that is bathed needeth not save to wash his feet, but is clean every whit" (xiii. 10). "The servant is not greater than his lord; neither is one that is sent greater than he that sent him" (xiii. 16).   "The servant knoweth not what his

---

[1] Cf. the following parabolic sayings from the Logia: concerning the city set on an hill which cannot be hid (Matt. v. 14); the unclean spirit, which, after having been expelled, returns with greater power (Matt. xii. 43 ff.); the importance of the condition of the eye for enlightening the whole body (Luke xi. 34 f.); the watching of the householder, who knows the hour in which the thief will come (Luke xii. 39); of the punishment meted out to the servant in accordance with the measure of his knowledge of his master's will (Luke xii. 47 f.); the prognostication of the weather from the clouds and wind (Luke xii. 54 f.); of the desirableness, even at the last moment before the judicial decision, of seeking a friendly settlement with the adversary (Luke xii. 58 f.); of the exchange of places at the marriage-feast (Luke xiv. 7 ff.); of the servant who, for the work due by him, receives no special reward from his master (Luke xvii. 7 ff.); of not desiring new wine, after having drunk mellow old wine (Luke v 39); of the freedom of the king's sons from tax-paying (Matt. xvii. 25 f.).

lord doeth" (xv. 15).   "A woman when she is in
travail hath sorrow, because her hour is come : but
when she is delivered of the child, she remembereth
no more the anguish, for the joy that a man is born
into the world" (xvi. 21).   Here also we may refer to
the parables at the beginning of chap. x., concerning
the door leading into the sheepfold, through which
one must pass who would take charge of the flock
(vers. 1–5); the thief who comes only to steal and to
destroy; the good shepherd who gives his life for the
sheep; and the hireling who leaves the flock in the
lurch in time of danger (vers. 10–13).

The second kind of parable used by Jesus has its
distinctive mark in this, that it refers, not to some
frequently recurring general fact, but to a single
event which has occurred in quite definite circumstances.   The parables are detailed here by way
of example.   Whilst parables of the former class are
drawn from the actual world, those of this sort, so far
as they refer to concrete persons or circumstances,
belong to the domain of pure fancy.   Yet the concrete details being, in the case of all these parables,
conditioned by their argumentative purpose, are
not contrived by a mere arbitrary fancy.   They are
always such as could happen in actual life.   In Mark
we find parables of this sort in the account of the
Sower whose seed fell upon grounds of different
quality (iv. 3 ff.), and that of the unfaithful Husband-
men (xii. 1 ff.).   From the numerous parables belonging to this category, derived apparently from the Logia
sources, and given in our first and third Gospels, I may
single out, as examples, the parable of the wise man

who built his house on a rock, and the foolish man
who built his house upon the sand (Matt. vii. 24 ff.),
that of the servant whose debt of ten thousand
talents was forgiven him, but who would not forgive
his fellow-servant a debt of one hundred pence (Matt.
xviii. 23 ff.), of the two sons sent into the vineyard
(Matt. xxi. 28 ff.), of the two debtors of one creditor
(Luke vii. 41 ff.), of the barren fig-tree (Luke xiii.
6 ff.), and that of the Prodigal Son (Luke xv. 11 ff.).

In the discourses of the fourth Gospel we find
no parables of this kind. As in those discourses
we miss the mode of teaching by examples, so also
we miss the expansion of the comparison into an
imaginary concrete example.

5. In regard to all the parables of Jesus, the
principle holds good that they are not to be regarded
as allegories in which, by way of illustration, an
event is figuratively described, and in which, therefore, an ingenious meaning can be drawn out of
every detail. They are rather comparisons whereby
a familiar relation or mode of conduct serves as a
basis on which to found some judgment or parallel
rule in regard to a relation or mode of conduct in a
different sphere, yet so that the analogy shall hold
good only in one important particular, whilst the
remaining details may present no analogy.[1] For
example, in the parable of the Ten Virgins (Matt.
xxv. 1 ff.), we have not to ask who are specially
meant by the bride and the oil merchants, or what

[1] Cf. on the distinction between allegory and parable, and on the
unjustifiableness of allegorising the parables of Jesus, *vid.* Jülicher,
die Gleichnissreden Jesu, p. 59 ff. B. Weiss has rendered good service
in rejecting the allegorising method of explaining the parables.

by the oil in the lamps, or even the slumbering of the wise virgins, etc. ; we must rather attend to the main thought, that only those virgins will be admitted to the marriage-feast who keep themselves in readiness, even though the coming of the bridegroom be unexpectedly late; and that those virgins, even though invited to the supper, shall be excluded from participation in the marriage festivities, who have foolishly failed to make preparation for the unexpectedly late arrival of the bridegroom. Only we have to make application of this main thought to the analogous case of the disciples of Jesus, who, in their uncertainty as to the time of the second advent, must keep themselves in a state of preparation, even though the returning Messiah come unexpectedly late, lest through unreadiness they lose eternal blessedness. Since in all the parables some circumstance or mode of conduct must be represented as specially analogous to the circumstance or mode of conduct which requires to be explained or enforced, it seems most natural to interpret the chief persons and circumstances in the parable from the persons and circumstances in regard to which Jesus is giving instruction. For example, in the parable of the Ten Virgins, the coming bridegroom is interpreted as Christ at His second advent, the virgins as those disciples who shall be on earth at the time of His coming, and the marriage as the heavenly life in the perfected kingdom of God. To make a similar application of all the particular features of the parable, and to bring out all possible analogies in the details of the parallel cases, appears very inviting, and even justified and necessary in seeking to bring out the whole wealth of thought which Jesus sought to convey in this parable. But such an allegorising interpretation is the more impossible, the more the story of the parable is detailed. The reason is that the two things compared belong to a wholly different sphere, and it is impossible that the two cases should be found exactly parallel down to the minutest details. No doubt in some cases the allegorising interpretation holds good to a very wide extent, as, for example, in the parable of the Prodigal Son, where this mode of interpretation is favoured by the fact that Jesus saw in the relation between father and son the most fitting emblem of the relation between God and man. Yet even in such a parable as that, the possibility of allegorising all the details of the narrative has its limits ; and generally the quest of allegorical meanings, though justifiable in some of the parables, especially the shorter, leads often to arbitrary interpretations and over-subtleties, sometimes even to absurdities. Yet caution must be exercised in bringing out the analogy between the principal persons and circumstances compared, even where that analogy seems quite natural and obvious. Certainly the comparison cannot be made (except in one particular aspect) where the analogy in the parable aims at an argument *a minori ad majus* or *a pejori ad melius*. This case occurs in the parable of the prudent Steward, who is intentionally called the "steward of unrighteousness," and whose wisdom is described as that which the children of this world employ in their generation (Luke xvi. 8); so also in the parable of the Judge and the Widow, the former of whom is expressively depicted as the godless "judge of unrighteousness" (Luke xviii. 2–7). To interpret, in the first case, the faithless steward simply as a genuine member of the kingdom of God—"a child of light" (Luke xvi. 8), or, in the latter case, to interpret the ungodly, dishonest judge simply as God, would be contradictory to the fact that Jesus expressly accentuates the difference of character between the two persons. In these cases, keeping out of view the vast contrast between the children of this world and the children of light, and between the unjust judge and God, we see that, in the former case, it is only the prudent forethought of the "children of the world" which can be compared with the wisdom which the children of light (though for a very different purpose, and by using very different means) ought to cultivate; and in the latter case it is the fulfilment of the importunate widow's petition by the unrighteous judge which is analogous to the fulfilment by God of the long-continued supplications of His elect ones. In a certain sense this is the case with all the parables taken from nature and ordinary human life, where the doctrine in regard to the kingdom of God must be founded analogically on an argument *a minori ad majus* (cf. the striking instance Luke xi. 13). Therefore the analogy between the principal persons and objects in a parable of Jesus, and the corresponding persons and circumstances of the kingdom of God, even where the comparison may be very easily and patly drawn as to external features, must ever be limited in range. Indeed, if we wished in brief compass to give the meaning and scope of a parable, it would be right simply to equate the principal persons and circumstances of the parable with the corresponding persons and circumstances to which they referred, in so far as this can be done without violence or over-subtlety. At all events, Jesus Himself has often so proceeded, *e.g.* in the parable of the Sower, Mark iv. 14 ff., or when, in practically applying the teaching of the parables, He continues, in figurative expressions, the use of some ideas of the parables (*e.g.* Luke xvii. 10; Mark xiii. 35 f.). The exegete must be well aware, however, that such equating of particular ideas can only be carried out in a compendious and peculiarly inexact way, and that it is allowed in each parable exactly to compare only one point which does not refer so much to particular persons and things in the parable, as to some relation or action depicted in it whereon some religious judgment or precept may be founded. Only by bearing this in mind can the exegete be preserved from an arbitrary play of ingenuity, in seeking to carry the allegorising mode of exposition into separate details, with the risk of finding in his failure a stumbling-block.

6. This very fact of the applicability of the comparison to only one main point in the parable, is the reason why Jesus has so often given His parables in pairs. The second parable is supplementary; in it some point of importance, which could not be sufficiently brought out in the first parable, receives special attention in the second. In Mark we find the two parables of the New Cloth on the old garment and of the New Wine in old bottles

standing in this complementary relation to each other
(ii. 21 f.). The former brings out the idea that the
new relation which Jesus teaches His disciples,
cannot be brought in merely over above the Jewish
traditional mode of righteousness, so that this latter
is regarded as remaining intact. But in this first
parable only the one idea can be exhibited, viz. that
in such a patchwork, the antiquated system, instead
of being renovated as it requires, would be brought
to complete dissolution. A new thought, viz. that
even the new system would be injured by such a
combination, required to be set forth in the second
parable of the New Wine, which, being poured into
old bottles, would not only burst these, but would
itself be lost. So, too, the parable of the Sower
(iv. 3 ff.) is supplemented by that of the Light, which
is not meant to be put under a bushel or under a bed,
but upon a stand (iv. 21). The former parable teaches
that the gospel remains inefficacious in all who, from
whatever cause, are unsusceptible. The additional
thought that the gospel is not meant, however, to
remain inefficacious, but the reverse, is brought out in
the supplementary parable. In the Logia we also find
such a pair of parables in the case of the Mustard-
seed and the Leaven (Luke xiii. 18–21), the former
illustrating the marvellously rapid growth, and the
latter the pervading and assimilating power, of the
kingdom of God. There, too, we find the twin parables
of the Treasure hid in the field and of the Pearl of
great price (Matt. xiii. 44-46), both which illustrate
the truth that the quest of all other goods must yield
to the endeavour to gain sure possession of the

greatest treasure which has been found; but with this difference, that in the one parable the treasure is accidentally found, while in the other it is expressly sought. Then we have the parables of the Lost Money and the Prodigal Son (Luke xv. 8–32), both which set forth the joy experienced in recovering something that was lost; but in the first case the recovery is exhibited as the result of a search, whilst in the second it is the result of a voluntary and penitent return. Further, we have the parables of the Faithful and Wicked Servants and of the Wise and Foolish Virgins (Matt. xxiv. 45–xxv. 13), of which the former inculcates the necessity of readiness for the master's return in case of his coming sooner than was expected, the latter shows the need of readiness even though he return later than was anticipated.[1]

Also in the discourses of the fourth Gospel we find such a pair of parables, viz. those of the Shepherd

[1] On the ground of the observation of this frequently employed method of Jesus, in thus setting together two mutually complementary parables, we can in one case conclude that a parable handed down in the form of a single narrative has been pieced together out of two originally connected parables. In another case we can assume the original juxtaposition of two parables which have been handed down to us in separate places. The *first* case is presented by the parable of the Marriage-feast (Matt. xxii. 1 ff.), where the concluding narrative of the expulsion of the guest who had not on a wedding-garment does not quite accord with the earlier one, which describes how, instead of the persons first invited, the host had drawn others by compulsion to his feast. This concluding part was originally a self-contained, supplementary parable (cf. *Log.* § 20e, *L. J.* i. p. 134 f.). The first of the two parables, which Luke (xiv. 16–24) gives separately, is intended to show that those who are first called will be shut out from the kingdom of God if they do not directly obey the call; whilst others who originally appeared the most unlikely would be brought in; the second of the two parables then shows that they who do not present conditions worthy of the kingdom shall be excluded.

The *second* case occurs in the parables of the Wise Steward (Luke and the Flock in the beginning of chap. x. The first of these parables (vers. 1–5) describes how the sheep obey and follow only the shepherd who enters by the door into the sheepfold, whilst the one who breaks in by another way is a stranger and a robber, from whom the sheep flee. Its application, according to the explanation in vers. 7–9, is that Jesus is the one essential Mediator of salvation for men : "I am the door: by me if any man enter in, he shall be saved, and shall go in and out, and find pasture" (ver. 9). But since this comparison of Jesus to the door of a sheep-fold, which in a merely passive sense gives entrance to the flock, makes no account of the devoted care with which Jesus ministers salvation to His people, there-fore this additional idea is brought out by a second parable (from ver. 10), in which the same figure of a sheepfold is employed in another relation. As the good shepherd, in contrast to the robber who will only injure the flock, and in contrast to the careless hireling who leaves it in the lurch in time of danger,

xvi. 1 ff.) and of the Faithful and Unfaithful Servants (Matt. xxv. 14 ff. ; Luke xix. 12 ff.), whose original connection is established by the fact that Luke makes the sayings in regard to the reward of those who are faithful or unfaithful in few things (xvi. 10–12)—sayings which corre-spond in meaning with the latter parable—follow immediately after the former parable (cf. *Log.* § 26*b*, *L. J.* i. p. 146). Whilst the former of the two commends the wisdom of providing, by means of present goods, for future welfare, the other enjoins faithfulness in the management of goods entrusted to us, as being the right means of attaining the end thus wisely aimed at. Also the two parables of the Tares among the Wheat (Matt. xiii. 24 ff.) and of the good and bad Fishes in the Net (Matt. xiii. 47 f.), appear to have originally been presented as such a pair of parables (cf. *Log.* § 44*b*, *L. J.* i. p. 179) ; the former shows that the separa-tion of the bad element from the good must not be prematurely under-taken, for fear of destroying the good with it ; the latter shows that the separation will be effected with perfect certainty at the appropriate time.

devotes his life for the welfare of the sheep; so Jesus
exhibits Himself as the true Saviour, in lovingly
devoting His life for them. That the form in which
those two parables are put, and the allegorical application made of them, differs somewhat in type from that
of the synoptical parables, is not to be denied. But
I cannot see that those two parables, either in regard
to their relation to the point of instruction to be
brought out, or in their complementary relation to
each other, are distinctly different from, *e.g.*, the
parables of the New Piece of Cloth and of the New
Wine (Mark ii. 21 ff.).[1]

7. If the copious employment of examples and
parables on the part of Jesus was designed to make
His mode of teaching popularly intelligible, so also
the way in which He selected and amplified them

---

[1] The meaning of those two parables in John x. 1 ff. and their relation
to each other are usually understood in a different way from my view.
For, while one and the same figure of the flock and the shepherd is used
in both, expositors have usually proceeded upon the presumption, supposed to be self-evident, that in the former as well as in the latter the
flock stands for the Church, and the shepherd for the church-leader.
But since that presumption is opposed to the explanation in vers. 7–9,
where Jesus compares Himself rather to the door which admits the
sheep, some have felt impelled by criticism to look upon the explanation, vers. 7–9, as a non-authentic allegorising interpretation of the
evangelist (B. Weiss in *Meyer's Commentary*, at this passage); others, to
condemn the authenticity of the whole of the two parables, saying that
the interpretation which makes Jesus at one time the door, at another
the shepherd who enters by it, is a piebald one, harmonising neither
with parable nor proper allegory (Jülicher, *die Gleichnissreden Jesu*,
p. 119 f.). We arrive at a much more satisfactory result by strictly
following out the explanation of the two parables indicated in the text,
viz. that Jesus is first compared to the door and afterwards to the
shepherd. For from this fact we must conclude that the other ideas in
the two parables, which correspond as to expression, do not really apply
to the same things. Therefore it is necessary to separate the two parables
absolutely, and explain them independently of each other. If we had
only the first parable, vers. 1–5, with the interpretation vers. 7–9, no one

was wholly governed by the purpose of giving them an impressive pregnancy.   One can speak of a fixed principle to which He had regard in the shaping of His examples and parables for that purpose : I might designate it as *the principle of aiming at the greatest clearness in the briefest compass.*

This principle first of all appears in the fact that, in selecting examples, He chose such as brought out into the most vivid relief the general rule to be illustrated. I may mention that example whereby, in the Logia discourses, Jesus, in speaking of the true righteousness, illustrates His precept in regard to inner freedom from anger and hatred, and an inner purity to regulate outward acts.   He selects the case of one who, in bringing his gift before the altar, remembers that

could doubt that the meaning intended was this : that as the door of the fold is related to the sheep which the shepherd (or, on the other hand, the thief) seeks to lead after himself, so Jesus is related to the salvation which men aspire after ; He is the only way of entrance, the only Mediator.   This explanation, however, will not be invalidated or rendered improbable by the view that in a further parable beginning with ver. 10, Jesus teaches that, as the good shepherd shows a devoted zeal for the interest of the flock, so Jesus devotes Himself for His people's salvation.   If but one coherent allegory were given in vers. 1–16, such a change in the meaning of certain of its figurative members would of course be inadmissible.   But if it is rather the parable that is here employed, with the purpose of comparing, not particular persons or objects, but one analogous relation or action, it is quite admissible that the comparison drawn from the shepherd and the flock is used in two parables with different objects.   And if we then sought to interpret the parable by giving the application of the main ideas (which, as we have seen at p. 124, must be done in brief undetailed form), the same ideas must here be interpreted differently in the two parables.   That here we have a real parable and not an allegory, is confirmed by those features of the narratives which cannot be allegorically interpreted, viz. the porter who opens the door to the shepherd, and the other sheep which are represented as gathered in the same fold with the shepherd's own sheep, whom he calls by their names (ver. 3).

his brother has something against him (Matt. v. 23 f.). From the fact that reconciliation with a brother is necessary even where that brother is in the wrong, He makes it clear that it is wrong to cherish anger, not merely in the case of anger arising from our own evil nature, without offence being given us, but even where offence *has* been given, and where it may seem natural to repay the offender with hatred. But by supposing this enmity to be remembered at the moment of bringing an offering to the altar, and by requiring that the gift should be left in order to go and effect reconciliation, Jesus brings vividly out the absolute obligation to cherish a forgiving spirit. Every other duty must yield to that. Even the religious act—so highly regarded by the Jews—of bringing an offering to the temple, must take second rank alongside of this most urgent duty. The absoluteness of the command to abstain from hatred and be ready for reconciliation could not be more briefly and clearly enforced.

The principle above noted also comes out in the fact that, in dealing with the special cases selected for examples, Jesus avoids all considerations and circumstances, which, though neither nullifying nor limiting the general precept to be taught, would in any degree obscure it. In regard to many of His declarations and precepts, which strike us at first as hard and strange sayings, we find a satisfactory explanation in this method of dealing with examples. Otherwise we are speedily tempted to regard them as overstrained and unpractical, or to smooth away their edge on the ground of their being figurative. We have an example of this method of Jesus in the precepts which He laid down in opposition to the earlier rule, "An eye for an eye, and a tooth for a tooth" (Matt. v. 39 ff.). He sought to inculcate the general principle that, in the kingdom of God, men must repay evil with undeserved kindness instead of with retributive vengeance; and that the injury which is inflicted, or the concession which is demanded, by another, must not be held as a motive for hostility against him, but should rather prompt us to be cheerfully ready to meet his wishes and further his interests. To make this precept vivid, Jesus shows its application to particular cases, wherein, in one form or other, whether by brute violence or legal form, by rude demand or simple request, the will or wish of another is directed towards our injury. In such cases it is the world's way to defend one's own rights by active opposition to our opponent, or by turning coldly away from him. But the rule laid down by Jesus is: "Whosoever smiteth thee on thy right cheek, turn to him the other also; and if any man would go to law with thee, and take away thy coat, let him have thy cloke also; and whosoever shall compel thee to go a mile, go with him twain. Give to him that asketh thee, and from him that would borrow of thee turn not thou away."

The strikingly characteristic feature of these precepts of Jesus lies in this, that in the supposed cases the form of friendly attitude enjoined by Jesus towards another, corresponds to the form of the intentions or wishes of that other directed to our own hurt. By this correspondence it is made possible immediately to compare the duty with its supposed occasion. It is made plainly and absolutely manifest that our duty is just the reverse of revenge or jealous watch over our merely selfish interests, and that our obligations to another are not adequately met by our merely suffering from him, or doing for him, what cannot be avoided : rather we must maintain a spontaneous readiness to promote his interests.[1]

Could Jesus, then, have really meant that His disciples ought, in all circumstances, to fulfil in this outward corresponding way, and even to exceed, the violent demands of another to yield up to him, or to do for him, whatever he might desire ? He Himself frequently refused the unjust demand or prayer of another (*e.g.* Mark i. 37 f.; iii. 31 ff.; viii. 11 f. ; Luke xii. 13 f.). An exception, necessitated by the very scope and purpose of the precept, occurs in the case of a demand, the compliance with which would be a violation of just love, being in reality hurtful to the other, or involving an infringement of the duty owed to a third person. In ordinary life, indeed, the disciples of Jesus would generally be led by such considerations, founded in the duty of love, to defend themselves from violence, to bring the aggressor to punishment, to refuse an unjust demand or prayer, and to employ a line of conduct different, from an external point of view, from

---

[1] In the case where the mere utterance of a request on the part of another is supposed, a double fulfilment of his desire is not commanded, because in such a case where no force is attempted, the spontaneity of the compliance is sufficiently shown by a simple granting of the request.

that enjoined by Jesus. But all circumstances and considerations which, from our very recognition of the law of love, require us to punish or repulse an assailant or to refuse his demand, are kept out of view by Jesus. For, by taking account of such considerations, Jesus would neither have really limited, nor made more fully manifest, the rule, that the members of the kingdom of God must be wholly free from revenge, and ever ready to show gratuitous kindness, even in the case of an unjust demand or of spoliation on the part of another. While leaving out such qualifying considerations, Jesus chose His examples so as to bring out, in the briefest and clearest terms, the rule He means to lay down. On the same principle, we have also to explain the Beatitudes pronounced upon the poor, the hungry, the mourners, the persecuted; the woes pronounced upon the rich, the full, those that laugh and those who are praised of all men (Luke vi. 20 ff.);[1] also His injunction to cut off hand or foot, and to tear out the eye, if they be a cause of stumbling (Mark ix. 43 ff.; Matt. v. 29); His command, above all things, not to swear, but to let your speech be yea, yea, and nay, nay (Matt. v. 34 and 37); to enter the closet and shut the door when they pray (Matt. vi. 6); and many such like sayings of a specialising kind.

We must, I think, understand such peculiarities in Jesus' form of teaching from their opposition to the casuistical method of the Jewish scribes. Their mode of explaining the law was indeed founded throughout on the principle of applying the law to special cases,

[1] Cf. *Log.* § 2*a*, *L. J.* i. p. 53 ff.

and deciding its precise application, or non-applicability, to the various possible circumstances. They showed what one who is afraid of transgressing the law must do and leave undone, and also how far he might go without violating the letter of the command. This casuistical treatment, with all its quibbling and fine distinctions, did not really lead to an enlightened upright walk, but rather to obscuring and in many ways nullifying the true meaning and purpose of the command. We can well imagine how one so profoundly upright and so keen of discernment as Jesus, would have a genuine abhorrence for this casuistical method of the scribes. Now, He certainly did not renounce that effective means of popular intelligibility, derived from the specialising of general judgments and rules, and applying them to concrete cases ; but He used that means in a way quite opposed to the casuistical method. He did not seek to enumerate as fully as possible the particular cases to which the rule applied, or to denote the special circumstances which call for exceptions or limitations of the rule ; but He notes the cases in which the meaning and purpose of the given rule are most sharply brought out, and He purposely omits all the circumstances through which the extent and importance of the rule are less clearly apparent. Every loophole of escape, and every pretext for making convenient exceptions, on the part of the hearers was to be cut off.

In the parables of Jesus, this principle of aiming at the greatest clearness in the shortest compass, comes out in His investing the case selected for comparison with those circumstances under which the relation or action, which forms the point of comparison, and on which the purpose of parable turns, may stand out at the clearest. Only by attention to this principle of the parables of Jesus, we are led to avoid entirely the allegorising mode of interpreting them. For, at all events, we may justly assume that Jesus, whose mode of teaching is so pregnantly expressive, did not interweave meaningless details into His parables for the mere purpose of embellishment. Now, it is a proper inference from this assumption, not that all the accessary circumstances of the narrative permit of being compared directly, but rather that these circumstances are meant to set in the clearest light the main point of the comparison, an object which by no means accords with the allegorising interpretation.[1] For example, in the parable of the Ten Virgins (Matt. xxv. 1 ff.), the circumstance that all the virgins fall asleep is necessary in order to bring out as strongly as possible the value of prudent preparedness even for an unexpected tarrying of the bridegroom. It was necessary to relate that the foolish virgins fell asleep, in order to make it clearly apparent that they were not sensible of the evil consequences of their want of forethought, until at the last critical moment, when it was too late to supply the want.

[1] In regard to the copiousness of similes, the discourses of Jesus may be compared with the Homeric similes. For these also the rule holds good, that we must not carry out their meaning in an allegorising way, but must also inquire for their *tertium comparationis*. But the principle which is so important for the composition of the parables of Jesus, viz. that their details are wholly governed by the object of making as clear and effective as possible the one decisive point of the comparison, cannot be observed in the same way in the Homeric similes. The poet delights much more in pictorial details, even when they are of no moment for the comparison.

That not only the foolish but the wise virgins fell asleep, is, however, a detail which as little fits the allegorising interpretation as it strikingly serves to bring out the value of forethought on the part of the wise. For if these five wise virgins had been represented as remaining awake, their wakefulness as well as their wise forethought would have appeared to the hearers another reason for esteeming them more worthy than the five foolish virgins of participating in the marriage-feast ; and thus the value of their having made preparation even for the case of the unexpectedly late return of the bridegroom would not have been so clearly brought into relief as their one chief point of superiority.

Further, we find the parable of the man who applied to his friend for bread (Luke xi. 5 ff.) invested with circumstances which do not at all lend themselves to an allegorising mode of interpretation, but, on the other hand, serve to bring out with the utmost clearness the one point which the parable is designed to illustrate, viz. the value of implicitly trustful prayer. It is midnight ; the door of the friend's house is shut, so that the petitioner cannot enter and get the bread for himself, but the other must be awakened from sleep that he may rise and give it. The friend's children are lying with him in the same bed, so that getting up is a difficulty and a trouble for him ; thus the circumstances are specially unfavourable for granting the request. But just through the unpropitiousness of the circumstances, the greatness of the petitioner's faith, and the power of his faith to achieve the granting of his request, come most clearly out.

Again, in the parable of the Wise Steward (Luke xvi. 1 ff.), the same principle is indicated by the fact that the steward is designated as unfaithful. Jesus sought in that parable to bring out the value of wisdom, which aims at securing future welfare by means of present opportunities. In the supplementary instruction appended by Him, He showed that for the disciples, whose great object of striving was the heavenly life of blessing to be vouchsafed by God, the right conduct for attaining this end consists in the diligent and faithful use of the worldly goods entrusted to them by God.[1] In this line of thought, it would not have been at all so suitable to represent the steward —by whose example He sought to bring most clearly out the value of wisdom—as an upright, faithful man, though thereby the offence might have been avoided which would be caused by this man's dishonesty under the allegorising interpretation of the parable. For if the steward had been distinguished for fidelity, frugality, diligence, or some other excellence, these virtues would have come into consideration along with his wise forethought in order to insure him a good livelihood when thrown out of his situation. When, however, he was represented as a dishonest spendthrift (ver. 1) and lazy fellow (ver. 3), it is evident that in his forethought alone lay the ground of his further well-being. The value of wise forethought is also most strongly accentuated by its being exhibited as isolated from other virtues. We have again, in a similar way, to explain the parable of the unjust Judge and the poor Widow (Luke xviii. 2 ff.).

[1] Cf. the note on p. 127 f.

The fact that the judge is here described as neither fearing God nor regarding man, is not to be accounted an inappropriate or at least indifferent *trait* of the narrative, which is only used to make the story of greater external interest ; for it is of essential import-ance for bringing out the main point, and thereby also the peculiar purpose of the parable. The value of importunate prayer has to be set forth. Now, were the qualities of justice or of the fear of God or man pre-supposed in this judge, these would appear to conduce to the fulfilment of the widow's prayer. But inas-much as he was lost to all moral and religious feeling, and even to all fear of public opinion, the importunity of her prayer is set quite apart from all concurrent motives, and its unaided efficacy is brought vividly to light.

This principle, so characteristic of the method of Jesus, of seeking the greatest clearness in briefest compass, is not so discernible in the fourth Gospel as in the synoptical discourses. In the Johannine dis-courses, as we have already remarked, there is a lack of specialising and exemplifying exposition, as well as of parables, which set forth a single conceived case with its concrete circumstances. But then the chief material, in which we find examples of this principle of the teaching of Jesus in the discourses in Mark and the Logia, is lacking in the Johannine discourses.

8. The impressive pregnancy of the style of Jesus is shown not only in His use of examples and parables, but even when He expresses general judgments and instructions in general form. He delights in putting such judgments and instructions in the form of crisp,

pointed sentences, containing specially an antithesis
or corresponding relation. A style of that kind is
very effective for the purpose of being clear and
memorable. Jesus, in this, has manifestly followed
the traditional form of the proverbial wisdom of
the Jews, which, as proved by the treatise in the
Mischna entitled Pirke Aboth ("Sayings of the
Fathers"), was also employed by the scribes in the
time of Jesus. But He does not present a long series
of sentences which contain variations on the same
thought; He rather gives in a single utterance the
substance or the confirmation of what He means to
inculcate, the practical inference from a parable, the
answer to a question, or the solution of a difficulty.
Often he takes a current proverb, when some idea, of
special import in its bearing on the kingdom of God,
can be rendered more vivid from the fact of its agreement with a general rule enshrined in proverbial form.
Such are the following sayings, recorded in different
connections, and independently of each other, in the
Gospel sources : [1] "Nothing is hidden that shall not
be made manifest; nor was anything made secret, but
that it should come to light" (Mark iv. 22 ; cf. Matt.
x. 26) ; "With what measure ye mete, it shall be
measured unto you" (Mark iv. 24; cf. Matt. vii. 2) ;
"For he that hath, to him shall be given ; and he
that hath not, from him shall be taken away even that
which he hath" (Mark iv. 25 ; cf. Matt. xxv. 29);
"Many that are first shall be last; and the last first."
(Mark x. 31 ; cf. Luke xiii. 30 ; Matt. xx. 16); "For
every one that exalteth himself shall be humbled, and

[1] Cf. *L. J.* i. p. 197 ff.

he that humbleth himself shall be exalted" (Luke xiv. 11; xviii. 14; Matt. xxiii. 12).

Of the other sayings of this sententious stamp the following may be given :—From the Gospel of Mark: "I am not come to call the righteous, but sinners" (ii. 17); "The Sabbath was made for man, and not man for the Sabbath" (ii. 27); "There is nothing from without the man that, going into him, can defile him; but the things that come out of him, those defile the man" (vii. 15); "Whosoever would save his life shall lose it; and whosoever shall lose his life for my sake and the gospel's shall save it" (viii. 35; cf. Matt. x. 39; Luke xvii. 33); "Whosoever shall be ashamed of me and of my words in this adulterous and sinful generation, the Son of man also shall be ashamed of him when He cometh in the glory of His Father with the holy angels" (viii. 38); "If any man would be first, he shall be last of all, and minister of all" (ix. 35; cf. x. 43 f.); "He that is not against us is for us" (ix. 40); "Render unto Cæsar the things that are Cæsar's, and unto God the things that are God's" (xii. 17); "God is not the God of the dead, but of the living" (xii. 27); "The spirit is willing, but the flesh is weak" (xiv. 38). From the Logia : "I came not to destroy, but to fulfil" (Matt. v. 17); "All things whatsoever ye would that men should do unto you, even so do ye also unto them" (Matt. vii. 12); "Judge not, that ye be not judged" (Matt. vii. 1); "Ask, and it shall be given you; seek, and ye shall find; knock, and it shall be opened unto you" (Matt. vii. 7); "He that is not with me is against me; and he that gathereth not with me scattereth" (Matt.

xii. 30); "Many are called, but few are chosen"
(Matt. xxii. 14); "To whomsoever much is given,
much shall be required; and to whom they commit
much, of him will they ask the more" (Luke xii. 48);
"He that is faithful in a very little is faithful also in
much; and he that is unrighteous in a very little is
unrighteous in much" (Luke xvi. 10). Also the saying of Jesus, quoted by Paul in his address at Miletus,
"It is more blessed to give than to receive" (Acts
xx. 35), may be mentioned.

In the discourses of the fourth Gospel, also, some
general utterances of Jesus, similarly pregnant in form,
are preserved: "That which is born of the flesh is
flesh; and that which is born of the spirit is spirit"
(iii. 6); "God has not sent His Son into the world to
judge the world, but that the world should be saved
through Him" (iii. 17); "God is spirit; and they
that worship Him **must** worship in spirit and in truth"
(iv. 24); "For judgment came I into the world; that
they which see not might see, and that they which see
might become blind" (ix. 39); "He that loveth his
life shall lose it; and he that hateth his life in this
world shall keep it unto life eternal" (xii. 25); "He
that receiveth whomsoever I send receiveth me; and
he that receiveth me receiveth Him that sent me"
(xiii. 20). In direct reference to a current proverb,
Jesus says to His disciples: "Herein is the saying
true, One soweth, and another reapeth" (iv. 37).
In general, however, it is true that this proverb-
like pregnancy is not in the same measure peculiar
to the sayings of Jesus recorded in John's Gospel
as in those of the synoptical Gospels; and this

difference is of great importance for the general view of the distinctiveness of the Johannine discourses.

9. Finally, we must note the abundant use made by Jesus of *figurative forms of expression.* These imply some mental comparison serving to illustrate the thought. What in them is characteristic, however, is that the form of comparison is not expressed; but another conception is directly substituted for the one intended, and is given figuratively instead of that latter. This figurative mode of expression, from the striking way in which Jesus employs it, contributes greatly to the distinctness and impressiveness of His ideas. For by a single figurative expression with which ideas of well-known quality and value are connected, or else some well-known relation or action, something can be shortly and graphically expressed which, without figure, would require a much more extensive description. That the form of expression is figurative, and what is the literal truth to be expressed by it, is usually made clear directly from the context. Some of the figurative expressions had also already become current out of the Old Testament.

The following are examples of this figurative form of expression : " Beware of the leaven of the Pharisees" (Mark viii. 15); "Are ye able to drink the cup that I drink? or to be baptized with the baptism that I am baptized with?" (Mark x. 38); "The Son of man is come to give His life a ransom for many" (Mark x. 45); "When thou doest alms, sound not a trumpet before thee; . . let not thy left hand know what thy right hand doeth" (Matt. vi. 2 f.); "Beware of false prophets, which come to you in sheep's clothing, but inwardly are ravening wolves" (Matt. vii. 15); "Go ye to the lost sheep of the house of Israel" (Matt. x. 6); "Come unto me, all ye that labour and are heavy laden, and I will give you rest; take my yoke upon you" (Matt. xi. 28 f.); "The good man out of his good treasure bringeth forth good things" (Matt. xii. 35); "They bind heavy burdens, and grievous to be borne, and lay them on men's shoulders; but they themselves will not touch them with the finger" (Matt. xxiii. 4); "Let the dead bury their dead" (Luke ix. 60); "Fear not, little flock" (Luke xii. 32); "I am come to cast fire on the earth; and what will I if it be already kindled? But I have a baptism to be baptized with; and how am I straitened till it be accomplished!" (Luke xii. 49 f.); "Go ye and tell that fox" (Luke xiii. 32).

If a figurative form of expression is extended, so that not merely a single conception, but a complete thought, or chain of thoughts, is presented as a unity in a figurative form, we have then an allegory. Occasionally in the discourses of Jesus we meet with figurative ideas thus allegorically expanded. Thus He speaks of the narrow gate that leadeth into life (Matt. vii. 13 f.); of the plenteous harvest for which the labourers are few, and the lord of the harvest sending forth more labourers (Luke x. 2); of the wish to take out the mote from a brother's eye, while a beam is in the man's own eye (Matt. vii. 3 ff.); of the giving of that which is holy to the dogs, and the casting of pearls before swine (Matt. vii. 6); of the looking back on the part of one who has put his hand to the plough (Luke ix. 62). Since the figurative mode of expression always depends on some mentally drawn comparison, it very easily connects itself with a parable: Jesus seizes the occasion of some figurative turn of speech to subjoin a parabolic saying corresponding to the figure; or, in drawing the practical conclusion from a parable, He uses, in a further figurative way, the terms employed in it. So, when He addressed the Syrophenician woman: "Let the children first be filled; for it is not meet to take the children's bread and to cast it to dogs" (Mark vii. 27); when, in reference to the false prophets, He says: "By their fruits ye shall know them; do men gather grapes of thorns?" etc. (Matt. vii. 16–20); when He condemns false teachers: "Ye be blind leaders of the blind; but if the blind lead the blind, both shall fall into the ditch" (Matt. xv. 14); when He exhorts His disciples: "Let your loins be girt about, and your lamps burning; and ye yourselves like those who wait for their lord at his return from the wedding," etc. (Luke xii. 35 f.); when He practically concludes the brief parable of the salt: "Have salt in yourselves" (Mark ix. 50); or when He gave the parable of the man about to take a journey, who left his house, and gave authority to his servants, and to every man his work, and commanded the porter to watch, — He proceeds in the wholly allegorising conclusion: "Watch ye therefore: for ye know not when the master of the house cometh, at even, or at midnight, or at the cock-crowing, or in the morning; lest, coming suddenly, he find you sleeping.

And what I say unto you, I say unto all, Watch!"
(Mark xiii. 34 ff.).

The use of this figurative mode of expression also
comes out strikingly in the discourses of the fourth
Gospel. We remember expressions like the following:
" Destroy this temple, and in three days I will raise it
up (ii. 19); "This is the condemnation, that light is
come into the world, and men have loved the darkness rather than the light" (iii. 19); "I have meat to
eat which ye know not of; . . . my meat is to do the
will of Him that sent me" (iv. 32, 34); "John was a
burning and shining light, and ye were willing for
a season to rejoice in his light" (v. 35); "Labour not
for the meat which perisheth, but for the meat which
endureth to life everlasting, which the Son of man
shall give you : for Him hath God the Father sealed"
(vi. 27); "I am the bread of life : he that cometh to
me shall never hunger; and he that believeth in me
shall never thirst" (vi. 35); "If any man thirst, let
him come unto me and drink; he that believeth on
me, as the Scripture hath said, out of his belly shall
flow rivers of living water" (vii. 38); I am the light
of the world : he that followeth me shall not walk in
darkness, but shall have the light of life (day)"
(viii. 12); "In my Father's house are many mansions"
(xiv. 2) ; "I am the way" (xiv. 6); "I will not leave
you orphans" (xiv. 18).

It is only to be remarked that, on the one hand,
the figurative phraseology used in the Johannine discourses is less varied than that met with in the
synoptical discourses ; and that, on the other hand,
the figures used are pretty often expanded in an

allegorising way.   For example, the figure of water :
" Whosoever drinketh of the water that I shall give
him shall never thirst ; but the water that I shall give
him shall be in him a well of water springing up unto
everlasting life" (iv. 14 ; cf. vii. 38) ; the figure of the
harvest : " Lift up your eyes, and look on the fields ;
for they are white already to harvest.   And he that
reapeth receiveth wages, and gathereth fruit unto life
eternal : that both he that soweth and he that reapeth
may rejoice together," etc. (iv. 35 – 38) ; the oft-
recurring figure of the light : " Yet a little while is
the light with you.   Walk while ye have the light,
lest darkness come upon you : for he that walketh in
darkness knoweth not whither he goeth.   While ye
have the light believe in the light, that ye may be
children of light" (xii. 35 f.; cf. ver. 46 ; iii. 19 ff. ; viii.
12 ; ix. 4 f.) ; the figure of the shepherd, allegorisingly
expanded in the parable of the Good Shepherd who
devotedly cares for the flock (x. 10 ff.) : " I am the
good shepherd, and know my sheep, and am known
by mine, . . . and I give my life for the sheep.   And
other sheep I have which are not of this fold : them
also I must bring, and they shall hear my voice ; and
there shall be one fold, and one shepherd" (x. 14–16 ;
cf. ver. 26 ff.) ; and the figure of the vine stock : " I
am the true vine stock, and my Father is the husbandman.   Every branch in me that beareth not fruit,
He taketh away ; and every branch in me that
bringeth forth fruit, He purgeth it, that it may
bring forth more fruit," etc. (xv. 1–6 ; cf. vers. 8,
10).   The allegorical extension of figurative expressions, as our previous examination of the employment

of this mode of speech in the other sources goes to prove, was not an exclusive peculiarity of the Johannine discourses. But along with less variety in the figures generally used, there is a greater frequency in their use, and more instances of the allegorising extension of particular figures than in the synoptical discourses, and their more frequent use is all the more conspicuous from the paucity of parables proper in the fourth Gospel.

10. Our review of the characteristic features of Jesus' method of teaching proves what a wonderful art and power of popular eloquence He possessed. He avoided pedantic modes of teaching and the petty arts of the scholastic learning. The particular methods He employed by preference were not indeed new, but were rather the customary and natural means of popular discourse ; yet He handled them with greater ease and precision, and with higher originality in details, than other teachers.[1] A rich fancy and an acute judgment were His equipment,—a fancy which provided Him with ever fresh material for His examples, pictures, and similitudes; acuteness of judgment, which enabled Him to grasp the essential point in the instance on hand, and to find the fittest phraseology and forms of presentation whereby the weightiest thoughts should be most forcibly expressed. We can well understand how the discourses of Jesus, even apart from the significance of their contents, would fill the hearers with admiration by their natural, lucid, and pithy style, and force the declaration from

[1] On the special originality of the parables of Jesus, cf. Jülicher, *die Gleichnissreden Jesu*, p. 149 ff.

their lips : "He speaks as one that hath authority, and not as the scribes" (Mark i. 22); that is, not from a limited stock of traditional apparatus laboriously applied, but in sovereign disposal of an abundance of power, like a true orator "by the grace of God." The examples and parables of Jesus, by their typical memorable forms, preserve even yet their living freshness of illustration and lucidity of demonstration. The brief striking statements and figures of Jesus are to a great extent proverbially used in our own day apart even from their religious use. Jesus has imparted a classical stamp to those forms of speech, and through them His discourses have acquired a perennial popularity. One can compare them with the Epistles of Paul, who, without being a rhetorician of the schools, possessed a powerful natural eloquence kindled by enthusiasm, and who by no means addressed himself to the "wise after the flesh." But how difficult would it still be for our laity—how hard must it have been even for those of Paul's time!—to become familiarly acquainted with the Pauline terms, not only those of his doctrinal discussions, but even in his hortatory teaching! How immensely higher in popular efficiency stands Jesus' method in its plain simplicity, which yet detracts nothing from its depth of thought!

What, however, is above all wonderful here is, that the man who had such rich material of popular eloquence at command, has used it ever in strict subservience to the purposes of the religious thoughts to whose announcement He devoted His life. Throughout His recorded discourses we never find that He has given free play to His fancy in order merely to please Himself and others, or for the sake of showy embellishment. Never has He employed His sharpness of judgment for the mere purpose of exercising His dialectic skill upon His own thoughts or those of others, or beyond what was called for in order to the illustration or exposition, the establishment or confutation, of those thoughts. The artistic form of speech was never with Him an end in itself, so as to turn attention upon itself and away from the matter of discourse. The one aim of Jesus in regard to style and method was to make His meaning plain, and show the importance of His ideas. Therefore He never used the arts of speech in order to beguile His hearers by too lightly carrying them over the difficulties of His teaching, or smoothing over its offensive strictness. On the contrary, He has everywhere spoken with perfect plainness, and has uttered, with the utmost strictness, unpalatable declarations and hard commands, which practically followed from His teaching, without ever palliating them or making concessions. He employed, indeed, all His skill and power of speech in order to convince His hearers of the truth of His statements and the rightful authority of His precepts. It was no object of His to present His teaching as something specially novel and peculiar, and, because of its higher and supernatural theme, as something strangely contrasted with natural and earthly knowledge. He has, indeed, intentionally emphasised the relationship of what He taught and commanded to the ordinary earthly phenomena and the common modes of human conduct.   No facts of nature or of human life appeared too small to be unable to aid Him in bringing His teaching of the kingdom of God home to the human understanding.

By the form which He gave His teaching, Jesus bore witness to the universality of character and aim which He ascribed to His teaching.   It was no private doctrine, designed for a narrow circle of the initiated ; nor was it a scholastic or scientific doctrine, designed for the scholarly and the cultured.   It was a message of universally intelligible import, designed for all classes of people, rich and poor, young and old, if they would but hearken and receive it.

CHAP. II. IDEAS OF JESUS CONCERNING THE NATURAL ORDER OF THE WORLD.

1. The subject - matter of the teaching, which it was the chief aim of Jesus to disseminate among the people, was the kingdom of God.   But this did not prevent His giving expression to many ideas not directly referring to that subject, but rather to the natural order of the world, or creation in its widest sense.   In treating the subject of the kingdom of God, the question constantly occurs in regard to God's will and ways toward the world and men, and, reciprocally, of man's proper deportment in the world towards God.   Hence it was to be expected that Jesus would be continually expressing ideas in regard to the natural world, and would be presupposing the same in His hearers.   Abundant occasion was

presented, also, by the parables, which He loved to employ in confirming and illustrating His teaching, for referring to what had happened or was happening in the world.

The extent, indeed, to which the ideas of Jesus of this kind have been preserved in the Gospel narratives must be accidental, since it was not the purpose of the writers to give us direct information on the subject. It is certainly interesting for us to gather every item of information concerning such ideas of Jesus traceable in His recorded words and discourses, and thereby to gain a glimpse of this department of His inner life. Our understanding of certain of those ideas, for example, the anthropological, is also important for the interpretation of some of the religious utterances of Jesus. But still more important than even the careful determination of the extent and meaning of the ideas of Jesus on this subject, is the knowledge that He had not made them a matter of independent research or learning, but had acquired them partly on the ground of His personal observation and experience, and partly by accepting the current modes of thought and traditions of His countrymen.

That Jesus, in spite of the keen faculty of observation which He possessed, and the independence of His judgment, abstained from any attempt at criticising the popular ideas concerning the order of the world, whether in the way of correcting or of completing them, must be regarded as a course intentionally pursued by Him in prosecuting His mission of proclaiming the kingdom of God. The self-limitation of Jesus in this respect proceeds on the same principle according to which He rejected the appeal of the man who claimed His help in the matter of dividing the inheritance with his brother (Luke xii. 13 f.). He was conscious of His special Messianic vocation of announcing the kingdom of God, and wished to devote Himself to the fulfilment of this God-given task. In so far as He might have occupied Himself with more exactly determining the order of the world, or with rectifying the popular conceptions in regard to it, He would have withdrawn His interest and His powers from His special vocation, and would have turned aside the attention and intelligence of His hearers from the essential subject of His Messianic preaching. Therefore we must regard all expressions of Jesus in reference to the order of creation as belonging to the externals of His doctrine, and not give them a position among the organic members of His teaching in regard to the kingdom of God. Jesus Himself has intentionally prevented their becoming independent branches of the teaching essential to His mission, and employs them merely as means in aid of that teaching. No doubt the course followed by Jesus in regard to this subject is the same in the discourses of the fourth Gospel as in the discourses of the synoptical Gospels; therefore it were a needless pedantry if, in treating of this class of ideas, we kept the different sources strictly apart.

2. A series of utterances will be remembered in which Jesus expresses ideas gathered from *simple observation of natural phenomena.* He speaks of the sun which God causes to rise, and the rain which

God sends (Matt. v. 45); of the lightning which falls
down from heaven (Luke x. 18), which comes out of
the east, and flashes to the west (Matt. xxiv. 27); of
the clouds in the west which portend rain, and of
the south wind which brings scorching heat (Luke
xii. 54 f.); of the rain-burst which swells the streams,
and brings ruin to the house built on a sandy foundation, whilst the house founded on a rock stands firm
(Matt. vii. 24–27); of the wind which blows where
it listeth, whose rushing is heard without its origin
or destination being known (John iii. 8).   He speaks
of the grain of wheat which only multiplies if it is
laid in the ground and dies (John xii. 24); of the
seed whose growth and increase depends upon the
nature of the ground, and which, if it fall on the way-
side, will be eaten by the fowls, if on stony ground
with light soil, will quickly spring up, but with little
root, and will therefore be scorched by the sun's
rays; if it fall among thorns, it will be choked by
the quickly growing thorns before it is ripe; but if it
fall upon good ground, will spring up, and grow high,
and bear fruit, some thirty-fold, some sixty-fold, and
some an hundred-fold (Mark iv. 4–8).   Further, He
mentions the seed, which the earth spontaneously and
without man's knowing how, causes to sprout into
the green blade, which grows into the ear, and finally
ripens to the full corn in the ear (Mark iv. 26–28);
of the fruit, which, from its nature, good or bad,
indicates the nature of the tree on which it has
grown (Matt. vii. 16–18); of the mustard-plant, which,
springing from the least of seeds, becomes the greatest
of garden herbs, under whose twigs the birds of the

air find shelter (Mark iv. 31 f.; Luke xiii. 19); of
the fig - tree, whose twigs become tender at the
approach of spring, and put forth leaves (Mark xiii.
28), and if it be unfruitful can be fertilised by being
dug about and manured (Luke xiii. 8); of the vine-
branch, which, so long as it remains in union with
the stock, can bring forth fruit, and which, through
the pruning of the husbandman, can be rendered
more fruitful (John xv. 2-4); of the lilies of the
field, which, without toiling or spinning, are more
gloriously arrayed than Solomon (Matt. vi. 28 f.); of
the reed which wavers in the wind (Matt. xi. 7). He
refers to the wisdom of the serpent, and the harm-
lessness of doves (Matt. x. 16); to the foxes which
live in dens, and the fowls which have nests (Luke
ix. 58); to the hen which gathers her brood under
her wings (Luke xiii. 34); to the ravens, which, without gathering stores, are fed by God (Luke xii. 24);
of the eagles, which gather round the carcase (Luke
xvii. 37); to the wild dogs and swine, which, if one
cast them a pearl, which they do not value and cannot
eat, would but trample upon it, and even attack the
giver (Matt. vii. 6); to the sheep, which know the
voice of the shepherd, and the names by which he
individually calls them, which follow him, while they
flee at the unknown voice of a stranger (John x.
3-5); and of the wolf, which harries and scatters the
sheep (John x. 12; Matt. vii. 15). He mentions the
salt, which, if it once become insipid, cannot regain
its savour through anything else, and is not even fit
for the dunghill (Mark ix. 50; Luke xiv. 34 f.); also
the leaven, a small quantity of which is sufficient to

leaven three measures of flour (Luke xiii. 21); the wine, which, when new, bursts an old skin‑bottle, but when old, is of mellower taste than the new (Luke v. 39); and the patch on unfulled cloth, which shrinks and tears the surrounding portion of the older cloth (Mark ii. 21).

3. The *anthropological ideas* imbedded in the discourses of Jesus are less in amount, though of greater importance, than those pertaining to natural history. Those ideas entirely correspond to the popular conceptions and modes of speech of the Old Testament which were current among the Jews in the time of Jesus. They were in a plastic, undeveloped state, and form by no means a scientifically elaborated system. First of all, the body and the soul in man were distinguished (Matt. vi. 25; x. 28). The *soul* (ψυχή) was regarded as the seat of the life, of the Ego in the widest sense. It was, in particular, the vital force of the external earthly life which animates the body, and distinguishes man and other animals from lifeless nature. It was refreshed and strengthened by food and drink, and was summoned away at the death of the man (Luke xii. 19-22). To love, to seek, and to save the soul, or to hate and lose it (Mark iii. 4; viii. 35; Luke xiv. 26; Matt. x. 39; John xii. 25), means—to attend to and preserve the earthly life, or to injure or lose it. To yield up or to lay down the soul (Mark x. 45; John x. 11, 15, 17; xiii. 37 f.; xv. 13), means to offer up the external earthly life. So far, however, as the idea of continued existence after death was thought of, the *soul* appears to have been regarded as the seat of the Ego, which is not subject

to the conditions of earthly life, and which eventually becomes the subject of the higher heavenly life. In this sense Jesus can describe the violent deprivation of the earthly life as a killing of the body, with the express addition that men are unable to kill the soul (Matt. x. 28). In these distinct meanings which the notion of *soul* could bear, lies the solution of the paradox contained in those sayings of Jesus recorded in harmony in our three chief sources : "Whosoever would save his life shall lose it ; and whosoever shall lose his life shall save it" (Matt. x. 39 ; Mark viii. 35 ; Luke xvii. 33 ; John xii. 25). Here, in the antecedent clauses, the preservation and yielding up of the external earthly life is meant ; and, in the concluding clauses, it is the loss or gain of a higher personal life, whose well-being is independent of the circumstances of the earthly life. By "ease of soul" we must understand, at one time, the rest of the earthly vital forces (Luke xii. 19) ; at another time, the inward peace which the godly obtain, in spite of toil and burdens, through humble submission to the Divine will (Matt. xi. 29).

When Jesus refers to the conscious spiritual activity of man, He uses by preference the conception of the καρδία. It is to be noted, however, that this conception as employed by Jesus, and, indeed, as used in the New Testament generally, being the equivalent of the Old Testament לֵב, does not correspond in meaning to the popular use of our German word *Herz* (heart).[1]

---

[1] Cf. the notices upon the Old Testament and Pauline modes of speech in my treatise, *Die Begriffe Fleisch und Geist im Biblischen Sprachgebrauche*, pp. 30 f. and 133 f.

For we are accustomed to understand by heart, as distinguished from understanding and will, the seat of the disposition, of the feelings, and specially the seat of the good friendly feelings and frames (cf. the current expressions : to have a heart or inclination for something; to have the heart in a matter; hearty, heartless, etc.). The καρδία of the New Testament, however, corresponds much more to our notion, *Sinn* or *Gesinnung* (mind); that is, it denotes in general the seat of all kinds of spiritual activity, and has as little a good as a bad sense attached to it. In the καρδία, that is, the mind or inner man, reside the reasoning powers (Mark ii. 8) ; out of it proceed evil thoughts, unchastity, theft, murder, adultery, etc. (Mark vii. 21 f.) ; in it dwells lust, for example, that referred to in Matt. v. 28 ; it is the seat of doubt or of trust in God (Mark xi. 23) ; it experiences unrest, fear, sadness, and joy (John xiv. i. 27 ; xvi. 6, 22) ; it can be hardened or overcharged with intoxication of the senses or by pressure of cares (Luke xxi. 34), so that the vigilance and intelligence of men are impaired ; it lies with a man's treasure, that is, the goods on which his thoughts and desires chiefly dwell (Matt. vi. 21). An essential characteristic of the καρδία is its inwardness (Mark vii. 21) ; ταπεινὸς τῇ καρδίᾳ (Matt. xi. 29) is one who is lowly in his inmost thoughts ; that is, one who keeps himself obediently and humbly submissive, in distinction from one who is merely in a lowly external position, and from one who only puts on the appearance of humility without being truly humble. The hidden contents of the inner being express themselves in the words (Matt.

xii. 34 f.) or the actions of men (Mark vii. 21 f.).
Those expressions can indeed be hypocritically
deceptive : the lips can honour God, whilst the
heart is far from Him (Mark vii. 6 = Isa. xxix. 13).
But God sees the real state of the heart (Luke
xvi. 15).

The relation of the καρδία to the soul must not be
conceived as if each stood independent of the other.
But the soul comprises the whole of the spiritual
nature of man, and the whole conscious spiritual
activity can be referred to it. The disposition of
restfulness, or of unrest, is attributed in certain utterances to the soul (Matt. xi. 29 ; John xii. 27), as it is
elsewhere imputed to the heart (John xiv. 1; xvi. 22).
Also in the words, Mark xii. 30, in which Jesus
renders the passage, Deut. vi. 5 : "Thou shalt love
the Lord thy God with all thy heart (καρδία), and with
all thy soul (ψυχή), and with all thy mind (διάνοια),
and with all thy strength" (ἰσχύς), *heart* and *soul*
do not denote two distinct spiritual faculties. But
only in order to bring out as strongly as possible the
completeness with which all departments of man's
inner being must be brought under the sway of the
love of God, the inner nature is pleonastically denoted
by different expressions. Under the first of these
the *inwardness* of the spiritual life is emphasised, by
the second its *individuality*, by the third its faculty
of *intelligent thought*, and by the last its *strength* or
intensity.

The notion of *the spirit* (πνεῦμα), which Jesus often
employs with reference to the Divine spiritual power,
He uses only three times of man's spiritual life, where

a special occasion was presented for so doing.[1]   In
those words to the disciples in Gethsemane, " The
spirit indeed is willing, but the flesh is weak" (Mark
xiv. 38), He describes the weakness of the disciples,
not simply as a condition caused by their physical
frame, but more generally as caused by man's state
as a creature.   Therefore He here chooses the term
" flesh," which, following an Old Testament usage, is
employed by synecdoche to denote the frail, perishable nature of man as a creature.   By expressly con-
trasting the idea of " flesh," according to this meaning,
with "spirit," it was natural that, by this latter term,
Jesus should characterise that side of His disciples'
nature in which He discerned a courageous and joyful
alacrity, which, however, in view of the weakness of
the flesh, He judged to be in need of Divine support.
For, according to Old Testament usage, this term
" spirit " was applied to the inner spiritual life of man,
the soul, especially when it was not considered in
respect of its individuality, but of its higher Divine
nature and origin.[2]   This expression " spirit," therefore, forms the specific antithesis of the term " flesh,"
which brings out the frailty of man as a creature.

---

[1] The expression οἱ πτωχοὶ τῷ πνεύματι, Matt. v. 3, would fall under
this head, if we should not take the simple οἱ πτωχοί of Luke vi. 20 as
more exactly rendering the text of the Logia (cf. *Log.* § 2*a*, *L. J.* i. p.
53 ff.).   Besides, the οἱ πτωχοὶ τῷ πνεύματι would not signify "the poor
of (as to) spirit," but, according to the analogy of ταπεινὸς τῇ καρδίᾳ,
Matt. xi. 29, and similar Old Testament expressions, "the poor *in*
spirit," that is, the humble - minded, those who not merely are and
appear externally poor, but who feel and know themselves poor and
needy.   The expression, Luke ix. 55, "Ye know not what manner of
spirit ye are of," does not, for reasons of textual criticism, fall under
consideration.

[2] Cf. my treatise, *Die Begriffe Fleisch und Geist*, etc., p. 27 f.

Under the term "spirit" in the passage referred to, we must not, indeed, understand a really different faculty than that which is elsewhere expressed by the term soul or καρδία, though certainly that faculty is meant under a different point of view, viz. in respect of its being the higher and divinely-originated nature, in opposition to the weak creature nature. So also, in that utterance of Jesus on the cross, recorded only in Luke (xxiii. 46), and connected with Ps. xxxi. 6, "Father, into Thine hands I commit my spirit," this idea of "spirit" is used when it concerns the resigning to God of the life given by Him. Finally, in that saying of Jesus to the woman of Samaria, handed down from the Johannine source, "The true worshippers shall worship the Father in spirit and in truth; . . . God is spirit, and they who worship Him must worship in spirit and in truth" (iv. 23 f.), the use of the notion "spirit" to designate the organ whereby man must worship God, was required in order to bring out the mutual relation as to character between the organ and the object of worship. But here, also, nothing more is really meant by the spirit in which prayer is to be offered, than is meant in Mark xii. 30 by the whole heart and soul and mind and strength with which man must love God.

4. In regard also to *supernatural spiritual beings*, whether good or bad, and their relation to men, Jesus has followed the traditional ideas. No doubt He has taken quite a different view from that of His Jewish contemporaries of the significance of these spiritual agencies for the restoring or hindering of the health-giving intercourse of man with God. This point,

however, will meet us farther on in the exposition of the special contents of the teaching of Jesus.   But so far as their existence, nature, and ordinary mode of activity are concerned, He has simply accepted the current ideas of His countrymen.

We learn but little from the well-attested sayings of Jesus as to His ideas concerning the angels.   He calls them the "holy angels" (Mark viii. 38), "the angels in heaven" (Mark xii. 25 ; xiii. 32) ; thus He considers them as belonging to God, and in holy fellowship with Him.   His sayings to the Saddu- cees, that they who have risen from the dead neither marry nor are given in marriage, but are as the angels in heaven (Mark xii. 25), shows that He does not invest them with such a sensuous nature, nor does He ascribe to them such sensuous desires, as those of men on earth.   Therefore He does not regard them as bearing towards each other relationships such as those founded on the sensuous nature of man.   That He ascribes to them a higher intelligence than that of men, but still with limited knowledge, is evident from the expression, "But of that day, or that hour (of the Parousia), knoweth no man, no, not the angels in heaven" (Mark xiii. 32).   He makes them the representatives of the glorious power of God, when He says that the Son of man, at His second com- ing, will appear in the glory of His Father with the holy angels (Mark viii. 38).   He looks upon them as helpful agencies, who communicate to men the blessings appointed by God, when He tells us in His parable of poor Lazarus whom angels carried to Abraham's bosom (Luke xvi. 22).   The

saying[1] (Matt. xviii. 10), " Take heed that ye despise
not one of these little ones : for I say unto you, That
in heaven their angels do always behold the face of
my Father who is in heaven," conveys the idea
of guardian angels (cf. Acts xii. 15), who belong
individually to particular human beings, whose welfare they oversee.   In those words of Jesus, reported
only by our first evangelist, as spoken at His arrest
to the disciple who smote impetuously with his
sword, " Thinkest thou that I cannot now pray to
my Father, and He shall give me more than twelve
legions of angels?" (Matt. xxvi. 53), the angels are
represented as mediating agents of the mighty power
of God.

In contrast with the holy angels who work for the
welfare of men, according to Jesus' view, stand Satan
and his angels, the demons and impure spirits.   These
are regarded by Jesus as beings of supernatural
powers, united by common interests in a kingdom at
war with the kingdom of God (Mark iii. 23 ff.).   He
presupposes that they exert upon men an agency
prompting to evil, and corresponding to their own
evil nature.   He regards Satan as bringing about
situations which furnish a strong allurement to sin.
In that account of His temptations, given in our first
and third Gospels, and founded probably upon intimations given by Jesus Himself (Matt. iv. 1 ff. ; Luke
iv. 1 ff.), the perverse ideas and motives which, at the
period after His baptism, threatened to shake His
certainty of His Messianic calling, were represented

---

[1] On the possibility that the saying was handed down in the Logia,
cf. *Log.* § 28*b*, *L. J.* i. p. 154 f.

as temptations of the devil.   Mark (viii. 33) gives
the expression wherewith Jesus rebuked Peter when
the latter sought to turn Him from the idea of the
necessity of His suffering and death: "Get thee
behind me, Satan!"   The Logia (Luke xxii. 31)
inform us that Jesus, referring to the conflict impending for His disciples, said to Peter at the last
supper: "Behold, Satan hath desired to have you,
that he may sift you as wheat."   And, according to
the Johannine source (xiv. 30), He said, in reference
to the conflict connected with His coming sufferings
and death: "The prince of this world cometh, and
hath nothing in me."   We notice specially from the
passages, Mark viii. 33; John xiv. 30, that Jesus, by
the simple brevity of the expression, speaks as if
Satan were to assault Him in direct form, whereas
the temptations referred to took place manifestly in a
natural way through the words and acts of other men.
Here He expresses the view that the motives and
persuasions, by which men tried to make Him untrue
to the fulfilment of His Messianic calling, sprang from
an evil principle hostile to God, and tended to an evil
and godless end.   And, according to ideas common
to Himself and His disciples in regard to Satan as
the personal principle of evil and enmity to God,
He makes it appear as if Satan was the immediate
tempter.   I am far from thinking that He does so in a
mere figurative way.   Beyond all doubt Jesus accepted
the contemporary ideas as to a real existence of
Satan, and accordingly, in the particular cases referred
to, He supposes a real Satanic co-operation.   Still it
must be inferred from the mode of expression in the

passages, Mark viii. 33 and John xiv. 30, that, in relating to His disciples the temptations of Satan by
which He was assailed immediately after His baptism,
Jesus did not, as a matter of course, mean that Satan
himself came in a direct visible way, however natural
such a misunderstanding might be on the part of His
hearers, from the drastic way in which He stated the
principle He sought to bring out.   Under the designation of " the prince of this world," which occurs in
the Johannine source, in xii. 31 and xvi. 11, besides
the already quoted verse, xiv. 30, the devil is described
as the leader or ruler of the world so far as it
stands in hostile opposition to the will and character
of God.   And the same idea is presented in John
viii. 44, where the devil is declared to be a murderer
from the beginning, who continues, not in righteous-
ness ($\dot{a}\lambda\eta\theta\epsilon\dot{\iota}\dot{q}$), but speaks lies; and where He pronounces the unbelieving Jews to be the offspring of
the devil, because they have the same evil nature
and exhibit the same evil disposition as Satan.

Besides this allurement to sin, Jesus recognises
another mode of Satanic and demoniac agency towards
men, namely, the infliction of all sorts of evils upon
men.   The devil is the enemy *par excellence*, who, in
conformity with his own evil character, seeks to bring
mischief upon men (Luke x. 19).   Strange as the idea
may appear to us, of connecting with the conception
of the devil and demons any other sort of evil activity
than that directed to the moral and religious injury
of men, it is clear that Jesus quite fully accepted the
idea of demoniac influences aiming, not at immorality,
but at the misery of men.   Jesus has not, indeed, un-

folded this idea as something original on His part, but has adopted it from the popular mode of view of His countrymen.[1] In accordance with this popular conception, He specially regards sicknesses as resulting from demoniac influence. This mode of view was applied in a general way to all sicknesses. For example, the woman who, for eighteen years, had a spirit of weakness, by which she was bowed down and unable to rise (Luke xiii. 11), Jesus declares to have been bound by Satan for eighteen years (ver. 16). But especially in the case of certain extraordinary morbid phenomena, such as intermittent diseases, it was supposed that the person was so possessed and indwelt by the demon, or, in particularly bad cases, by many demons, as to be made the powerless object of their pernicious dealings and the involuntary organ of their utterances (cf. especially Mark v. 2-5 ; ix. 17 f., 22). That Jesus had much to do during His ministry with sick persons, who, in this special sense, passed for demoniacs, that He regarded and treated them as possessed with real demons, and that He saw in their seizures a special task for Himself and His disciples, cannot, according to our authorities, be held doubtful (cf. Mark i. 23 ff., 34; iii. 11 f., 15, 22 ff.; vi. 7 ; Luke x. 17-20; xi. 14 ff.; xiii. 32). This mode of view finds very characteristic expression in the parable of the Demon, which, at his return to the man from whom

---

[1] Compare Paul's reference to that agency of Satan, or of Satan's angel, whereby the flesh was injured, with no moral or religious detriment, since it tended to the salvation of the spirit in the day of judgment in the case of the man judged on account of moral corruption (1 Cor. v. 5) ; while in the case of the apostle himself, when tempted to spiritual pride, such agency tended to preserve his humility and trust in Divine strength alone (2 Cor. xii. 7).

he had been expelled, brought with him seven other
spirits more wicked than himself (Matt. xii. 43 ff.).[1]
In order to bring this declaration home to our modern
intelligence, we must exchange the mode of view
employed by Jesus to that current among us, and
speak of a sickness which, after it has yielded to
treatment, but yet has left a lingering predisposition
behind, assails its subject anew, so that the relapse
becomes more violent than the original sickness.
Such, according to Jesus, would be the experience of
His unbelieving contemporaries.   Far as they now
seemed beyond the reach of those judgments which
had formerly visited Israel, they were about to undergo
a still heavier visitation (ver. 45b).   It is clear that it
was not the unhappy subjects themselves of this demoniacal possession, but the demons who maliciously
tormented them, who were regarded as morally evil.

We can easily lay down the general ground on
which the ideas of Jesus in regard to sicknesses and
other evils, as caused by demoniac agents, was based.
Jesus, as well as His Jewish contemporaries, lacked
that conception of the universal correlation of earthly
phenomena through natural law, which forms the
modern basis of natural research.   The impulse
to attain a knowledge of the natural causes of particular phenomena, and the self-evident presupposition of the existence of such natural causes even
where they are unknown, were not then current
as they are now.   The common natural phenomena,
in which the connection between the determining
causes and the corresponding effects is clearly appar-

[1] Cf. *Log.* § 12e, and at § 12b, *L. J.* i. p. 101 ff.

ent, were, of course, apprehended by Jesus in the
same naturalistic way as by us. Take an instance in
the account of the seed, whose germination and fruit-
fulness are conditioned by the quality of the soil and
by other circumstances (Mark iv. 3 ff.). But the universal correlation of earthly phenomena in conformity
with natural law, which has formed the progressive
result of later scientific research, in regard to outward nature and our own faculties of perception—
continued down to our own time—lay quite outside
the circle of ideas held by Jesus. Therefore, in
the case of uncommon and mysterious phenomena,
the explanation readily presented itself to Jesus,
as to His contemporaries, that those striking effects
were produced by the superior power of an invisible
being. The pious mode of contemplation, which sees
in all earthly events the immediate agency of the will
of God in order to insure the welfare of His children,
was, in the case of Jesus, as we shall afterwards see,
absolutely unaffected by the degree of His idea of the
natural interrelation of things.

5. To the domain of ideas simply borrowed from
the popular mode of view in regard to the system of
the created universe, belongs also the idea of Hades
as employed by Jesus in the narrative of the Rich
Man and Lazarus (Luke xvi. 22 ff.). Certainly it was
not His aim in that parable to give information in
regard to the conditions in Hades, but rather to bring
out that the judgment of God as to individual men by
no means necessarily corresponds with the reputation
they bear among their fellow-men, but may be dia-
metrically opposed to that (Luke xvi. 15). He

illustrates this thought from the example of two
men, far removed from each other in earthly position and fortune, who after death, when apparently
the judgment of God overtakes them, come to have
their original positions directly reversed. It is
with the contrast between the position of those
two men on earth and after death that Jesus is
concerned, and He depicts that contrast in a way
corresponding to the ideas current among His hearers
in regard to the conditions of existence in the world
to come. Lazarus, as well as the rich man, enters
Hades; but this Hades is no longer, like the Old
Testament Scheol, a region of darkness and misery
without distinction for its inhabitants, among whom
even the good can no longer praise God. With
Jesus, as in the more advanced Jewish conception,
Hades appears divided into two parts, adjacent, yet
separated from each other by an impassable gulf—a
place of bliss and a place of misery. Lazarus passes
into Abraham's bosom, that is, into the highest part
of the abode of the blessed; the rich man enters the
place of woe, where he suffers thirst in burning flame.
Whether, also, the idea that the inhabitants of both
the separate parts of Hades can see and converse
with each other, were founded on a prevalent Jewish
view, must be left undecided. It is very probable
that Jesus Himself has used this idea with imaginative licence merely for the purpose of carrying out
the parable, viz. in order that His view of the case
narrated, and the practical lesson to be drawn from it,
should not be appended to the narrative as a supple-
mental reflection, but should be inwoven with the story.

No other sayings of Jesus as to Hades have come down to us which add anything essential to the view presented in the narrative of Lazarus. The words of Jesus to the thief on the cross, " To-day shalt thou be with me in paradise," where under paradise is understood the place of happiness in Hades, occur only in Luke (xxii. 43). When Jesus, as reported by the Logia, declared of Capernaum, that, though exalted to heaven, it would be thrust down to Hades, He uses the term Hades—as denoting a far-down subterranean region—figuratively to express a position of the utmost abasement. Also in those words to Peter, which we may consider as perhaps reliably recorded, " Thou art Rock, and the gates of Hades shall not prevail against thee" (Matt. xvi. 18);[1] "the gates of Hades," which keep irrevocably all who pass through them into the realm of the dead, is a popular expression for the greatest steadfastness.

6. Finally, we have, in this connection, to consider the ideas of Jesus relative to the events of past history. These are confined to the historical occurrences recorded in the Old Testament; and here also there is but one point that is specially noteworthy. Jesus has found no occasion, in connection with His work, to apply criticism to the historical traditions which were unquestioningly received by His countrymen. He refers to the murder of Abel (Luke xi. 51 ; cf. John viii. 44) ; to the deluge, and the destruction of Sodom (Luke xvii. 26 ff.; cf. x. 12); to the introduction of circumcision by the patriarchs, and its sanction by Moses (John vii. 22) ; to the joy of

[1] Cf. *Log.* § 47, *L. J.* i. p. 180 f.

Abraham at receiving the Messianic promise (John viii. 56); to the vision seen by Moses at the burning bush (Mark xii. 26); to the eating of manna in the wilderness (John vi. 49, 58; cf. ver. 31 ff.); to the lifting up of the brazen serpent by Moses (John iii. 14); to David's partaking of the shewbread in the house of God (Mark ii. 25 f.); to Solomon's glory (Matt. vi. 29); and to the visit of the Queen of Sheba in order to hear his wisdom (Luke xi. 31); to the sending of Elias to the widow of Sarepta, and to the healing of the leprosy of Naaman by Elisha (Luke iv. 25 ff.); to the preaching of righteousness by the prophet Jonas to the Ninevites (Luke xi. 29, 30, 32); to the continuous persecution of the prophets by the Israelites, down to the murder of Zachariah in the temple court (2 Chron. xxiv. 21) at the close of the Old Testament period (Luke xi. 47–51; xiii. 33 f.). To this simple reception of the historical material handed down in the Old Testament, naturally corresponds the adoption of the traditional ideas in regard to the origin of the Old Testament writings. For Jesus, Moses is the author of the whole legal system (Mark i. 44; vii. 10; x. 3 ff.; xii. 26); David is the writer of Ps. cx. (Mark xii. 36).

Wherever, in short, the ideas of Jesus in regard to the natural order and previous history of the world are brought under consideration, the view finds confirmation that He has never sought to investigate, correct, or extend those ideas. He had to employ them in His teaching, but He has not made them special themes of that teaching. He has accepted them as they were given to Him and His compatriots through simple observation or through tradition. He did not so accept them in order to give them the sanction of revelation, but only to concentrate the attention of Himself and His hearers wholly upon that which formed the true theme of His revealed message, the gospel of the kingdom of God.

THIRD SECTION.

PREACHING OF THE KINGDOM OF GOD IN GENERAL.

———◆———

CHAP. I. THE THEME OF THE PREACHING OF JESUS, AND ITS DETAILS IN GENERAL.

1. AT the beginning of his narrative Mark describes the substance of the preaching with which Jesus set out, as follows (i. 14 f.): "Jesus came into Galilee, preaching the gospel of the kingdom of God, and saying, The time is fulfilled, and the kingdom of God is at hand: repent ye, and believe in the gospel." The glad tidings which Jesus proclaimed were tidings of the kingdom of God. In delivering this message, He, on the one hand, proclaimed the fact that the kingdom was beginning to be set up; and, on the other hand, He announced the requirements to be fulfilled in view of that fact. The whole contents of the teaching of Jesus can be classed under this general theme and the two points of view from which He expounded it. His preaching in regard to the kingdom of God contained, partly, instruction as to the existence of the kingdom, its nature, its realisation and development; and partly, exhortations to

173

the fulfilment of the conditions of membership. For Jesus sought to impart no mere theoretical knowledge of the kingdom of God as something of no personal concern to the hearers. His object was to establish that kingdom practically among His hearers; and therefore He continually aimed at inciting them to become members of it. Although, in the discourses of the fourth Gospel, this title of "the kingdom of God" occurs only in one place (iii. 3 and 5), yet, in reality, the whole contents of those discourses, their testimony to His Messiahship, and their exhortations to faith in Him, can be ranked under the general subject of the kingdom of God, and the two aspects under which He expounded it.

The idea of the kingdom of God was familiar to the Jews in the time of Jesus. For them it signified that condition of things which would insure the realisation of God's kingship over His people (Dan. ii. 44), after which the pious in Israel ever aspired as the normal relation between them and God (Ex. xix. 6). Along with this they expected the fulfilment of the promises of the Old Testament and all the religious hopes of the Jewish people.[1] But though Jesus took this well-known idea as the central point of His preaching, and proclaimed that the kingdom of God was at hand, He was quite aware from the first

---

[1] As to the employment of the term kingship or kingdom of God by the Israelites of the earlier period, as well as those of Christ's own time, cf. Schürer in the *Jahrbüchern für protestantische Theologie*, 1876, p. 166 ff., and *History of the Jewish People*, ii. p. 453 (trans. Div. II. vol. ii. p. 170); Cremer, *Bibl. Theol. Lexicon of N. T. Greek*, under the word βασιλεία.

that this kingdom as He viewed it did not at all correspond to the contemporary Jewish conception of it. In adopting this idea, He sought to set His preaching in an intelligible relation to the hopes of salvation which His contemporaries built upon the prophetic promises of the Old Testament, and He claimed that, in the kingdom of God which He announced, those hopes found their true and express fulfilment. For He was thoroughly assured that, in the new order which He proclaimed and was introducing, the general idea of the kingdom of God would be fully realised, that is, *the idea of a Divine dispensation under which God would bestow His full salvation upon a society of men, who, on their part, should fulfil His will in true righteousness.*

This preaching of Jesus, which made the highest claim and awakened the greatest expectations, would at first naturally appear a great mystery to all who heard it. What authority had He for such a message; how far was it true; and in what sense must it be understood? These were questions which must have occurred not only to those who could not believe in the humble unlettered carpenter of Nazareth, who doubted His having prophetic illumination to enable Him to cast light upon the subject of the kingdom, and His power to contribute aught towards setting it up. They must also have occurred to those who trustfully welcomed His preaching and sat as disciples at His feet. We must also remember, what we have already noted in our account of the Jewish hopes in the time of Jesus, that the idea of the kingdom of God was not a clear, definite conception in the mind of His contemporaries.   On the contrary, we find that those hopes presented manifold and important divergences on such points as the expectation of the Messianic King, the personal salvation hoped for by individuals as related to the national Messianic hope, and the stress laid upon the moral-religious character of that coming dispensation.   In relation to their attitude towards each of these points, a problem was raised by Jesus' announcement that the kingdom of God was at hand.   His message required a more exact explanation and verification.

2. For understanding the organic connection in which Jesus Himself apprehended and presented the teaching which helped thus to explain and confirm the tidings of the kingdom of God, it is specially important to consider that He did not proceed from the assertion of His own Messiahship and the chief realisation of the kingdom of God in His own person as Messiah, and upon that basis found His teaching in regard to the kind of salvation and the nature of the righteousness to be found in the kingdom which He was to establish.   On the contrary, He first sought to make clear the special kind of deliverance and the nature of the righteousness of that kingdom, as well as the conditions of membership, whilst He purposely kept His own Messiahship in the background.   In opposition to the idea of the fourth evangelist, as it had become prevalent in Church tradition, according to which Jesus was openly proclaimed the Messiah by John the Baptist and by Himself from the outset, the clear and consistent account by Mark must be held as authoritative.   According to Mark, Jesus, at

the beginning of His ministry, was recognised neither by the Baptist nor by His own disciples as the Messiah, nor did He refer to Himself as such. He suppressed the premature announcement of His Messiahship by the demons. Only at a comparatively advanced stage of His ministry, and in the inmost circle of His disciples, did He begin to be recognised as the Messiah; and even then He expressly forbade the general publication of that truth. At length, just at the close of His ministry, and in view of the impending catastrophe, He openly claimed to be the Messiah, and, as such, openly accepted the homage of His disciples.[1] The less Jesus has sought to give systematic order to His doctrine otherwise, the more significant is the fact, that He methodically kept back the course of His teaching in regard to His Messiahship, of which He was undoubtedly conscious since His baptism. He did not, from the outset, directly proclaim that truth; but gradually paved the way for its being understood by teaching the nature and coming of the kingdom in general. He thus sought to call forth, wherever possible, a spontaneous recognition of the truth on the part of others, not by their mere acceptance of authoritative assertions, but from an enlightened understanding of its grounds. Had Jesus declared Himself quite plainly to be the Messiah, there would have been associated with His person, in accordance with the prevailing Jewish ideas of the nature of the Messianic kingdom, expectations which He neither could nor would fulfil. But if He first elicited an understanding of the nature of the

[1] Cf. *L. J.* i. pp. 3 ff. and 311–316.

M

Messianic kingdom as He meant it, then also the paradoxical form in which He Himself realised the ideal of the Messiah would be understood as the true and necessary one, in conformity with the genuine nature of the kingdom of God.

We need not suppose, indeed, that Jesus had from the first a fixed purpose of keeping back the open declaration of His Messianic claim during the greater part of His public ministry. We must rather consider how exceedingly short His public life was, and how premature — according to human judgment — was its close, as if, measured by the standard of the career of other reformers and founders of religions, it was still in its introductory stage. After the first flow and ebb of the tide of success, Jesus had gained only a small band of followers, who, from a trustful knowledge of the kingdom of God as preached by Him, derived the knowledge of His Messiahship. It was not so much because He perceived His death to be impending, that Jesus, at the close of His life, proclaimed His Messiahship; but that catastrophe was rather brought about because Jesus, after having trained His disciples to a right understanding of His Messiahship, began openly to claim that dignity. Thus the preparatory period of His work, during which He did not publicly claim the Messiahship, but laid the foundation of a deep and real knowledge of it, was really the main part of His ministry ; whilst His public claim to be the Messiah, which, according to human judgment, ought to have formed the point of transition to His public Messianic career, in reality brought that career to its earthly close.   Certainly I do not mean that Jesus, when He openly came forth as the Messiah, in particular at His Messianic entry into Jerusalem, did not anticipate His approaching death. According to our Gospel sources, He had already, at an earlier period, clearly foreseen the end; and on that account set the necessary proclamation of His Messiahship designedly in relation to His death. I only wish to say that the fact—so remarkable at first sight—of His abstaining from giving open testimony to His Messiahship until shortly before His death, in spite of His consciousness of being the Messiah, and of His endeavour to be recognised as such, loses its psychological singularity when we think that the period of this abstention was a comparatively short one, His whole ministry being so speedily brought to a close.

It was because the contemporary Jewish conception of the latter-day salvation was not absolutely and always connected with the expectation of the Messiah,[1] that it was possible for Jesus to withhold for a time the announcement of His Messiahship, whilst proclaiming the kingdom of God, without express reference to the Messiah. The general view of the latter-day salvation, although usually, was nevertheless not universally modified by the special Messianic idea, and therefore the omission of this idea was not felt to imply the lack of an essential and self-evident mark of the kingdom of God. The announcement of the kingdom by Jesus would naturally awaken on the part of His hearers the

[1] Cf. p. 62.

question of what relation He bore to the Messiah in that kingdom. But it was not necessary for Jesus to answer this question from the beginning.

The objection need not be urged, that, as Jesus in any case regarded Himself as the founder of the kingdom, on whom its earthly existence depended, and in union with whom alone other men could become its true members ; and as, in His own case, the knowledge of the kingdom of God as a present reality had sprung out of the consciousness He attained of His Messiahship, it would have been the true method of preaching the kingdom to others, to teach them first to recognise Him as the Messiah, and so lead on to the kingdom of God as founded by Him. It is sufficient to say in reply to this, that, by the Jews in general as well as by Jesus, the Messiah was always conceived as the means whereby the kingdom of God was to be set up. Even though in reality the means precedes the end to be subserved by it, yet, in the matter of recognition, the understanding of the end must precede the understanding of the means which in its nature is adapted for producing that end. Even Jesus Himself did not attain His Messianic consciousness without preparation. This preparation consisted in having, from childhood, known and loved God as His Father, and in having been conscious of possessing Divine endowments, and in having striven to fulfil God's will in upright obedience. Only by having lived and moved in this relation to God, which He deemed the normal and natural one, could the knowledge have come upon Him at baptism with the sun-burst of a revelation, that on this very relation the peculiar nature of the expected kingdom of God rested, and that He Himself, in whom that relation was thoroughly realised, had been called to be the founder of the kingdom of God. In analogy with this growth of His own Messianic consciousness, He had also to awaken in others the true recognition of His Messiahship. He had first to impress upon them those spiritual relations between God and men which He now perceived as the essential foundation of the kingdom of God. He had also to produce in them the conviction that where this relation had come to exist, there the kingdom of God was realised. He could then mature in their minds the self-evident truth that He was the Messiah, the perfect founder of the kingdom of God, and that in union with Him men must become genuine citizens of this kingdom. Certainly it was on the ground of their knowledge of His Messiahship that the disciples could alone attain the full knowledge of the realisation of the kingdom of God ; but their understanding of the true nature of the kingdom, and of the general law of its realisation, already formed the foundation of the knowledge of His Messiahship.

3. The representation of the contents of the teaching of Jesus which we now seek to give, must be based, as to its arrangement, on the method of the course followed by Jesus in His teaching. We must take as our starting-point the teaching of Jesus as to the nature of the kingdom of God. Jesus nowhere, however, described its character by giving short, concise formulæ, but by more precisely defining and explaining, in His peculiar sense, the points which

the Jews in general conceived to be of essential moment in the kingdom of God, viz. the ideas concerning the salvation to be brought into full realisation in God's kingdom, and the ideas concerning the righteousness through which the members of the kingdom would bring the reign of God to full recognition. This Jesus effected on the ground of the special view which He entertained and proclaimed of the character of God. From a close examination of those ideas of Jesus as to God, and the saving benefits and righteousness of His kingdom, which are found continually as the underlying basis of His judgments and precepts, we can determine the true sense in which He announced the coming of the kingdom of God, and can understand the conditions of membership in it. Here, however, we must not overlook the question, if He Himself, during the period of His ministry, passed through a course of development in His apprehension of the nature and coming of the kingdom of God. Afterwards we shall have to discuss, on the one hand, the personal testimony of Jesus to His Messiahship ; and, on the other, His statements concerning the further development of the kingdom of God on earth,—statements which He pronounced on the ground both of His idea of the nature and coming of the kingdom, and of His own personal Messianic experiences. Already, in connection with Mark i. 14, we have noted the circumstance, that Jesus made His practical exhortations in regard to God's kingdom go hand in hand with declarations as to the actual existence of the kingdom ; and, in conformity with this, just as our first main section issued in a practical consideration of the general conditions of membership of the kingdom, so also the two following sections conclude with a consideration of the conduct which Jesus enjoined in relation to Himself as Messiah, and in relation to the further extension which He foresaw for the kingdom of God on earth. The contents of our second and third main sections are related to the contents of our first main section, as the more special exposition and application are related to the general rule. The announcement by Jesus of His own Messiahship, as well as that of the future further extension on earth of the kingdom of God, might be classed under the general theme of the announcement of the kingdom of God, since they define more precisely how the kingdom of God is developed. But we must deal with those two subjects as separate branches, apart from the general teaching of Jesus concerning the kingdom of God; for this reason, because He Himself, on good grounds, refrained from making them from the outset a subject of teaching, in the same way as He taught the general view of the nature and coming of the kingdom of God and of the conditions of its membership. In keeping separate these three main sections, we will, in my view, best express the inner connection of the thought of Jesus, as well as the historical progress in the announcement of His doctrine, so far as it is on the whole observable.

CHAP. II. GOD AS THE FATHER.

1. Speaking paradoxically, we can say that Jesus taught no new doctrine of God, but adopted and built upon the Old Testament Jewish view; and, at the same time, that His conception of God stands on a specifically higher level than the Jewish view; and that in the distinctive peculiarity of that conception lay the root of all the new elements of His teaching, and of the whole divergence of the Christian religion from that of the Old Testament. Jesus, indeed, taught no new doctrine of the particular attributes of God; also His conception of the character of God, taken as a whole, was already formed and recognised by certain Old Testament declarations. Yet that conception had only found occasional expression in the Old Testament, and had not been completely carried out in its consequences, whilst Jesus established it as the normal and standard conception of the Divine character, and with unsurpassable clearness exhibited it in its practical results.

The God of whom Jesus speaks is the one God of Israel (Mark xii. 29), the God of Abraham, Isaac, and Jacob (Mark xii. 26). Jesus has based His view upon the Old Testament revelation of God; and the knowledge of the nature of God, as derived from this revelation, He accepted as valid. Nowhere do we find Him stating and teaching anything as to the nature of God which was impossible on the basis of the Old Testament religion. When He declared that with God all things are possible (Mark x. 27; xiv. 36), or when He spoke of God as being perfect (Matt. v. 48), or when He affirmed

that none were good but God only (Mark x. 18),
i.e. so far as God is the eternal essence of the good,
and does not undergo such a process of striving
and struggling in approximating the good as is the
case with the best of men, He sought thereby to un-
fold no new view as to God, which would have required
a special explanation and basis for the Jewish mind.
But He appealed to those features of the Divine
character whose recognition He could take for
granted, and from which He sought to draw only
such conclusions as were postulated by the line of
thought in which they occurred.

The significant point with Jesus is the conception
of the character of God, taken as a whole, which He
regarded as the standard of all religious knowledge and
of all religious life. He has not defined the sum of the
attributes of God otherwise than before His time, but
He has apprehended in a peculiar way their relation
to each other in the character of God. He has not
sought to give a precise exposition of this general conception of God by means of theological notions, but He
has made it generally intelligible by usually employing
the name of Father to designate God. He has used
this name as a foundation whereon to base weighty
teaching in regard to God's gracious action, and the
right mode of piety on the part of men.

Of course it is not the mere name of Father,
but the idea bound up in it, that is important.
His abundant and frequent use of that name
would be meaningless were it employed from a mere
habit. We can see, however, that He purposely
meant to denote thereby a peculiar general view of

the Divine character ; and what is original here is the dominant significance for His whole teaching which was given to the idea indicated by the name.

Frequently in the Old Testament God had already been designated as Father.   In the first place, He is called the Father of the people of Israel, whom in His love He has chosen and brought up as His people (Hos. xi. 1 ; Isa. i. 2 ; Deut. i. 31 ; viii. 5 ; xxxii. 6 ; cf. Tob. xiii. 4 ; 3 Macc. vi. 3).   So far as they thought of other nations having their existence also from God, still Israel was called the first-born son of God, to set forth that this people is the peculiar object of the Divine love (Ex. iv. 22 ; Jer. xxxi. 8 ; Sir. xxxvi. 14).   In this paternal relationship of God to His people lies also the motive for His redemptive manifestation to them in the future ; Jehovah Himself refers to this in His gracious assurance : " Is not Ephraim my dear son and my pleasant child ? For I well remember still what I have said to him ; therefore my heart breaks towards him, and moves me to have mercy upon him " (Jer. xxxi. 19).   And the godly Israelites appealed to it in their urgent prayers for redemption : "Art Thou our Father, though Abraham knoweth us not, and Israel doth not acknowledge us ? Thou, O Lord, art our Father, our Redeemer ; from everlasting is Thy name " (Isa. lxiii. 16 ; cf. lxiv. 8). On the other hand, in this fatherhood of God lay the motive binding the Israelites to obedience to God : " Should not a son honour his father, and a servant his master ? If, now, I am a father, where is my honour ? and if I am a master, where is he that feareth me ?" (Mal. i. 6).   The realisation of the ideal

religious relationship between Jehovah and the people
in the longed-for latter-day was indicated by the fact
that the people should be called the "sons of the
living God" (Hos. ii. 1), and that God should be
called by them "my Father" (Jer. iii. 19).   Whilst
in these passages God is termed Father in relation to
the people in general, sometimes also the theocratic
king, who was the apex and representative of the
people, was spoken of as standing in a special relation
of sonship to God (2 Sam. vii. 14 ; Ps. ii. 7 ; lxxxix.
27 f.).   Finally, in certain post-exilic passages God was
also called Father in relation to the individual Israelites, as in Mal. ii. 10 : " Have we not all one Father ?
has not one God created us ? " and in the prayer of
the son of Sirach : " Father and God of my life "
(xxiii. 1, 4 ; cf. also li. 10), where only the relation of
God to individuals as Creator is suggested.   In the
Wisdom of Solomon, however, the very significant
declaration is found in the mouth of the ungodly, that
the pious boasted of God as their Father, and regarded themselves as the sons of God (ii. 16–18).   On
the other hand, the name of Father is once in the
same writing applied to God as He rules in His
providence (πρόνοια), and directs the vessels of men
through the pathways of the sea (xiv. 3).

But even this glance at the Old Testament use of
the name of *Father* as applied to God, sets clearly
before our eyes that this was by no means the
customary and prevalent designation of God by the
Israelites.   Nowhere in the Psalms, which were the
most direct expressions of reverence to God as taught
in the Old Testament, was God addressed as Father

of the people of Israel or of individual Israelites.
Rather we find there, as elsewhere, that the customary
title under which God was designated, in view of His
position and attitude toward Israel, collectively and
individually, was that of *King* (Ps. v. 3 ; x. 16 ; xxiv.
7 ff.; xxix. 10; xliv. 5; xlvii. 3, 7-9, etc. ; cf. Jer. vi. 5;
xxxiii. 22; xli. 21 ; xliv. 6) ; and, in correspondence
with this, the Israelites style themselves the *servants
of God* (Ps. xix. 12, 14; xxvii. 9 ; xxxi. 17; xxxiv. 23 ;
xc. 13 ; cxix. 122 ff.; cxliii. 2, etc.).   Also in Deutero-
Isaiah, the personification of the pious Israel, by whom
God would bring into existence the full and longed-
for redemption, is called the *Servant of Jehovah.*
This predominance of the kingly designation of God
is not accidental, but arises out of the conceptions
which the pious Israelites had of the government of
God.   They knew well that God showed grace and
mercy, patience and faithfulness, and that, in virtue
of these attributes, He had chosen and led His people
Israel, and would bring them to perfect well-being, as
well as protect and bless individual saints.   But these
attributes, nevertheless, did not appear to them as
determining the whole character and action of God.
For, on the one hand, God showed those attributes
only towards His chosen people Israel, not to other
people ; on the other hand, the Old Testament saints
knew other forms of dealing on the part of God
towards the people Israel and individual Israelites,
which were not an outcome of His redemptive grace
and faithfulness, but were merely manifestations of
His absolute power and greatness.   The many
lamentations of the devout, that God had forsaken

them, individually or nationally, in spite of their not having turned aside from His ways; and their questions of surprise and impatience as to why, and how long, He would abandon them to undeserved sufferings; had their foundation in this, that even the devout Israelites could not take for granted the constant and unconditional reign of Divine grace and faithfulness, but must reckon with the possibility of God manifesting His power arbitrarily towards them.   The despairing utterances of Job, who, conscious of innocence, yet felt himself exposed, in his creature-weakness, to the power of God which overwhelmed him with sufferings (cf. especially chap. ix.), give a touching expression of the idea that God does not use His power absolutely in the service of His grace and faithfulness, but may let it go forth arbitrarily even towards the godly.   Moreover, the final answer of God to Job, which only appealed to His absolute power and wisdom as Creator, to show that man must not expostulate with God (chap. xxxviii. ff., especially xl. 2 ff.), sanctions the right of that view on the ground of the Old Testament.   Besides, they were taught to practise abundance of ceremonial duties towards God, which had no motive except in the holiness of God, so far as this attribute was conceived as resting upon His separateness from terrestrial and transient nature, especially from certain of its substances and processes.   On these grounds, the name of King must have appeared to the Israelites as the fittest designation for God, and as the most general characterisation, in view of His position and His mode of working.   Through this title the thought of

the grace and long - suffering, the faithfulness and
righteousness of God, were by no means excluded.
An absolute monarch may also care, even in a fatherly
way, for his people, and may bestow lasting favours
upon those of whom he makes choice ; and thus it is
quite intelligible how the Israelites, in conceiving of
Jehovah as the heavenly King, who graciously ruled
over His people, and had pity on them that feared
Him, " as a father pitieth his children " (Ps. ciii. 13),
would sometimes attach to Him the name of Father.
Nevertheless, the kingly name still remained the
peculiar and ordinary title for God, since it expressed
that, in their view of His character, His absolute
power and transcendence were regarded as the highest
qualities, for which independent scope was given in
the ways and commands of God, along with the
manifestation of His ethical attributes.

In later Judaism, down to the time of Jesus, there
was by no means a development of the conception
of God, in the line of more strongly accentuating the
dominant significance of grace and faithfulness for the
character and working of God, and accordingly of in-
clining to a more prevalent use of the name of Father.
The development proceeded rather in the way of
enhancing to the utmost the ideas of God's transcendent greatness and judicial authority over men.
According to the Pharisaic view, the moral relation
of man to God was one of legal subjection.   And
in that servile relationship on which they supposed
man's claim to a share in God's blessings to be
founded, the main stress was laid on ceremonial
duties, in which respect was paid to the greatness

of God, and His separateness from the transitory world. If we take note of this tendency of Jewish theology in the time of Jesus, and consider how ready it lay to the hand of Jesus, in view of the traditionary notion of the "kingdom of God" which He accepted, to designate God as the King of His kingdom, we gain a right estimate of the fact that Jesus chose much rather the use of the name of Father, for Himself and for His disciples, as the usual term for God, and has made the idea of the paternal love of God the foundation of His proclamation of the kingdom of God. No doubt He found the basis of this apprehension and appellation of God in the Old Testament, but His original and significant achievement was that, in opposition to the religious tendencies of His time, He should have so taken hold of that connecting link, as to bring into a position of sole and sovereign authority in His teaching that view of God which exalts His gratuitous love and faithfulness, and which, therefore, uses the name of Father as its comprehensive expression,—a view which till then had only appeared in fragmentary form, and had been only incompletely thought out.

2. Jesus knew God first as His own Father. The assurance which He early attained, on the ground of His religious consciousness, that He was the object of the pure fatherly love of God, remained as the principle of His Messianic consciousness, and attended Him through His whole active ministry. He addressed God in prayer as " Father" (Matt. xi. 25 f.; Mark xiv. 36; Luke xxiii. 46), and spoke of Him as *His own* Father (*e.g.* Matt. x. 32 f. ; xi. 27 ; xviii. 19,

35 ; Luke xxii. 29). But yet He did not regard God as being *only* His own Father. Rather it appeared to Him self-evident that the fatherly love of God, whose object He knew Himself to be, was not a limited condition of the character and government of God, manifesting itself merely to some, or only to a single individual, but that it was universally and always present with God, and constituted the highest principle of His will and working. Therefore, for Jesus, God was above all else " the Father" (Mark xiii. 32 ; Matt. xi. 27 ; Luke xi. 13). Whilst, in the Old Testament, God is regarded as the Father specially of the people of Israel as a whole, so far as He had chosen that people in unmerited grace, and had in mercy led them, Jesus regarded God by no means in an analogous way as the Father over the kingdom of God as a whole, but rather as the Father of all mankind, and therefore as the Father of single individuals. He taught His disciples also in their prayers to address God as Father (Luke xi. 2) ; and in His teaching, to whatever hearers, He called Him "your Father" and "thy Father" (Matt. v. 45, 48; vi. 1, 4, 6, 18, 32; x. 29; xxiii. 9 ; Luke xii. 32 ; Mark xi. 25). For God bestows His fatherly care and love on every individual (Matt. vi. 31 f.; Luke xi. 13), and sets store by the least individual (Matt. xviii. 14). It would not be according to the mind of Jesus if we regarded God as Father only in relation to the individual members of His kingdom, and not to others also. His view of the matter is shown by the words with which, in the discourse on Righteousness, He describes the motive for the duty of undeserved forgiving love :

"Love your enemies, and pray for them that persecute you : that ye may become sons of your Father who is in heaven; for He maketh His sun to rise on the evil and on the good, and sendeth rain on the just and the unjust. . . . Be ye therefore perfect, as your heavenly Father is perfect" (Matt. v. 44 f., 48). God does not *become* the Father, but *is* the heavenly Father even of those who *become* His sons.

This idea would be inconceivable, if in the Fatherhood and Sonship the mere relation of procreator and procreated were understood; for manifestly the Fatherhood of the one implies also the existence of Sonship in the other. But, for the consciousness of Jesus, it is not the relation of God to man as Creator which primarily is taken into account in His name of Father, but His unmerited, bountiful, forgiving love. This relation He maintains always and universally, in that He bestows His benefits on the good and on the evil. His very perfection consists in this love; and it can as little be conceived that God *is* not eternally and always Father, and does not always act as such, as it can be conceived that God requires to *become* perfect. This ethical apprehension of the notion of Father, however, also corresponds to Jesus' apprehension of the notion of Sonship. Man is a true son of God, not from the fact of being indebted to God for existence, and in experiencing all kinds of benefits at His hand, but from the fact of his comporting himself as a son of God, in obediently fulfilling the will of his heavenly Father, and in resembling the ethical nature of God in will and deed. It is thus

intelligible, that whilst God always *is* the loving
Father of all men, nevertheless men must *become*
sons of the heavenly Father by attaining His spirit
of gratuitous forgiving love. Though very far from
conceiving of God as first becoming the loving and
gracious Father of men from the time of the founding
of the kingdom of God, or perhaps in consequence of
the atoning death of the Messiah, yet Jesus can declare
that only the members of His kingdom who live as
becomes God's children are true sons of God. The
principle, that the sons of an earthly king are free
from payment of tribute to the king, He in this sense
applies to Himself and Peter and to all His disciples,
whom, in contrast with the Jews who do not yet belong
to the kingdom of God, He regards as the sons of
God, and therefore as not subject to the obligations
corresponding to the relation of servants (Matt.
xvii. 25 f.).

By the view of God which Jesus briefly expressed
through the name of Father, the thought that God's
will is the absolute authoritative standard of human
duty, and that men are bound to fulfil the Divine will
in unconditional obedience, is not excluded, but rather
included. For authoritative commands and guidance
on the one side, and willing obedience on the other,
are natural and characteristic in the reciprocal relation
of father and children. Therefore it was by no
means contradictory of the view already indicated,
as that mainly taken by Jesus of the character and
working of God, that He should, in several instances,
illustrate and establish His statements and precepts,
bearing on the attitude of God towards men and of

men towards God, by means of parables which refer
to the mutual relationship of earthly masters and
servants (Matt. xviii. 23 ff.; xx. 1 ff.; xxv. 14 ff.; Luke
xii. 47 f.; xvi. 1 ff., 13; xvii. 7 ff.); or that, in connection with those parables, He should plainly designate
His disciples in figurative language as "servants" of
God (Luke xvii. 10), and their obedient fulfilment
of the will of God as "service" (Luke xvi. 13). For,
in regard to the matter of obedient fulfilment of the
father's will, the relation of child is analogous to that
of servant (cf. Matt. xxi. 28–31). Nevertheless, we
must not conclude from this that the sovereignty of
God over men has been with Jesus the determinative
idea for His conception of God, and for His view of
the relationship between God and men. But, as in
the Old Testament, in spite of particular instances
in which the name of Father is applied to God, His
kingly relation is nevertheless the peculiarly characteristic one; so also with Jesus, in spite of various
cases in which He likens the mutual relationship
between God and man to that existing between
master and servant, nevertheless the paternal idea
of God is for Him the characteristic one. The fact
that God requires obedience from man, as a master
does from his servant, is not incompatible with His
position as Father. On the contrary, Jesus has so
emphasised and expanded the significance and consequences of the fatherly relation of God, that no room
appears to be left for such commands and acts of will
on God's part as characterise a despot in distinction
from a father.

But further, Jesus' conception of God as Father

does not prevent His often speaking of a "reward" which the godly either have or may expect in heaven from their Father for their righteousness, a reward which the true workers of righteousness will not lose (Mark ix. 41; Luke vi. 23; xiv. 14; Matt. v. 46; vi. 1; x. 41). For a father can also give his children a reward for their obedience and acceptable conduct; and thus also the assurance given by Jesus that every service of love, even the smallest externally, and all righteous acts, will find their reward in heaven, is a perfectly intelligible expression of His certainty that all true fulfilment of the Divine will on the part of the godly has value in God's eye, and that God, in His faithfulness, will, in a fitting manner, manifest His appreciation of their conduct.

But this certainty in the consciousness of Jesus did not imply any character of legalism corresponding to the Pharisaic Jewish view of the relationship between God and men. For the point of importance is, that God does not *only* recompense men's righteous acts with corresponding rewards, whilst He denies His blessings to those who do not render such obedience, but that He rather, in His fatherly kindness, freely dispenses immeasurable bounties to the unworthy, and is ready fully to forgive the guilt of the penitent. God, as the heavenly Father, sends sunshine and rain even for the evil (Matt. v. 45); He gives good things to those that ask Him (Matt. vii. 11), not for their previous obedience, but merely for their prayers. And, as Jesus declares in the parable of the Labourers in the Vineyard, who were hired at different hours of the day, and received the same reward (Matt. xx.

1–16), He bestows the salvation of His kingdom not according to the measure of merit, but of grace alone. He bestows it, not as due remuneration for previous service, but in equal measure, even where there can be no question of corresponding merit, and without any one being allowed to dispute with Him about the amount of those blessings. The parable of the servant who was released from his great debt by his lord, and who yet showed himself pitiless in regard to the trifling debt of his fellow-servant (Matt. xviii. 23 ff.), teaches that from God the Father all members of His kingdom receive such boundless forgiveness, that they are bound to grant unlimited forgiveness to their offending brethren, whilst there is no comparison in value between their generosity and the Divine grace they have experienced.

In the parable of the Prodigal Son (Luke xv. 11 ff.), Jesus has, in the most beautiful and clearest way, given expression to the contrast between the view of God implied in the name of Father, and the legal apprehension of the relation between God and man. The object of this parable is by no means to give an allegorical representation of the degradation of man in his estrangement from God and in the misery of sin, his penitent return, and his gracious reception by God, to which the conclusion drawn from the envy of the elder brother would have formed a pendant peculiarly superfluous from the nature of the subject; but the purpose is rather to exhibit the pardoning, bountiful grace of God vouchsafed to the sinner on condition of his penitent return, as the natural, self-evident procedure of God, in opposition to the legalistic view, which supposes that God can only reward righteous actions by a strictly equivalent recompense, and must punish all sin by withholding salvation, without giving room for pardoning grace. With reference to this purpose of the parable, the account of the displeasure of the elder son at the loving and joyful reception of his brother by the father, and of the father's disregard of that displeasure, is not superfluous. On the contrary, the peculiar object of the parable is gained by this part of the narrative, and the whole preceding story only serves to depict a situation in which, on the one hand, the ready and joyful reception of the son by the father seems to find its motive in the penitent return of the prodigal, but in which, on the other hand, occasion is given, through the greatness of the offence of the son, to elicit blame, from the legalistic standpoint, for vouchsafing pardon and overwhelming the returning prodigal with kindness. The perversity of this mode of judgment, applied from the legalistic standpoint, is at once apparent, when it has to do with the relations between the father and the son. The retributive justice which punishes according to desert, and coldly repels the returning penitent, would, in the father, have been an unnatural denial of his fatherly love; even as the envious aloofness of the elder son from his returning brother violates the moral sense, and does not correspond to the brotherly relationship. If God stand related to men as a Father, it then becomes certain and self-evident that He receives the penitent sinner in grace, and is ready to grant him new and rich blessings; and, on the other hand, that merely to apply retributive justice to right and wrong cannot be God's method of dealing with men. Were this not the case, the parable would have no demonstrative power. And it is very significant that Jesus enters into no discussion as to whether God really is the Father of men, but proceeds upon the certainty of it, as upon an undoubted axiom, and only draws the practical consequences ensuing from it for the dealings of God with men.[1]

3. The fact that such stress was laid by Jesus on

[1] If we seek to expound the parable of the Prodigal Son in an alle-gorising way, we encounter the difficulty that the previous relationship of the elder son to the father is represented as an entirely blameless one. For the son's personal testimony, that he had never transgressed the command of the father (ver. 29), and the acknowledgment on the part of the father, "Son, thou art ever with me, and all that I have is thine" (ver. 31), do not properly apply to the legalistic Pharisees, and those generally who aspire after external righteousness, by whom evidently the elder son must be indicated. In that case we should require to look upon that fulfilment of the father's commands, so boast-fully referred to by the son, as confined to mere external acts, and also the continual fellowship with the son, referred to by the father, as a mere external participation of life and goods, whilst their hearts re-mained far asunder. If, however, we consider that the important thing in every parable is in regard to one leading thought in which lies the point of comparison, whilst the remaining details are so given as to be the most serviceable for the illustration of that main thought (cf. above, p. 135), we perceive that the description of the elder son in this parable, just inasmuch as no blame is cast upon his previous conduct, is in thorough accordance with the purpose of the parable. For the main thought, whose illustration is the aim of the parable, is this : that the demand that one should follow a line of conduct which is merely to be rewarded according to its merits, does not comport with the relationship between father and son. This thought would be expressed in a far less telling way, if the representative of this legalistic demand were depicted as one who had no right, on account of his own frailty and guilt, to require the rigorous enforcement of retributive justice in regard to a brother ; whilst, on the other hand, the validity of that thought is all the more clearly brought out if that legalistic demand were made by one who was sufficient as to personal merit. Even in this case that demand appears unnatural and ill befitting the relationship between father and son. But as to whether there exist such sons of God as are really entitled to make that claim of personal merit, this parable is neither fitted nor intended to cast any light.

the fatherly relation of God to men, by no means
excluded from His consciousness the recognition of
the holy supremacy of God over the world, which the
Jews regarded as His pre-eminent attribute. In the
prayer which He has given as a model to His disciples, He makes these words—" hallowed be Thy
name "—follow immediately after the invocation to
the Father, meaning thereby that the Divine name
should be reverently acknowledged as to its sacred
majesty, and as separate from all that is profane
(Luke xi. 2). When His disciples address themselves
to God in prayer, their use of the name of Father,
by which they express their trust in the loving and
gracious disposition of God, far from detracting from
the idea of His supermundane majesty, and bringing
Him down to a level with creation and with man,
must rather be accompanied by the desire at the
same time to recognise the sovereign majesty of Him
who is addressed as Father. For the Jewish consciousness the name is the significant designation of
the recognised nature of the thing named ; the hallowing of the name of God is the reverent recognition
of the majesty of the revealed character of God. But
since, in the view of Jesus, the name denoting the
most important side of the Divine nature is that of
Father, and the idea of His fatherly character is not
merely added as a secondary and more precise designation of the idea of the Holy One, but, conversely,
the hallowing of the name of God refers to the pre-
fixed name of Father, that very fact shows that for
Jesus the hallowing of the name of God has another
and higher sense than the hallowing of the Divine

name as it was conceived and employed by the Jews.
The nature of God was regarded by the Jews as
severed to the utmost from all transitory, natural
qualities, and as specially opposed to certain forms
and conditions of matter; and they abstained as far as
possible from using the name Jehovah, as well as the
Divine names in general. But in the consciousness
of Jesus the holiness of God has no longer an independent significance alongside of His ethical attributes; but it is in that purity and magnitude of His
paternal love in which He has His perfection (Matt.
v. 48; cf. ver. 45), that His holy exaltation above the
world consists. Jesus has not, indeed, anywhere
uttered this thought directly in this form, but He
has virtually expressed it, by inferring as a consequence the incorrectness of all the ideas derived
from the Jewish conception of the holiness of God
in regard to the effect of natural influences, or, on
the other hand, of rites of external purification in
profaning or sanctifying men (Mark vii. 14–23).

Similarly, the thought of the almighty operation of
God upon the world is not diminished in the mind of
Jesus by the idea of Fatherhood, but is rather raised
into higher significance. Jesus has represented the
Father as the Lord of heaven and earth (Matt. xi.
25), with whom all things are possible (Mark x. 27;
xiv. 36), governing the course of the world and
human life in their totality, knowing the day and the
hour when the world shall come to an end (Mark
xiii. 32), penetrating the inmost thoughts of men
(Luke xvi. 15), fixing the limits of human life (Luke
xii. 20), having the power to destroy the soul and

body of man in hell (Matt. x. 28), and capable of creating new forms of life such as man cannot now conceive (Mark xii. 24). But He had also a very vivid idea of the immediate determination of even the minutest things on earth by the will of God, and indeed by His loving fatherly will. It is the heavenly Father who sends sunshine and rain to men (Matt. v. 45), who feeds the ravens and clothes the lilies of the field, and who knows also the wants of men and provides for them (Matt. vi. 25-32) ; not a sparrow falls to the ground without Him, and even the hairs of our head are all numbered by Him (Matt. x. 29 f.). With the Jews in the time of Jesus, the tendency to set God at the utmost possible distance above the world, led them to regard God's active relationship to the world as limited, and to seek in angelic powers the media of the connection between God and the world and men. But Jesus has been led by His view of the supreme significance of the fatherly love of God for the Divine character, to conceive of God's immediate providential operation on the world and men. He has indeed accepted the traditional Jewish view of the existence of angels, and of their activity in the service of God for the help of men ; but, on account of the difference of His conception of God, the angels have a very different significance for His system of religious ideas than for that of the Jews. They appear to Him not as necessary and desirable mediators, in order to conceive of the sacred exaltation of God as undisturbed by His operation upon the finite and transient world, for they effect nothing more than what God also immediately effects.

4. From this view of God entertained by Jesus, as we find it in the Logia of Matthew and in Mark's Gospel, there is no divergence in the view of God exhibited in the discourses of the fourth Gospel. Here also the name of Father is the ordinary designation of God ; and, indeed, Jesus employs this name *first of all*, though by no means *only*, in the sense of designating Him as His own Father. His Father, to whom He knew Himself bound by a mutual relationship of love (v. 17-23), is also *the* Father of all ; and this name is used with a practical end in view, when Jesus speaks of the true way of honouring God (iv. 23), and of the certain hearing of the prayers of His disciples (xv. 16 ; xvi. 23, 26 f.).

His statements in regard to particular attributes or aspects of the nature of God, other than those which are implied in the name of Father, are only occasional, and are not given for the purpose of expressing something new and hitherto unknown in regard to God. When Jesus says of the Father that He is *spirit*, and as such requires spiritual worship (iv. 24) ; when He speaks of Him as *living* (vi. 51), as *having life in Himself* (v. 26), as He who *quickens the dead* and *makes alive* (v. 21) ; or when Jesus imputes to the Father the attribute of *holy, i.e.* exalted above the world (xvii. 11), and *righteous, i.e.* working in true consistency (xvii. 25), — He appeals only to well-known characteristics of God. His aim in these utterances is not to give direct teaching about God as such, but to point to practical inferences founded in those Divine attributes and dispositions.

It is peculiarly worthy of note, that in the passage,

xvii. 11, the invocation "Holy Father" expresses
the motive for the prayer addressed to God for such
sanctification of the disciples as consists, not in their
external withdrawal from the world, or in their being
preserved from all sorts of defiling physical influences
and conditions in the world, but in their being kept
from the evil that is in the world, in their being
maintained in rectitude (ἀλήθεια) through the revealed
word of God (vers. 11–19). The ethical sense in which
this sanctification of the disciples, that is, their being
raised above the world in consecration to God, is
here understood, indirectly indicates the ethical sense
in which the holiness attributed to the Father is to
be apprehended. We see clearly, though indirectly,
that Jesus here conceives the holiness of God in
another way and on a different basis than that in
which the Jews apprehended it ; just as we infer the
same from the declaration in Mark vii. 14–23, that not
what passes into a man from without, but that which
arises out of his inner nature, defiles him. In His
conception of the holiness of God, Jesus retains the
general idea of exaltedness above the world. But,
from the supreme importance of the attribute of
fatherly love, for His view of God, that holy exaltation
is now conceived as resting, not on some sort of
relation of physical opposition to the world, but on
the moral elevation and purity of the Divine will.
The utterances of Jesus in His farewell prayer,
preserved in the Johannine source, show the moral
superiority of Jesus' view of the Divine holiness,
just as we recognise it in that discourse in Mark's
Gospel.

Of special interest here is the saying by which Jesus (John v. 17) justified His acts of healing on the Sabbath (cf. vii. 23), which had so offended the Jews : " My Father worketh hitherto, and I work." The Sabbath-rest on which God entered at the close of creation, and on which man's consecration of the seventh day was primarily based (Gen. ii. 2 f.), did not imply entire cessation of activity on God's part, since He had been working uninterruptedly down to that present hour. On this sure basis Jesus founds the lawfulness, yea the duty, of being employed, like the Father, in active usefulness on the Sabbath. This idea of the continuous activity of God was not indeed necessarily strange or offensive to the Jews. They did not object to this idea ; yet it was somewhat opposed to the tendency of the Jewish mode of viewing the Divine character. For the stress which they laid upon the transcendent exaltation of God led, on the one side, to a diminished view of the immediate operation of God on the world, and to an exaggerated idea of God's resting in the sense of keeping aloof from created things. On the other hand, it led to a higher estimate of the religious duty for man, by abstinence of various kinds, but especially by abstinence from all activity on the Sabbath, of setting Himself in a right attitude of consecration to God. Jesus, on the contrary, found, in His view of God as Father, the motive for emphasising the continued activity of God in the world, and accordingly, for claiming His own right to be actively co-operating with His Father even on the sanctified seventh day. We can give no fitter illustration of the sense in

which Jesus regarded the continued activity of His
Father, than by referring to those expressions
recorded in the Logia of Matthew in which He
speaks of the feeding of the ravens, the decking of
the lilies, the protection of the sparrows, as the work
of the all-embracing love of the heavenly Father,
and thence derives the absolute certainty of God's
provident care for the being and well-being of men
(Matt. vi. 25 ff. ; x. 29 f.). Jesus does not by any
means think merely of God's creative and preserving
agency in nature, or merely of His gracious redemptive work for men, but of the universal activity of
His love as it manifests itself in creating life in all
departments (John v. 21). The idea of God as
the Father, in whose nature love is the supreme
characteristic, necessarily led Jesus to emphasise the
unresting Divine activity springing out of that love.[1]

5. If we seek to gain a correct impression of the
significance which the conception of God, attested
by the Gospel sources as peculiar to Jesus, and briefly
expressed by the name of Father, must have had in

[1] The harmony shown between the conception of God presented in
the Johannine and the synoptical discourses would be essentially
limited, if it were true that in the discourses of the fourth Gospel a
general dualistic view prevails, and that the redemptive agency of God
is represented as extending to only a part of the race, whilst all the
rest are looked upon as from the first and conclusively subject to a
God-opposing evil principle. In my opinion, this dualistic view of the
Johannine discourses is only apparent, not real. But the passages
which present the aspect of a dualism refer specially to the possibility
of faith in Jesus given to one man and wanting to another. It will
therefore be appropriate to consider those passages when we come to
treat of the conditions of entering the kingdom of heaven, specially
with reference to faith in the Messias ; and there we shall take occasion
to meet the objections that might be raised against the assertion of
the harmony of the conception of God in the Johannine discourses and
that presented in the synoptical Gospels.

the religious consciousness of those Jews who were converted from the prevailing Pharisaism to the gospel of the kingdom of God taught by Jesus, we must glance at the Christian doctrine of Paul. What its significance was for them we do not fully learn from the Gospel narratives; for Jesus Himself did not come from under the shadow of Pharisaism to reach His religious standpoint. In virtue of the foundation which He knew was laid in the Old Testament for His conception of God, He has rather presupposed the obvious and self-evident truth, for His hearers, of that conception, than laid stress on its difference from the Pharisaic conception. But the testimony of Paul, who had come under the full influence of the Pharisaic view, and had felt its oppressive weight upon his spirit when striving after the fellowship and favour of God, brings clearly out what a great and reorganising advancement the view of God taught by Jesus must have implied for the Pharisaic consciousness, and what a blissful emancipating effect it must have exercised upon their spirit. In Paul's view, the gospel of the grace of God meant the abrogation of the hitherto binding Mosaic ordinances (Rom. iii. 21 ff.). Instead of servitude to God, whose yoke had hitherto burdened men, there now came in the filial relationship in which Jesus Christ stood, and upon which, for His sake, all believers enter (Gal. iii. 23–iv. 7; v. 1; Rom. viii. 14–16). Instead of servile fear, and the unhappy feeling of inability to keep the Divine commands, and being exposed to the curse of the law for all transgressions (Gal. iii. 10; Rom. vii. 14–24), there now came in

the feeling of freedom and gladness in relation to
God. There was a consciousness that power for
every good work, and for the greatest tasks, was
granted by God, and a trust, accompanied by assur-
ance of salvation and joyous hope, was awakened in
regard to all experiences of the present and the future
(Rom. v. 1–11 ; viii. 17–39).   In the supplicatory cry,
" Abba, Father!" which Paul represents (Gal. iv. 6 ;
Rom. viii. 15) as the utterance of the "Spirit of
Adoption" shared in by all believers, we hear only the
answering echo of the address which Jesus Himself
uses in His prayers to God, and which He taught
His disciples also to use.   As the retention of this
Aramaic word "Abba" by Mark (xiv. 36), in his
account of the agony of Jesus in Gethsemane, is
certainly to be explained by the indelible impression
which the tone of this appeal to the Father made
upon His disciples in that hour, in a similar manner
we must explain the remarkable fact that Paul has
twice used this word "Abba," not merely as his own
personal utterance, but as the characteristic invocation used by all Christians.   Doubtless the address
to God as Father, which the first disciples were
accustomed to hear so significantly used by Jesus,
had remained unchanged as the common symbol of
prayer in the apostolic Church, and so had been
adopted into current use even by the Churches in
heathen countries.

We may condense into the following statements
the result of our consideration of the conception of
God entertained by Jesus.   Whilst Jesus as a rule
designated God as Father, and regarded fatherly love

as the attribute of God peculiarly manifested towards men, He has developed the Old Testament conception on those lines which were fittest to meet the *religious* comprehension and needs.   For, as the religious interest always aims at obtaining blessings or salvation from God, the emphasising of the fatherly love of God, in which lies the most potent, spontaneous, and continually efficacious motive for extending blessing to men, most directly appeals to the religious understanding and need.   The prevailing tendency of Judaism in the time of Jesus to regard the holiness of God, in other words, His transcendent exaltation above the world, as the principal aspect of the conception of God, on the one hand, led to the religious relation of men to God being regarded, by Pharisaism, as a legal servitude, and the chief religious duties as external ceremonies; and, on the other hand, by Alexandrianism, the religious intuition was transformed into philosophical speculation.   But the high significance which Jesus imparted to the moral quality of fatherly love in the conception of God, enabled Him to regard the religious relation between God and men as entirely moral, and to understand in its highest and purest sense the holy exaltation above the world inseparable from the idea of God.   As surely as Jesus found in the Old Testament, and in the Jewish teaching founded on the Old Testament, a real basis for His conception of God, so surely did an epoch-making advance beyond the limits of the Old Testament religious consciousness lie in the certainty, clearness, and fulness with which He first apprehended and announced the Fatherhood of God.

CHAP. III. THE SAVING BENEFITS OF THE KINGDOM
OF GOD.

1. In Jesus' conception of God as the loving Father,
lay the foundation of His idea of the benefits of the
kingdom of God.   He found in God's paternal love,
first of all, the pledge of the certain bestowal of these
benefits upon all those who trustfully and prayerfully
seek them from God.   For the heavenly Father
must be willing to grant good things (Matt. vii. 11)
to them that ask Him; yea, the highest good, the
kingdom of God: "Fear not, little flock; for it is
your Father's good pleasure to give you the kingdom" (Luke xii. 32).   And the Father grants His
blessings, not only to the righteous who have earned
a right and title to them, but also to sinners who
come to Him in penitence.   Jesus assumes that all to
whom He brings the gospel of the kingdom of God
are sinners, and are thrown on the forgiving grace of
God.   Forgiveness of sins appears, therefore, to Him
to be a gift of Divine grace, through which every
blessing of the kingdom of God is received, and in
which all have a share who turn with trustful decision
to the kingdom of God.   In this sense He proclaimed
forgiveness to the palsied man, who on one occasion,
when Jesus was teaching in his place of abode (Mark
ii. 1 f.), in order that he also might listen to that teaching
(ver. 5),[1] succeeded, through the greatness of his faith

---

[1] The explanation of this narrative, usually regarded as self-evident,
is that the sick man got himself conveyed to Jesus only in order to be
miraculously healed.   The account given in Matt. ix. 1 ff. must be so
understood, as it tells nothing about Jesus being engaged in the house
teaching.   Luke, who, as well as Mark, relates this latter circumstance

in the gospel of salvation taught by Jesus, in overcoming all obstacles caused by his sickness and the
pressure of the crowd. Thus it was also with the
sinful woman at the Pharisee's house, who gave evidence of the greatness of the forgiving grace she had
received, through the greatness of the thankful love
she showed to Jesus (Luke vii. 47 f.). Accordingly,
He declares that, for all His disciples, an immeasur-
ably great gift of Divine forgiving grace forms the
foundation of their saved state, and of the unconditional duty of readiness to forgive others (Matt.
xviii. 22–35). He assumes also that His disciples
must constantly pray for the forgiveness of sins, while
at the same time trustfully expecting the fulfilment
of their prayer if they themselves heartily fulfil their
duty in the kingdom of God, specially the character-

(Luke v. 17 ff.), immediately adds that "the power of the Lord was
present to heal," in order to connect the bringing of the sick man with
the healing power, not with the teaching activity of Jesus. But if we
read Mark's account without being biased by the parallel reports, the
view becomes plain that the sick man only wished to hear the teaching
of Jesus. His longing to hear the gospel of the kingdom of God was so
great, that when he could approach Jesus by no other way to hear His
word, got himself lowered through the roof into the room where Jesus
taught. This faith, which was directed, not towards bodily health, but
the salvation preached by Jesus (cf. Mark i. 15), Jesus rewarded by
assuring the man that his sins were forgiven,—not that the palsied man
was a specially great sinner, or that his sickness had been brought on
by sin, but only to give him the comforting assurance that he would
certainly receive from God the Divine saving grace, after which he had
displayed so earnest a desire. This assurance of the forgiveness of
sins was not, however, a mere foretoken of the fulfilment of the sick
man's special desire, but it implied the highest satisfaction of that
desire. The subsequent healing of the man was occasioned by the
offence taken by the scribes at the declaration of forgiveness, as Jesus
sought to prove to them His right to pronounce forgiveness of sins by
visibly demonstrating His right to pronounce upon the man another
Divine blessing (vers. 6–11).

istic duty of forgiving love (Luke xi. 4; Mark xi. 25; cf. Matt. xviii. 35).

But now, wherein consist, in the view of Jesus, the benefits which God, in forgiving their sins, will vouchsafe to the members of His kingdom? We can answer, in the first place, that Jesus indicated the kingdom itself as the highest blessing of God. For He represented this kingdom as the Good which the Father purposed to give to His disciples (Luke xii. 32), which should be the object of their quest before all earthly goods (Luke xii. 31), and whose coming they should plead for in their prayers before all petitions for particular gifts and blessings from God (Luke xi. 2). He compared this kingdom to a treasure and a goodly pearl, for whose sake its finder may well part with all his other possessions (Matt. xiii. 44-46).

But the kingdom of God itself appears to be the highest Divine gift only in so far as a state of ideal and blessed fellowship of God with a people attached to Him in true obedience, a state such as is denoted by the notion kingdom of God, insures the highest welfare for all its members. To be exact in our thinking, however, the benefit itself which is realised in the kingdom is still to be distinguished from the kingdom of God. Wherein, then, we repeat, consists, according to the conception of Jesus, this benefit of the kingdom of God?

2. In any case, we can say at the outset that Jesus has included no particular earthly happiness, power, and glory with this saving good. No doubt, so far as we are able to judge from our Gospel sources, He

did not from the very outset of His ministry announce
that great earthly trials and persecutions were in store
for Himself as well as His disciples, but rather it was
on the ground of the experiences which He encountered in the course of His ministry that He obtained
a view of, and so proclaimed, the severe outward
tribulations to be expected by the members of the
kingdom of God (cf. Mark viii. 31; ix. 12 f., 31;
x. 33 f. ; xiii. 9–13 ; Luke xvii. 22 ff.).   But it by no
means follows from this that He had in prospect, for
Himself and His disciples, any external earthly power
and glory of the kind that the Jews expected in the
kingdom of God.   For, between the two extremes of
those severe earthly persecutions and trials, and this
desire for extraordinary earthly splendour and happiness, lies the mean of ordinary earthly life, with its
external benefits distributed in varied measure by
God to men.   These good things of ordinary earthly
life Jesus has never regarded as incompatible with
the kingdom of God.   He has even expressly prescribed to His disciples a petition for these things.
They were to trust that these would be given, yet in
due subordination to their endeavour after the kingdom of God.   But nowhere in His utterances that
have come down to us, has He expressed the expectation or the promise that the members of the
kingdom of God would attain any extraordinary
external good fortune or well-being, any particular
eminence in political or social relations on earth, or any
wonderful earthly power and glory.   When He said
to Peter that all renunciation of earthly goods for His
sake and the gospel's would find a reward in kind of

a hundred-fold in the present life, He significantly
added—"with persecutions" (Mark x. 29 f.).   He
thereby made it clear that He was not thinking of the
mere profit acquired through the wonderful increase
of external earthly goods.   So it was also with His
assurances to His disciples that all their prayers
would find an answer (Matt. vii. 7 ff.; xviii. 19;
Mark xi. 24), and that they would be preserved from
all danger and harm (Luke x. 19).   This, as we shall
afterwards more fully see, manifestly did not imply
that His disciples might hope for the unlimited
bestowal of all earthly good things they might desire,
or any wonderful preservation from all earthly
dangers.   We must here consider the importance
which the idea of a future miraculous earthly prosperity, and of outward power and glory, for the nation
and individual Israelites, had in the Messianic hopes
of the Old Testament prophets as well as of the Jews
in the time of Jesus, in order to measure the greatness of the innovation when Jesus, in proclaiming the
kingdom of God, looked quite away from all promise
of earthly happiness, power, and glory.   And what an
offence the lack of this promise in His teaching must
have caused to His Jewish contemporaries!

Jesus sought to turn away His disciples' aspirations
from earthly things, by pointing out the more trivial
and transitory value of these (Matt. vi. 19).   At
their best and fullest, these cannot insure personal
life for men: "For what doth it profit a man, to
gain the whole world, and to lose his soul? (that is,
his personal life).   For what can a man give in
exchange for his soul?" (Mark viii. 36 f.).   He

admonishes His disciples to "Take heed, and keep yourselves from all covetousness : for a man's life consisteth not in the abundance of the things which he possesseth," — that is, these possessions, even where existing in the greatest abundance, cannot insure earthly life.   And in proof of this axiom He sets before them the example of the Rich Man, whom all the earthly goods, accumulated and intended for a long life of prosperity, could not maintain in life when God's summons suddenly came to him; nor could he prevent his possessions passing into the hand of others (Luke xii. 15–21).   So He pronounces these earthly goods "the unrighteous Mammon," as being only counterfeit and foreign goods for men (Luke xvi. 11 f.).

In contradistinction to the collection and possession of earthly treasures, He knew of a "being rich towards God" (Luke xii. 21),[1] in possessing a treasure

---

[1] In explanation of the expression, Luke xii. 21, οὕτως ὁ θησαυρίζων αὑτῷ καὶ μὴ εἰς θεὸν πλουτῶν, I might note the following.   We must first bring out that in the words ὁ θησαυρίζων αὑτῷ the emphasis by no means lies on the αὑτῷ, so as to make it stand in opposition to εἰς θεόν in the second half of the verse.   The idea of "laying up treasures *for himself*" could only stand in opposition to "laying up treasures *for others*." That this opposition is not intended, however, appears from the idea of πλουτεῖν in the second half of the verse, which denotes the having of treasure for himself, howsoever the adjoining words, εἰς θεόν, may be interpreted.   We must also emphasise, "who layeth up *treasure* for himself." The idea of laying up treasure for himself, which, though expressed in a quite general way, is shown, from its connection with what goes before, to refer definitely to earthly goods, is contrasted with the idea of being rich, which is more precisely defined by the addition of εἰς θεόν.   Of this idea there are three explanations which seem to yield an appropriate sense : (1) to be rich for God—*i.e.* to have a riches whose purpose has reference to God ; (2) to be rich according to God—*i.e.* to have a riches which God recognises as such ; (3) to be rich with God—*i.e.* to have a riches which in some sense is deposited with God.   In order clearly to decide among these possible explanations, we require to consider, on the one

in heaven, and He admonishes His disciples to direct their efforts towards these heavenly riches : "Lay not up for yourselves treasures upon the earth, where moth and rust doth consume, and where thieves break through and steal; but lay up for yourselves treasures in heaven, where neither moth nor rust doth corrupt, and where thieves do not break through nor

hand, the custom of the language, and, on the other, the connection of the context. Both these considerations, however, make for the third explanation. Whereas scarcely any analogy can be adduced for the interpretation of εἰς in either the first or second sense, in taking the εἰς in the third way, we can point to the very frequent use in the New Testament of the εἰς in composition with verbs which denote situation where we would expect ἐν, but where the εἰς is required in view of the motion whereby the situation was entered upon (*e.g.* Mark xiii. 16; Luke xi. 7; Acts ii. 5; vii. 4; cf. Winer, *Grammatik d. N.T. Sprach-idioms*, § 50, 4*b*). Thus the pregnant expression in this passage has arisen from the co-operation of the two ideas—having treasure with God, and bringing in treasure to God, and, indeed, from carrying out the analogy of what was specially related in the parable, as to how the rich man sought to lay up his earthly treasure in earthly storehouses. The context of the passage confirms this explanation, inasmuch as no expression is given in it to the thought that man must give his goods a reference to God as their end (apply them to the service of His kingdom; cf. Luke xvi. 9; Matt. xxv. 14–20), nor to the thought that man must not strive after a kingdom of human estimation, but after one which God recognises (cf. Luke xvi. 15 prev. and 19 ff.); but rather the thought that, instead of perishable riches on earth, man should seek to lay up an imperishable treasure in heaven (ver. 33 prev.; Matt. vi. 19 f.; cf. *Log.* § 15*d*, *L. J.* i. p. 118). In this thought, which concludes the whole passage which opens with the warning against the quest of earthly riches (Luke xii. 15), lies the explanation (afforded by the context) of this saying, ver. 21. The want of preciseness in the form of this saying comes out with special clearness when we compare it with the form given in Matt. vi. 19 f., where the exact antithesis to the being rich in heavenly treasure with God is not given by the general notion of gathering *treasure* for one's self, but by the special one of gathering *earthly* treasure for one's self. But the reason of this unprecise general notion in ver. 21, as we have already remarked, lies in the fact that, from the foregoing context, no doubt could prevail as to the application of the general notion, "gathering treasure," to *earthly* treasure, according to the ordinary meaning of the word. And the formal unpreciseness of this expression is not removed even if the εἰς θεόν be otherwise explained.

steal " (Matt. vi. 19 f.).   The contents of these heavenly riches, which, on account of their imperishableness, are designated the genuine riches which truly belong to man (Luke xvi. 11 f.), are the "eternal life," which in the future Aeon will be shared in by the devout (Mark x. 30), or simply "the life," in opposition to everlasting destruction in Gehenna (Mark ix. 43, 48; Matt. vii. 14).   Because Jesus was aware that His faithful disciples, in common with the saints of earlier times, who shall rise again (Luke xiii. 28), would attain this everlasting life, even though they should die before the beginning of the future Aeon, He could encourage them to make confession of His doctrine without fear of those who indeed kill the body, but are unable to kill the soul (Matt. x. 28), and He could declare that whosoever should lose his soul (*i.e.* his life) for His sake and the gospel's would save it (Mark viii. 35 ; Matt. x. 39), and that whosoever in the impending persecutions should endure unto the end (*i.e.* according to the foregoing words, till they had suffered a violent death) would be saved (Mark xiii. 13).

This everlasting life, which is the proper life of man, implies a perfect, unclouded blessedness.   Indeed, what is in the highest degree wonderful, Jesus has not concerned Himself with any precise imaginative picture of the forms and conditions of this eternal life and its blessedness.   But He has illustrated the general idea that this future life would bring a blissful enjoyment, by depicting the position of the blessed under the figure of participation in a feast (Luke xiii. 29 ; xxii. 30 ; cf. Mark xiv. 25).   In the blessedness of that future life lies the reward destined, and in a manner stored up, by God for the just—a reward whereby He will recognise and requite the true right-eousness which is pleasing to Him (Luke vi. 23; Matt. vi. 1–6, 16–18; x. 41; Mark ix. 41). Since this in-heritance of eternal life insures an incomparably rich reward for all sufferings of the earthly life, Jesus could, at the beginning of His discourse on the true righteousness, pronounce the poor, the hungering, the mourners, and the persecuted to be blessed, in view of their future participation in the heavenly bliss of the kingdom of God. He does not here mean that the ground of attaining future welfare lies merely in earthly poverty or unhappiness, any more than, in afterwards pronouncing woes upon the rich, the full, those that laugh, those who are praised of men (vers. 24–26), He makes earthly well-being in itself the cause of being subjected to future misery. He only seeks to bring out as clearly as possible that the sole true and perfect blessedness is that of the future, in com-parison with which earthly afflictions are of no account, and earthly bliss is but a shadow. There-fore, in view of their expected participation in the future weal, He declares those to be blessed who, from an earthly point of view, are miserable, since the absolute worth of that future weal is most clearly evident in their case. Therefore, also, in view of the expected future misery of those who, from an earthly point of view, are happy, He pronounces a woe upon them, since in their case the worthlessness of earthly good fortune comes most clearly out.[1]

---

[1] I have sought (*Log.* § 7*a*, *L. J.* i. p. 53 ff.) to demonstrate for what reason the form of the Beatitudes conveyed to us by Luke is to be held as more original than that in Matthew. We need not approach

3. Generally, Jesus has not precisely explained and justified the certainty of the eternal heavenly life which He spoke of in His teaching, since, for the majority of Jews at that time, the idea of the resurrection of the just from death to a blessed life had a recognised authority. All the more valuable for us, therefore, is that conversation of Jesus with the Sadducees which has been preserved for us, in which, in opposition to those adversaries of the resurrection hope, He set forth His reasons for that hope and His ideas of the nature of the resurrection life (Mark xii. 18 ff.). When the Sadducees, in order to push His idea of the

these Beatitudes, as Luke presents them, with the preconceived idea which is usually brought to them on the ground of the text of Matthew, viz. that the Beatitudes indirectly indicate the conditions of participating in the heavenly welfare of the kingdom of God. In the first place, the whole main substance of the great discourse of Jesus that follows the Beatitudes, is to show the true nature of the righteousness belonging to the kingdom of God, and constituting the condition of receiving reward from God. But the introductory beatitudes and woes were only meant to make more clearly apparent the absolute value of this Divine saving good. When, in accordance with this purpose, Jesus declared the poor and sorrowing to be blessed in view of their obtaining the welfare of the kingdom of God, and pronounced woes upon the rich and fortunate in view of their future retribution, which was to be expected, these utterances of Jesus appear to us one-sided and exaggerated, in so far as we reflect that mere earthly misery does not make men worthy of eternal welfare, just as earthly happiness in itself does not necessarily expose men to future punishment. But this apparently rough and one-sided form of speech is quite in accordance with many other utterances of Jesus. He followed the principle of aiming at the greatest significance in the shortest form (cf. above, p. 130 ff.). Where, therefore, He seeks to illustrate the general idea that the future bliss of the kingdom of God is the true blessedness for men, He takes examples from those classes of men in whose case, on account of their earthly circumstances, the idea is most plainly perceptible. That Jesus has presupposed the poor and the suffering whom He apostrophises to be really pious, and therefore fit candidates for heavenly felicity, and the rich and fortunate whom He addresses to be ungodly, and therefore unmeet for any reward from the heavenly Father, is clear enough from the subsequent part of the discourse. But it did not lie within the scope of His purpose to emphasise this thought in the introductory part of His discourse.

resurrection to absurd consequences, propounded to
Him the question of how, in the case of a wife who,
in accordance with a Mosaic enactment, should have
successively married seven brothers, her marriage-
relationship must be conceived as standing at the
resurrection, He answered : " Is it not on this account
that ye err, because ye know not the Scriptures, nor
the power of God ? For when they shall rise from
the dead, they neither marry, nor are given in
marriage ; but are as the angels in heaven. But as
touching the dead, that they are raised ; have ye not
read in the book of Moses, in the place concerning
the Bush, how God spake unto him, saying, I am
the God of Abraham, and the God of Isaac, and the
God of Jacob ? He is not the God of the dead, but
of the living : ye do greatly err " (vers. 24–27). In
regard to the craftily conceived difficulty by means of
which the Sadducees wished to make out the impos-
sibility of the resurrection-life, Jesus pointed to the
power of God, which would establish for those who
have risen again quite new forms of life, unlike those
of the earthly life. The error of those Sadducees
was founded on their limited ideas of the power of
God, leading them to suppose that the future new life
could only be a sense-life, like the present earthly
existence, with the same appetites and forms of intercourse occasioned by man's sensuous nature. The
decisiveness with which Jesus here repudiates the
idea of the earthly sensuous character of the future
life, and conceives it according to the analogy of the
heavenly state of the angels, is very significant in its
contrast, not only to the hypothetical idea entertained
by the Sadducees of the resurrection-life, but also to

the popular Pharisaic teaching on the resurrection.
For if, among the Jews of that period, there were
representatives of a doctrine of the resurrection in
which the future life was viewed as one purely
heavenly and eternal, beginning only at the expira-
tion of the whole world-period,[1] yet at all events the
prevalent popular resurrection-hope was directed to
the reawakening of the pious dead to a participation
in the Messiah's kingdom, and to that kingdom as
one to be established on earth, and to insure earthly
dominion and glory, and conceivable sensuous and
external felicity. The clear utterance of Jesus in the
above passage in regard to the unlikeness of the
resurrection - life to the life of sense on earth, also
confirms our view, that when Jesus spoke of a reclining
at table and eating and drinking in the future kingdom of God (Luke xiii. 29; xxii. 30; Mark xiv. 25),
He was using figurative terms to express a blissful
enjoyment in fellowship with others, and that no idea
of any kind of satisfying of real sensuous needs was
thereby intended.

Nevertheless, His reference to God's power to
establish such a supersensuous angelic resurrection-
life only substantiates the *possibility* of the godly
being awakened from the sleep of death by God.
Jesus grounds the *certainty* of obtaining the heavenly
resurrection-life, as against the Sadducees, by appeal-
ing to a word of God taken from that very "book of
Moses," from among whose legal statutes they had
drawn their objection against the conceivableness of
the resurrection. In the words of God to Moses, "I
am the God of Abraham, and the God of Isaac, and

[1] Cf. above, p. 72.

the God of Jacob," Jesus finds a deeper sense than the thought that God, in revealing Himself to Moses, wished to describe Himself as the same God who some hundred years before had appeared to the patriarchs, and who had been worshipped by them as God. If God thus solemnly declared His relation to those patriarchs in order to signify to Moses what He *is*, and not merely what He *was*, He must have meant this relation as one not merely belonging to the past, but as still continuing. But God is not a God of the dead, but of the living ; if He declared His communion with the patriarchs to be still continuing, they must, in spite of their dying, have entered upon a state of existence corresponding to fellowship with God. In regard to this argument of Jesus, it is to be noticed that what was to be proved by it was not a general idea of continued existence after death, such as that of the dead in Scheol according to the Old Testament view, and such as even the Sadducees would not have controverted, but it was the rising again out of Scheol to a life of well-being. On the other hand, it is evident that the "life" involved in the very conception of standing in communion with God is not the resurrection-life directly, since the godly who live on earth partake of such a "life" as seems compatible with thus belonging to God. We must not conclude, however, from the words of Jesus, that He regarded the patriarchs as having ascended immediately after death to a resurrection-life with God in heaven. This would not accord with the idea of Jesus in regard to the abode of Abraham and the blessed dead in Hades, as we find it expressed in the narrative of the Rich Man and Lazarus (Luke xvi. 23 ff.). On the other hand, we must not infer that Jesus regarded the condition of the dead saints in Hades as an unhappy, cheerless, shadowy existence, but as already a condition in fellowship with God, and as the possession of such a life as, like even that of the godly here upon earth who are in fellowship with God, contains in itself the germ of an everlasting heavenly life towards which it tends, and therefore leads by an inner principle of necessity to a resurrection. It is certainly true that Jesus, in His interpretation of the Divine utterance (Ex. iii. 6), has understood that spiritual relation of proprietorship in the patriarchs on the part of God in a deeper sense than that which the words were at first meant to convey. All the more characteristic, therefore, is His interpretation of that Old Testament passage for the peculiar view which Jesus entertained of the basis of the resurrection-hope—a view which was so clear and self-evident to His mind, that even on that account He found it expressed in the passage in question. He had the certainty that fellowship with God is a life-bringing relation. Whoever truly belongs to God, so that God regards that one as His, cannot really experience the destructive power of death or be in an unblest condition, but must have and maintain a blessed life granted by God. Such a one, by virtue of this enduring life in fellowship with God, in spite of earthly death and in spite of Hades, shall at length be awakened to a heavenly life with God.

No doubt, Jesus, in His doctrine of the resurrection of the just, followed the Pharisaic Jewish doctrine, which on this point had made an important step in advance of the Old Testament view. He also found a basis for His conception of the supersensuous heavenly nature of the resurrection - life in at least certain branches of the Jewish theology of His time. Nevertheless we must bear in mind that He has imparted to the idea of the future eternal life in heaven such significance, as an organic element of His view of the kingdom of God, as found no analogy in the doctrines of His Jewish contemporaries. It showed, indeed, a specific advance of His peculiar general view beyond that of Jewish religious tradition. In our introductory notice of the religious hopes of the Jews in the time of Jesus, we have seen how the hope of personal salvation on the part of the godly, so far as it referred to a future resurrection-life, was on the point of becoming detached from the national hope directed to the Messianic kingdom.[1] For the Messianic kingdom was expected, on the ground of Old Testament prophecy, as a kingdom of earthly happiness, power, and supremacy, to be established on earth through a reorganisation of all earthly relations, and therefore, in the popular ideas, it implied even a rising of the pious dead to a share in this earthly Messianic kingdom. In proportion, however, as the personal hope of salvation failed to find full satisfaction in this prospect of resurrection to a new and wonderfully enriched earthly life, and therefore looked more to the ideal of a heavenly resurrection-life in a mere transcendental form, the hope of personal salvation became detached in thought from that of the Messianic kingdom.

[1] Cf. above, p. 72 f.

But with Jesus, who did not at all include wonderful earthly prosperity, external glory, or political power among the blessings of the kingdom of God, the eternal heavenly life, which He regarded as the crowning blessing of that kingdom, became once more connected with the highest ideal of salvation which the godly personally hoped for.

4. Still more important, however, in their bearing on His view of the experiences of the present earthly life, are the consequences which resulted for Jesus from the certainty of the future eternal life. For it would be very absurd merely to say, in characterising His doctrine of the blessedness of the kingdom of God, that He has removed the scene of that bliss entirely from this earth and laid it on the other side of the grave. The essential point rather is, that Jesus, in making the fatherly love of God to men His primary principle, and in accordingly maintaining the certainty for God's saints of a future heavenly life of eternal welfare, could also draw the still wider conclusion that God's saints even on earth obtain absolute protection against all evils and dangers, an absolute bestowal of all necessary good things, and a true and pure felicity. We must distinguish, however, between a felicity of a mere earthly kind and a happiness which may be experienced on earth. The blessedness of God's kingdom as Jesus conceived it, does not essentially consist in earthly prosperity and splendour, such as the Jews expected under the Messiah's reign ; and yet it may well enough include possessions and conditions bestowed upon mankind already on earth, whilst the complete blessedness of the kingdom of

God must still be waited for in the heavenly life beyond.

The thought that God will grant to the just ones who trust in Him a true and lasting happiness, not merely in the future, but now in the present, appears to Jesus, from His idea of the fatherly love of God, as self-evident. Again and again, in the hearing of His disciples, He gave such unlimited assurances of blessedness in reference to this life, as appear altogether exaggerated according to the ordinary views of happiness or unhappiness. But this seeming exaggeration disappears when we consider how differently Jesus estimated things as valuable or worthless, wholesome or pernicious, for man on earth from the way men usually judge.

When the disciples whom He had sent to publish the proclamation of the nearness of the kingdom of God, were giving expression, at their return, to their joy that even the devils were subject to them in His name, He replied, according to the account given in the Logia : " I beheld Satan fallen as lightning from heaven : behold, I have given you authority to tread upon serpents, and over all the power of the enemy ; and nothing shall in anywise hurt you. Howbeit, in this rejoice not, that the spirits are subject unto you ; but rejoice that your names are written in heaven " (Luke x. 18-20). That joy of the disciples because of gaining, in particular cases, wonderful victories over such baneful, evil agencies as the demons and " the enemy " Satan,[1] He contrasts with the assurance that the disciples had gained such absolute

[1] Cf. above, p. 165 ff.

dominion over these hostile powers as to be no longer liable to any injury from them. Had Jesus here sought to indicate any miraculous gift of external preservation from earthly harm, or any external conquest over the powers of evil which war against earthly life and well-being, His unlimited assurance of further immunity for His disciples would have been chargeable with strong exaggeration. Nor would such an assurance have found much justification in the instances related of a miraculous gift of healing and of a miraculous immunity from harm enjoyed at a later date by the apostles. For that assurance would still have stood in glaring contradiction to the hard, lifelong sufferings and persecutions predicted for His disciples by Jesus Himself, and actually experienced by them. The real sense in which Jesus gave that absolute assurance appears from His adding, that what should form the proper object of their joy was, not their power over demons, but the fact that their names were written in heaven. For this inscription of their names in heaven, which we are not to understand in the general sense of their being members of the kingdom of God, but in the more special sense of their possessing the sure title to a future life of blessedness, furnishes the explanation of that absolute power over evil agencies, and their consequent immunity from harm. All hostile powers, all earthly ills and trials, cannot harm the disciples, but are subject to them, so far as those evils cannot take away or impair their title to that highest heavenly blessedness. The true welfare of the disciples does not rest upon miraculous power to exorcise evil spirits, so that

these may do no more injury, and may appear from
an external point of view to be subdued.   Such
external victories over evil are transient ones, and
do not insure true life and true happiness.   But the
certainty of being destined of God to eternal life and
citizenship in heaven is the foundation of true blessedness.   Not only does it hold out for the future a welfare which cannot be destroyed by any hostile power
or any earthly ill, but it insures present immunity from
real injury, from all that might touch man's spiritual
and eternal well-being.   It would not accord with a full
appreciation of the high idealism of Jesus' religious
conception, to interpret the "authority over all the
power of the enemy" and the immunity from all hurt,
promised to His disciples, in a mere figurative or
indirect sense.   For this would be to follow that
external and earthly mode of view which was so
directly in conflict with that of Jesus, viz. that the external earthly life and welfare of man is his true life
and welfare.   No doubt, in ordinary secular human
speech, welfare and prosperity, or the reverse, are
spoken of in a purely mundane, external sense ; but
Jesus implies that the godly, or the members of the
kingdom of God, know better than the worldling
what true welfare and real evil are.   When Jesus
declared, speaking from the same point of view as in
the text we have been considering, "Whosoever
would save his soul (*i.e.* his life) shall lose it ; and
whosover shall lose his soul for my sake and the
gospel's shall save it" (Mark viii. 35 ; cf. Matt. x. 39),
He does not regard that life which can be lost on
account of the gospel as man's true life, and the life

which can be won through the loss of earthly life He designates as life only in a borrowed sense ; but, conversely, He regards the latter as the true life of man. Similarly, in regard to the text we have just been considering, by security against evils, even though that does not imply insurance against loss of earthly life and prosperity, He would have us understand immunity against evils in the strictest and highest sense, since He takes true heavenly life and welfare as the measure of what constitutes real evil.

That this mode of view does not hold good for Jesus merely in the general, but that He also uses it in a special way in that passage, Luke x. 18–20, and that His certainty that all earthly evils and sufferings had no more power or consequence for His disciples was ultimately founded on His knowledge of the fatherhood of God, is proved from the words which, according to the Logia account, were uttered by Jesus immediately after that saying addressed to His disciples (Luke x. 21–24 ; Matt. xi. 25–30).[1] As He had been occupied with the subject of the authority given by God to His people over all hostile powers, He addresses the Father as " Lord of heaven and earth," and gives Him thanks because He has, not to the worldly wise, but to babes, revealed " these

---

[1] Cf. *Log.* § 8, *L. J.* i. p. 90 ff. The composition of this Logia-passage, as shown by a consideration of the reports, partly parallel and partly supplementary of each other, of our first and third evangelists, furnishes a particularly clear instance, not only of the relation in which these two evangelists stand to the Logia-source and of the critical method by which, by help of the means supplied by these evangelists, we may reconstruct the contents of the Logia-sources ; but especially it brings out the importance of this critical labour for the exact Biblico-theological understanding of the teaching of Jesus.

things "—that is, the power over all enemies and the preservation from all evils, granted even here upon earth to His disciples whose names are inscribed in heaven (Luke x. 21). Then He has indicated Himself as He to whom all things have been delivered of the Father (that is, according to the context, He has received absolute power and dominion over all things from God), and as He who alone knows perfectly the Father in His character, and can alone reveal Him to others (ver. 22). And now, in immediate connection with this, He proceeds to give the exhortation: "Come unto me, all ye that labour and are heavy laden, and I will give you rest. Take my yoke upon you, and learn of me; for I am meek and lowly of heart; and ye shall find rest unto your souls. For my yoke is easy, and my burden is light" (Matt. xi. 28–30). In these words Jesus shows how, amid the woes and troubles of this earthly life, it is possible to find true rest and solace, and how to make the hard and pressing burdens become soft and easy, viz. by sincere, humble submission to the will of God. This teaching He presents as a revelation which He has derived from His perfect knowledge of the fatherly character of God ; for whoso has come to know God, the Lord of heaven and earth, as Father, can be humbly submissive in view of all earthly trials and burdens, since he can have the trust that even the externally hard and evil experiences laid upon him by his heavenly Father are yet wholesome and good. In this saying in regard to the transformation of the heavy burdens into light, and of distress into comfort, by means of genuine humility, Jesus gives the true explanation of

His assurance to His disciples that all hostile powers would be subject to them, and would by no means do them harm. The declaration that He Himself was the model after whom men should learn meekness and humility, did not, in His consciousness, contradict, but rather explained and established, the foregoing declaration that all things were delivered to Him by the Father. For He does not conceive of that power conferred on Him by God as an ability to ward off, in a miraculous external way, the earthly trials and evils, but as the ability to overcome these earthly troubles through humble submission. Similarly to this, He has conceived of the power granted to His disciples over all hostile and hurtful agencies, not as one which would insure them against earthly troubles and burdens, but as the power to triumph, after His own example, over earthly crosses and losses through genuine humility, so as, in spite of them, to maintain inward rest and holy joy.[1]

But Jesus judged, not merely that earthly evil and earthly death could inflict no real injury upon His disciples, but also that all that was really helpful and

---

[1] I cannot deem it justifiable to understand by the κοπιῶντες καὶ πεφορτισμένοι specially those who are oppressed by the law and heavy laden under its burden (Weiss, *Matthäus-evangelium*, p. 307). The fact that in Matt. xxiii. 4 the Pharisaic legal ordinances were figuratively spoken of as heavy burdens, cannot prove that, in the passage above quoted, where, in the whole context, there is no question of legal ordinances, the general idea should be understood with special reference to the law. For, clearly as Jesus could pronounce the statutes of the Pharisaic scribes to be intolerable burdens, He had yet no thought of representing the righteousness which He taught as something easier than that pursued by the scribes and Pharisees (cf. Matt. v. 17–20). What He meant, however, in proposing Himself, in so far as He was meek and lowly, as the pattern for the weary and heavy laden, was not to bring out the contrast between the yoke of inward

salutary for them was granted them by God even in the present. This latter idea is the essential complement of the former. As absolute as His assurance that no evil should in any way befall them, is His assurance that all things which they will ask in trust from their Father in heaven shall be granted. " Ask, and it shall be given you ; seek, and ye shall find ; knock, and it shall be opened unto you : for every one that asketh receiveth ; and he that seeketh findeth ; and to him that knocketh it shall be opened. Or what man is there of you, who, if his son shall ask him for bread, will give him a stone ; or if he shall ask for a fish, will give him a serpent ? If ye then, being evil, know how to give good gifts unto your children, how much more shall your Father which is in heaven give good things to them that ask Him ? " (Matt. vii. 7–11). " I say unto you, that if two of you shall agree upon earth as touching anything that they shall ask, it shall be done for them of my Father " (Matt. xviii. 19). " Verily, I say unto you, Whosoever shall say unto this mountain, Be thou taken up and cast into the sea ; and shall not doubt in his heart, but shall believe that what he saith

righteousness and active love which He imposes, to the weary yoke of external and ceremonial performances. Nor was it the contrast between the joyous spirit of filial freedom (cf. Matt. xvii. 26), and the ever unsatisfied spirit which struggles under bondage to servile legal ordinances. When He indicates meekness and humility as the features of character which the weary and heavy laden should learn of Him in order to find solace, He must refer to labours and burdens of a kind which find relief and comfort in a meek and lowly spirit. But those are not the pressure and burdens of the law, but such as arise from earthly bondage and earthly trials. This view, which is already suggested by an isolated study of the passage, is most clearly verified if we consider the connection of the passage with the preceding utterances of Jesus to His disciples, as shown in the Logia, Luke x. 18–20.

cometh to pass; he shall have it. Therefore I say unto you, All things whatsoever ye pray and ask for, believe that ye have received them, and ye shall have them" (Mark xi. 23 f. ; cf. Luke xvii. 6 ; Matt. xvii. 20).[1]

These general promises certainly cannot mean that all the disciples' wishes without distinction, even those which are unwarranted and pernicious, shall be fulfilled. It is certainly significant that Jesus, in the first-mentioned passage, has only in general declared that the asking and seeking shall find answer. But the answer may not be precisely what they sought. He only gives assurance that the heavenly Father will give good things to them that ask : He does not exclude the proviso that what is granted may be different from what was asked. But similarly in the other passage in which He directly promises the good things asked, He takes for granted that the disciples as members of the kingdom, and as true children of God, would shape their requests according to their heavenly Father's will, and ask for nothing adverse to the kingdom of God and their own true welfare. God's fatherly love, which had such supreme significance for Jesus, was itself the cause of this limitation in answer to prayer. Jesus, indeed, does not assure His disciples that all their arbitrary wishes shall be granted ; but, presupposing the general bent of their aspirations to be towards the kingdom of God, He seeks to express as clearly as possible that the greatness of the request and the difficulty of their obtaining the things sought are no barriers whatever to the Omnipotent God, who has established His

[1] Cf. *Log.* § 29, *L. J.* i. p. 157 f.

kingdom of grace upon earth for the very purpose of
bestowing upon His children, even upon earth, all
that they truly need.

5. Wherein, then, consist those good things which
are to be obtained even during this earthly life ?
Among these, in the first place, we reckon the means
of earthly livelihood, in the measure which God
judges to be necessary for individual men. Not that
the means of earthly livelihood forms by itself an
independent good, or a blessing of absolute worth
alongside of the spiritual good of God's kingdom ;
but if the disciples make the kingdom of God the
first object of their aim, they receive earthly blessings
in their due measure into the bargain ; "for your
Father knoweth that ye have need of all these
things" (Matt. vi. 25–33; Luke xii. 22–31).[1] Though
Jesus knew the worthlessness of all earthly good
things for the establishing and maintaining of man's
true life and welfare ; and though He emphatically
declared the sole true value of heavenly blessings,
and strove to exclude the notion of earthly prosperity
and glory which clung to the Jewish ideal of the
Messianic kingdom, He was yet far from simply
despising and rejecting the gifts needed for preserving earthly life, and from imposing on Himself and
His disciples a severe ascetic abstinence from them.
He rather taught that these gifts also should be
thankfully received from God. And He directed
His disciples to pray for them (Luke xi. 3), and trustfully to expect them from Him. Here we have a
grand proof of that soundness of judgment which

[1] Cf. *Log.* § 15*b*, *L. J.* i. p. 116 ff.

tempered things in due proportion, and also of the purity in which He conceived the supermundane character of the benefits to be bestowed by God. Had He regarded these benefits as only being a higher kind of physical life and sensuous happiness, He would have viewed them as standing in a direct opposition to the earthly life and its necessaries. And He would have prescribed the task which afterwards, to so wide a circle of Christendom, appeared the main object of the imitators of Jesus, of mortifying, as far as possible, the earthly life, and foregoing the necessaries of physical existence, so as to approach as nearly as possible during this earthly lifetime to the blessedness of the heavenly life. But in His view fatherly love was the leading principle of the Divine nature : in it the perfection and majesty of God consisted ; and therefore He regarded the heavenly welfare vouchsafed by God to men as primarily a life in the moral nature and power of God. Hence, while He esteemed the earthly life and natural blessings of no absolute value in themselves, He could regard them, in the measure of their bestowal by God, as not only harmless and indifferent in relation to the higher life, but even as a means to that end. The two mutually supplementary parables of the prudent Steward (Luke xvi. 1–9) and of the diligent faithful Servants and the wicked unfaithful Servant (Matt. xxv. 14–29),[1] are designed to inculcate the truth that the right use of earthly goods in the present life can and shall secure reward in the future heavenly life. The former parable shows the

[1] Cf. *Log.* § 26, *L. J.* i. p. 143 ff. ; and above, p. 128 (note).

value of that wisdom which remembers the future in the present, and seeks to insure future well-being with present means. But such an unfaithful mode of using earthly goods entrusted to one, as would appear to the "children of this world" a wise means of insuring future *earthly* well-being, would, of course, for the "children of light" be quite an unwise mode of using them in order to securing them a *heavenly* reward from God. But in order that the godly, in reference to *their* purpose, may show a wisdom analogous to that of the "children of the world," they must act in the opposite way in regard to earthly goods; that is, they must, according to the will of God, and with true fidelity and assiduous diligence, use the goods entrusted to them by God. These thoughts are set before us in the parable of the faithful Servants. Earthly goods are subservient to man's eternal welfare in so far as he uses them faithfully, and in a way corresponding to God's will, and so far as he shall, through fidelity in the use of these things, foreign and unessential as they are to his true life, make himself worthy of having the true riches committed to him (Luke xvi. 10–12). Through this idea of the educational significance of the earthly life and the use of earthly goods, it was impossible for Jesus to set store by an asceticism which spurns earthly blessings for the sake of the heavenly.

But since, in the view of Jesus, the good things of this life may be possessed by the disciples alongside of the Divine gifts of saving grace, since those may help in the development and confirmation of the

disciples' fidelity to the will of God; therefore the
grace bestowed by God on His children in this life
must in part consist in His preserving and strengthening them against all temptations that threaten to
impair their fidelity and the condition of their obtaining eternal life in heaven. Jesus teaches His
disciples to pray and confidently to expect from the
Father that He will not lead them into temptation
(Luke xi. 4); that is, will not bring them into such a
position in life, or set before them such tasks and
dangers, as will be too hard for them in proportion to
their strength, and as will furnish them with too great
an allurement to sin. That the negative idea of
"not coming into temptation," as expressed by Jesus,
is equivalent to the positive idea of " the (subjective)
rejection and overcoming of the (objectively presented) possibility of, and allurement to, sin," and
that the "not leading into temptation" is equivalent
to the positive "giving of power to overcome the
temptation," is clear from the words of Jesus to His
disciples in Gethsemane : "Watch and pray, that ye
enter not into temptation" (Mark xiv. 38). He had
clearly foreseen that they would by no means be
spared the external circumstances of temptation, but
yet they would not "come into temptation" if they
had the power to resist the dangerous occasion of
falling into sin. Even this power, however, God
gives to them that ask; and therefore the disciples,
on account of the weakness of their "flesh," must
turn for succour to God in prayer. In the same
sense Jesus taught His disciples to trust that, in the
persecutions that awaited them in the future, they

would be upheld by God through the power of His Spirit that they might witness a good confession. If brought before the council for His sake, they were not to take anxious thought as to what they should say, since it was not they who were to speak, but the Holy Ghost (Mark xiii. 11). Jesus cannot here mean that the disciples would be helped by the Spirit to such a defence as would lead to their external liberation and deliverance from threatened death.[1] Rather He expressly adds that the result of those persecutions would bring death to the faithful (ver. 12). But He certainly meant that when the disciples were discouraged in prospect of such deadly persecutions, if they could, under those trying circumstances, so give testimony to the Messiah as was incumbent upon them (ver. 13 ; cf. viii. 38), they could rely upon the Holy Ghost for support, and He would bear witness through them.

To the declaration of Peter, that they, the twelve, had left all and followed Jesus, He answered : " Verily

---

[1] In this sense Luke (xxi. 12 ff.) has altered the thought and diction of that saying of Jesus as recorded by Mark. Whilst, according to Mark, the arraignment of the disciples before tribunals and earthly powers would happen to them for a testimony, that is, would serve the purpose of presenting a testimony to the Messiah before rulers, according to Luke xxi. 13, that appearance before the tribunal would turn out for a testimony to the disciples themselves ; that is, instead of their being convicted of a punishable offence, it would lead to a demonstration of their integrity and innocence. This change of the thought corresponds with Luke's mode of indicating that the disciples in order to their defence,—and, indeed, their successful defence,—so that further opposition and gainsaying on the part of their adversaries would become impossible (ver. 14 f.), would not need to premeditate what they should say, since higher support would be granted them for that purpose. Here, instead of προμεριμνᾶν, " to be anxious beforehand," the word used in Mark xiii. 11, Luke has the by no means equivalent expression προμελετᾶν.

I say unto you, There is no man that hath left house, or brethren, or sisters, or father, or mother, or wife, or children, or lands, for my sake, and the gospel's, but he shall receive an hundred-fold now in this time, houses, and brethren, and sisters, and mothers, and children, and lands, with persecutions; and in the world to come eternal life" (Mark x. 28–30). Here the idea of an hundred-fold increase of relatives in a literal sense would be an absurdity, and so also the hundred-fold increase of house and lands may also be understood in a non-literal sense. In what an ideal way Jesus could estimate earthly things, and could judge of things externally different as if they were alike, is shown in the matter of the widow's mite, which He said was "more" than all the great gifts which the rich poured into the temple-treasury (Mark xii. 43); and in His saying to His relatives, who came to call Him from His zealous labours (Mark iii. 21 and 31 ff.), as He pointed to the circle of hearers who sat about Him: "Behold my mother and my brethren! For whosoever shall do the will of God, the same is my brother, and sister, and mother" (ver. 34). Rightly, therefore, that saying of Jesus in regard to the hundred-fold increase which would be reaped on earth in consequence of every act of renunciation for His sake and the gospel's, has been explained as referring to the community of goods, and the close tie which would bind together the members of the kingdom of God in the bond of mutually helpful love. Only, we ought not, I think, to restrict the application of the expression *solely* to the gain derived from the love of the other members of God's kingdom. Along with that, we must consider all the other experiences, goods, and powers, temporal or spiritual, in which the disciples shall, through the fatherly love of God, become sharers. The gain thereby received does not, from an outward and earthly point of view, constitute a state of good fortune. Nay, from the persecutions connected with their testimony to the Messiah and His gospel, its value may appear far less than that of the goods and relationships they had forsaken. These latter, however, judged from the higher standpoint of the kingdom of God, are far surpassed in value by the new goods and relationship which tend to true welfare and everlasting life.

6. The result of our whole inquiry as to how Jesus represented the benefits to be granted by God in His kingdom, may be shortly summed up as follows. The blessings of God's kingdom He did not regard as consisting in any special prosperity and glory of an external earthly kind, such as, on the ground of Old Testament prophecy, the great majority of the Jews expected as the benefit to be realised in the Messianic latter-day; but primarily in the future, spiritual, heavenly, and eternal life which God has prepared for His own in His kingdom. Yet the benefit of the kingdom of God is not merely a future one, which only begins in the life to come. But the heavenly Father permits His children already in the present life to share only in that, and in all that, which tends to insure their true and heavenly well-being. Neither can earthly evils and distresses do them real harm and disturb their inward rest and contentment; nor, if they but trust in and pray to God, will this world's

good things and the powers of the spiritual life be
denied them, in so far as these are means of their
proving their fidelity to the will of God upon earth.
In this sense Jesus recognises a blessedness granted
by God to His children even on earth,—a blessedness
which we can by no means understand if we do not
firmly grasp the connection which this earthly life is
meant to have with the future, everlasting, heavenly
life.   But they whose names are written in heaven
recognise it as a truly blessed life, and have joyful
experience of it.   The epoch-making advance made
by Jesus in His idea of blessedness, beyond that of the
Psalmists and Prophets, as well as of the Jews of His
time, lay in the fact that He not merely conceived the
highest ideal of bliss as one wholly supermundane,
spiritual, and purely heavenly, but that, through His
conception of true blessedness, He attained a different
estimate of the world and earthly life, according to
which it was possible for the godly to have, not merely
a sure *hope* of future blessedness, but also an abundant *experience* of blessedness in this life.   The Old
Testament saints lacked the prospect of the future,
heavenly, eternal life, and therefore also the possibility
of estimating the true value of earthly happiness or
adversity in its relation to that heavenly goal.   But the
Jews in the time of Jesus, though they had attained
the prospect of a future life, and referred the hope of
resurrection, not merely to a reawakening to a new
earthly life, but to an exaltation to eternal life in
heaven ; yet, on account of their legal conception of
the religious relation between God and man, could not
advance to the conclusion which Jesus formed.   They

could only estimate this earthly life from the point of view of having to perform laborious works of right-eousness and of self-denial, in exchange for which they would receive the reward of bliss in the life to come. They thought that, in cases of particular earthly trial, men suffered the just punishment of their personal or hereditary faults (cf. John ix. 2; Luke xiii. 2 and 4). Only through Jesus replacing this legal conception by the idea of fatherly love as pertaining to the character and dealings of God, could He seize the thought that even this life is full, to the godly, of manifestations of God's grace, that is, full of all that affords a fitting preparation and education for obtaining the heavenly eternal life.

7. What relation does Jesus' view of the blessings of the kingdom, as recorded in the fourth Gospel, stand to that we have been considering, as testified to by the Logia of Matthew and the Gospel of Mark? We must, in order to answer this question, abstract the circumstance that in the discourses of the Johannine source those blessings are presented almost throughout as something specially granted through Jesus and obtained by means of faith in Jesus; whilst in the Logia of Matthew and the discourses of Mark, this mediating significance of Jesus in order to our obtaining blessing by no means appears in like pro-portion. We may examine this peculiarity of the view of saving blessing in the Johannine discourses somewhat later. At present we will only inquire how far the contents of the blessings set forth in these Johannine discourses of Jesus correspond with the

nature of the benefit of the kingdom of God taught by Jesus, according to the accounts given in our other sources.

The frequently employed general term for this benefit in the Johannine discourses is "life," or "eternal life" (*e.g.* iii. 15 f. ; iv. 14; v. 24–26 ; x. 28; xvii. 2). But the impression that this designation of the benefit of the kingdom guarantees an essential agreement of the idea of the contents of that benefit with that given in the discourses of the Logia and Mark, since there, also, eternal life is represented as the true and highest blessing, is counteracted by the circumstance that Jesus sometimes, in the Johannine discourses, speaks of eternal life as decidedly a present possession of the believer : "Verily, verily, I say unto you, He that heareth my word, and believeth on Him that sent me, hath everlasting life, and shall not come into condemnation ; but is passed from death unto life. Verily, verily, I say unto you, The hour is coming, and *now* is, when the dead shall hear the voice of the Son of God; and they who hear shall live" (v. 24 f. ; cf. iii. 15 f. ; vi. 40, 47, 53 f. ; vii. 38). In the Logia and the sayings in Mark the eternal life is regarded as a future and heavenly one (cf. especially Mark x. 30) ; but when, in the Johannine discourses, it is spoken of as something already possessed in the present, the conclusion forces itself upon us, that under the same designation something different is there expressed than in Mark and in the Logia. Wherein consists, then, the nature of this eternal life as spoken of in the Johannine discourses ?

In that expression in the prayer of Jesus as high

priest, "This is life eternal, that they may know Thee, the only true God, and Jesus Christ, whom Thou hast sent" (John xvii. 3), seems to be found an authentic explanation of the nature of eternal life, according to its meaning in the Johannine discourses.[1] The knowledge of God, and of His Son, whom He has sent, has been communicated to men by Jesus; and, so far as men believingly receive the message of Jesus, there exists for them, in the knowledge so obtained, and in the inward apprehension of the Divine nature as revealed by Him, an already existing eternal life. But, so far as this knowledge and the spiritual apprehension of God have their continuance and completion after their earthly death, they have thereby also a future eternal life. But legitimate doubts arise in regard to this interpretation, if we consider a series of other sayings, which stand in the closest formal analogy to that declaration of John xvii. 3. Jesus says He Himself is the resurrection and the life (xi. 25; cf. xiv. 16); His word is spirit and life (vi. 63); the commandment, given to Him by the Father to speak, is eternal life (xii. 50); He says of the Holy Scriptures that the Jews thought they had eternal life in them (v. 39); whereby He does not declare that the existence of eternal life in the Scriptures, but that the possession of this life by the Jews, was only a supposition of theirs. From a comparison of these passages with one another, and from the context, we clearly infer that Jesus is not there stating wherein eternal life exists *as to its essence*, but wherein lies *the means of obtaining it*.

[1] Cf. B. Weiss, *Handbook of the Biblical Theology of the N.T.* § 146b.

Jesus Himself is the resurrection and the life, so far as He is the *Mediator* of the resurrection-life. His words, in relation to His Divine call to proclaim them, are eternal life, so far as they are the *medium* of eternal life for men. In the Holy Scriptures the Jews thought they had eternal life, so far as they regarded the instructions of Scriptures as the means of certainly obtaining eternal life. The pregnant mode of expression in all these passages has been chosen, in order to indicate that the above - named means for obtaining eternal life is not merely a possible one alongside of other means, but is the sole possible one which fully guarantees the end striven after.[1] Thus it follows that the declaration also, xvii. 3, that to know God and His Sent One is eternal life, is not to be understood as meaning that in that knowledge itself *consists* eternal life, but as meaning that that knowledge is the means, and indeed the exclusive and perfect means, of obtaining eternal life. For the question, wherein the essence of this eternal life consists according to the view presented by the Johannine discourses, no answer is here afforded.

From the conversation with Nicodemus (John iii.),

---

[1] The same form of expression is exhibited in the following Pauline passages :—1 Cor. i. 30: "Christ is made of God unto us wisdom, and righteousness, and sanctification, and redemption"—that is, Christ has been made for us the Mediator, and, indeed, the sole and perfect Mediator, of those benefits ; Col. i. 27: "Christ in you, the hope of glory"—that is, Christ who is the sole and perfect foundation and support of our hope of glory ; Col. iii. 4 : "When Christ, who is your life, shall be manifested"—that is, when Christ, who is the sole and perfect founder and mediator of your life, shall be manifested ; Rom. viii. 6 : "The mind of the flesh is death, but the mind of the spirit is life and peace"—meaning, not that the mind of the flesh *consists* of (or, in) death, nor that it has death *for its object*, but that this mind *certainly leads* to death, as the other to life and peace.

as it appears to me, it is possible to find such an answer. The difficulty of establishing a connected unity in the discourse of Jesus to Nicodemus, or of seeing what inner relation it bears to the appeal of Nicodemus to Jesus, is solved, if we consider how the idea of the new birth through God's Spirit in the first part of the discourse corresponds with the idea of eternal life in the second. The purpose of the discourse is to set the more perfect statement, that Jesus was sent of God to impart eternal life to believers (ver. 16 f.), in opposition to the saying of Nicodemus, that He was a teacher sent from God (ver. 3 f.). To lead up to that statement, Jesus first declares that the necessary condition of participation in the kingdom of God lies, not merely in a new knowledge, but in a new birth; and not in a creaturely new birth, through which only a creaturely nature, *flesh*, would be produced, but in one effected by God's Spirit, through which Divine *Spirit* would be produced (vers. 3-8). To the doubting question of Nicodemus, how such a new birth through God's Spirit is possible (ver. 9), Jesus replied that His testimony to this heavenly fact was grounded on personal experience (vers. 10-12), and that, in virtue of the unique perfection of this heavenly experience of His, He was also the sole medium of a similar experience for others, that is, for all who believingly acknowledge Him (vers. 13-15). For God had sent Him in order that He might be the mediator of eternal life to all that believe (vers. 16, 17); so that whoever does not reject this faith for the furtherance of his own immoral conduct, thereby virtually rejecting eternal life, but rightly presents it, has already entered upon a state of justification (vers. 18–21).

A survey of this line of thought makes it evident that the eternal life, which Jesus knew He was sent of God to bestow, is regarded as identical with the new nature consisting of Divine Spirit, which is produced in man through the new birth effected by God's Spirit. We are led to the same result by the conclusion of the discourse in John, chap. vi.   For in this latter Jesus declares Himself, and that just in so far as He is flesh and blood — that is, a human creature — to be the medium of bestowing an already present eternal life upon all who believingly receive Him (vers. 35, 40, 47, 51, 53, 54).   The paradoxical form of this asser- tion, by which He gave offence to the Jews, found its solution in His closing saying, that the flesh or creaturely nature has no worth whatever : " It is the Spirit that quickeneth ; . . . the words which I have spoken to you, they are spirit, and they are life" (ver. 63).   Here also the idea of the Divine Spirit and eternal life correspond to one another.   Jesus set up His claim to be the medium of eternal life in so far as He was conscious that a Divine spiritual power operated through His preaching—a power shared in by all who received His message in faith.

Eternal life, as that term is used in the Johannine discourses, is a mode of being, not of a creaturely, but of a Divine character, and consists in the possession of the Spirit of God.   Eternal life can, in this sense, be possessed by man even during the present earthly life.   This Jesus declares to be His own present possession, just as He promises it as a present possession to those who believe in Him. "As the Father has life in Himself, even so gave He to the Son also to have life in Himself" (v. 26); "For as the Father raiseth the dead and quickeneth them, even so the Son also quickeneth whom He will" (v. 21); "He that believeth hath eternal life" (vi. 47; cf. ver. 54; v. 24).

But this Divine form of life which may be obtained in this world, is so truly an eternal life, that it cannot die with the creaturely life. It is therefore not *merely* a life in the present world, but it has continued existence in spite of earthly death, which, for all who have become partakers of that higher life, loses its significance as a real death. Thus Jesus, in regarding the believing reception of His message as the means of obtaining eternal life even in the present world, could draw the conclusion that whoever kept His word would never see death (viii. 51), and said that "whosoever believeth on me, though he die, yet shall he live; and whosoever liveth and believeth on me shall never die" (xi. 25 f.). He can also declare that whoever, through unbelief, debars himself from the present possession of eternal life, has thereby already entered into the state of condemnation, seeing that he has rejected the means of possessing that higher life which, beginning in this world, endures to eternity (iii. 18).

8. We justly lay stress on the fact that, in the Johannine discourses, Jesus, in employing the idea of eternal life, not only exhibits a peculiar use of language, but also a peculiar thought not occurring

in the sayings recorded in the Logia and in Mark,— the thought, namely, of a higher Divine form of life already existing in believers, as the foundation of the life which eternally endures beyond the grave. Yet we can only properly estimate that fact, if we take into account that this peculiar use of language and this pregnant thought by no means occurs all through those discourses in John in which the blessing to be brought in by the Messiah is treated of, but only at particular altitudes, whilst close by we find such a mode of thought and speech in regard to that subject as thoroughly accords with that of our two other main sources.

In the first place, the idea of eternal life is used in several passages simply in the sense of the *future* heavenly life, which begins after the earthly life. When Jesus says that the water which He gives shall become, in the receiver, a well of water springing up unto eternal life (iv. 14), or when He calls upon men not to labour for the meat which perishes, but for that meat which endures to eternal life (vi. 27), or when He promises that whosoever hates his soul (that is, his life) in this world, shall keep it to life eternal (xii. 25), He manifestly regards that eternal life simply as a future state of existence, for whose attainment the gifts bestowed in the present by the Messiah, and, in a relative sense, the gifts pertaining to the natural life, are the means. This future heavenly life of bliss, this entrance into the mansions prepared in the Father's house (xiv. 2), and this participation in the heavenly glory of the Messiah (xvii. 24), He represents as the peculiar goal to which He prepares

the way for His disciples (xiv. 3 f. and 6), and whose
attainment by them is the object of His desire.   But
He also points out to them, not only the future goal
of bliss, but present experiences of blessing, whose
nature He more definitely describes just as they are
described in the reports of the Logia and Mark.   In
spite of His setting before His disciples the prospect
of dire persecutions from men and of distresses in this
world (xv. 18 ff. ; xvi. 1 f., 33), and of His promising
them anything but unclouded earthly felicity, He yet
repeatedly gives them promises of a perfect granting
of all their prayers (xiv. 13 f. ; xv. 7, 16 ; xvi. 23 f.).
The condition subjoined by Him, that they pray in
His name, *i.e.* with reference to their being His
(cf. Mark ix. 41), or to their abiding in Him and
His words abiding in them, *i.e.* in regard to their
holding fast the truth He taught (xv. 7), is no other
than the condition which is presupposed by the like
promises in the discourses of the Logia and Mark,
namely, that the disciples pray as true members of
God's kingdom, having the supreme bliss of God's
kingdom as the highest object of their aspirations.
The unlimited promise, founded on the fatherly love
of God to the disciples (xvi. 26 f.), of the hearing of
all true prayers, corresponds to the similarly unlimited
assurance of abiding peace and perfect joy even
during their earthly lifetime (xvi. 24).   The disciples
should also attain to the same joy and peace which
Jesus possessed, and which He was able to conserve
even in the near prospect of inevitable death :
" Peace I leave with you, *my* peace I give unto you :
not as the world giveth, give I unto you.   Let not

your heart be troubled, neither let it be afraid"
(xiv. 27) ; "This have I spoken unto you, that my joy
might be in you, and that your joy may be full"
(xv. 11) ; "Now ye have sorrow ; but I will see you
again, and your heart shall rejoice, and your joy no
one taketh away from you" (xvi. 22). "This have I
spoken unto you, that my joy may be in you. In the
world ye shall have tribulation : but be of good cheer;
I have overcome the world" (xvi. 33). This victory
over the world, which Jesus proclaims at the very
moment when, judged according to outward appearances and earthly standards, He was subjected to the
hostile powers of the world, this victory and the joy,
indestructible and perfect, which the disciples should
possess, even as He Himself possessed them, can be
understood by us in no other sense than those words
recorded in the Logia, in regard to the power of the
disciples (those whose names were inscribed in
heaven) over all hurtful and hostile earthly forces
(Luke x. 19 f.), and in regard to the rest which all
the labouring and heavy laden shall find, if they
become, like Him, meek and lowly in heart (Matt.
xi. 28 ff.). Just as the meaning which we found previously in those words of the Logia is confirmed
by these parallel utterances of the Johannine discourses, so the authenticity of these latter utterances
is certified by the testimony of those words furnished by the Logia-sources. Finally, we find in the
Johannine discourses such encouraging promises of
support to the disciples by the Holy Spirit, as are
analogous to the promise in Mark xiii. 11. As Jesus
promises there the help of the Spirit to the disciples

in case of their being called upon to give testimony
to His Messiahship in the midst of deadly persecutions, so He here designates the Holy Spirit as their
advocate, who, in His (Jesus') own room, should
continue His instruction among them (xiv. 16 f. ;
xvi. 13 f.), bring all things to their remembrance
which Jesus had taught them (xiv. 26), and through
their means would bear a true testimony for Him
before the world (xv. 26 ; xvi. 7 f.).

In examining the points of agreement between the
view of salvation borne witness to in the Johannine
and that given in the synoptical discourses, the question of how we are to interpret that peculiar idea of
the Johannine discourses, that even upon earth believers receive a higher form of existence—an eternal
life—through the operation of the Holy Spirit, must
assume the following form. Must we say that this
idea, in relation to Jesus' conception of salvation
which is harmoniously attested elsewhere as a consistent unity, forms an element so new and strange
that it cannot be ascribed to the simple and uniform
mode of thought of Jesus, but must be regarded as a
gloss of the evangelist, who freely manipulated or
supplemented the words of Jesus ? Or must we
admit that this idea stands in a relation so intimate
and direct to the elsewhere recorded views of Jesus,
that it might very well have been advanced by Himself as the central point of His teaching in regard to
the Messianic salvation, and so might have been seized
and preserved for us by the disciple who stood nearest
to Him, and had most intimate communion of spirit
with Him ? It is not a question as to the form of words

in which this idea is couched in the Johannine discourses ; for we can readily conclude from the similar
form of the expression in the First Epistle of John
(iii. 14 f. ; v. 11–13), that this form of the thought—the
application of the notion " eternal life " to indicate the
super-terrestrial state of life already enjoyed on earth
by the believer—cannot be ascribed to Jesus Himself,
but to the apostle.   But in regard to the thought
itself which is clothed in this form, we ask if, on the
ground of internal probability, it must or must not be
denied to Jesus Himself.

To my mind, even were we to accept the former
solution of this problem, we by no means thereby
set our seal to the opinion, in regard to the fourth
Gospel, that it has not thereby sprung from a genuine
apostolic source, and does not generally contain true
and valuable reminiscences of the actual discourses of
Jesus.   However, I confess that for me that solution
is neither at all certain nor necessary.   The thought
that all salutary gifts and experiences which the
heavenly Father grants to His children here upon
earth are inwardly connected with their obtaining the
future heavenly life and prepare them for it, is at
least of essential importance to Jesus in His view of
salvation.   This thought is not altered, but rather
further developed and completed, by the idea that,
even during the present earthly life, a permanently
higher form of life, depending on the Holy Spirit's
power, is begun in the disciples, the possession of
which warrants the continuance of life in spite of
earthly death.   And if we consider the teaching of
Jesus, not in an isolated way, but in its historical

connection with the doctrinal development which was its preparation and starting-point, it becomes in the highest degree probable that Jesus Himself held and expressed this thought which carried forward and completed His view. For, on the one hand, John the Baptist, in re-connecting himself with the early prophets who had promised the bestowal of the Spirit of God with purifying and renewing power for the people of God in the latter days, had declared the blessing to be expected from the coming of the Messiah to be a baptism of the Holy Spirit. In thus laying particular emphasis on the inward benefit proceeding from true righteousness, John the Baptist set himself in characteristic opposition to the Messianic hopes of his Jewish contemporaries, hopes which were primarily directed to terrestrial happiness and temporal power. On the other hand, the idea that every Christian is equipped even on earth with a Divine power and a Divine life, has formed even from the apostolic period an essential element of the Christian consciousness. Not only has Paul magnificently expressed this idea in his doctrine of the Holy Spirit, who is, for believers, the principle of all Christian knowledge and conduct, of prayer and of hope, as well as the pledge of future life (1 Cor. ii. 10 ff. ; xii. 3 ff. ; Gal. v. 22 ff. ; Rom. viii. 4-27), but also in the Epistle of James, which we must set in the front rank as a witness for the early apostolic Church, we find fundamentally the same idea, only under another title. There it is said that God gives "wisdom" liberally, and without upbraiding, to them that ask (i. 5) ; and that this wisdom from above is not

earthly and sensuous, but furnishes man with power
for every virtue and good work (iii. 15, 17). Were
we to suppose that Jesus, conscious as He Himself
was of an equipment of Divine spiritual power
(Mark i. 10), did not teach that a similar and continual endowment of Divine power would be shared
in by His disciples, to animate and strengthen them
in the knowledge of the Divine will, and that thereby
the heavenly life of the future would be implanted in
their hearts, we should (through such a supposition)
lose an important link in the chain of historical
development, viz. the intermediate link between the
Old Testament prophetic idea of the Baptist and this
idea of the apostolic time.   Already in the first
generation after the apostles, the promised effusion of
the Spirit in the Messianic times was specially understood of the gifts of prophecy and of tongues as they
were manifested in the Christian Church ; and one
prophecy of the risen Jesus has been handed down,
which referred to the first miraculous appearance of
the gift of the Spirit in the apostolic Church (Luke
xxiv. 49 ; Acts i. 8).   But the prophecy of the coming
of the Spirit, when taken in this sense, does not
correspond exactly with the thought which we must
postulate, in the teaching of Jesus, as deducible from
Old Testament prophecy and John Baptist's teaching,
and as the presupposition of the original apostolic
view.   Therefore, if the thought, which it thus
appears necessary to postulate, is found in the discourses of the fourth Gospel, we have certainly no
right to reject it as not authentic merely because it is
not attested by the two other chief Gospel sources.

On the contrary, we have every reason to regard the recording of this thought as one evidence of the independent value of these Johannine discourses of Jesus for the supplementing of our other documentary sources.[1]

CHAP. IV. THE RIGHTEOUSNESS OF THE MEMBERS OF THE KINGDOM OF GOD.

1. In that paternal love which is an essential attribute of God, we must seek the sole and ultimate ground of Jesus' view of salvation, and of its certain bestowal, as well as of the exact nature of the blessings implied in that salvation. In the same feature of the Divine character we have to seek the ruling principle of His idea of the righteousness of the members of the kingdom of God.

[1] I would refer the reader to *L. J.* i. pp. 249 ff., 252 f., 267, where I have offered reasons for my opinion that the fourth evangelist, who edited, and brought into a historical setting, the sayings of Jesus reported in his Gospel, was not quite familiar with, and did not understand, this idea of the already present bestowal of "eternal life" or of the Holy Spirit to believers through the Messiah. He has sought expressly to explain away this idea where he found it. To the saying of Jesus, v. 24 f., he has added the by no means equivalent explanation by the idea of the future general resurrection, ver. 28 f., which interrupts the train of thought between ver. 26 f. and ver. 30. And he has, in the same sense, added small statements of similar import in reference to the future resurrection (vi. 39, 40, 44, 54). He has also interpreted the saying of Jesus, vii. 38, in regard to the streams of living water that would flow from within those who believe on Him, by an addition, ver. 39, referring to the future bestowal of the Holy Spirit after Jesus should be glorified, since the Holy Spirit was not yet given. Hereby the evangelist plainly betrays that he belonged to the sub-apostolic generation, and also that he did not originally conceive and formulate that thought, so clearly expressed, of the present bestowal of eternal life, but rendered it according to a received tradition whose meaning was strange to him. This tradition evidently appears to us to be of genuine apostolic authority.

But we must first take up the etymological questions connected with the idea of *righteousness*.

We must bear in mind that, in the Old Testament phraseology, which governed the religious language of the Jews in the time of Jesus, and which He Himself adopted, the word "righteousness" had a wider signification that that of the Greek word δικαιοσύνη as used by profane authors. For it denotes, not only the idea of legality, equity, impartiality in judgment and retribution, but a normal disposition or mode of action which, while certainly including that judicial virtue, means something more.[1] As applied to men, "righteousness" specially denotes a disposition for action which takes the will of God as its supreme norm. Righteousness in this sense is the most general designation for the pious God-pleasing disposition or conduct of men which is opposed to sin (cf. *e.g.* Mark ii. 17; vi. 20). The term then also comprises in its meaning that pious disposition which has God as its direct object, as well as the moral disposition which, according to God's command, is to be shown to other men. When, *e.g.*, Jesus teaches that righteousness must not be done before men to be seen of them, He adduces such examples of righteous conduct as alms-giving, praying, and fasting (Matt. vi. 1 ff., 5 ff., 16 ff.).

Further, it is here to be noted that, in the discourses of the fourth Gospel, righteousness, so far as it implies a dutiful conscientious disposition, is usually indicated by the word ἀλήθεια. This usage, which appears

---

[1] Cf. E. Kautsch, on the derivates from the stem צדק in Old Testament use of speech, *Programm*, Tübingen, 1881, p. 27 ff.

peculiar to us, is nevertheless not arbitrary and strange. It is founded on the fact that the Septuagint has rendered the Hebrew word אֶמֶת by the Greek ἀλήθεια, although the meaning of the two words is not strictly the same, as the Hebrew word has a wider signification than the Greek term. For אֶמֶת means originally "steadfastness," and then, as applied to knowledge, speech, and actions, or to persons, so far as they think, speak, or act, it means "rectitude," which exactly corresponds to something given or existing. Thus the term can, on the one hand, denote intellectual rightness or truth, in the sense that utterances or manifestations in word or deed, and that appearances or ideas, correspond to the reality. This is the sense in which the word coincides with the peculiar meaning of the Greek ἀλήθεια, and for the sake of which the Seventy have used this word in general to render the sense of that Hebrew term. On the other hand, the Hebrew word can, however, denote also the moral and legal rightness of actions, sayings, or thoughts so far as these correspond duly and faithfully to the claims which arise from given acts or relations. Now, since the LXX. generally translate the Hebrew word, even when used in this sense, by ἀλήθεια, whilst the word אֱמוּנָה, which has not at all the meaning of intellectual truth corresponding to reality, they render as readily by ἀλήθεια as by πίστις, we shall not, for our part, translate ἀλήθεια, when used in this sense, by simple "truth." We must rather choose a general expression, such as will denote, not only the intellectual truth, but at the same time the quality or disposition duly corresponding to what is required in the exist·

ing relations—for example, "rectitude" or "the right."
In conformity to the influence of the Septuagint
on the formation of the religious use of Greek by
the Jews, which is quite analogous to the influence
of Luther's translation of the Bible upon the German
religious phraseology, the wider meaning which we
have just mentioned as attached to the use of ἀλήθεια
has passed into the New Testament idiom, where we
can plainly recognise it in the Pauline Epistles as well
as the Johannine writings. There is nothing remarkable in its use where ἀλήθεια has the ordinary meaning
of "truth," though, of course, we cannot say that in
those cases the phraseology of the Septuagint has
been departed from, since the idea of "truth" is not
excluded by the Septuagint usage, but rather included, and occasion is left for the use of the word in
its peculiar sense. On the contrary, the deviation of
the Old Testament use of the word from the common
usage is clearly apparent, where its conjunction with
certain ideas which are closely united in the Old
Testament, or where its opposition to the idea of sin
or wrong, shows that it is not the idea of the rightness
of intellectual truth, but the rightness of faithful and
dutiful conduct that is meant. This is the case in
the prologue of the fourth Gospel, i. 14 and 16, where
the conjoined terms χάρις καὶ ἀλήθεια are a translation
of the Hebrew terms חֶסֶד וֶאֱמֶת or חֶסֶד וֶאֱמוּנָה, and
where also ἀλήθεια denotes rightness, not in the
special sense of intellectual truth, but of faithfulness,
corresponding to certain obligatory relations or to
certain promises. For this faithfulness, along with
spontaneous mercy and grace, is mentioned exceed-

ingly often in the Old Testament as the characteristic
attribute of the God who reveals Himself in blessing
His people (cf. Rom. xv. 8 f., ὑπὲρ ἀληθείας θεοῦ and
ὑπὲρ ἐλέους). Also in the Johannine discourses of Jesus
we must, not only in the passage iii. 21, understand
the idea ποιεῖν τὴν ἀλήθειαν, which stands in opposition
to φαῦλα πράσσειν, in the sense of "to do the right,"
i.e. to act dutifully or conscientiously (cf. LXX.
Gen. xxxii. 10; xlvii. 29; Josh. ii. 14; 2 Sam. ii. 6;
Neh. ix. 33; Isa. xxvi. 10; Tob. iv. 6; xiii. 6); but
also in the passages viii. 32, 40, 45, 46, and xvii. 17
and 19, where the connection also shows the antithesis
of sin or evil, ἀλήθεια must be understood as "the
right" in the moral sense (cf. in Paul: 1 Cor. v. 8;
xiii. 6; Rom. ii. 8; 2 Thess. ii. 10–12). In view of this
fact, when we are dealing with other passages, such
as xiv. 6, 17; xv. 26; xvi. 13; xviii. 37 f., where the
antithesis of sin is not directly indicated, we cannot
take it for granted that ἀλήθεια has the meaning of
intellectual "truth." We must here, in the first place,
suppose that it is used in the wider sense of "rectitude" or "the right;" and then we must ask if,
according to the connection of the passage, or according to Jesus' mode of view exhibited elsewhere, the
word is to be here taken in the more special sense
of intellectual truth or in that of dutiful conduct, or
if it is to be understood in the general sense which
embraces both those meanings.[1]

---

[1] Cf. *L. J.* i. p. 300 f., and my treatise, "The use of the words ἀλήθεια,
ἀληθής, and ἀληθινός in the New Testament investigated on the ground
of the Old Testament usage of speech," in the *Studien und Kritiken*,
1883, p. 511 ff. I must hold to the view there presented in opposition
to Cremer in his *Lexicon of N. T. Greek*, vid. ἀλήθεια. The LXX. have

2. After these introductory remarks on the linguistic question, we can now enter upon a consideration of the teaching on the subject of righteousness. Generally the Jews were convinced in their religious consciousness that mankind owed to God the performance of righteousness and the fulfilment of His will, so that Jesus generally had not to impress this upon them. But the Pharisaic mode of view set in the foremost place the performance of righteousness

rendered the word אֱמוּנָה, when used in reference to God, only three times by πίστις, and at other times by ἀλήθεια; but when it has reference to men, it is, as a rule, translated by πίστις. How Cremer can infer from this that the LXX. have not taken ἀλήθεια = πίστις, and have not thought of using ἀλήθεια in the sense of "good faith" (p. 112), is to me logically inconceivable. The right conclusion seems to me to be just the converse. Cremer concludes his discussion on the LXX. usage by the declaration : "ἀλήθεια retains the meaning of 'truth' and 'veracity' only in a much wider sense than is ordinary in Greek ;" but if the latter important admission is made, involving as it does the real state of the case, the question as to whether ἀλήθεια does or does not retain the meanings of "truth" and "veracity" becomes merely a matter of words. For we can, of course, as readily hold that truth and veracity have been taken in an unusually wide sense, as that the LXX. have used the word ἀλήθεια in a wider sense than is usual in Greek. For us as theologians, who must make the original meaning of the Holy Scriptures intelligible for the present generation, it is only of importance that we should explain in the ordinary language that unusually wide sense of the words truth and veracity ; and that I seek to do in maintaining that what in the Greek of the LXX. and of the New Testament is called ἀλήθεια, and what in modern translations has been rendered by "truth," is something more general in signification, viz. "rectitude," under which the rectitude of faithful and dutiful conduct can also be expressed. With reference to the New Testament use of language, Cremer, in my opinion, adopts from the first an unjustifiable position when he thus states the question : how far the intellectual sense of the idea (i.e. = truth) employed in classical Greek is applicable in the New Testament usage, and how far there may be a remainder which must be referred to the Old Testament usage? In this examination Cremer finds only a slight remainder, specially in the Johannine writings, John i. 14 and 16 ; iii. 21 ; 1 John i. 6, where he cannot deny the influence of the Old Testament *form of expression;* but he will not also admit here an influence from the *substance of the thought* of the Old Testament in the sense of service on which a claim for reward could be founded, and thereby undermined the consciousness of the bounden duty of doing right. In opposition to this, Jesus emphasised in a significant saying the simple duty of the universal fulfilment of God's will. Referring to the servant who received from his master no special thanks for the performance

idea. It is here to be observed, however, that the use of the word in the intellectual sense, which corresponds to the classical Greek meaning, is by no means excluded, though the Old Testament usage of the LXX. was the standard one. According to the latter usage, ἀλήθεια bore also, and indeed primarily, the sense of intellectual rectitude, *i.e.* truth in the ordinary sense. The remark which Cremer, in another place, has made in regard to the idea δίκαιος in the New Testament holds good here, however, namely, that the employment of this word, not in a religious, but in the purely social sense corresponding to its use in profane Greek, "the Biblical idea does not acquire a twofold use; for the Biblical conception does not exclude the profane sense as such, but prevents its limitation." The vast range of agreement, also, observable between the New Testament use of ἀλήθεια and its use in classical Greek, furnishes by no means a sufficiently solid basis for the assertion that New Testament Greek has been moulded according to the profane Greek usage, from which no departure has been made except where, in certain special instances and for weighty reasons, there is a recognisable influence of Old Testament usage. But a sufficiently weighty reason for presupposing the Old Testament usage in connection with ἀλήθεια, and even for asserting it in cases where there is no departure from the profane usage, lies in the certainty of the predominant influence of the LXX. on the formation of the religious Greek modes of speech of the Jews and the New Testament writers. Therefore the possible sense of rectitude as referring to faithful conduct, according to the peculiar LXX. usage, will be everywhere unhesitatingly accepted where either the analogy, certain Old Testament forms, or the line of thought, indicate this possible signification. I confess that to me Cremer's opposition to this aim of explaining, as far as possible, a New Testament idea on the ground of its Biblical development, is only intelligible from the supposition of a certain, perhaps unconscious, anxiety lest the precious thought that Jesus Christ and His announcement of the "truth" is the revelation of the reality κατ᾽ ἐξοχήν, would be impaired, if one did not find it expressed in the Johannine utterances which assert the ἀλήθεια of Jesus and His words. But for me that precious thought is elsewhere sufficiently established in the New Testament, and specially in the utterances of Jesus in regard to Himself, as the present treatise can testify.

of the work committed to him, He thus addressed His disciples : " So likewise ye, when ye have done all that is commanded you, say, We are unprofitable servants : we have done that which was our duty to do " (Luke xvii. 7-10).   Jesus did not here mean to exclude the thought, which He has elsewhere so often expressed, that the faithful performance of the Divine will obtains a reward from God,—a reward after which men may and ought to aspire.   For even an obedience for which a reward is promised, whereby stimulus and encouragement is afforded, may at the same time be a perfectly obligatory duty, which a man is not free to omit without blame, and on whose performance he cannot pride himself as if he had done something specially meritorious.   In Jesus' view, such an unassuming sense of duty ought to accompany all works of righteousness.

But Jesus understood the contents of this righteousness which is man's duty, and which corresponds to the will of God, in a different way than did the Jews of His time.   The Jews regarded the revelation of God's will in the law and the prophets as the standard of true righteousness, and that in the sense handed down by the scribes, who were occupied in explaining and applying the doctrine of the law.   The Pharisees of that period appeared to their countrymen the models *par excellence* of this righteousness, from the stress they laid upon the correct observance of the traditional doctrine of the law.   Jesus, indeed, still upheld the permanent value and authority of the Old Testament revelation of the Divine will, and could appeal to certain statements of the Mosaic law as a compendious expression of the abiding commands of God (Mark x. 19; xii. 29–31). But, at the same time, He claimed the power to raise the law and the prophets to a perfection they had not already attained (Matt. v. 17). And He set this perfecting of the law, which applied to all who entered the kingdom of heaven, in opposition to the legal traditions and the modes of righteousness of the scribes and Pharisees: "I say unto you, If your righteousness exceed not the righteousness of the scribes and Pharisees, ye shall not enter the kingdom of heaven' (Matt. v. 20).

If we sought to give an account of this perfect kind of righteousness, as it was conceived and taught by Jesus, we might in the following way suitably classify the abundant material found in the evangelical narratives. We might first take up those sayings of Jesus which lay stress upon this aspect of all manifestations of righteousness, that they must have their root in the inner being, and have their value according to whether they exist within the man. Then, in connection with the fact that Jesus designated the double command of love to God and one's neighbour as the greatest commandment (Mark xii. 29–31), we must examine how Jesus has set forth in His teaching the righteous conduct to be observed directly towards God, and that to be observed towards men. In the formal co-ordination of the righteousness to be shown towards God and that to be shown towards men, we must, of course, take into account that the righteousness exercised towards men is at the same time a mode of piety towards God. For this thought is

already involved in the idea of righteousness, that is,
the disposition and mode of conduct which corresponds to the will of God.

A.—*Righteousness as seated in the Heart.*

3. All through His teaching, Jesus has held that
the existence and value of righteousness are solely
determined by the inward man or the heart (καρδία ;
cf. above, p. 157 f.).   In the eyes of men we may
pass for righteous from our external words and acts ;
but God sees in the secret places (Matt. vi. 4, 6, 18),
and knows the heart (Luke xvi. 15).   He judges
according to the state of the heart.   The Pharisee
who accounted himself righteous, and in an ostentatious prayer appealed before God to the greatness of
his outward good works in comparison with those
of other men, is judged by God as less righteous
than the publican, who neither had nor claimed the
external appearance of righteousness, but only begged
for God's merciful forgiveness of his sins (Luke xviii.
10–14).

Jesus was certainly not the first who laid stress on the
significance of the heart for true righteousness.   That
God searches the " heart," and that the purity of the
heart is the condition of a state pleasing to God, was
a truth often enough expressed by the Psalmists and
Prophets (*e.g.* 1 Sam. xvi. 7 ; Ps. vii. 10 ; v. 2 ; xxiv. 4 ;
li. 12 ; cxxxix. 23 ; Jer. xvii. 10 ; xxxi. 32) ; and this
view was largely current in Judaism in the time of
Jesus.   But not only was this view becoming more and
more obscured through the theory and practice of the

scribes and Pharisees, who, or at least the greater number of them, had allowed the pursuit of righteousness to sink into gross externalism; but even in the Old Testament itself that thought does not occur in such a general consistency, that it could be represented as the only authoritative principle for the whole conduct commanded by God. What was new and significant in the teaching of Jesus on this point, lay in the fact not only of His energetically combating the teaching and practice of external righteousness as it had become prevalent among His contemporaries, and of seeking to restore to a seat ot supremacy the deeper and more inward conception of righteousness taught by the prophets; but ot His carrying out this latter view in as strict practical consequence as He had declared it to be the exclusively right and authoritative conception. This had not been done in the prophetic period. And although this stage of progress made by Jesus did not establish an original thought, but was the consistent carrying out of a conception whose truth had previously in many aspects been recognised, still we cannot lightly estimate that progress. For the difficult and important thing here was just the consistent application and exclusive use of the ethical principle. The idea that the heart has important significance for the value of the conduct before God and men, must be intensified with every stage of advance in moral insight; but the idea that the heart *alone* is the basis of the existence and value of the religious conduct to be practised towards God and men, and that all merely external deportment is worthless before God, corresponds to the highest ethical mode of view, which can only be attained along with the highest ethical conception of God.

The great discourse of Jesus on Righteousness, which in the Logia stands at the beginning of the discourses and sayings of Jesus, has its unifying principle in the purpose of showing that all precepts of righteousness are insufficient, and all forms of righteousness are worthless, which do not correspond to the principle that rectitude must prevail in the heart, and consequently must equally regulate the whole course of the conduct. Jesus has here adduced various particular examples of righteousness, and accordingly this discourse affords rich material for a knowledge of the special modes of conduct which pertain to the righteousness of the kingdom of God. Yet the peculiar purpose of the discourse does not lie in setting forth those special modes of conduct, but in the rejection of certain general standards of righteous conduct which do not harmonise with the view that the whole inner man must be directed towards the right.[1]

Jesus, in the first place, sets His precepts of righteousness in opposition to the earlier injunctions which were limited to forbidding gross outward acts of sin, whilst they passed over impurity of heart and

---

[1] Cf. *Log.* § 2, *L. J.* i. p. 52 ff. The chief motive that has led to the insertion of the large passage (Matt. vi. 19–34) by our first evangelist in that discourse, appears to have been, that he aimed, not only at opposing the perverted standard of righteousness, but at exhibiting the principal forms of manifesting the true righteousness. For in that case, along with the exercise of love, to which several passages of the discourse refer, trust in God required to be mentioned as a principal form of manifesting a pious spirit.

manifestations of it which were insignificant in appearance. He Himself judged that an impure heart, even when manifested in the smallest outward acts or not at all, was as culpable as the gross acts of sin condemned by the earlier precepts. "Ye have heard that it has been said by the ancients, Thou shalt not kill; and whosoever shall kill shall be in danger of the judgment: but I say unto you, Every one that hateth his brother shall be in danger of the judgment; and whosoever shall say to his brother, Raca, shall be in danger of the council; and whosoever shall say, Thou fool, shall be in danger of the Gehenna of fire" (Matt. v. 21 f.). "Ye have heard that it has been said, Thou shalt not commit adultery: but I say unto you, That every one that looketh upon a woman to lust after her, hath committed adultery with her already in his heart" (ver. 28). With such intensity should the mind be directed to righteousness, that no act should appear to it too troublesome or difficult, and no sacrifice too great, in order to achieve that mode of character and to overcome evil. Jesus illustrates these thoughts by examples which He subjoins to His precepts. Whoever, on bringing his offering to the altar, remembered the hostility of his brother, far from finding in this remembrance a motive for repaying that brother with hatred, ought rather to be prompted, by a spirit of spontaneous love, to set aside the performance of the intended act of worship in order to become reconciled to his brother (ver. 23 f.).[1] And similarly, if the eye offend,—that is, from the context, if on beholding a woman occasion is given

[1] Cf. above, p. 130.

for sinful desire,—the spectator must pluck out his eye and cast it from him. The meaning is that the mere thought of sin must be held so essentially grave, that the most painful sacrifice ought not to be shunned in order to remove that occasion of sin (ver. 29).

According to the same general principle, Jesus sets in opposition to the earlier precept, not to perjure one's self, but to fulfil what has been promised by oath, His precept, not to swear at all, but to let one's word be yea, yea; nay, nay (vers. 33 f., 37). If untruth and falsity to promise were only forbidden with reference to oaths, untruthfulness would then appear permissible in the case of promises without oath. Jesus, on the other hand, would have men feel unconditionally bound by even the simplest saying and promise. He deemed that every confirmatory addition to the plain,[1] simple affirmative or negative arose "from the evil one;" for it is a consequence, and an indirect expression of an evil mode of view, that a man should not be held as pledged to the truth by the simple yea or nay. Even in the Pharisaic view of righteousness, it was regarded a duty to abstain as far as possible from swearing by the name of God, in order not to use needlessly that sacred name. But for swearing by the Divine name they substituted swearing by other things, the appeal to which could have no other meaning than an indirect appeal to the name of God. Jesus denounced this abuse, and specialised His general command against oaths by forbidding

---

[1] This idea of plainness is brought out by Jesus through the duplication of the yea and nay.

even those periphrastic formulæ : " I say unto you, Swear not at all : neither by heaven ; for it is the throne of God : nor by the earth ; for it is the footstool of His feet : nor by Jerusalem ; for it is the city of the great King. Neither shalt thou swear by thy head, for thou canst not make one hair white or black " (vers. 34–36). Jesus showed that this Jewish mode of avoiding oaths was not what He meant, since that is found to be no better than an ordinary oath when the principle is applied to it of judging, not by external standards, but by the state of the heart. For the meaning of that form of speech is still an appeal to God as a witness of the truth and the avenger of those who forswear themselves ; and in using it, the heart which does not hold itself pledged to the truth without an oath could still cherish deceit.

But in order to avoid any conclusions drawn from this precept of Jesus, which are out of harmony alike with the general view of Jesus elsewhere expressed in regard to the true righteousness and with His own practice, we must fix our attention upon the purpose He had in view in thus prohibiting swearing. That purpose is plainly shown from the line of thought running throughout the discourse on righteousness. It was the inculcation of a righteousness having its root in the heart, and therefore requiring to be unconditionally observed in the simplest outward acts. An oath and solemn affirmation which a man may employ before his fellow-men, since, in their inability to read his inward truthfulness, they cannot put full confidence in his word if it be not solemnly asserted, are quite different in their nature and inward motive from the oath and protestation with which a man accompanies his word, because he would not feel absolutely pledged to truth and faithfulness by his simple word and promise. From the whole tenor of His teaching in regard to the righteousness of the kingdom of God, there is no reason to conclude that the members of the kingdom were forbidden the use of such confirmatory forms of speech towards others or an appeal to God as witness to the truth of their words. Perhaps we cannot refer to the fact that Jesus Himself, at His trial before the high priest, answered by oath (according to the adjuration of the high priest) the question whether He were the Messiah, since, according to the original account in Mark (xiv. 61 f.), the high priest did not put his question in the form of an adjuration. Still we can point to the fact that Jesus, according to the testimony of all our sources, frequently strengthened His statements by the addition of "verily," in order to awaken a closer attention in His hearers and greater trust in His word (e.g. Matt. v. 18; Mark iii. 28; viii. 12; ix. 1; John iii. 3; v. 19, 24 f.). When we consider the matter, it is certainly true in a certain sense that the absolute prohibition of oaths can only find its full realisation in the perfected kingdom of God, where the disciples have no longer dealings with men who mistrust them, and whom they must themselves mistrust. But, to my mind, we cannot say that Jesus consciously made this prohibition only for the future ideal state of the perfected kingdom, or only for His disciples in their intercourse with one another. For He addressed His precept to the then present hearers of His discourse, and that in regard to their speech in general, and not merely to their speech among other members of the kingdom. We must, however, bear in mind that principle which is so often to be observed in the discourses of Jesus, of aiming at the greatest clearness in the shortest compass. According to this principle, in order to make the meaning and scope of a rule as plain as possible, He abstracted from all the circumstances of ordinary life which tended in any way to obscure that meaning and scope, yet without really setting up an exception to the rule.[1]

According to the tenor of the discourse, the point intended here is to substitute, for the earlier command to be faithful and true in regard to oaths, the higher command to be true and faithful in regard to the smallest word. The prohibition of oaths and all confirmatory additions to the simple statement, is in this connection only meant to apply to the use of oaths and other protestations, as expressing the reservation that one is not pledged to truth and faithfulness by the simple and ordinary form of speech. Jesus sought with the greatest clearness to forbid, universally and unconditionally, such protestations made with this reservation, and so far as they arose out of a deceitful spirit. This unlimited prohibition holds good, not only for the ideal state of the perfected kingdom of God, but for all His hearers in the present, and not only for their intercourse with other members of the kingdom, but with all men, even the evil and untruthful. The prohibition of all oaths, arising from an evil deceitful spirit,

[1] Cf. above, p. 130 ff.

is not really limited by the right to confirm speech by a solemn adjuration, where it is called for in the circumstances in order to make what is said more credible and impressive to others. In seeking to accentuate His prohibition of oaths in consideration of the absolute duty of truthfulness, Jesus here abstracts from all circumstances which warrant the solemn affirmation of words by oaths.

After Jesus had set His higher commandment of unselfish forgiving and gratuitous love, even towards those who injure and are hostile to us, in opposition to the earlier principle of retribution of injury, and of love to our neighbour (Matt. v. 38–48), He proceeds, in the same discourse, to characterise as worthless all external acts of righteousness which do not spring out of an upright pious mind, and which are only used as a means of gratifying a selfish desire for honour and admiration. "Take heed," He says, "that ye do not your good works before men to be seen of them; otherwise ye have no reward of your Father" (vi. 1); and He shows how this precept is to be followed, by giving three illustrative examples. When a man gives alms he is not to sound a trumpet before him (in German the same thought is figuratively expressed by the proverbial expression, *an die grosse Glocke hängen*, to hang on the great bell, or to blaze abroad). On the contrary, his left hand must not know what his right hand does; that is, he must not let his alms-giving be accompanied by the least act (the hand being the organ of activity, and showing therefore his "knowledge" in acts) which may serve to make his act of benevolence known (vers. 2–4).

When a man prays, he must not ostentatiously plant himself where he can be seen by many, but should go into his chamber and shut the door (ver. 5 f.). When he fasts, he must not hang his head with a doleful air, but should appear to others as if he were not fasting (vers. 16–18). The external deportment which Jesus enjoins in these three examples is, of course, not meant as obligatory in all circumstances. But here, too, Jesus forms His examples on the principle of the greatest clearness in the shortest compass; that is, He abstracts from all the possible circumstances which might justify the public performance or announcement of good works, such as doing a thing as an example to others, public confession or fellowship with others, Jesus Himself being accustomed to pray aloud in presence of His disciples. But He put the matter in the way which should most plainly show that so far as the publicity of the act implied the desire to be seen and applauded by men, it was by all means to be avoided.

Similarly, Jesus regarded all zeal for improving others morally or religiously, which did not begin with self-reformation, as mere hypocritical show and not real righteousness. For a true inward zeal for righteousness would, in the first place, begin its work in a man's own character. It is thus that Jesus forbids the disposition to see and remove the mote out of a brother's eye, and is unconscious of, and fails to remove, the beam which is in his own eye (Matt. vii. 1–5). This applies to those who perceive and judge and seek to put right the faults of others, whilst they overlook their own gross faults, and do not labour to remove them. So, too, He warns against "false prophets, who come in sheep's clothing, but inwardly are ravening wolves "(ver. 15); that is, teachers who come forth to teach righteousness, and have the appearance of virtue and piety and of being true prophets, whilst in heart they are evil, and out of their heart rise evil deeds which do not harmonise with their teaching. Jesus gives the rule: " By their fruits ye shall know them " (ver. 16),—meaning that the actual works of those teachers of righteousness will prove if they are true prophets sent by God, or false prophets who have taken their pious teaching only as a mask for self-seeking purposes.

But since, in Jesus' view, the existence or non-existence of righteousness depends on whether or not the heart is set on righteousness, He estimates the greater or less merit of good works and the culpability of sins according to the heart, and not according to the external appearance. No doubt, generally, the greatness of the external action, good or bad, is intimately related to the goodness or badness of the heart. On this ground, Jesus, in heightening the early commandment against murder by forbidding even the thought of hatred, makes the following gradation: " Every one that is angry with his brother shall be in danger of the judgment; and whosoever shall say to his brother, Raca " (that is, " Thou good-for-nothing "), " shall be in danger of the council; and whosoever shall say, Thou fool" (that is, "godless"), " shall be in danger of the Gehenna of fire" (Matt. v. 22). He presupposes that the hatred expressed in word is greater than that which is unuttered, and that the violence of the language corresponds to the intensity of the hatred. But Jesus was also well aware that the degree of outward expression was no decisive standard for judging the heart. Therefore He laid special emphasis on the significance which the mere word has as an utterance of the inward mind. Though mere good words, unaccompanied with corresponding acts, do not suffice for true righteousness (Matt. vii. 15 f.), yet an evil word of itself, even if unaccompanied with an evil action, is a valid proof of an evil heart and a culpable fault. Jesus applies this to the Pharisees, who, blaspheming His work, pronounced it to be of the devil ; and declares that the use of such an expression of opprobrium is a very culpable form of enmity : "Ye offspring of vipers, how can ye, being evil, speak good things ? for out of the abundance of the heart the mouth speaketh. The good man, out of his good treasure, bringeth forth good things ; and the evil man, out of his evil treasure, bringeth forth evil things. And I say unto you, That every idle word that men shall speak, they shall give account thereof in the day of judgment. For by thy words thou shalt be justified, and by thy words thou shalt be condemned" (Matt. xii. 34–37). So also it holds good in regard to works of righteousness, that their value is not to be measured by their external greatness. Jesus sets the highest store by externally insignificant acts if they have sprung from a pure and good heart. The poor widow who cast two mites into the temple treasury, gave, in Jesus' estimation, more than all the others who cast in of their abundance ; because in making her small offering, which constituted her whole means of living, she showed a more self-sacrificing spirit than the others (Mark xii. 41 ff.). Analogous to this is the way in which Jesus spoke of the reception of a little child, which also is an externally insignificant act.   If it were done in His name, that is, with conscious reference to Himself (since His disciples are bound to love), this act had the same value as if men should receive Himself and the Father who sent Him (Mark ix. 37 ; cf. Matt. x. 41 ; xxv. 40).   Again, whosoever shall give even a cup of cold water to His disciples, because they belong to the Messiah, shall not lose their reward (Mark ix. 41). Even the smallest act of love, though uncostly and of no value from an external point of view, and though not worthy of reward, if prompted by a spirit of friendliness to the Messiah and His kingdom, has value in God's eye, and has a sure reward from Him.

4. We can well understand how Jesus, on the ground of this truly ethical mode of judgment, which determined the quality of all righteousness from the state of the heart, should feel driven to abhor and severely condemn that external legalism, so austere and petty, never sincerely honest, nor taking into account the true spirit of the law and the heart of men, which the scribes and Pharisees had made so prevalent in Judaism at that period.   Here He encountered a form of righteousness which bore the most pretentious appearance of piety and regard for the fulfilment of the will of God, but whose leading motives were in reality vanity and self-seeking, and its result human self-complacency.   Jesus saw in it a mighty hindrance to their attaining the ideal and

practice of piety belonging to the true kingdom of God. In His moral indignation against the use made of the temple-worship for purposes of covetous traffic, and against the degradation of the house of God—"the house of prayer"—into a den of thieves, He executed the condemning act of cleansing the temple (Mark xi. 15 ff.). He also again and again with words of stern rebuke castigated the false piety of the Pharisees and Pharisaic teachers of the law, namely, in the discourses, Luke xi. 39–52; Matt. xxiii. 13 ff.,[1] and also Mark vii. 6–13; xii. 38–40; Matt. xxiii. 1–7. Besides the point which we must more particularly consider afterwards, viz., that the Pharisees, by their legal ceremonies, set aside and annulled the moral duties of love to their neighbour, Jesus directed His accusation to this other point, that their legal zeal was merely external, and did not spring from a true interest in the Divine law. Therefore He not only called them "blind" (Matt. xxiii. 16, 17, 19, 24, 26), since, with all their supposed knowledge of the will of God, they were wholly in the dark on the subject; but He characterised them as "hypocrites," that is, actors in a special sense. For they concealed their real character under a mask, and appeared before men other than they really were. He applied to them the words of Isaiah (xxix. 13): "This people honour me with their lips, while their heart is far from me" (Mark vii. 6). He compared them to whited sepulchres, which have a fair outward appearance, but within are full of dead men's bones and all uncleanness (Matt. xxiii. 27). He reproached the Pharisaic scribes for

---

[1] Cf. *Log.* § 13, *L. J.* i. p. 104 ff.

the impure and selfish by-ends which they aimed at
in their doctrine and actions : " All their works they
do to be seen of men : for they make broad their
phylacteries " (pieces of parchment carried by the Jews
on their forehead and arm to remind them of the law),
"and enlarge the borders of their garments " (worn
upon their tunic for the same purpose) (Matt. xxiii. 5).
In other words, with those visible signs they paraded
their zeal for the law, and, by making them specially
large, they made the greater pretension to strictness.
" They love to walk in long robes, and to have saluta-
tions in the market-places, and chief seats in the
synagogues, and chief places at feasts ; they who
devour widows' houses, and for a pretence make long
prayers," that is, the forms of piety were used by
them as a cloak for covetousness (Mark xii. 38–40).
Jesus perceived that they were not truly occupied
with the will of God, since they disregarded the
commands of God, and substituted for these their
own human traditions (Mark vii. 8 ff.).   He adduces
as a striking example of the pure externalism of their
teaching as to the law, their absurd distinctions in
regard to the binding character of different forms of
oaths : " Woe unto you, ye blind guides, which say,
Whosoever shall swear by the temple, it is nothing ;
but whosoever shall swear by the gold of the temple,
he is a debtor !   Ye fools, and blind ! for whether is
greater, the gold, or the temple that hath sanctified
the gold ?   And, Whosoever shall swear by the
altar, it is nothing ; but whosoever shall swear by the
gift that is upon it, he is a debtor.   Ye blind ! for
whether is greater, the gift, or the altar that sanctifieth

the gift ? He therefore that sweareth by the altar, sweareth by it, and all things thereon. And he that sweareth by the temple, sweareth by it, and by Him that dwelleth therein" (Matt. xxiii. 16–21). Further, He shows the essential falseness of their zeal for the law, by the contrast between what they taught others and their own works : " They bind heavy burdens, and lay them upon men's shoulders; but they themselves will not touch them with their finger " (Matt. xxiii. 4). By adducing this contrast, He can well enough exhort His disciples to do and to hold all which the scribes teach when sitting in the chair of Moses, but not to act according to their works : "for they say, and do not " (Matt. xxiii. 2 f.). Yet, in other places, we find Him declaring that these blinded teachers, who were not themselves imbued with true piety, could not lead others to genuine righteousness; for " if the blind lead the blind, both shall fall into the ditch" (Matt. xv. 14). Therefore He pronounces woes upon the Pharisaic scribes, who shut the kingdom of heaven against men, whilst they neither entered in themselves nor suffered those who would enter to go in; who compassed sea and land to make one proselyte, and when he had become so, made him twofold more a child of hell than themselves (Matt. xxiii. 13, 15). Having clearly discerned the essential difference between this external zeal for righteousness on the part of the Pharisaic scribes, and the inward righteousness which He prescribed to all who enter the kingdom of heaven, and having noticed the malign influence which these vaunted authorities

and patterns of righteousness exerted against the
success of His preaching, Jesus compares those who
imagined themselves to be the true representatives
of the law and the prophets, to the enemies and
murderers of the prophets. In bitter irony, He takes
the zeal for the erection and adornment of the tombs
of the prophets as the sign of their continuing the
work of the murderers of the prophets: "Your
fathers killed them, and ye·have built (their tombs)"
(Luke xi. 47 f.).

One can regard as classical the way in which Jesus
characterised and, by His very description of them,
condemned the false and external Pharisaic piety
which thus ministered to by-ends. It would certainly
be far wrong to suppose that Jesus meant His re-
proaches to apply without distinction to all the
Pharisees. The example, given by the case of Paul,
of a Pharisee who struggled after the highest ideal of
righteousness, certainly proves that this party had
representatives of a better kind. It was the vain
hypocritical kind of righteousness, prevalent among
the great mass of the party at that period, which
Jesus has depicted with such incomparable vividness
and irony, that He has made the Pharisees for all
time a type of false and merely external piety and
morals.

5. By regarding the heart as the sole seat and
standard of true righteousness, Jesus was led into
conflict, not only with the perverted righteousness
of the degenerate piety of His time, but with an
important element of Jewish legalism founded in the
Pentateuch—in other words, with the whole tendency

to maintain or set up the so-called Levitical system of purity. This referred to the Old Testament Jewish precepts of purification, which arose out of the idea of the incompatibility of the holiness of God with certain material conditions, which, as we have already seen,[1] were supposed, by profaning the man, to put him out of fellowship with God. On the ground that this Jewish principle of defilement had no necessary connection with the heart, and did not really profane the man, Jesus pronounced the ceremonial rites founded upon it to have no value in relation to the righteousness of the kingdom of God. On one occasion the Pharisees and scribes from Jerusalem reproached the disciples of Jesus because they ate with unwashen hands. According to the account in Mark (vii. 1 ff.), Jesus summarily dismissed the objection of the Pharisees and scribes, on the ground that their zeal for righteousness did not rest on a true interest in the commandments of God, but only on an interest in their own human traditions (vers. 6-13). Then, having called the multitude together, He laid down a principle of judgment, which applied not only to the legal and Pharisaic precepts regarding food, but indirectly also to the Levitical precepts as to purification in general : "Hearken unto me every one of you, and understand : There is nothing from without a man, that entering into him, can defile him : but the things which come out of him, those are they which defile the man" (ver. 14 f.).[2] Having entered the house, He

---

[1] Cf. above, p. 48.

[2] Mark calls this saying of Jesus a παραβολή (ver. 17), since Jesus did not speak directly of food which a man partakes of, nor of the utterances of thoughts, but figuratively of the things which pass into and come out

gave His disciples the following explanation of this principle : " Perceive ye, that whatsoever from without goeth into the man, it cannot defile him ; because it goeth not into his heart, but into his belly, and goeth out into the draught, purging all meats ? That which proceedeth out of the man, that defileth the man. For from within, out of the heart of men, proceed evil thoughts, fornications, thefts, murders, adulteries, covetings, wickednesses, deceit, lasciviousness, jealousy, railing, pride, foolishness : all these evil things proceed from within, and defile the man " (vers. 18–22).

It is here noteworthy how Jesus does not regard this primary thought—that purity or impurity, sanctification or non-sanctification, in the sight of God depends solely on the state of the heart—as in any way standing in question ; but He takes it as the self-evident basis of His explanation. In admitting this proposition, it is clear that, whatever passes into man from without, as food and mere physical influences, cannot impair man's nature in the sight of God, since it does not enter the part of his being according to the state of which God judges the

of him, thus leaving His hearers to judge what those things were. It is from the figurative form of this saying that we can explain the paradoxical light in which it appeared to His disciples, and which gave occasion to their request for an explanation of the saying (ver. 17). For it appeared at first glance as if that which passes into a man, and which he assimilates, co-operates in the formation of his nature and worth ; whilst that which comes out of him, and no longer belongs to him, is of no further consequence for his nature and worth. But Jesus solves the paradox, by showing that the thing which passes into the man is his food, and that it is only in him temporarily ; whilst the things which come out of him—viz. his actions and words—are the expressions of his inner character, and determine his religious condition and worth.

man, but is only temporarily incorporated with the external, and in God's sight non-essential, part of man's being. Those things that enter from without can indeed become for men occasions of sin; but the ground of that sinfulness and defilement does not lie in the things themselves, but in the evil inward disposition finding in these occasions of activity. On the other hand, in admitting that proposition, it is also clear that what comes out of the inner man, the evil words and deeds, defile him before God, not from the mere fact of their emanating from him and passing away, or as if the evil thoughts and desires that remain hidden in the heart were not sinful and defiling, but they are defiling, because, proceeding from the inner man, they testify to the state of the heart, which is God's sole criterion for judging men.

In order to estimate the full significance of this principle of Jesus, — that man is profaned, not by external things that pass within without taking root in the heart, but by that which proceeds from his inner being,—we must form some idea of the extraordinarily weighty part the Levitical laws of purification played in the religious consciousness and life of the Jews. We must consider what a powerful influence they had in shaping the ordinary everyday life of the Jews, and in the satisfaction of the needs of natural life, and the whole compass and forms of social intercourse. That principle of Jesus laid the foundation for the loosening of the conscience from the bonds of merely physical conditions; and this loosening meant, not merely an emancipation of the religious consciousness and life from heavy burdens, but a deliverance of the physical and social life from narrowing restrictions. That principle opened a pathway of far-reaching consequence for the progress of human culture. But why, then, was it that Jesus could, with such clear assurance, use that idea—that the heart is the sole criterion of righteousness—for condemning and abrogating those prescribed purifications? And why, on the other hand, did not the fact that these prescriptions were sanctioned by the revelation of the law, rather lead Him somewhat to doubt, and to restrict the significance of the inner nature as the sole standard of judging in regard to righteousness? Our answer must be, Because of the purity of His view of the ethical nature of God. Jesus knew from His own personal experience that the highest and surest revelation of God consists in a knowledge of the fatherly character of God; and He regarded the Divine holiness and perfection as depending upon the supremacy and perfection of the Father's goodwill. Therefore it was inconceivable to Him that God would make His fellowship with men dependent upon any kind of merely external physical conditions. Neither could He imagine that the Divine commands would have any other object than men's assimilation with the moral and spiritual character of God.

6. Is it then only by *us* that this inner relation is established between Jesus' conception of God and His doctrine of righteousness as founded on the state of the heart, and was Jesus Himself aware of this relation? Even had no positive assertion that Jesus was aware of this been handed down to us, we should have to take

the fact for granted; for His clear exposition of the consequences resulting from His conception of God— not as to this one point only, but all through His teaching—cannot be attributed to His having only accidentally hit upon the truth, since His whole line of thought exhibits an organic unity of clearly conceived truth. It is not expressly declared in the Logia and the Gospel of Mark, that Jesus was conscious of this necessary connection of thought. But we find a significant passage of the Johannine discourses which appropriately supplements the deliverances of the other main sources, so far as they have reference to this point. That principle of Jesus in regard to the founding of righteousness on the state of the heart does not elsewhere occur in the Johannine discourses. And, indeed, as those discourses belong to the closing period of Jesus' ministry, they do not deal so much with His conflict with the Pharisees touching the nature of righteousness, as with His conflict with the priests at Jerusalem in regard to His Messiahship. But in His conversation with the woman of Samaria at the well, Jesus has given a deliverance in regard to the right mode of worship to be observed in the Messianic time, wherein He has clearly expressed the reciprocal relation existing between spiritual worship and God's spiritual nature: "The hour cometh, and now is, when the true worshippers shall worship the Father in spirit and in truth: for the Father seeketh such to worship Him. God is spirit, and they that worship Him must worship Him in spirit and in truth" (iv. 23 f.).

According to the occasion which prompted it, this

utterance directly refers only to the honouring of
God by *worship*. What makes such worship genuine
(οἱ ἀληθινοὶ προσκυνηταί) and conformable to God's
requirements, is not that it should take place in a
definite spot and according to definite external forms,
but that it should be practised in the minds of men.
So far as it is expressed by external words and acts,
it must be done in truth, *i.e.* it must be a genuine
product of the inner being. Indirectly, however, this
utterance refers to *piety of conduct* in general, such as
the Father would accept as true veneration from men.
Since God is spirit, and has nothing limited or
material in His nature, and since He stands related
to those who worship Him as a Father who seeks
that His children should possess the same nature as
He Himself has, therefore He claims from them a
truly spiritual reverence, and can attribute no value
for that end to any merely external conditions, places,
and acts.

B.—*The Righteous Conduct required towards God.*

7. When Jesus was asked by one of the scribes
which was the first of all the commandments, He
replied: " The first is this, Hear, O Israel ; The Lord
our God is one Lord : and thou shalt love the Lord
thy God with all thy heart, and with all thy soul, and
with all thy mind, and with all thy strength. The
second is, Thou shalt love thy neighbour as thyself.
There is no other commandment greater than these "
(Mark xii. 28–31).

We do not enter now upon the question as to why

Jesus in that answer indicated not the first of the commandments only, but the first and second ; nor as to the inner relation in which, according to His view, the commandment of love to our neighbour stands towards that of love to God. Here we shall only consider the first half of that answer. It shows that Jesus included in the idea of a righteousness accept-able to God something more than what is embraced by the due fulfilment of the Divine law of love to our fellow-men—something, namely, that has direct refer-ence to God Himself. And this necessary inward attitude towards God He found comprehensively expressed in the phrase, *love to God with the whole inner being*, as it was taught in the Mosaic command, Deut. vi. 4 f.—that "Schma" which by the Jews was regarded as the most holy.

Certainly it is not accidental that Jesus is not wont to employ the idea of love to God in other parts of His teaching, where He had not special occasion, as in replying to that question of the scribe, to follow the Old Testament phraseology.[1] That idea of love to God certainly corresponds to the childlike relation which, according to Jesus, should be cherished by men towards their heavenly Father. That idea emphatically indicates the moral inwardness of man's due attitude to the will of God, in contrast with mere external worship — a mere servile obedience or a mercenary legality. Yet, on the other hand, the conception is so general, that it does not adequately express that special kind of relation of men to God

---

[1] Cf. A. Ritschl, *Doctrine of Justification and Reconciliation*, 3rd German ed. ii. p. 99 f.

demanded by the knowledge of His full sovereignty
over them, the greatness and gratuitousness of His
fatherly love towards them, and the immensity of
His power placed at the disposal of His love. So
far as these latter qualities were involved in His
conception of God, it was a matter of course that
Jesus should enjoin upon men that disposition and
peculiar relation to God which, according to its
very idea, includes both the attitude of spirit towards God and the acknowledgment of His infinite
love and power, and the humble yet happy assurance of His salvation — I mean *Trust* (πίστις,
πιστεύειν).

With Jesus the opposite of the idea of trust is not
doing or knowing, but timidity and fear in regard to
dangers and evils (Mark iv. 40; v. 36), and doubt
as to the obtaining of good things (Mark xi. 23 f.).
The object to which this trust—that is, the boldly
confident and happy expectation of good things—
refers, is not specially the forgiveness of sins, but
more generally the grace of God or the glad tidings
of the kingdom of God, which include the proclamation both of the love and of the blessings of God.
Jesus requires of His hearers and disciples trust in
general (Mark i. 15; xi. 22)—trust that God will
set up His kingdom, and grant in it all grace to
His people: "Fear not, little flock; it is your
Father's good pleasure to give you the kingdom"
(Luke xii. 32). But He also requires trust that the
Father will grant, to those who seek His kingdom,
all the earthly blessings they need. In this sense He
forbids disquieting care on His disciples' part as to

wherewithal they shall be clothed and nourished in the future. He would by no means preclude wise and careful forethought (πρόνοια), whereby men have regard for the future in the present, and strive to insure their future through the means and resources at present possessed ; but He would exclude all depression and faint-hearted anxiety (μέριμνα) to which men are prone to give way if they do not see themselves masters of the situation for the future as well as the present, and do not find resources and means capable of meeting the exigencies of the future. From such anxious care the disciples must be preserved by the trustful assurance that their Father knows what they have need of, and that the God who feeds the fowls of heaven, and arrays in splendour the transient flowers of the field, shall much more give to them, His human children, whatsoever they may need (Matt. vi. 25–32).

According to the whole mode of view of Jesus, it was self-evident that trust could not be opposed to pious submission to the Divine will, and the endeavour after obedient fulfilment of His commands. It was no less self-evident that trust for the obtaining of earthly blessings from God, or preservation from earthly want and danger, must be absolutely subordinated to the seeking of His kingdom and His everlasting grace (cf. Matt. vi. 33; Luke xii. 31). But with this reservation, already implied in the conception of trust directed towards God and His grace, Jesus holds out an unlimited warrant for trust and for expecting great results therefrom. For on account of His conception of the greatness of the fatherly love of God, and of the world-controlling power of God, it was impossible for Him in this respect to admit any limit. To the man who prayed for his son, who was under demoniacal possession, in the doubting, conditional words, " If Thou canst do anything, have mercy on us and help us," Jesus answered, " If thou canst? —all things are possible to him that believeth " (Mark ix. 22 f.). In the same general terms in which, through these words, He ascribes unlimited power, not only to Himself, but to every one who has faith, He has done so in the drastic saying which the Logia (Luke xvii. 5 f.) and Mark (xi. 22 f.) have harmoniously recorded : Whosoever has faith as great as a grain of mustard-seed, might say to the sycamine tree or to the mountain, Be removed ; and it shall be done. He does not mean that we may call upon the supernatural power of God to do our own pleasure, and, by means ot a magical, miracle-working faith, can remove all things in the sphere of earthly nature which appear to thwart us, and to arrange all things as we wish. How little do such ideas accord with the humble and pious mode of thought of Jesus, which was directed, not to earthly, but to heavenly ends, and how little with His own mode of action ! But He has made it unmistakeably clear that no reason can exist, either in the greatness of the blessings sought, or the greatness of the apparently necessary outward means, or the greatness of the external difficulties that lie in the way, for our not obtaining what is trustfully asked of God, since to the Divine power, which faith appeals to, all things are subservient. Of the universal correlation of natural phenomena, and the calculable regularity of their sequence throughout the whole order of nature, Jesus had as little idea as His contemporaries.[1] But for this very reason it could not occur to Him to suppose the effective power of trust in God limited by natural law. We should proceed very unhistorically were we to explain away out of the view of Jesus the idea that man can effect and experience miracles through trust in God. He had undoubtedly the consciousness of having, through trust in God, obtained and imparted wonderful Divine help in manifold circumstances and for manifold purposes of His earthly mission. But He has looked for the same kind and the like power of faith in others. And we need not say that in His view the trust of others ought to be directly placed in Himself, the Messiah, and in His peculiar miraculous power. He welcomed such a trust in Himself, so far as it did not proceed from a mere love of external miracles, but from the general trust in regard to the saving grace of God's kingdom as proclaimed by Him,—a trust which was therefore directed to Him as the proclaimer and bringer of that Divine saving grace. He highly commended the faith of that heathen centurion who thought he had no need to beg that Jesus should personally come and heal his son, since the higher healing power obtained through the intervention of Jesus must be miraculously effective even by a word (Matt. viii. 5–13; Luke vii. 2–10).[2] Similarly in the case of the woman with

---

[1] Cf. above, p. 168.

[2] Cf. *Log.* § 3, *L.J.* i. p. 70ff. The usual way of explaining the greatness of the faith which Jesus commended in the case of that heathen centurion, is to regard it as consisting in his having believed Jesus capable,

the issue of blood, who in natural shame would not speak of her trouble, and was yet confident that without speaking to Him she was able to obtain healing from Him; and, in the case of the blind man near Jericho, who implored the Nazarene by the title of "Son of David" to have mercy on him, Jesus made mention of their faith as the ground of their being made whole (Mark v. 34; x. 52). But He by no means regarded this relation of trust in Himself and His intervention as essential : He rather virtually taught and directed, in the first place, that the faith which is sufficient for all things, even for removing mountains,—a faith which all could and should have,

not only of a miraculous influence upon those immediately present, but also of working miracles at a distance. This explanation presupposes that all the healing power which Jesus exercised, and which men sought from Him, was manifestly of a purely miraculous kind. This supposition has certainly already found its way into our Gospel narratives. But, in the oldest sources, there are many indications that this is not altogether correct, and that we must rather suppose that the healing activity of Jesus was primarily a philanthropic ministry of love to the sick which He consciously carried on in dependence on Divine help, but which only in certain circumstances amounted to miraculous agency. The conflicts which Jesus had with the Pharisees, in regard to His works of healing on the Sabbath, would have been quite inexplicable if the help He gave to the sick had been purely miraculous, and most plainly show that His method of healing had the external aspect of a helpful medical process, when it could be represented by the Pharisees as a work unlawful to be done on the Sabbath (cf. *Log.* §§ 19 and 22, *L. J.* i. pp. 128 and 138). Our narrative, also, of the heathen centurion, as recorded in the Logia, indicates indirectly this character of the ordinary healing art exercised by Jesus. When Jesus promised the centurion, who had acquainted Him with the sickness of his son, that He would come and heal him (θεραπεύειν, Matt. viii. 7), He did not express His intention of bringing miraculous, but medical, help. The greatness of the centurion's faith, therefore, consisted in the fact of his trusting, *not merely in the medical, but the miraculous*, ability of Jesus in healing. Nor was this miraculous ability, in the view of the centurion, a merely physical one belonging to and exercised by Jesus, but one which depended on higher powers which stood at His command, and which could be called into exercise merely at will or with a word.

—must be immediately directed to God (Mark ix. 23 ; xi. 22 f.). He rebuked His disciples for their little faith, when they could not, without His aid, help the father who besought them on behalf of his son, since they did not consider that trustful prayer to God is the one all-powerful means of bringing help in such cases (Mark ix. 19, 23, 28 f.). He rebuked them on the occasion of the storm on the lake, because, full of despair and the fear of death, they awoke Him from sleep, when they ought to have known that they were in God's safe-keeping, and should have depended on God's help for victory over the menacing elements: "Why are ye so fearful? how is it that ye have no faith?" (Mark iv. 37–40). It is an arbitrary, unjustifiable limitation of the general idea of "faith," or "trust," here used by Jesus, to explain that He here blames His disciples for their want of faith in His Messiahship or His Divine mission, since they should have been certain that, through their connection with Him, the Messiah and Sent One of God, they were secure from the shipwreck which was threatening them. Of His Messiahship, His disciples at that time knew nothing, since Jesus as yet designedly abstained from announcing to them His unique Messianic significance. But trust in God, which Jesus, as a prophet sent from God, taught them to cherish, they not only ought to possess, so far as they found themselves externally in relationship with Him, but so far as they knew themselves to be under the protection of the heavenly Father, without whose will no sparrow falls to the ground, and by whom even the hairs of the head are all numbered

(Matt. x. 29-31). We may certainly say that the word of reproof, "Why are ye so fearful? how is it ye have no faith?" would have applied to the disciples had their courage failed in the storm even in the absence of Jesus.

8. We have to establish this positive aspect of the faith taught by Jesus (that it must be directed *to God* in an unrestricted way), by bringing out a very significant point of difference between it and the Jewish view then prevalent. We find with Jesus no trace of the idea that the spirit of devout trust must address itself to the angels, or that it could suffer any limitation on account of the agency of demons. We must consider what importance the idea of the agency of the angels and demons had for the popular piety of the Jews of that period, and how it arose among them from the tendency to conceive the idea of God in the most abstract and transcendental form, so that the idea of the number and potent influence of angelic beings ever increased and appeared more necessary, in order to mediate between that God who was absolutely exalted above the world, and who stood in essential opposition to all that is material and transient. We must remember, also, how the heightened ideas of the extent and power of the dominion of evil spirits led to a practically dualistic conception of the world, and that individual Jews stood in constant superstitious fear of the inevitable and arbitrary, malicious and hurtful influence of these diabolical powers. Thus we shall be able to measure the importance and grandeur of this point in the teaching of Jesus, that He has allowed neither the idea of

angels nor of devils to exercise influence on the
devout trust of men. We ought not, in discussing
the teaching of Jesus, to lay stress on the fact that
He adopted the Jewish ideas of the existence of
angels and their activity in the service of God; but
we must above all emphasise the fact that, all through,
He found no support for faith in the thought of
angels, far less did He allow trust in angels to take
the place of trust in God. His trust and that of His
disciples was to be directed immediately and solely
towards God, whom He did not conceive as dwelling at
the utmost distance from the world, but as the Father
whose love furnishes the living impulse towards beneficent agency and care on behalf of His creatures.
In a similar way He has divested the Jewish idea of
demons of its importance, which was detrimental to
faith. We of the present day, to whom that whole
idea of the influence of demoniacal spirits on human
life, and of their special relation to certain forms of
disease, has become so foreign, are apt to treat too
summarily the thought that Jesus held the current
ideas as to the existence and agency of demons.
What is peculiarly significant and instructive, however, is not that idea in itself, as He simply adopted
it from His contemporaries, but rather the fact that
it did not tend with Him, as in their case, to superstitious fear and cowardice in regard to the supposed
evil spirits. He associated that idea with the absolute
certainty of having, by Divine power, such mastery
over those evil spirits that they must hearken and
yield to Him and cease to do injury. Jesus set aside
the practical dualism to which the Jewish demonology

led.   He did not merely entertain the hope that in the future, at the end of the world, the dominion of Satan would be overcome by the kingdom of God; but He was assured that, even then, Satan was being completely hurled from his place of power, and that He, Jesus, was that Stronger One who was able to overcome Satan, the strong man armed, and spoil him of his possessions (Mark iii. 27).   In this assurance He sought, and with success, to bring Divine help to the demoniacs whom He met; and, conscious of victorious power, commanded the evil spirit with a voice of authority.   He has regarded this power of ruling over evil spirits as similarly belonging to all His disciples (Luke x. 18 ff.).   For that certainty of this power was but the reverse side of trust in the love and power of God which He required in unlimited measure in all His disciples.

9. Through thus considering the relation in which Jesus' doctrine of trust in God stood to the Jewish views as to angels and demons, we are led on to the question how far we are to recognise in the strongly emphasised command of absolute trust in God a new and peculiar feature in the teaching of Jesus.   Our remembrance of so many beautiful expressions of fearless trust in God, in the Psalms, makes us at first inclined to regard that trust, as Jesus taught it, as an expression of piety quite current among the Jews of His time, and readily intelligible by them.   And so Jesus Himself has exhibited His command to trust in God, not as a new commandment, which, like His precept to found righteousness only in the heart, and His injunction to love even one's enemies, was

to be set over against an earlier and opposing command. But however much the Psalms, as a portion of Holy Scripture, possessed an authoritative value for the religious consciousness of the Jews, we cannot at all conclude that the piety of the contemporaries of Jesus corresponded exactly to that expressed in the Psalms. We must bear in mind how much the piety of later Judaism was influenced, not only by the already strongly-marked tendency to conceive the holiness of God as consisting in an abstract aloofness from the world, but especially by the tendency to regard the religious relation of individuals to God as a legal one, in which service and reward strictly corresponded. By this prevalent attitude of Jewish piety, the note of simple joyous confidence in the Divine mercy and faithfulness, which is heard in the Psalms, is overborne by the tone of anxious legalism and of self-righteous and mercenary pretentiousness towards God, or even, in the case of the deeper and more earnest characters, by a timorous, unrestful fear of the righteous judgment of God.

We must estimate the significance of this exhortation of Jesus to trust in God, by its opposition to that "spirit of bondage" (Rom. viii. 15), tending to fear, which prevailed in Jewish piety. By that exhortation Jesus struck once more a note which rang clearly in the classic period of Israelitish piety, but had afterwards grown dumb; and we can well understand that the encouragement He gave for trusting the heavenly Father, and His assurance of the boundless power and unlimited results yielded by such a trust, as well as His own example of a faith which recoiled before no duty and no danger, but undertook the seemingly impossible with courage and confidence of victory, made a mighty and marvellous impression upon those who were moved with continual apprehension on account of all possible known and unknown offences against the holiness of God, and thought they could expect no grace or blessing from God unless they had first earned a title to it by meritorious service. Whilst, however, we bring out the real affinity existing between the trust in God taught by Jesus and that expressed in the book of Psalms, which was its early prototype, we must directly add that the trust taught by Jesus was, nevertheless, fuller and more absolute than the latter. He founded it on a higher and purer conception of the love of God and of the salvation provided by God for men, than that possessed by the Old Testament saints. In the Psalms, expressions of joyous trust alternate with expressions of sad despondency, with complaints and questions as to why God's face was turned away when the devout were in earthly troubles and oppression, and especially when they were in danger of death, after which no more experience of the Divine favour was to be expected. Such a degree of trust as is expressed in those words of the psalm, "Nevertheless I am continually with Thee; Thou hast holden my right hand. Thou shalt guide me by Thy counsel, and afterward receive me to glory. If I have Thee, I ask nothing more in heaven or in earth; when my heart and my flesh fail, God is still the strength of my heart, and my portion" (Ps. lxxiii. 23 ff.), is, however, even in the Psalms, a singular phenomenon; since, for such absoluteness of trust, the general religious view of the Old Testament saints did not yet furnish all the prerequisites. But those requirements were present in the religious view of Jesus.

10. In the consciousness of Jesus trust in God and prayer were essentially connected ideas (cf. the relation of these conceptions to one another in the passages, Mark ix. 23, 29, and xi. 22–25). For trust in God finds its natural expression in the words of prayer directed to God ; and, conversely, prayer should always and altogether be founded on trust. Jesus repudiates the idea that the power and prevalence of prayer depend at all on external excellences : "When ye pray, do not babble as the heathen do; for they think they shall be heard for their much speaking" (Matt. vi. 7 ; cf. Mark xii. 40). So also He declares that united prayer does not depend for success on the number of worshippers : when two, that is, the smallest possible number for a meeting, agree in petition, their prayer shall be granted (Matt. xviii. 19 f.). But He teaches that what gives value and efficiency to the prayer is the trust of the worshipper. From the parable of the man who acceded to the request of his friend for bread, even when that request was presented at the most unseasonable time and in the most unfavourable circumstances, and who granted the prayer, not because the suppliant was his friend, but above all, because of the persistency of his suit (Luke xi. 5–8), and from the lesson drawn from it, how it is impossible for an earthly father, though being evil, to give his children worthless and hurtful things instead of the good things asked from

him, Jesus sought to encourage His disciples to address their prayers trustfully to their heavenly Father (Luke xi. 9–13; Matt. vii. 7–11). We need not here repeat in what sense or under what conditions, necessitated by the idea of true pious trust, Jesus promised a certain fulfilment of the prayer of His disciples.[1] Unceasingly, day and night, must they pray to be kept before the judgment of God shall come upon the ungodly and impenitent at the end of the world, and to attain the eternal salvation which shall then be consummated for God's chosen ones (Luke xxi. 36 and xviii. 2–8);[2] for this ultimate salvation must form the goal to be continually and absolutely aimed at by devout faith. How all prayer for earthly goods and preservation from earthly evils must, on the other hand, be expressed, Jesus shows by the example of His own prayer in Gethsemane: "Abba, Father, all things are possible unto Thee; take this cup from me : nevertheless not as I will, but as Thou wilt" (Mark xiv. 36). Jesus has full assurance of the fatherly character and almighty power of God, who alone knows what is best for the purpose of His kingdom and for the glorifying of His Son. Hence He derives from His humble, trustful submission to the supreme will of God, a sufficient motive for making His prayer for preservation from the greatest trials conditional.

[1] Cf. above, pp. 233 f. and 290.

[2] In regard to the connection of the passage, Luke xviii. 1–8, with the foregoing utterance on the Second Coming, xvii. 22 ff., and in regard to the special reference thus given to the admonition to continual prayer, xviii. 1 ff., and further, in regard to the apparent relationship of the passage, Luke xxi. 34–36, to the Logia-fragments, given Luke xvii. 22–xviii. 8, cf. *Log.* § 33*c* and *d*, *L. J.* i. p. 162 ff.

When Jesus was asked by one of His disciples to teach them to pray, as John also had taught his disciples, He set plainly forth the manner and matter of true prayer by giving them an example of it. He puts this pattern prayer in the simplest and concisest form, in opposition to the voluble style of heathen prayers. But few as are its words, this wonderfully comprehensive prayer expresses the sum and substance of all the petitions which a fully trustful disciple of Jesus is prompted to express in prayer. The original scope of this prayer, as recorded in the Logia - source, is certainly given more faithfully in Luke's redaction, though the more extended form given in Matthew deserves the preference in certain particulars.[1] The original tenor of the prayer seems to have been the following : Father! Hallowed be Thy name! Thy kingdom come! Give us this day our appertaining[2] bread! And forgive us our debts

---

[1] Cf. *Log.* § 11*a*, *L. J.* i. p. 97 t.

[2] By this expression " appertaining," I seek to render the Greek word ἐπιούσιος, whose general sense, from the connection, scarcely admits of doubt. Its etymological derivation, however, will probably never be decided with perfect certainty. The derivation from ἡ ἐπιοῦσα, scil. ἡμέρα, " appointed for the following day," must, in my view, on account of its inappropriate sense, be ruled out of court. The derivation from ἐπί and οὐσία, with the signification, " requisite for existence or life," I hold to be possible, since H. Cremer (*Bibl.-theol. Dictionary of N.T. Greek*, 4th German edition, 1885, p. 344 f.) has adduced proof that οὐσία can, as matter of fact, bear the signification " existence." But I confess that, with Kamphausen (*The Lord's Prayer*, 1886, p. 97 ff.) and others, I regard as the most probable the derivation (given by Leo Mayer in Kuhn's *Zeitschrift für vergleichende Sprachforschung*, vii. 401 ff.) from ἐπί and the participial stem ὀντ, with the signification " being to "=" pertaining to," after the analogy of περιούσιος = " being over "— *i.e.* superfluous. Though Leo Mayer has recently (in the *Report of the Royal Scientific Society at Göttingen*, 1886, p. 245 ff.) retracted this opinion, since in it the idea of life or livelihood, to which the relative idea " pertaining " refers, must be mentally supplied, I cannot regard this reason as valid.

as we have forgiven our debtors! And lead us not into temptation!

As we have already treated the main ideas of the invocation and the particular positions of this prayer in the account we took of the conceptions of God and salvation in the teaching of Jesus, it remains for us here only to consider the arrangement and scope of the prayer as a whole.

The usual division of the Lord's Prayer into two parts, the first of which has direct reference to the things of God, whilst the second expresses desires relating directly to one's own welfare, does not appear to me quite justified. The words, "Hallowed be Thy name!" appear to my mind to have the closest connection with the invocation "Father!" With the same meaning and motive, they form a supplement

For, on the one hand, it is clear, in view of the connection of the notion "pertaining to" with the notion "bread," that the former has the closest relation to the support of life, for which bread comes into account as a means; just as in the complex idea, "superfluous bread," it is self-evident that the notion of *superfluity* stands related in thought to the support of life, and that one's need of the means of life furnishes the measure of the superfluity. On the other hand, I find in the very fact that this relation to the support of earthly life is not expressly mentioned, a peculiar and intentional delicacy of thought and expression. For thereby the proviso is left open which holds good for all prayers of Jesus' disciples, viz. that their quest of earthly goods must be subordinate to their quest of the kingdom of God. Though the need of earthly livelihood is the natural and ordinary standard according to which the bread appertaining is measured, yet for the consciousness of Jesus and His disciples it is not the ultimate and highest standard. The earthly bread must subserve the earthly life so far as the latter has as its object the attaining of eternal and heavenly life. Therefore, the prayer of the disciples must be for the bread "appertaining" in general —*i.e.* the bread which in God's view corresponds to their need and is helpful to their higher welfare. Certainly Jesus has in this sense adopted the expression לֶחֶם חֻקִּי of Prov. xxx. 8, which was rendered by the Greek-speaking Christians, in full accordance with the tenor of the words, by ἄρτος ἐπιούσιος.

to that invocation, just as the appeal to the Father in Mark xiv. 36 is supplemented by the words, "All things are possible unto Thee," and in the words of the prayer, Matt. xi. 25, by the apposition, "Lord of heaven and earth." The worshipper who invokes God under the name of Father, and realises the gracious, beneficent love of God, must at the same time remember and recognise God's glorious majesty, which is neither annulled nor impaired, but rather intensified supremely, through His fatherly love. An appeal to God as Father, if not associated with reverent homage before the Divine Majesty, would betray a want of understanding of the character of God. The importance of a due expression of the idea of God in the invocation, lies in the fact that it contains the motive prompting the petitions which follow. The nature of the contents of the prayers in Mark xiv. 36 and Matt. xi. 25 made it necessary for Jesus to lay special stress on the almighty power as well as the Fatherhood of God ; but, in the prayer which He sets before His disciples as an example, He has, in accordance with the general character of the contents of the prayer, reverently acknowledged, in the most comprehensive terms, the high superiority of God above the world as well as His Fatherhood. If the Fatherhood of God involves the motive to a childlike trust which turns towards Him, expecting the fulfilment of its desires and the vouchsafement of all blessing, the acknowledgment of God's hallowed name which follows prompts the worshipper to cherish no wishes incompatible with humble submission to the Divine will, and not to offer requests for mere earthly goods,

but for such as are in harmony with the holy nature
of God. The reference to the hallowing of God's
name is not made in the form of a simple statement,
such as "Father, *whose name is holy or to be hallowed*,"
but in the form of a wish. The reason of this is that
the worshipper regards the hallowing of God's name
as a personal duty which he dare not say he fulfils or
will fulfil, but rather that he wishes it fulfilled. In
this form of a wish the words are made to correspond
in form with those of the petitions which follow. But
along with this correspondence in form, there is this
difference, that the proper petitionary part of the
prayer begins afterwards, whilst this wish, "Hallowed
be Thy name!" belongs rather to the introductory
invocation.

After the disciple has thus, in the invocation and
its appendix, compendiously expressed the true idea
of God, which is also the basis of the true idea of
salvation and of trust, a petition follows for that
good which must form the highest goal of the
Christian's aspirations, and which involves in its
answer the obtaining of the highest welfare, viz.
Thy kingdom come. Certainly the coming of the
kingdom is also the ultimate object of God's own
will; and the believer, in thus praying, takes for
granted that God's purpose tends to that end. But
we ought not on that account to separate this petition
from the following ones for bread, for forgiveness of
sins, and for deliverance from temptation, as if the
former was in a special way prompted by zeal for the
interests of God's cause, while the latter were directed
to man's own welfare. The worshipper prays for the

coming of the kingdom as insuring all well-being for him in a way which accords with the Divine will, just as he knows that he expresses the good pleasure of God in addressing petitions for daily bread, forgiveness of sins, and preservation from temptation. God's interests and the real interests of the believing worshipper are regarded as coinciding; but in prayer the worshipper asks those benefits for his own sake, though with a regard to the will of God.

The prayer for the coming of God's kingdom is not, however, co-ordinate in significance with the three following petitions. The latter are subordinate to the former, although in the very simple form of the prayer this real subordination is not specially expressed. By a twice-occurring "and" the three following petitions are set in close relationship. They are directed towards the special blessings which may be hoped for by the believer, who aspires after the kingdom of God. He can ask for the portion of bread for the day, but not for long earthly life and riches, as if these held out a blessedness worthy of the Christian's aim. Yet he may ask for the means of maintaining the earthly life for the space of time in which God grants it, and certainly for the *portion* of earthly livelihood which in God's judgment is requisite for present sustenance, and which is most useful for him in relation to the eternal life to which the present life is subordinated.[1] And then, as being humbly conscious of demerit and of positive and oft-repeated offence against God's holy will, whereby he has estranged himself from God's fellowship, and yet as

[1] Cf. the observations on p. 302 f.

being desirous of remaining in health-giving fellowship with God, he should pray for the forgiveness of
his sins. But also with reference to the future he
should cherish the desire and purpose of fulfilling
God's will in sincere obedience; and, deeply sensible
of his own weakness, that wish and resolve should be
expressed in the prayer, *Lead us not into temptation.*
This means that he may not be placed in such dangerous situations of life, and have such difficult tasks set
before him, as his own feeble strength will be insufficient to cope with. Not that he must pray for
easy circumstances which will spare him true conflict
against temptation, and earnest striving after good;
but he must, in humility becoming in a suppliant,
realise that he is unfit successfully to accomplish his
tasks, and be victorious in the conflicts, unless God
defend and help him.

In this account of the order of thought in the Lord's
Prayer one portion is still left out of account, which
might easily appear unimportant and unnecessary,
and hence, in view of the pregnant brevity of the rest
of the contents of the prayer, somewhat strange : we
refer to the addition to the prayer for forgiveness of
sins : *as we have forgiven our debtors.* Certainly this
analogy of his own forgiveness is not brought in by
the suppliant to indicate the measure of Divine forgiveness which he craves, but only that he may not
appear so unworthy of the Divine mercy. But why
then, it may be asked, must such an analogy be
alluded to in this prayer, whose tone seems better to
accord with a humble, trustful petition for unmerited
forgiveness? Without doubt, nothing was further

from the purpose of Jesus than to prompt a self-com-
placent side-glance at the worshipper's own righteousness, which had been shown in the peculiarly difficult
duty of forgiving another's offences. How thoroughly
Jesus disallowed all self-righteous thought in prayer,
is plainly taught by the example of warning given by
Him in the case of the self-righteous Pharisee, and of
the conscience-stricken publican, who only begged for
Divine mercy, and who alone of the two found acceptance with God (Luke xviii. 10–14). He has certainly
not sought to represent the relation of man's forgiving
love towards others to God's sin-pardoning grace, as
if the latter was wholly conditioned by the former,
and was not rather its primary source and constraining power. Jesus' own view of that relation, and His
object in appending the additional words to the
petition for forgiveness of sins, can be inferred from
His parable of the forgiven but unforgiving servant,
who was delivered over to punishment by his lord.
From that parable Jesus drew the conclusion: "So
shall also my heavenly Father do to you, if ye
forgive not every one his brother from the heart"
(Matt. xviii. 23–35; cf. Mark xi. 25). In the boundless pardoning grace of God, in which all His disciples
have a share, lies the constraining motive to the duty
of forgiving their brethren. If they do not fulfil this
duty, they thereby render themselves unworthy of the
grace they have received, and God will allow them
no further part in it. What Jesus inculcates by those
appended words, is the necessity of remembering in
prayer the duty of forgiving love, not in order to
merit Divine grace by the fulfilment of that duty, but

in order not to forfeit by its neglect the grace of
God, which they always need, and to which they
appeal in their very petition for forgiveness of
sins. All who would enjoy and retain the blessing
of God must earnestly seek to fulfil the will of
God. But whosoever cherishes feelings of hatred
and revenge against his brother cannot have God's
love and forgiveness. Hence in prayer the heart
must be free from all hateful and resentful thoughts
and impulses. If he has hitherto borne hatred
and enmity against his fellow-men who have wronged
and injured him, this violation of his own duty towards them (that is, in regard to forgiveness) forms
part of the debt for which the suppliant must ask
God's forgiveness. But he cannot get remission of
this debt, or of the other sins of daily life, until he has
eradicated[1] the last remnant of hatred and enmity
from his heart. This consciousness of a duty which
is bound up with true prayer, must in Jesus' view be
expressed in that addition to the prayer for forgiveness of sins.

11. The sole *direct forms of devout deportment*
towards God to which Jesus in general exhorted His
disciples, and of which He emphasised the necessity,
are trust and prayer out of a trustful heart. Certainly
He by no means rejected external ceremonies and
forms of the devout life altogether. He has rather

---

[1] If the perfect ἀφήκαμεν, which Matthew (vi. 12) gives, be understood
in this way, it is clear that it agrees in meaning with the present
ἀφίομεν in Luke (xi. 4). The perfect must not be taken as meaning that
the worshipper looks back on acts of forgiving love which he has done
within a longer or shorter period of his previous life, but that even now
in prayer, he so fully forgives all who have done him wrong, that he can
regard this forgiveness as a definitive transaction.

taken for granted that His disciples would take part in these, even as He Himself did. Yet these forms had a very different significance for His religious consciousness than they had for the Jews, and therefore He did not, like the Jews, make them objects of special instruction and admonition. What attitude He adopted towards the whole system of Jewish Levitical purifications we have considered in earlier passages (cf. p. 281 ff.). His great principle, that God takes account only of the state of men's hearts as the measure of righteousness and purity, led Him of necessity mainly to deny the worth of those ceremonial observances which had their *raison d'être* in the supposed incompatibility of the holiness of God with certain forms and conditions of matter.

In regard to the *ascetic exercises* which the Pharisees and Essenes, and even John the Baptist and his disciples, so highly esteemed and cultivated as special proofs of earnest piety, Jesus recognised only a limited value and conditional rightness. His own mode of life and that of His disciples was not ascetic. He could contrast Himself in this respect with John the Baptist, who "came neither eating nor drinking," while "the Son of man came eating and drinking" (Matt. xi. 18 f.). He certainly did not altogether forbid fasting; but He only recognised it as justifiable in a time of sorrow and as a real expression of inward grief. In this sense He answered the question of the disciples of John the Baptist and the Pharisees as to why His disciples did not join in the traditional practice of fasting, when He gave them the parable of the children of the bride-chamber, who could not fast so long as they had the bridegroom with them, but who would certainly fast when the bridegroom was taken from them (Mark ii. 18–20). He here takes up quite different ground as to the value of fasting from that of the Pharisees and John the Baptist's disciples. These prized fasting, not only as the expression of a sad spirit, and commanded it not only as a right observance when circumstances required that godly sorrow should be manifested, but they required fasting in itself as mere external abstinence from earthly enjoyment as a work of pious merit, whose frequent exercise would render God specially propitious. But Jesus did not recognise such acts of mere external piety.

In regard to the *conduct of worship*, Jesus has declared Himself in an analogous way. This, according to Jewish law, referred partly to keeping holy the Sabbath, and partly to participation in the temple services at Jerusalem. On the one hand, He has in general presupposed the permissibility of those legal forms and rites of worship (Matt. v. 23 f. ; cf. also xxiii. 19–22), and in particular cases He even expressly enjoined their observance (Mark i. 44 ; cf. Matt. xvii. 27). On the other hand, no special stress was laid throughout His teaching on mere formal expressions of piety. Neither were these an object of special interest to Himself, nor did He seek to engage His disciples' interest in them. We must gauge the significance of this negative fact by this positive one, that, for the religious consciousness of the Jews, the forms of worship had an importance of the first rank, and that, in the teaching of the Jewish scribes, the determination of particular cases in the matter of Sabbath observance and the traditions of the whole overgrown system of binding observances, were a subject of pre-eminent interest.

The absence of this interest on the part of Jesus, which must have appeared very strange to His country-men, finds, however, its elucidation in some of His recorded expressions, in which He has intimated His view of the true nature and basis of religious cere-monies. First of all, it is recorded that when He cleansed the temple He made an appeal to the words of Scripture : " My house shall be called a house of prayer for all peoples " (Mark xi. 17). Here we must not be contented with merely remarking that this declaration as to the temple being a house of prayer was made by Jesus in special reference to Isa. lvi. 7, and was introduced by Him as no new idea, but as one well known to and accepted by the Jews. Much rather we must dwell on the significance of the fact that, from among the abundance of Old Testament declarations and precepts in regard to worship, Jesus selected this prophetical utterance and made it the standard for judging the temple-service, in opposition to the inferior conception which prevails throughout the foundation and details of the whole legal system of the Pentateuch, as well as the teaching of the later Jewish scribes. Certainly it was no strange idea for the Jews to set prayer and oblation in a relation of analogy to each other. But it was a very different thing for the Jews to regard the offering as the primary thing, whilst allowing prayer, "the offering of the lips," to stand in place of the offering proper, in cases where it was impossible to bring this to the legal centre of worship and sacrifice at the temple ; and for Jesus, in connection with the prophetic saying, to make prayer the primary idea, and to regard the whole system of temple service, according to its meaning and purpose, to be an expression and form of prayer. This latter mode of view is the spiritual one, corresponding to the purely spiritual nature of God ; and its consequence is that a relative value for the worship of God can be attributed to the external offerings only in so far as they may be the expression, form, and means of true worship. As a supplement to this significant utterance of Jesus, we have the words with which He defended His disciples when they were accused by the Pharisees of unlawful conduct in plucking the ears of corn (Mark ii. 23 ff.). He first reminded them that David also, when he was in need, had, along with his companions, eaten of the shew-bread, which was allowed only to the priests. This act of David, who was a recognised representative of Old Testament piety, was sufficient to show that the prescribed ritual did not lay down an absolutely impassable limit to the devout (ver. 25 f. ; cf. Matt. xii. 5, where the legitimate activity of the priests on Sabbath was given as a proof that the duty of abstaining from work on Sabbath was not absolute). He then, however, brought in a principle which positively establishes the meaning and purpose of the Sabbath ordinance, and at the same time indicates the ground and measure of its observance : " The Sabbath was made for man, and not man for the

Sabbath" (ver. 27). He hereby taught that the existence and value of the Divine ordinance of a seventh-day rest did not lie in any superiority of that day over other days, or in abstinence from work being in itself pleasing to God, so that, in all circumstances, men must be under servitude to its strict observance. But He held that the Sabbath is appointed by God for the service of man, as a means for his benefit, certainly not for any self-indulgent and ungodly end, but for ends which are in accordance with God's will and man's true welfare. Such a purpose for which the Sabbath was made subservient, must be recognised in the worship of God, which requires a special time for assembling, and for rest and special opportunities for its common performance. Jesus Himself having, in the foregoing words, judged the question in regard to the right of infringing the Sabbath-ordinance, by bringing forward the analogy of a case of lawful infringement of another ritual ordinance, in the same sense we may extend this positive declaration of His, as to the purpose and value of the Sabbath, into a judgment in regard to the purpose and value of external ritual observances in general. None of these have been appointed for their own sake, as if God desired men unconditionally to employ certain outward forms of homage. They were all appointed for man's sake, in order to be forms, means, and aids to what constitutes the peculiar and chief end of his being, and which tends to his highest good, viz. for the service of God in the fulfilment of His will.

From this view Jesus must have derived a conscious inner freedom in regard to ceremonial acts and

ordinances which the Jews did not possess.   "The
Son of man is Lord also of the Sabbath," is the conclusion which He Himself drew from that principle in
regard to the purpose of the Sabbath (Mark ii. 28).
In conformity with that consciousness of freedom,
Jesus also, when the temple-tribute was demanded of
Him, propounded the question to Peter: "From
whom do the kings of the earth take custom or
tribute? from their children, or from strangers?"   And
on Peter's answering, "From strangers," He added,
"Then are the children free" (Matt. xvii. 25 f.).   He
did not feel Himself and His disciples inwardly bound
by the legal ritual of the Jews, nor obliged to maintain
and establish that ritual, since He well knew that on the
whole it expressed only a servile attitude towards God,
and not a position of sonship towards the heavenly
Father.   He has payed that temple-tax, "in order to
give no cause of offence" (ver. 27), as well as otherwise connecting Himself and His disciples with the
existing ritual.   But yet He preserved His conscious
inner freedom in regard to these ordinances, and His
sovereign right to use them for His purpose.   He
did not put Himself in a position of bondage to
them, but wherever, in given circumstances, they were
hindrances to His purpose of rightly fulfilling the will
of God, He set them aside.   That He regarded the
showing of merciful love as a duty superior to ceremonial performances, and as therefore authorising and
demanding the eventual discontinuance of these, we
shall afterwards have special occasion to show.   Thus
He has recognised the lawfulness of infringing upon
the Sabbath rest, in favour of acts of mercy and love,

without avoiding the offence for which He thereby gave occasion in the view of the scribes and Pharisees. He met the reproach of the Pharisees that He violated the Sabbath law, by pointing out the hypocrisy of their zeal for the Sabbath, in that they who angrily rejected as impious the giving of help to their fellow-men on Sabbath, did not avoid giving similar help to their cattle when it concerned their own interests (Luke xiii. 10-17; xiv. 1-6). He also gave a new turn to the whole question in regard to what is lawful on Sabbath, and led up to the right solution, which only a hardened conscience could fail to admit, by thus formulating that question : " Is it lawful to do good on the Sabbath, or to do evil ? to save life, or to kill ? " (Mark iii. 4). From the Jewish-Pharisaical point of view the former question sounded quite differently, viz.—Is it lawful to do work of a certain external magnitude on Sabbath ; and how great may it be and still be lawful on Sabbath ? But Jesus has not admitted this mode of stating the question. Not according to external magnitude, but according to its moral quality, must, in the view of Jesus, the rightness or wrongness of an act, its permissibility or non-permissibility, be measured. A mode of conduct which is in conformity with God's will, and truly helpful to men, is always to be followed, even on Sabbath ; and its omission on Sabbath is unlawful and evil.

We can now sum up shortly our discussion, carried out on the basis of the Matthew-Logia and the Gospel of Mark, as to the right conduct, which, according to Jesus, must be shown in direct intercourse with God.

Jesus has enjoyed *(ined)* an inward love, which, in accordance with God's supreme position as the Father,
must exhibit unconditional trust in respect of His
gracious gifts; He has prescribed a prayer to God,
which must proceed wholly from trust in Him; He
has allowed the validity of ceremonial and ritual acts
and observances, in so far as these can and will be
forms and means of true worship ; but He has denied
them any validity and worth in themselves, and He
has recognised His own power of setting them aside
with perfect inner freedom, so far as He found them
incompatible with such acts of pious conduct as His
knowledge of the fatherly will of God showed to be
His duty in regard to men.

---

12. This result of our inquiry upon this point will
in no single point be altered, if we take into consideration the teaching and exhortations contained in the
Johannine discourses. Since the same conception of
God prevails in these as in the synoptical discourses
of Jesus, so also the devout mode of conduct towards
God, which must be deemed suited to the nature of
God Himself, is harmoniously depicted in both. In
the first place, we call to mind how the farewell discourses of Jesus to His disciples are pervaded with
exhortations to trust in God and prayer. In view of
the impending catastrophe which the disciples do not
yet anticipate, but which Jesus clearly foresees, and in
view of the coming period when the disciples should
be left alone to the hatred and persecution of the
world, which they would experience like their Master
before them, Jesus exhorts them not to let them-

selves be afraid or faint-hearted, but to trust in God
(xiv. 1, 27 ; xvi. 33). Certainly He did not give
them ground to expect an earthly well-being and
deliverance, but He gave them the assurance that
He would prepare for them heavenly mansions
(xiv. 2 f.), and would send them His Spirit as their
advocate to teach and stand by them in their conflicts
with the world (xiv. 16 f., 26 ; xvi. 7 ff.). And so,
too, He exhorts them to prayer in His name, *i.e.* to
such prayer as they could present in His name as His
disciples, and also with a view to the salvation proclaimed by Him, and He promises them an answer
from God, " that your joy may be full " (xiv. 13 f. ;
xv. 16 ; xvi. 23 f.). He certainly calls upon them
here to trust in Himself as well as in God (xiv. 1, 12),
and to address prayer to Himself (xiv. 13 f.). This
corresponds to that Messianic and mediatorial dignity
which is claimed by Jesus throughout these Johannine
discourses, and which we may make the subject of
consideration later. That this mediation as Messiah
is at all events not meant in a sense implying any
lessening of direct trust in God, is made clear by those
words from this very discourse : " In that day ye
shall ask in my name : and I say not unto you, that I
will pray the Father for you ; for the Father Himself
loveth you " (xvi. 26 f.). To the certainty of the
love ot God corresponds a direct faith to be placed
in God.

Such an expression of this trust in God specially as
applied to the worldly calling and to the dangers
which threaten men in the pursuit of their calling, is
contained in the parable, with which, according to the

Johannine source, Jesus answered the disciples, when, at the announcement of the sickness of Lazarus, He was about to repair to Judæa, and the disciples tried to keep Him back because the Jews had sought to stone Him: "Are there not twelve hours in the day? If a man walk in the day, he stumbleth not, because he seeth the light of this world. But if a man walk in the night, he stumbleth, because the light is not in him" (xi. 9 f.). The meaning of this parable is, that whoever is engaged at his God-appointed task can suffer no harm in its fulfilment until the measure of it appointed by God has been accomplished, since he is protected by the safe-conduct of God; whilst he who is occupied apart from his God-appointed sphere must suffer harm, since he is not under Divine protection.[1]

[1] This parabolic saying must not be taken in an allegorising way, by making the day-time equivalent to the *period* of one's vocation. No satisfactory sense is thus obtained. For Jesus certainly did not lay down the principle without further conditions, that, so long as the period of a man's vocation lasts, he cannot stumble, *i.e.* cannot suffer harm or failure. Only if the man, during the period of his vocation, is occupied with the *work* of his vocation, can he trust to be insured against such stumbling. But it would be quite meaningless to say that the man, in walking beyond the period of his vocation, that is, after his earthly life, which, however, is equivalent to the whole period of his vocation, would stumble. It is necessary to apply the figure to the *work* of his vocation. Certainly in this interpretation there is this point of dissimilarity between the circumstances related in the parable and those to which we apply it, that the man's employment outside of the sphere of his vocation cannot take place *after* the completion of the work of his calling, as walking in the night takes place after the day-time; but it is the conduct of one who, in the time which ought to be devoted to the duties of his calling, shirks these duties, that is compared to walking in the night. This dissimilarity cannot cause difficulty, how-ever, if we bear in mind that, in all the parables of Jesus, it is not a question of allegorical interpretation, but of a *tertium comparationis*. In our interpretation also the preliminary question of Jesus, "Are there not twelve hours in the day?" is not without meaning. He seeks thereby to bring out that, as the day-time has a certain length, during

This declaration in regard to trust in God, Jesus used in the present instance in reference to Himself; yet it has also a general applicability for all men. This saying furnishes a peculiar and valuable supplement and commentary for the general exhortations to unconditional trust given elsewhere by Jesus, as well as for the promises of the certain obtaining of all blessings trustfully sought and prayed for. We refer specially to the condition presupposed by Jesus, that the man "walk in the day" and "have the light in him;" that is, he must, in all his purposes and acts, be engaged in the sphere marked out for him by God, and let himself be enlightened by the Divine will revealed to him.

Also in regard to the Jewish forms of worship, we find in the Johannine discourses certain sayings of Jesus, which quite confirm and supplement the other Gospel reports concerning His views on this point. We have first to notice that saying to the Samaritan woman, who wanted His opinion as to whether Jerusalem or Gerizim was the right place for the worship of God: "Woman, believe me, the hour cometh, when ye shall neither in this mountain, nor in Jerusalem, worship the Father. . . . The hour cometh, and now is, when the true worshippers shall worship the Father in spirit and in truth: for the Father seeketh such worshippers. God is spirit; and they that worship Him must worship Him in spirit and in truth" (iv. 21 and 23 f.). From the spiritual nature of God,

---

which a man can reckon upon the light and not stumble, so also the work of his calling has its God-appointed measure, which, under Divine protection, he can trust to be able to fulfil.

and the spirituality which accordingly must constitute the true essence of Divine worship, Jesus infers that true worship cannot be confined to one spot either exclusively or by preference. He expresses the assurance that in the new period, which had been already inaugurated by His proclamation of the kingdom of God, the full knowledge of God would do away with the narrow forms of worship to which the Jewish mind attributed an absolute and unchanging value. Here we have a magnificent expression of the same clear recognition of the fact that external acts and ordinances of worship have no value in themselves, and He, as founder of the kingdom of God, had freedom and sovereignty in regard to such forms of worship, which is decidedly expressed in those synoptical sayings in regard to the temple being meant for a house of prayer, and that the Son of man was Lord even of the Sabbath. And as Jesus, according to the synoptical accounts, practically showed His conscious freedom in regard to those external ceremonial ordinances, in that He had, in the exercise of active charity, broken in upon that Sabbath - rest which the Pharisees deemed so inviolable; so in the Johannine source a similar manifestation of freedom on the part of Jesus has been recorded, and that in conjunction with such special words of self-justification as coincide with the main line of defence, which, according to the synoptical accounts, He used in regard to His healing on the Sabbath (v. 1–17 ; vii. 15–24).[1]

[1] In regard to the original connection of the passage, John vii. 15–24, with the Sabbath-healing and the discourse in chap. v., and in regard

Jesus declared that, as His Father, in spite of the Sabbath-rest on which He entered at the completion of His works of creation, was still working up to that present hour, so He also, the Son, likewise worked (v. 17). His view of the Divine character afforded for Him the standard of what is right and God-pleasing : from it He derived His own principle of duty, and by it He criticised the traditional legalism. Assured that God does not keep far aloof from the world, but maintains relations of continuous loving agency in human affairs, He concluded that active benevolence on Sabbath well befitted a son of God. The Jewish idea, that work as such, or practical activity in the world, was something profane, received no support from His conception of God. He only took into account if His Sabbath activity, which in its general character as work was not wrong, were also in its special kind such as harmonised with the work and will of God. As by the question, Mark iii. 4, He led up to the principle that to do good and to save life on Sabbath must be lawful and necessary ; so here, in this Johannine passage, He sees in the benevolent character of His work a valid reason for its being done on Sabbath. Even the Mosaic law, by permitting circumcision to be performed on Sabbath, shows that the command to rest on that day was not absolute and in all circumstances binding, but admits exceptions in the case of work conducive to man's welfare ; how then should not this work,

to the original form which must have been borne by the narrative of the Sabbath-healing, v. 1–16, in order rightly to account for the words of Jesus, v. 17 and vii. 21 ff., cf. *L. J.* i. pp. 228 ff. and 266 f.

which has not merely tended to the purification of one bodily member, but has healed the whole man, be deemed by a righteous judgment, which judges not according to appearance, be lawful and right on Sabbath? (vii. 22–24).

Finally, we may refer to that saying of Jesus, recorded by the Johannine source, as given to the Jews who sought a sign to prove His authority for purifying the temple : "Destroy this temple, and in three days I will raise it up" (ii. 19). Here the lofty consciousness of the reformer found expression. He saw, on the one hand, how all reality in the legal worship represented in the temple was being destroyed by the hierarchy themselves, who ought to have been guardians of the true worship of God, but had degraded the house of God into a market-place (ver. 16). On the other hand, He felt in Himself the power to create and establish, after the briefest interval, a new form of worship.[1] But how far Jesus regarded this new temple which He was to set up as being, not wholly different from the old, but rather as a restoration of it, is a question to be discussed afterwards, when we consider more precisely the relation in which Jesus viewed His doctrine as standing to the Old Testament.

---

13. At the close of this section we may glance shortly at the influence upon the apostolic Church of this wonderful teaching of Jesus, so harmoniously

[1] That this is the real meaning of the saying, and that the signification attached to it by the evangelist (ver. 21) does not truly correspond to the verbal form and meaning of the saying, cf. *L. J.* i. p. 251 f.

attested by the evangelists, in regard to the true
nature of the worship of God. Stephen, the first
martyr of the Christian Church, had been accused of
having said that "this Jesus of Nazareth would
destroy this place (the temple), and change the
customs which Moses had given" (Acts vi. 14); and
he himself, in his extant apology, sought, by an
appeal to history, to justify the sayings of which he
was accused. He showed that, in point of fact, the
temple at Jerusalem was not necessarily or always
the seat of God's graciously manifested presence.[1]
In the position thus taken up by Stephen, we find a
direct trace of the powerful influence exercised on the
company of the disciples by the attitude of freedom
in regard to the Jewish ritual maintained by Jesus.
Even where the disciples in general continued to take
part in the prescribed forms and ordinances of the
Jewish worship, just as Jesus Himself had done,
they still had a more or less clear consciousness
(founded expressly on certain sayings of Jesus, and
still more deeply upon the whole conception of God
taught by Him) that those ordinances and rites were
not absolutely and for ever binding, but that the
community of His disciples would sooner or later
break loose from them. This is not the place to
inquire to what extent we can find traces of this
consciousness on the part of the early apostles.
We may only say that, when Paul went somewhat
later among the heathen as the apostle of assured
faith in God, first in relation to His pardoning grace,

---

[1] Cf., in regard to this meaning of Stephen's apology, my work, in
Meyer's Commentary, "on the Acts of the Apostles," at chap. vii. 2.

and next to the gracious management of the whole
life by God and the supply of all needed blessings,
and when he dissociated this faith from legal rites
and ceremonies, he did not thereby bring any new
element into Christianity. He only thereby adopted
and applied the ideas which Jesus, with marvellous
clearness, recognised as true, and as destined to be
carried into practical effect in the future.

C.—*The Right Conduct towards Men.*

14. In His answer to the question, " Which is the
first of all the commandments ? " Jesus, with the
precept of supreme love to God, connects this other :
" Thou shalt love thy neighbour as thyself" (Mark
xii. 31). What was new and significant in this
answer lay in the addition of this second commandment, which seemed uncalled for by the question—a
command which is not found in the Mosaic legislation
in the same connection with the former, and which
stood at no such high level in the consciousness of
the Jews. Jesus, however, wished emphatically to
bring out the close and essential connection of the
two commands, and to repudiate the idea of a merely
subordinate significance of the Divine command in
regard to our conduct to our fellow-men. Certainly
He did not mean that those two connected commands
of love to God and our neighbour merely stood at
the top of a series of commandments, the others of
which had an independent though inferior significance.
On the contrary, He regarded those two commands
as a compendium of the *whole* law of God. They

were first, because they were the most comprehensive, and formed the essence and kernel of all the others, which were but deductions from them. Thus the answer of Jesus conveyed a very characteristic correction of the stating of the question. The question had been prompted by the zeal of the scribes to ascertain which among the multitude of commands was the one which demanded the precedence in the matter of obedience. But Jesus replied by pointing out a double commandment, which in its universality gives a summary of the whole law. And He required that this whole law should be fulfilled.

We can estimate the value set by Jesus upon the command to love our neighbour as being an essential and imperative duty, from its opposition to the prevailing tendency in Pharisaic Judaism to set aside moral duties towards one's fellow-men.[1] To the spirit of externalism, these latter duties, though resting on commands of God, appear nothing more than a service done to men; whilst those ritual and ceremonial observances, which are regarded as constituting the immediate service of God, must as such take the foremost place. This tenet of the scribes and Pharisees has repeatedly been denounced by Jesus. He reproached them for neglecting the command of God in favour of their own self-devised traditions, in regarding ritual acts as of higher value than the fulfilment of filial duties to parents; for they taught that it is more meritorious to give as an offering to the temple, the sum that ought to be appropriated to the support of parents, than to bestow it as a practical

[1] Cf. above, p. 45 f.

proof of filial piety (Mark vii. 9–13).   He also charged
them with cleaning the outside of the cup and platter,
whilst the inside of these vessels teemed with extortion
and excess (Matt. xxiii. 25).   In other words, they
precisely observed, in preparing their food, the ceremonial rules for preserving their Levitical purity ; but
they did not avoid the moral defilement caused by
the unlawful acquisition of that food, and by using it
to minister to intemperance.[1]   Moreover, they tithed
mint and dill and cummin, and with the utmost strictness paid the taxes for the temple service; but the
weightier matters of the law, judgment and mercy and
faith, they left undone, thus straining out the gnat
and swallowing the camel (Matt. xxiii. 23 f.).   Jesus
regarded the moral obligations due to one's fellow-men

---

[1] In my view, we cannot say with Weiss (*Matthew's Gospel*, p. 493),
that by ἀκρασία we can only understand immoderation in the acquisition
of food (or gain) by violating the rights of others.   For then the ἀκρασία
would not be really distinct from the ἁρπαγή, whilst a really new and
important idea is brought in if immoderation in the *use* of the food, as
well as dishonesty in its acquisition, is expressed.   So far as the filling
of the vessels was caused by the preconceived purpose of immoderate
eating, the fulness of the vessels might well be said to have proceeded
from excess.   That the very contents of the dishes were spoken of as
defiled through extortion and excess, and as being the object of necessary
purification by the removal of that immorality (v. 26), is, of course, only
a figurative form of expression brought in to make this moral purity or
impurity quite analogous formally to that ceremonial purity or impurity
which was represented as adhering to the food.   That which is really
capable of defilement and of purity, in the view of Jesus, is the human heart
(cf. Mark vii. 20–23).   The saying of Jesus, Matt. xxiii. 26, "Ye blind
Pharisees, cleanse first the inside of the cup and platter, that the outside
thereof may become clean also," must be understood as meaning that
the putting away of immoderation in the acquisition and use of food
would serve to make the external ceremonial cleansing really appropriate.   He does not mean that the inward purifying made the
ceremonial cleansing superfluous ; for the use of πρῶτον along with
καθάρισον is opposed to this.   On the other hand, we must not, in our
interpretation, leave out of account the relation of the one purification to
the other as means to end.

as not at all inferior in rank and value to ritual and ceremonial observances, but, on the contrary, as more weighty and urgent. For He knew, on the one hand, that external, ritual, and ceremonial forms and observances had only a conditional value in the service of God, who is spirit, and are neither valuable nor essential for their own sakes. He knew, on the other hand, that active love to men corresponds directly with the character and will of the heavenly Father. Therefore He declared that active benevolence is greater than formal worship, according to the word of God in the prophet (Hos. vi. 6), "I will have mercy and not sacrifice" (Matt. xii. 6 f.);[1] and He enjoined that men should practically give the precedence to the fulfilment of duties of charity over ceremonial acts (Matt. v. 23 f.). What He considered higher than love to one's neighbour was not external worship, but inward love to God expressed in genuine trust and prayer. But that inward attitude towards God cannot, like the external ritual, come into any conflict with the divinely - required duty of love to men. The scribe whose question Jesus answered, perfectly well understood that the close connection of the command to love our neighbour with the first commandment concerning love to God, was intended by Jesus in a sense opposed to the precedence of ritual and ceremonial duties. His intelligent, assenting answer, that love to God and our neighbour was indeed more than all burnt-offering and sacrifice, Jesus received with the approving words: "Thou art not far

---

[1] On the original connection and meaning of this passage of the Logia, cf. my treatise on the *Log.* § 43, *L. J.* i. p. 177 f.

from the kingdom of God!" (Mark xii. 33 f.). We see from this how weighty and characteristic for the right comprehension of the kingdom of God Jesus Himself considered this point of His teaching, viz. His view that the moral relation of love to men is to be estimated as fulfilling a Divine command, higher than all ritual and legal laws. He was conscious that this point of His doctrine stood in direct and mutual relationship to that view of the nature of God which He recognised as true, and as determining the character of the kingdom of God.

15. In God's fatherly love Jesus found the inward constraining motive for man's love to his fellow-men. Since God Himself is full of goodwill to men, He is pleased with their love to one another; and this love forms an essential *trait* in the character of a true child of the heavenly Father. But the nature and intensity of God's love to men is also the standard of the love required of them towards one another. Since God, father-like, exercises spontaneous forgiving love, men are likewise bound to love, not merely those from whom they themselves receive or expect good, but to love freely and forgivingly even strangers and enemies. Jesus has clearly expressed this order of thought in His great discourse concerning righteousness in pronouncing upon that primary command, "Thou shalt love thy neighbour," to which scribal tradition had added, "And thou shalt hate thine enemy." Jesus says, on the contrary, "Love your enemies, and pray for your persecutors; that ye may be sons of your Father in heaven: for He causeth His sun to rise on the evil and on the good, and His

rain to fall on the just and the unjust" (Matt. v. 43–45). He has indicated the same line of thought in the parable of the servant to whom his lord out of pity forgave the great debt of ten thousand talents, but who, on his own part, would show no pity to his fellow by freeing him from his trifling debt (Matt. xviii. 23–25). Whoever, in his need of forgiving mercy, has sought and obtained it for himself, and so has experienced its value, must feel inwardly bound to show a like love to others according to his ability. That servant in the parable must have known that his want of mercy towards his fellow-servant was contrary to the mind and will of his lord, whose mercy he had implored and found. Gratitude for mercy experienced must have given him an impulse to exercise a like merciful disposition. Thus, according to Jesus, a man's remembrance of the infinite mercy of God shown to him must oblige and impel him to manifest a like spirit of spontaneous forgiving love towards his fellows.

Jesus thus taught man's love to his fellow-men as a supreme religious motive, — a motive which binds men to the greatest spontaneous love, as to an absolute duty, even where earthly relations and duties do not exist or are unjustly dissolved. Here we must recognise the characteristic and epoch - making pre-eminence of the teaching of Jesus on the ethical side over all previous expositions and demonstrations of the duty of love, either of the Old Testament or of all heathen religions and philosophies. It is not quite right to make the essence of this ethical advance of Jesus beyond the Old Testament and Jewish stand-

point consist in this, that whereas the latter applied
the command of love to one's neighbour exclusively
to the Jewish nationality and religion, Jesus has
given that command a quite universal application.
Certainly we are justified in inferring, from the nature
and intensity of the duty of love as Jesus taught
it, that it has a universal tendency.   But Jesus
has Himself only indirectly intimated this inference.
He has directly set forth and expounded only the
general duty of a love to others which is not conditioned and limited by acts of kindness already experienced or hoped for at the hands of others ; and
He has practically applied this duty, in the first place,
to the private intercourse of the Jews with their
countrymen and co-religionists.   The form of argument which Jesus appended to His precept of love
to one's neighbour and against hatred to enemies,
"Love your enemies," etc., shows clearly that He
was thinking, first of all, of the kindly love shown in
private intercourse : "For if ye love them that love
you, what reward have ye?" (that is, what value
has such a disposition, and therefore what recompense does God recognise as due to you for it?)
"do not even the publicans the same?   And if ye
salute your brethren only, what do ye more than
others ? do not even the Gentiles the same?" (Matt.
v. 46 f.).   "And if ye lend to them of whom ye hope
to receive, what thank " (what Divine favour) " have
ye ?   Sinners also lend to sinners, to receive as much
in turn" (Luke vi. 34).

The duty of spontaneous and merciful kindness
towards Israelites and towards the strangers dwell-

ing in the land, and the duty of forgiving love towards private foes, was not foreign even to the Old Testament Jewish consciousness, as will be evident from many expressions of the Old Testament (cf. *e.g.* Ex. xxiii. 4 f., 9 ff. ; Lev. xix. 9 f., 18, 33 f. ; Deut. x. 18 f. ; xv. 7-11 ; xxiv. 17 ff. ; Ps. vii. 5; xli. 2; Job xxxi. 16–22, 29–32; Prov. xx. 22; xxiv. 29 ; xxv. 21 f. ; Isa. lviii. 6 ff. ; Zech. vii. 9 f.). The ground of the originality and significance of the teaching of Jesus on this point, did not lie in His giving the command of love an application and extension hitherto unknown. Indeed, not only those Old Testament expressions in regard to widows and orphans, strangers and even enemies, but even utterances of heathen philosophers regarding universal human love, could be adduced to prove that in this respect the teaching of Jesus was not original. But the newness and importance of this teaching of Jesus lies in the fact that He has *established on a firm religious basis* this command of love, and specially of spontaneous, forgiving love, so that this duty has attained an essential place in the moral consciousness of men. His teaching in regard to love is related to that of the Old Testament, just as His doctrine of trust in God, as we have already seen, is related to that of the Old Testament. As we find in the Old Testament, alongside of many beautiful expressions of trust in God, many others expressive of mistrust, which are not in accordance with the exhortations of Jesus to unconditional trust, and as we necessarily attribute this to the fact that the Old Testament conception of the character and saving grace of

God does not yet furnish a complete basis for a continual unlimited trust in Him; even so we find, along with many Old Testament exhortations to mercy and love and forbearance, a great number of expressions of revenge towards enemies. Nor are such expressions by any means only directed against the enemies of the nation and religion of Israel. They were even made a matter of prayer to God, with no consciousness on the part of the suppliant that he was entertaining a disposition contrary to the Divine will—a clear proof that the Old Testament view of God did not furnish the motive for such absolute love even to enemies as was taught by Jesus. It will not do to say that the authors of the vindictive psalms did not themselves take vengeance upon their enemies, but only prayed to God to do so; for this would not alter the case according to the judgment of Jesus. He required that the heart should be free from hatred, and full of good-will towards others; and therefore He enjoined prayer on behalf of one's persecutors (Matt. v. 44). Such a prayer is in direct opposition to the prayers for vengeance and destruction upon enemies. We must thus conclude that the Old Testament and Judaistic consciousness lacked the capacity to appreciate spontaneous forgiving love, not merely as a noble and meritorious act required by God, but as an *inwardly constraining duty*. It is a very different thing for a man to show kindness to an enemy in order to heap coals of fire on his head, that is, to make him blush for shame (Prov. xxv. 21 f.), from his forgiving and benefiting an enemy, because the neglect of this duty would make him ashamed of himself. To the moral consciousness the paradoxical judgment is by no means immediately evident, that a disposition to purely spontaneous forgiving love is unconditionally binding upon man, the neglect of which involves guilt. This sense of duty can only be awakened through our relation to God, and specially to God's unmerited forgiving love to ourselves as well as others. For that servant to whom his lord had cancelled the great debt, the cancelling of the small debt of his fellow - servant was no longer an act of wonderful magnanimity, but a self-evident moral duty. Here, then, is a feature truly great and new in the teaching of Jesus, that, in His preaching of the fatherly love of God, whose boundless beneficence is the source of being and of well-being for mankind, He has established the consciousness of inward obligation to gratuitous forgiving love without any limit, as it can only be based on this conception of God.

16. If, according to the meaning and phraseology of Jesus, we answered the question, *To whom* a disciple of His is bound to show love, we must reply, To a *brother*. Already, from the foregoing discussion, it is clear that the idea of neighbour, being too narrow, is inapplicable. Certainly, in answering the question as to the first of all the commandments, Jesus names the neighbour as the one to whom, along with God, love is to be shown (Mark xii. 31). But there, from the very statement of the question, Jesus required to point to a command formally given in the law of the Old Testament; and

the reason why the command (Lev. xix. 18) appeared specially appropriate to be cited, lay in the fact that in it the point was brought out that a man must love others with the same intensity as himself. But then the question, Who were the others that ought thus to be loved? could not, from that Old Testament saying, find an answer expressive of the conception of Jesus. His saying in the discourse on Righteousness, in which He expressly contrasted the old command to love our neighbour with His higher command to love our enemies (Matt. v. 43 ff.), leaves no doubt as to this point.

We are wont to regard the parable of the Good Samaritan as teaching that, in the view of Jesus, the neighbour was not merely a member of the Israelitish nation and religion, but also every stranger who needed loving assistance. But this conclusion does not exactly correspond to the idea of Jesus, expressed in His concluding question, "Which of those three, thinkest thou, has become neighbour to him who fell among the robbers?" to which the answer was returned, "He who showed mercy on him" (Luke x. 36 f.). No doubt when the scribe had asked, "Who is my neighbour?" and had expected that Jesus, unless He put Himself in open contradiction to the Old Testament mode of view, would recognise the Israelite as the neighbour, Jesus, in that parable of the Good Samaritan, manifestly intended to force the scribe to admit that the idea of neighbour could not be narrowed down to that of Israelite. On being told how an Israelite in dire distress was mercilessly neglected by the priest and Levite,—special representatives of his nation and his religion,—but disinterestedly helped by the passing Samaritan, the scribe had to admit that, in this case, the Samaritan who charitably took the part of the distressed Israelite had become the neighbour of the latter, and that the Jewish priest and Levite, who had neglected their compatriot and co-religionist, stood farther from him than the Samaritan. And if the question were asked to whom that succoured Israelite was bound to show neighbourly love, he could not confine it to his own countrymen, but ought to set the friendly Samaritan in the front rank of those to whom he owed this duty. In this argument, Jesus, in connection with the term "neighbour," had seized upon the common and obvious notion of *standing near*, in opposition to that of *one standing far apart* and *stranger*. But, in opposition to the narrow Jewish view, He showed that, without respect to nationality, practical benevolence found a neighbourly relation of moral duties, and that the Old Testament precept of love to one's neighbour must eventually include non-Israelites. But even this extension of the idea of love to one's neighbour falls short of the application given by Jesus to the general duty of love. Not only the neighbours with whom we are allied, and from whom we receive kindness, are to be the objects of that love, but also the stranger who does not salute us, and the enemy who inflicts injury upon us. We should show love like that of the merciful Samaritan to the Israelite, who was not yet his neighbour, but a stranger; that is, a spontaneous love, which forms new ties, and turns the stranger into the neighbour, thus creating a mutual relation involving further duties.[1]

The particular conception under which Jesus viewed the person who was the object of this love, which was a binding duty for the disciples, He designated by the term *brother* (Matt. v. 22–24 ; vii. 3–5 ; xviii. 15, 21 f., 35 ; xxiii. 8). That conception is used in the wide sense, derived from the relation to God as the Father of men. In conformity with this relation, Jesus says to His disciples : " Be ye not called Rabbi : for one is your Master ; and all ye are brethren. And call no man father on the earth : for one is your Father " (Matt. xxiii. 8 f.). Jesus has nowhere in His recorded utterances expressly given a universality of extent to this idea of brother. Yet we can say decidedly that it would quite as little correspond to His view to limit the use of this idea to fellow-members of the kingdom of God, as to limit the term neighbour, as the Jews did, to members of the Jewish nationality and religion (cf. Lev. xix. 16–18). But, according to the view of Jesus, all are brethren who have God as their

[1] The parable of the Good Samaritan is therefore quite warrantably used in the pulpit as affording a pattern of Christian charity, as Luke himself has done by his closing words : " Go and do thou likewise" (ver. 37). For such disinterested charity to a total stranger must be the special object of Christian teaching and admonition, whilst the question as to the extent of the idea of neighbour has no longer the same piquancy for the Christian as it had for those Jewish scribes in the time of Jesus. Nevertheless, in our purely exegetical-historical exposition and use of this parable, we may point out that it did not concern Jesus in the given circumstances to set up the Samaritan as the pattern of true charity ; but His object was to create such a situation as would make it obvious to the scribe how one who was not an Israelite might become neighbour to an Israelite. Cf. on *Log.* § 9, *L. J.* i. p. 93 ff.

Father.[1] Now, it is no doubt true that men become true sons of the heavenly Father if they fulfil His will and appropriate His character (Matt. v. 45).[2] Hence Jesus recognises as His brother, in a peculiar sense, one who does the will of God (Mark iii. 35 ; cf. Matt. xxv. 40), and also the disciples of Jesus afterwards specially regarded and called the fellow-members of the Christian community their brethren. But, on the other hand, it was true in the conscious-ness of Jesus, that God, in virtue of His gratuitous love, is Father even of those who do not walk as His children. Accordingly, the term brother is applied to men independently of whether or not they comport themselves as becomes members of God's kingdom. In the passages where Jesus forbids words and deeds of hatred to a brother, and requires rather kindly remonstrance with and forgiveness of an erring brother, we must by no means restrict the application of the term brother to co-members of the kingdom of God. No privilege was reserved by Him of showing an unselfish and revengeful, an implacable and unloving spirit towards others. The reason why Jesus here uses the term brother is rather because it supplies a

[1] Whilst the idea of brother in its peculiar sense denotes one sprung from the same earthly parents as another, it can also be applied in a wider sense to denote kinship as to family and race. When Jesus uses the idea in this sense, He can include the kindness shown to the brother in the love shown to the neighbour, which He distinguishes from the love to be shown even to an enemy (Matt. v. 47). But it by no means follows that with Jesus the ideas of "brother" and "neighbour" are identical. In cases where He did not use the idea of brother in the peculiar natural sense (as, *e.g.*, Mark x. 29 f. ; xiii. 12 ; Luke xiv. 12, 26), He applies it to the spiritual relation to the heavenly Father ; and in this sense it includes, not only the neighbour, but the stranger and the foe.

[2] Cf. above, p. 192.

motive for the love which is commanded.   As when
He exhorts to unconditional trust in God under the
name of Father, this term supplies a motive for that
trust; so in exhorting to a love which forgives and
rewards evil with good, the term brother which He
employs contains the motive to that love.   For the
brother stands in such close relationship to the brother,
that unbounded love and goodwill to him is always a
natural duty.   But the brotherhood meant by Jesus
as the motive for love rests, not on a common earthly,
but on a common Divine parentage, and has its spring
in the love of God.

17. Jesus gives neither a definition of the love
which is to be shown towards others, nor a systematic
exposition of the different ways in which it must be
manifested.   But, from the various particular injunctions and admonitions given on different occasions,
we can derive a clear idea of how He conceived that
loving disposition in general, as well as in its particular manifestations.

First of all, as the opposite of that love, He forbade
the hatred and anger which wish harm and ruin to
others, even though unexpressed in act, and only
harboured in the secret thought, or uttered in abusive
and disparaging words (Matt. v. 22).   On the other
hand, He warned His hearers against a selfish wish
for exalting themselves above others, even when
that wish is not shown in a harsh, overriding, and
overreaching of others, but in the more refined
form of vain ambition of the regard and approbation
of men, and the desire for precedence, titles, and
honour from men (Mark xii. 38 f. ; Matt. xxiii. 5 ff.).

Instead of this, He exhorted His disciples to humble themselves and to serve others. When they had a strife as to which should be accounted the greatest, He said to them : " If any one would become the chief among you, let him be last of all, and servant of all " (Mark ix. 35). " Ye know that they which are accounted to rule over the Gentiles lord it over them ; and their great ones exercise authority over them. But it shall not be so among you : but whosoever would become great among you, shall be your minister ; and whosoever would be first among you, let him become servant of all. For verily the Son of man came not to be ministered unto, but to minister, and to give His life a ransom for many" (Mark x. 42– 45 ; cf. Matt. xxiii. 11). According to the Logia accounts, He handed the cup to His disciples at the last Supper to give them an example of service, add- ing this word of exhortation : " He that is greater among you, let him be as the younger; and he that is chief, as he that doth serve. For which is the greater, he that sitteth at meat, or he that serveth ? is not he that sitteth at meat ? But I am among you as he that serveth " (Luke xxii. 26 f.).[1] That para- doxical statement, so often verified in ordinary life, that whosoever exalteth himself shall be abased, and whoso humbleth himself shall be exalted, was to form a rule for His disciples, who should have regard to it in their aims and actions (Luke xiv. 7–11 ; Matt. xxiii. 12). His design in all these declarations is not to inculcate self-abasing service upon His disciples merely as a means in order to future exaltation,

---

[1] Cf. *Log.* § 39*b*, *L.J.* i. p. 172 f.

sought as an equivalent and reward for their humiliation. But they had to view the self-abasing service
as constituting in itself their peculiar greatness.
Certainly this is not greatness according to external
human standards of judgment; but it is true greatness
in God's estimation, which shall be manifested in the
future life (cf. Luke xvi. 15 and 19 ff.), in allotting
men's further destiny according to their true worth,
and in apportioning heavenly bliss to the worthy.
This declaration, that the greatness of the disciples
consists in lowly service, and that the first among
them was he that should perform most service, is
made by Jesus because He sees in lowly, self-abasing
service the specific righteousness of conduct belonging to the kingdom of God. For this self-abasing
ministry is identical with love to others. When Jesus
exhorts to self-abasement and service of others, He
does not mean it as a mode of conduct which goes
along with love, but as a periphrasis of the love itself.
He emphasises that bent of will and mode of conduct
which constitute the peculiar nature of genuine love.
That is, a man must not think of himself, of his
own importance, aggrandisement, and enrichment,
but must rather work on behalf of others for their
welfare, and be helpful to them by self-sacrifice and
self-renunciation.[1]

He does not mean a mere ascetic self-abasement
practised for its own sake and not in order to any

---

[1] We should specially note that this self-abasing service is not the
exact equivalent of humility. Humility is the conscious lowliness we
feel before God in view of His superabundant love and holy majesty, and
in contrast to our own unworthiness, guilt, and entire dependence on His
grace (cf. the exhortations of Jesus to such humility, Luke xvii. 10;

good purpose, but the self-denial practised in the service of other men. Nor does He mean a service consisting in outward subjection to others, or in outward obedience to their wishes and commands, but a ready helpfulness shown in assisting others and promoting their interests with one's own means and resources. For He Himself practised such self-forgetful service, and purposely set it before His disciples as an example to be imitated by them (Mark x. 45).

This self-denying, ministering love is manifested in gifts, in benevolence and friendliness shown to others, and not merely towards those who are or who may become our benefactors. "It is more blessed to **give** than to receive," is the saying of Jesus, of which Paul, at Miletus, as recorded in Acts xx. 35, reminded the Ephesian elders. "Give to him that asketh thee; and from him that borroweth, turn not thou away," Jesus enjoins in Matt. v. 42; but not in the sense that one ought to fulfil all the wishes of others, however absurd and hurtful they might be. Still less does He imply that all requests made to us by some one should be granted without regard to the duties of kindness owed by us to others; for so to grant those requests would violate the true spirit of love. He really implies that one ought not to refuse a boon desired of us by another merely in order to have the benefit of it one's self. Rather we ought to be ready to gratify with our own means the expressed wishes and

---

xviii. 9–14; Matt. xi. 29). This humility towards God is to be thoroughly distinguished from self-renunciation in our dealings with men. That humility before God certainly includes the motive binding us to helpful love to men, whereby, in dutiful obedience, we fulfil the Divine will; but the former is not identical with this lowly service.

wants of another in a self-denying spirit. But a
love ready to serve others will not only try to meet
the wishes and wants which are actually expressed,
but, thoughtfully sympathetic and quick to interpret,
from the analogy of one's own experience, the needs
and desires of others, it will seek to gratify even
the unuttered requests of others. This is what
Jesus meant when He gave the rule: "All things
whatsoever ye would that men should do unto you,
do ye even so unto them" (Matt. vii. 12).[1] What a
contrast is presented by this saying to the common
rule, so like it in external form, not to do for another
what could not be done for us by another! This
negative command is thoroughly compatible with a
selfish, niggardly inactivity; whilst the command of
Jesus contains the principle of the most extensive
and spontaneous activity of love towards others.
That love should disinterestedly render good even
to those who cannot repay, Jesus teaches in the
words: "When thou makest a dinner or a supper,
call not thy friends, nor thy brethren, nor thy kins-
men, nor rich neighbours; lest haply they also bid
thee again, and a recompense be made thee. But
when thou makest a feast, bid the poor, the maimed,
the halt, and the blind: and thou shalt be blessed;
because they have not wherewith to recompense thee:
for thou shalt be recompensed in the resurrection of
the just" (Luke xiv. 12-14). This precept in regard
to the bestowal of hospitable entertainment is, of

---

[1] In regard to the original connection (attested by Luke vi. 30 f.)
between this saying of Jesus and the precept to give to him that asketh,
as opposed to the separation of the two in Matt. vii. 12, cf. on *Log.*
§ 2*f*, *L. J.* i. p. 61 f,

course, an illustrative application of a general rule, which Jesus desires clearly to enforce. But it is not merely in bestowal of external benefits to others that Jesus enjoins disinterested kindness, nor does He estimate the value of love by the external amount of the service rendered to another. Embracing under the conception of love to others also the saluting of others, the showing of respect and expressing of good wishes, He directs us not to greet only those of our acquaintances who salute us in return (Matt. v. 47). As an example of unselfish service on which He sets the highest store, He instances the receiving of a child as He Himself did, by way of illustration, in taking a child in His arms, pointing out the smallest and simplest act of benevolence which claims no special notice nor thanks (Mark ix. 36 f.).

Since Jesus taught that the supreme and proper welfare of man is eternal life in the kingdom of God, and that the supreme evil, to which no earthly evil is once to be compared, consists in the loss of eternal life through sin (Mark ix. 43–48), we can understand the severity of His warning against inciting another to sin, and the command that one should seek to restore an erring brother. The Gospel of Mark and the Logia of Matthew record in harmony that saying of Jesus, that whosoever shall cause to offend, or allure into sin, one of the least of believers that is a member of the kingdom of God, who shall become an heir of eternal life), it were better for him that a millstone were hanged about his neck, and he were drowned in the depth of the sea (Mark ix. 42 ; Luke xvii. 1 f.). To cause such a one to stumble Jesus declares to be the greatest crime, and most worthy of punishment, because He sees in it the most hurtful injury to another, and therefore the gravest dereliction of the duty of love. The guilt incurred by thus imperilling the standing in salvation of the very least member of the kingdom of God is extreme. For God, in His love, cares for the salvation of the smallest individual members of His kingdom, just as the earthly owner of a hundred sheep will not permit a single one of that large number to be lost (Matt. xviii. 10–14).[1] In regard to the sin which one person observes in another, He warns against being too ready and hypocritically zealous to put that other right whilst a greater fault remains unheeded and uncorrected in one's own case (Matt. vii. 1–5). Again, His exhortation to the endeavour, in a spirit of love, to convince an erring brother of his sin, and seek to restore him, does not clash with this warning against an unloving censoriousness which carries a fair but deceitful show of zeal for righteousness. "If thy brother sin against thee, go and show him his fault between thee and him alone : if he hear thee, thou hast gained thy brother. But if he hear thee not, take with thee one or two more, that at the mouth of two witnesses or three every word may be established" (Matt. xviii. 15 f.). The best way of putting another right is when two are alone together. The exhortation to call in two or three witnesses, in case the admonition that has been given prove ineffectual, granting it to be a genuine saying of Jesus, must certainly not be understood as meaning that, by the

[1] Cf. *Log.* § 28*b*, *L. J.* i. p. 154, and on *Log.* § 25*a*, *L. J.* i. p. 140 f.

admission of witnesses, the matter thus dealt with in the presence of disinterested men shall afterwards be regarded as rightly settled. He rather means that the corrective discipline will be placed on a firmer footing by the co-operation of those witnesses and by the testimony of several voices. Thus the effect upon him who has done the wrong will be much more weighty and impressive than if produced only by the private dealing of one person.[1]

Further, we find Jesus laying special stress in His teaching on the duty of maintaining a loving spirit in the face of wrongs inflicted upon us by another. We are to keep perfectly free from any vindictive attempt to reward evil for evil, and to be ready to forgive and to renew friendly relations with him. We must not at all be prepared for reconciliation merely when the other desists from his hostility, begs forgiveness, and offers satisfaction. We must be the first to move, and to make advances towards the renewal of friendly relations. This is the import of that illustrative case adduced by Jesus in regard to one coming into the temple with his offering, and there remembering that a brother has somewhat against him, is hostile to him either in mind or acts. The former must leave his offering behind and become reconciled to that brother (Matt. v. 23f.). This example does not merely teach that one must forego his own enmity towards another, and strive as soon as possible to obtain his forgiveness. It demands something much greater and more difficult, namely, that when enmity is displayed by

---

[1] In regard to the probable spuriousness of the words which follow in Matthew's text (xviii. 17 f.), cf. on *Log.* § 28*c*, *L. J.* i. p. 155 f.

another, we must manifest our own friendliness and disposition towards reconciliation.   Irritability, rancour, hatred must be laid aside ; and overtures of forgiveness and reconciliation must be made.   From a natural point of view such an attitude is not looked upon as a duty, because the other has not merited it ; but it would rather be regarded as an extraordinary piece of magnanimity.   But the disciples of Jesus, prompted by the obligations of brotherly love, typifying the love of the heavenly Father, must esteem that course as an urgent duty whose fulfilment must take the precedence of acts of ceremonial worship.   But not only once or twice must such forgiving love be shown to an erring brother.   Not seven times, but seventy times, or, as Luke gives it, seven times in the same day, ought one to forgive a brother who has committed an offence against us (Matt. xviii. 21 f.; Luke xvii. 3 f.).   By such a formulated command Jesus does not mean to lay down the utmost limits of the duty of forgiveness, but only to show how unweariedly we must maintain a forgiving spirit.   This exhortation to continual readiness to forgive is not neutralised or limited, by the consideration that the oft-offending brother might thus be encouraged to a careless repetition of his unpunished fault, and kept from due knowledge and repentance of it.   Certainly these considerations must affect the answer to the questions, when and how one must show his forgiveness so as not to harm, but benefit the offending person.   Yet this very regard to the other's benefit is the proof of the forgiving mind commanded by Jesus. The duty of forgiving love towards an offending brother can have no limit if its ultimate motive lies in the love of God which one has experienced for his own salvation.

Forgiving love must not confine itself to mere freedom from the vindictiveness which seeks to recompense evil with evil. It must far surpass that point, by being ready to share one's goods with an enemy, and even to exceed his wishes. This rule has most clearly been set forth by Jesus in that saying: "I say unto you, That ye resist not evil: but whosoever shall smite thee on thy right cheek, turn to him the other also. And if any man will sue thee at the law, and take away thy coat, let him have thy cloak also. And whosoever shall compel thee to go a mile, go with him twain" (Matt. v. 39–41). We have already (p. 130 ff.), in discussing the form of the teaching of Jesus, explained the method, so frequently observable in connection with precepts of this kind, of setting forth with the utmost brevity and clearness, in the examples adduced, the main thoughts to be conveyed; we have shown how, without in the least impairing the force of the precept, He abstracts all the circumstances which prevent the essential idea standing clearly out; and we can now refer to this earlier discussion. If we glance at the formally analogous direction of Jesus, to go into one's chamber for prayer, and to shut the door (Matt. vi. 6), we see from the context that this is opposed to an ostentatious worship in order to be seen of men. But plainly He does not intend to exclude public prayer of a truly reverent kind. So, in a similar way, the exhortation to show spontaneous kindness to an enemy, and that even in excess of his wishes, must be understood in contrast with the rule or natural inclination, to return evil for evil, and in reference to the object of making as emphatic as possible the injunction of beneficent love towards an enemy. But plainly this precept does not preclude self-defence, or even the punishment of another, if prompted, not by selfishness and revenge, but by sincere love to him. We would, however, divest these precepts of their peculiar significance were we to confine their application only to the perfected kingdom of God, or to our dealings with fellow-Christians who would not inflict injury from real wickedness. Nor do they refer merely to such persons as are easily brought to a better frame of mind by our forbearance and a kindness which put them to shame. It is not only in those circumstances in which forgiving love is easiest and victory over self least costly, that men must recognise the obligation of rewarding evil with good. No reservation must be made in the case of non - Christians and those not easily put to shame. Jesus absolutely prohibits selfishness and revenge in the case of injury received. He positively commands that love be shown to those who do us wrong. His exemplification is to make perfectly plain this very point, that no form of offence or injury, however great or violent, and however directly it may be aimed against our welfare, can absolve us from the duty of forgiveness and beneficent love. The only valid reservation granted by Jesus is, that the mode of showing our kindness to evil-doers must be adapted to the circumstances. To answer the unjust, extortionate demands made by another, in the simple way of correspondence shown by Jesus in His examples, is not allowed, wherever a regard for the welfare of the evil-doer, as well as for others to whom we owe duties, requires another way of proving our love. Still, the main principle aimed at by Jesus is not touched by this proviso. Jesus also enjoins prayer for persecutors as an exhibition of due love to enemies (Matt. v. 44). Where no outward act of kindness to an enemy is possible, the spirit of forgiveness can still be exercised in prayer for him.

When we glance over all the various directions given by Jesus in regard to unselfish, serving, spontaneous and forgiving love, we are filled with wonder at the elevation and consistency of His conception of love. The thought that each individual must be freely and wholly, in will and deed, at the service of others, whether they belong to one's own circle or not, and that in a disinterested way, not as merely giving reward or expecting reward in return, but with loyal devotedness—this thought cannot be more grandly and purely conceived and applied, nor can it be more firmly based in religious conscience, than has been done by Jesus. And He has presented it in the most lucid and impressive form. The particular examples of a loving behaviour which He gives are so entirely typical, that the main points enjoined by Him stand out with the utmost clearness. If we cannot always carry out in everyday life the most of these particular examples, the reason is that, for the purpose of typical form, abstraction has been made in them from all considerations which conspire in practical life to determine the

special mode of conduct. The object of Jesus was
not to show in systematic detail how love must be
manifested in every particular instance and amid the
varied and complex relations of life. His purpose
was to make popularly intelligible the true idea of
practical love; and this He has accomplished with
masterly skill, not by laying down abstract general
rules, but by special, concrete, illustrative examples.
He has done this so that the whole length and
breadth of this duty, as demanded by a knowledge
of God's fatherly love to us, is seen with unmistakeable clearness.

18. By the weighty emphasis laid by Him upon the
duty of gratuitous forgiving love, Jesus has by no
means been misled into a depreciation of duties owed
to those most nearly related to us and to those who
benefit us. He no more meant that we should fail
to meet our obligations and to maintain due fidelity
in the relations and offices incumbent upon us, than
He meant us only to render kindness to those who
love us in return. When upbraiding the Pharisees
because, in their zeal for fulfilling the *minutiæ* of
ceremonial requirements, they neglected the weightier
matters of the law, He has mentioned among those
weightier matters, not merely mercy, but righteousness and fidelity (Matt. xxiii. 23). And He has, in
express statements, applied the duty of observing
righteousness and fidelity to those bound together by
the ties of established relationships. We must have
regard to these express directions all the more,
because they essentially expand and explain those
commands of Jesus, to be afterwards considered, in

regard to the duty of His disciples severing themselves for His sake from the nearest and dearest earthly ties.

First, in regard to filial duties, these, as resting on the command of God, are declared by Jesus to be inviolable, in opposition to the Pharisees, who taught that it was an act of higher merit to give a contribution to the temple offerings than to the support of needy parents (Mark vii. 10–13). Moreover, He has most emphatically declared the absolute duty of maintaining conjugal fidelity. He judged that the guilt of conjugal infidelity is incurred, not merely where it is manifested in outward act, but whoso even looks upon a strange woman to lust after her has committed adultery with her in his heart (Matt. v. 27 f.). In view of the culpable licence allowed by the Jews to the man who, when tired of his wife, breaks the marriage bond,[1] and of the question over which the different schools of the scribes disputed, as to how great or small must be the motive justifying the divorce of a wife by her husband, Jesus solemnly declares the duty of maintaining the indissolubility of the marriage bond. When the Pharisees appealed from Him to Moses, who permitted the putting away of a wife under the form of writing a bill of divorcement (Deut. xxiv. 1), He declared that this Mosaic ordinance had been given on account of the hardness of heart of the Jews. He meant that this ordinance did not prove that a man was really entitled to put away his wife, and would be held guiltless ; it only prescribed a legally valid form of the dissolution in regard to the actual cases

---

[1] Cf. the reproach uttered by Malachi (ii. 13 ff.).

of culpable dissolution.   But the original Divine
decree in regard to marriage was the word spoken
at creation, that a man and his wife shall become
perfectly one (Mark x. 2–8).   Where the union of
husband and wife thus rests on a Divine command,
a human divorce could not be justifiable (ver. 9).
The additional declaration of Jesus, "Whoso shall
put away his wife, and marry another, committeth
adultery against her" (ver. 11), has been recorded
in the same unlimited form in the Matthew-Logia
(Matt. v. 32; Luke xvi. 18),[1] and by Paul (1 Cor.
vii. 10 f.).   Jesus teaches with unmistakeable plainness the absolute duty of maintaining intact the
conjugal bond, and that it is sinful and adulterous
if a man put away his wife because she no longer
pleases him, or because he wishes to marry another.[2]
The observance of the proper legal form in such
a case does not prevent that act of putting away
being a culpable violation of the Divine command.
But it comes to be a special question if it is also
to be held as adultery on the part of a husband,
if, in the case of his wife's violating the marriage
bond and actually severing the conjugal relation,
he then carries out the separation in its full and
final, and legally-recognised form.   To this question
the clause added by our first evangelist, to the
effect that unchastity is a valid reason for dissolving
marriage (Matt. v. 32 ; xix. 9), gives a short, though,
relatively to the full meaning of Jesus, not perfectly

---

[1] Cf. *Log.* § 2*d*, *L. J.* i. p. 59 f.

[2] The same absolute obligation holds good in the case of the wife,
as Mark, in his additional words, x. 12, has specially indicated; cf.
L. J. i. p. 40.

complete answer.[1] Jesus needed not to give an answer to this question. For, in that supposed case of unchastity on the part of the wife, the sin which Jesus declares as adultery still exists; though it lies with the other, that is, the wife. If, according to Jesus, the lustful desire after a woman involves the guilt of adultery (Matt. v. 28), how much more the act of unchastity! The exception noted by the first evangelist is no real exception to the rule which Jesus so emphatically laid down, that the obligation of marriage is absolute, and no dissolution of it is possible without incurring the guilt of adultery.

We have next to take up the statement in regard to allegiance to Cæsar, with which He answered the Pharisees and Herodians, if it were lawful, or not, to

---

[1] It would exceed the limits of our historical inquiry, which must be based on the sayings of Jesus reported in the original sources, to discuss the question here as to whether, and under what special conditions of gross and continued violation of conjugal duty on the side of the one partner, and of consequent actual severance of the marriage tie, the other is morally and religiously warranted, according to the principles laid down by Jesus, in seeking legal confirmation of the severance which has actually taken place. Is the condition of this right only given in the case of unchastity? I wish only to say that the simple, unqualified statement, that to put away a wife on the ground of unchastity is not culpable adultery, does not correspond with the meaning of Jesus. For the idea that violation of conjugal duty and severance of the marriage bond in the case of one partner does not warrant the other to consider himself quite free from all conjugal claims, has been expressed in the saying added by the Logia of Matthew, "and whoso marrieth her that is put away committeth adultery" (Matt. v. 32 ; Luke xvi. 18). This means that the wife, who has been put away without fault of her own, and through the guilt of her husband, must still keep true to the union once formed, and be ready to renew conjugal relations with her husband. If she marry another, she herself commits adultery, and also her new husband. This idea of Jesus is to be applied also to the case of infringement of marriage duty through the unchastity of one of the partners. It would, in this case, be the primary duty of the other to be ready to forgive, and to seek reconciliation and restoration of the tie that had culpably been broken.

pay tribute to the Roman emperor (Mark xii. 13 ff.). This ensnaring question was framed on the assumption that the Messianic kingdom stood in direct opposition to the heathen Roman empire, and that, in claiming to be the Messiah and the founder of the kingdom of God, Jesus must, if He carried out that claim truly and fearlessly (ver. 14), cast off the Roman yoke and refuse allegiance to the emperor. But Jesus, after pointing to the image and superscription of Cæsar on the tribute-money, laid down the rule: " Render to Cæsar the things that are Cæsar's, and to God the things that are God's " (vers. 15–17). He has not at all merely drawn the conclusion, from His assurance of the supermundane character of the kingdom of God, that the payment of tribute in the Roman empire was indifferent to the fulfilment of one's duty in the kingdom of God, and was therefore allowed; but He also, in pointing to the image and superscription of Cæsar on the coin, declared that this money belonged to the sphere of Cæsar, that Cæsar therefore had a right to it, and that payment of tribute to him was a necessary duty. He did not further disclose His view of the relation in which the fulfilment of duty to the emperor stands to the fulfilment of duty to God. He simply directs that the one duty should be fulfilled as well as the other ; and He implies that this twofold duty can be simultaneously fulfilled without the one being hindered by the other. The ultimate ground of the clearness and certainty with which He took this principle for granted, must be sought in His general certainty, that God commands men to meet their obligations to their fellow-men, paying what is due to each, and therefore to the Roman emperor. Jesus could so freely and confidently command the payment of what was due to Cæsar alongside of the payment of what was due to God, because the former was included under the latter, and stood towards it, not in a co-ordinate, but a subordinate relation.

Finally, I might here refer to the command of Jesus to the healed leper : " Go, show thyself to the priests, and offer for thy cleansing what Moses commanded for a testimony " (Mark i. 44). The leper had transgressed the ceremonial law of the Jewish community, by having pressed into the house where Jesus was (cf. ver. 43 : " Jesus forthwith sent him out ") ; therefore Jesus expressly commanded him to go and strictly fulfil those ordinances which the law prescribed to the healed leper. We need not see in this command of Jesus such an estimate of external legalism and worship as contradicted His sayings elsewhere recorded, expressive of His freedom of spirit in relation to forms and ceremonies. His command to the leper was an application of the general rule, that His disciples should not throw off obedience to their regular duties in the human relations and societies to which they belong. That the healed man should give thanks to God by bringing a legal offering, was required, not directly for the sake of God, but in respect to the rules of the national and religious community of which he was a member. In this sense Jesus gave as a reason for the command, " for a testimony unto them." Here, too, there was no incompatibility between the fulfilment of the human ordinance and the religious duty to God. The fulfilment of the former corresponded in Jesus' view to the fulfilment of the Divine command, and was therefore so far a religious duty.

———

19. On the basis of the Matthew-Logia and Mark's Gospel, we have now considered the ideas of Jesus in regard to man's conduct towards other men, as commanded by God, and as therefore belonging to the sphere of righteousness. We have seen how He has based on the fatherly love of God the duty of a purely unselfish love ever ready to help others. The boundless intensity of that love must be manifested in forgiving and kindly treating those who do us evil. At the same time, He requires that this should not be done to the detriment of any of the duties incumbent upon us from the relationships in which we stand to others. We are now in a position to institute a comparison between those ideas and the utterances of Jesus on the same theme as recorded in the Johannine discourses. Here the existing material lies in very small compass. It consists in that repeated exhortation of Jesus, given in the farewell address to His disciples, that they should love one another as He had loved them (xiii. 34; xv. 12), along with His short explanatory comment thereupon. The universal duty of love is not here applied by Him to concrete particular cases by examples, such as give vividness to the precepts of the synoptic discourses. Yet He refers them to His own example; and here also He gives them a striking practical example in illustration of the teaching He meant to convey (xiii. 12–17, 34;

xv. 12–17 ; cf. Mark ix. 36 f. ; x. 44 f.). But, in spite of the comparative shortness of the exposition, we recognise the fact that He not only here clearly indicates those points which strike us as the most characteristic features of the same precepts as recorded by the Synoptists ; but, here as well as there, the high estimate in which Jesus held obedience to those precepts is emphatically brought out.

It is noteworthy what stress is laid, in these Johannine discourses, on service as the real proof of love. It is no mere sentimental affection or inclination which is required, but a practical ministering to others. This is the meaning of the washing of the disciples' feet by Jesus, in order by this act of ministry to set them the example of washing each other's feet (xiii. 14 f.). What we stated above in regard to the synoptical commands of Jesus to His disciples to abase themselves and serve others — namely, that those commands are not to be referred to humility as a duty existing side by side with the duty of love, but to the duty of love itself, whose chief feature He meant to denote — is here verified, where the service of washing the feet is regarded as a model of unselfish trouble taken in a peculiarly lowly form in order to the good of others, and where this act of service given as an example, and the exhortation to imitate this example, form the introduction to the wider exhortation of Jesus to His disciples to love one another as He had loved them.[1]

---

[1] On the connection between the exhortation to wash each other's feet and the exhortation to love one another, xiii. 14 f. and 34 f., between which the historical passage about making known the betrayer,

Then it is important to notice how Jesus indicates
the intensity of the ministering love which He
teaches, by pointing to His own love as the example
for His disciples.   On the one hand, He refers to the
entirely devoted character of that love : " Greater love
hath no man than this, that a man lay down his life
for his friends " (xv. 13).   On the other, He points
out the *gratuitous* character of His love.   When He
calls the disciples, to whom His love was given, His
friends, He does not mean that His love for them
was that mere friendly love which depends on reci-
procation, and which is inferior in rank and value to
the love shown to strangers and enemies.   For they
were not such friends as might have drawn Him to
them, and, by communicating of their own to Him,
obliged Him to love them in return.   He had *made*
them His friends by drawing them to Himself, and
by giving them the highest He possessed : " I have
called you friends; for all things that I have heard of
my Father I have made known unto you.   Ye have
not chosen me, but I have chosen you " (xv. 15 f.).
His command, that they should practise a love of like
nature and intensity to that which He had showed
them, He calls a new commandment which He gives
them (xiii. 34).   This did not imply that the command
to love was now given absolutely for the first time,
as if there was no precept in regard to neighbourly
love in the Old Testament law.   Nor do we find it
indicated by the context that this newness of the

xiii. 21–30, is an interpolation of the evangelist, whilst the reference to
His approaching glorification merely makes the command to love one
another a farewell command, cf. *L. J.* i. p. 279 f.

commandment consists in the universal reference of Jesus' command in regard to love, as contrasted with the national limitation of the Old Testament command. But, in truth, the nature and intensity of the love which Jesus taught, and which He Himself manifested, were such as had as yet no sure basis in the Old Testament knowledge of God, and as had not yet been recognised as belonging unconditionally to the righteousness commanded by God. Therefore this commandment of love, as He had Himself practised it, could be characterised by Jesus as a new commandment (cf. Matt. v. 43 ff.).

Finally, we must notice what emphatic stress is laid, in these Johannine sayings of Jesus, on the peculiarly high significance, beyond the conception of it in the Old Testament, which is ascribed by Jesus to love in relation to the whole range of the pious life. He declares the high value which the fulfilment of this duty had for the disciples, not only by esteeming them happy if they fulfil it (xiii. 17), and by declaring that to receive His messengers with love was equivalent to receiving Himself and God (xiii. 20);[1] but also by representing this commandment of love as the only one which comprises all other precepts which He has to give His disciples, by obeying which they remain in fellowship with Him (xv. 10, 12, 17), and by indicating love as the characteristic feature whereby His disciples may be known by men (xiii. 35). In order to estimate at its true greatness the fact that Jesus did not indicate, as the

---

[1] On the original connection between vers. 17 and 20, interrupted by the disturbing interpolation of ver. 18 f., cf. L. J. i. p. 221 ff.

distinguishing mark of His disciples, a certain doctrine
of God or a certain mode of worshipping God, but
the love which they should have one to another, we
must bear in mind how strongly, in these very farewell
utterances in John, Jesus expressed His consciousness
of being the messenger and mediator of the true
knowledge of God (xiv. 6 ff. ; xvii. 3, 6 ff.)   And,
along with this, we must consider how the *worship of
God* is the natural expression of the knowledge of
God, and how the adherents of other religions and
founders of religions were known and distinguished
by the peculiar doctrine of God and mode of worship
which they followed.   No one who understands these
farewell addresses, with their accentuation of the inner
fellowship in which the disciples of Jesus ought to
stand towards God, and with their exhortations to
trust in God and to pray to Him, can suppose that,
in thus declaring brotherly love as the characteristic
mark of His disciples, Jesus meant to set the specific
religious duties in the background, as compared with
the manifestation of these moral duties towards men.
We can only explain that declaration of Jesus from
the clearness of His consciousness that the peculiar
kind of worship which corresponds to the knowledge
of God, imparted by Him to His disciples, does
not essentially and necessarily consist in external acts
of worship which can be taken note of by men ; and
also, that the exhibition of love to men of the kind
and intensity enjoined by Him, is essentially and
necessarily connected with the conception of God
proclaimed by Him, and is therefore a direct and
decisive proof of the recognition of that special con-

ception of God. This utterance of Jesus in regard
to the significance of love as the distinctive mark of
His disciples, has its proper explanation in the synoptical utterances, which attest, on the one hand, the
inner freedom in which Jesus stood towards external
forms and ordinances of worship, and His subordination of acts of outward worship to acts of love, and
which, on the other hand, lay down the knowledge of
the infinite, gracious, and forgiving love of the
heavenly Father as the foundation of the unconditional duty of gratuitous forgiving love to others.
We can say that the utterances of Jesus in regard to
the necessity of love on the part of His disciples, as
given in John, form a compendious expression of the
views and exhortations of Jesus in regard to the duty
of love which are given in the synoptical discourses.
They rest on the same principles as these latter, and
they stand at the same elevation.

20. I need not show in copious detail how the
influence of the peculiar teaching of Jesus in regard to
right conduct towards men comes clearly out in the
apostolic literature, and bears indirect witness to the
contents of the teaching of Jesus. For, all through
this special department of the New Testament, it is
most expressly recognised and commanded that love,
and specially the unselfish love that, without any
limit, spontaneously serves and forgives others, should
be cultivated as the conduct that is most characteristic
of the Christian. It may be specially noted how, according to the consciousness of Paul, the law which
the Christian must fulfil (not, indeed, for the purpose

like other earthly kingdoms. Because the Pharisees proceeded upon such an idea of the nature of the kingdom, they were in no position to recognise that it was then already in existence, and so they asked when it would come. Therefore, in His reply, Jesus first pronounced this idea of the nature of the kingdom of God to be a perverted one, to prepare for the declaration that the kingdom of God was already in existence.

I suspect that the warning of Jesus to His disciples, " Take heed, beware of the leaven of the Pharisees, and the leaven of Herod " (Mark viii. 15), also referred to the external political tendencies and ideals, which the disciples could not commingle in the smallest degree with their ideas and hopes of the kingdom of God without perverting the whole. What is singular in this saying of Jesus, is His here classing together the Pharisees and Herod, who in general pursued very different interests, and that He warned His disciples against any dangerous tendency which those two possessed in common. Jesus must have been thinking of some point in regard to which those two could be compared in spite of their standing so far asunder in most things—some point, characteristic of each, which formed a barrier to the right understanding and reception of the message of Jesus, and which, if the disciples did not avoid, would bring them danger and ruin. But what the Pharisees and Herod had thus in common, was setting their heart upon external-political power, and on a national-political kingdom. With the Pharisees, this attitude of mind, and the Messianic ideal corresponding to it, was one main reason which drove them to hostile misconception of and contempt for the kingdom of God as proclaimed by Jesus. With Herod, again, it was the selfish solicitude for his own power and sovereignty which prevented his recognising and appreciating the significance of the teaching of Jesus, and which inspired his wish to make away with this prophet who troubled him (Luke xiii. 31). Thus we can understand how Jesus deemed this tendency towards earthly power and glory, and towards an earthly political kingdom, to be an element both foreign and hostile to the kingdom of God (cf. Mark x. 42), and that He sought to warn His disciples against the slightest mixture of such externalistic views, Pharisaic or Herodian, with their aspirations after the kingdom of God.[1]

[1] The question as to what Jesus meant by the figurative expression "leaven," which His disciples, in their care in regard to bread, understood in a literal sense (Mark viii. 16), does not admit of being answered with perfect certainty from our defective knowledge of the special circumstances which gave occasion for the warning. In any case, the expression leaven is a proverbially figurative term for anything which though present in small quantity, quickly assimilates with something else. It may be thus employed in a good as well as a bad sense (cf. Luke xiii. 21 ; 1 Cor. v. 6 ff.). Since the Pharisees, as well as Herod, stood in several relations in antagonism to Jesus and His announcement of the kingdom of God, there are several ways in which it appears possible that Jesus may have used the term "leaven" in warning His disciples. If, however, we proceed upon the supposition above indicated, that Jesus must have meant some quality or mode of conduct possessed in some degree in common by the Pharisees and Herodians, and characteristic of each, we are led with great probability to the view given in the text. The Pharisaic *doctrine* in general cannot have been here meant (cf. Matt. xvi. 12), since Herod was not also the representative of a form of doctrine. Nor, on the other hand, can the unrighteous views and conduct of the Pharisees and of Herod have been meant in a general way, since these present different features in the Pharisees and in Herod. Neither can we say that the "hypocritical" zeal for external righteousness (cf. Luke xii. 1), which Jesus condemned in the Pharisees, was also characteristic of Herod ; nor can we say that the austerely legal Pharisees could be reproached with such worldly frivolity as that of Herod. But

2. But while Jesus has not represented the kingdom of God as one of a political kind, of external earthly splendour, He has at the same time viewed it as not a purely transcendental and heavenly one. No doubt there also existed in the Jewish Apocalyptic of that period a tendency of thought to withdraw the saving blessings they religiously hoped for entirely from the range of things earthly, and to conceive their realisation as something purely heavenly; and it is certain that this tendency exercised a pretty considerable influence in the formation of the circle of Christian thought in the apostolic and sub-apostolic period.[1] But, so far as we can judge from our sources, Jesus Himself has kept also from such an extreme in opposing the external and sensuous modes of thought and of hope. We can say that He had too direct and personal experience of fellowship with God and of possession of heavenly blessings already in His earthly life, to make it possible for Him to judge of the kingdom of God as being *merely* something future, far-distant, and heavenly, and as standing in entire contrast to the forms and circumstances of the present earthly life.

Certainly He regarded the kingdom of God as being *also* a future and heavenly one; and, as we shall afterwards see more precisely, He certainly

the point in regard to which the Pharisees and Herod could be compared, and which in the one as well as in the others caused opposition to Jesus and His preaching, was such a zeal for external power and glory, and for the establishment or maintenance of a political kingdom, as was incompatible with zeal for the heavenly benefits of the kingdom of God.

[1] Cf. Schürer, *Geschichte des jüdischen Volkes,* ii. p. 422 f., and W. Baldensperger, *das Selbstbewusstsein Jesu,* pp. 75, 85 ff.

reckoned upon a comparatively early advent of the future Æon, when the kingdom of God should attain its heavenly form. As He regarded eternal life in heaven as the highest blessing for individual saints, so He looked to the future heavenly state for the perfect form of the kingdom of God. Therefore He could employ the notion, kingdom of God, also with reference to the heavenly state, inasmuch as He re- garded the perfected form of the kingdom of God as being the true and proper form. The expression " to enter into the kingdom of God " could be used by Him as simply equivalent to entering into life or eternal life (Mark ix. 47, cf. vers. 43 and 45 ; x. 23, cf. vers. 17 and 21).[1] When, in connection with the intimation of His coming again in heavenly glory, He says that some of those present should not taste death till they saw the kingdom of God coming in power (Mark ix. 1); or when He speaks of "that day" when the "workers of iniquity" among the Israelites should see Abraham, Isaac, and Jacob in the kingdom of God, and they themselves thrust out ; and when men would come from the east and from the west and recline at table in the kingdom of God (Luke xiii. 28 f.) ; or when He refers at the Last Supper to the new repast which He and His disciples would enjoy in His king- dom (Mark xiv. 25 ; Luke xxii. 29 f.),—the kingdom of God plainly means only that perfected heavenly state.[2] We must regard it as a special proof of the

---

[1] Cf. also the relation in which the idea of the kingdom of God, Luke xiii. 28 f., stands to the idea of "life," Matt. vii. 14 (=Luke xiii. 24), in the Logia-fragment § 20*b* and *c*, *L. J.* i. p. 130 f.

[2] The expression "kingdom of heaven," which is generally given by our first evangelist in the discourses and sayings of Jesus instead of

uniformity of Jesus' view, that He did not represent
the eternal heavenly life, in which He saw the highest
and ultimate ideal of blessing for individuals, as being

"kingdom of God," cannot be made use of in drawing conclusions as
to the nature of the kingdom of God as taught by Jesus. The view we
must take of that expression depends primarily on the Gospel Criticism ;
for according to the results of this must be decided the question
whether, according to the testimony of the oldest sources, that expression can be held to have been used by Jesus. So also must be decided
whether the perceptible difference of thought which is indicated by that
phrase, as distinguished from the title "kingdom of God," is to be considered in treating of the peculiar teaching of Jesus Himself, or is rather
to be taken up in connection with an investigation of the circle of
Christian thought in which our first evangelist moved. From the
critical results which I have set forth and established in the first part
of this work, the conclusion cannot be regarded as doubtful that the
expression "kingdom of heaven" is of secondary importance, and did
not belong to Jesus. For since Luke, not merely where he follows
Mark, but also where he repeats fragments of the Logia-source, has
only the phrase "kingdom of God ; " whilst, on the other hand, the first
evangelist, not only in his fragments from the Logia, but where he
follows Mark, gives the term "kingdom of heaven ; " we must conclude
that the Logia-source did not supply this latter expression, but that our
first evangelist has inserted it here even as he has done in the text
borrowed from Mark. In regard to the meaning of this expression, I
go along with Schürer (*Jahrbücher für Prot. Theol.* 1876, pp. 171 ff. and
178 ff. ; cf. the explanation in the *Theol. Literaturzeitung*, 1883, p. 581,
and *Geschichte d. jüd. Volkes*, ii. p. 454) in explaining that it is only in the
Jewish custom of using some circumlocution for the name of God, and
of specially using the term heaven for that purpose (cf. Mark xi. 30 ;
Luke xv. 18), that we must seek the reason for interchanging the terms
"kingdom of God" and "kingdom of heaven." The peculiar meaning
of the notion "kingdom of God" would not be modified or specialised
by this transposition. It would neither specially denote the heavenly
origin of the kingdom nor its perfect realisation in heaven, but only that
the kingdom belongs to heaven, that is, to God in heaven, and that it
is governed from heaven, that is, by God. And just because that expression must be explained by the Jewish custom of circumlocution, and
was by no means an original term as used by the evangelist, but was
adopted by him out of the current phraseology of his contemporaries ;
and further, because this expression simply meant, in the consciousness
of the first evangelist, the same thing as the term "kingdom of God,"
and did not bring out any peculiar aspect of thought ; we can understand that the evangelist was not always consistent in the use of that
expression, but sometimes unconsciously employed alongside of it the
expression "kingdom of God" (vi. 33 ; xii. 28 ; xix. 24 ; xxi. 31, 43).

essentially independent of the kingdom of God to be established on earth, and as only succeeding to the realisation of this kingdom, but that He regarded the kingdom of God as including the highest Divine blessings, and also as comprising and perfecting in itself the eternal heavenly life of individuals.

But as Jesus viewed the saving blessings that God had in store for men as being not merely future and heavenly, but taught that God, in accordance with His unchanging fatherly love, grants all good things to men even in their present earthly life, and preserves them from every evil; so He was certain that the blissful kingdom of God was not *merely* in the future state in heaven, but would be realised even on earth among the true children of God, who experience His saving grace and fulfil His will in righteousness. The afore-mentioned reply of Jesus to the Pharisees, who inquired when the kingdom of God should come, and were told by Him that this kingdom was already in existence among them (Luke xvii. 20 f.), is corroborated by other utterances which clearly testify to the same thought. In the synagogue at Nazareth He read that passage in Deutero-Isaiah which announces the salvation hoped for in the latter day: " The Spirit of the Lord is upon me; because He has anointed me to bring good tidings to the poor: He hath sent me to proclaim release to the captives, and recovering of sight to the blind, to set at liberty them that are bruised, to proclaim the acceptable year of the Lord " (Isa. lxi. 1 f.); and He declared that those words were that day being fulfilled to His hearers in their ears, that is, whilst they were hearing His words

(Luke iv. 17–21).   He not only considered, according to the harmonious testimony of the Logia and Mark's Gospel, that the prophetic promise of the coming of Elias before the advent of the kingdom of God, in order to prepare the way for the new order of things, was already fulfilled in John the Baptist (Matt. xi. 14; Mark ix. 11–13), but He has expressly contrasted the period of prophetic prognostication of the kingdom of God, which extended down to the time of John the Baptist, with His own day, when men were laying hold of the kingdom of God : " All the prophets and the law prophesied until John ; . . . and from the days of John the Baptist until now the kingdom of heaven suffereth violence, and the violent take it by force. . . . He that hath ears to hear, let him hear" (Matt. xi. 12–15 ; Luke xvi. 16).[1]   The time of waiting and hoping for the future kingdom of God was over, and the time of its actual realisation had come, when it behoved men with energetic resolution to make themselves members of the kingdom. Also in giving expression to His assurance that the sway of Satan and the demons over men was broken, so that He (Jesus) Himself and His disciples were superior to them and could not at all be injured by them, He announced that the kingdom of God was at that present time being realised.   When the Pharisees declared that His expulsion of the demons was done through demoniac agency, He not only pointed out that this statement implied a contradiction in thought (Mark iii. 22–27), and was inconsistent with their estimate of the acts of members of their own class who cast out

---

[1] Cf. *Log.* § 4*b*, *L. J.* i. p. 75.

demons (Luke xi. 19), but He showed the just inference which should be drawn from His conquest of the
devils : " If I with the finger " (that is, with the power)
" of God cast out devils, no doubt the kingdom of God
is come unto you "[1] (Luke xi. 20). So also when
His disciples had returned from their preaching tour,
and reported their success over the wicked spirits, He
declared that He had beheld Satan as lightning fall
from heaven; that is, even in the course of His disciples' mission to spread the gospel of the kingdom
of God, He had gained the clear knowledge of the
breaking of the commanding power of Satan (Luke
x. 18). And then, after promising His disciples
unlimited sway over all hostile and hurtful powers
(ver. 19 f.), and brought out His own significance as
mediator of this state of grace (ver. 21 f.; Matt.
xi. 25–30), He added the words : " Blessed are the
eyes which see what ye see : for I say unto you, Many
prophets and righteous men " (cf. Matt. xiii. 17) "have
desired to see what ye see, and have not seen it; and
to hear what ye hear, and have not heard it " (Luke
x. 23 f.).[2] This closing statement corresponds with
the opening one in regard to the fall of Satan : as the
power of Satan will not be broken at some future
period, but had already at that present time become
decisively broken, so the goal of the hopes and wishes
of prophets and saints, namely, the establishment of
the kingdom of God, lay no longer in the future, but
the disciples had it present with them, and had a

[1] With this meaning of ἔφθασεν, "is already come," cf. 1 Thess.
ii. 16 ; 2 Cor. x. 14; Phil. iii. 16 ; οὐκ ἔφθασεν (Rom. ix. 31) means "it
is not yet come."
[2] Cf. Log. § 8d, L. J. i. p. 93.

blissful experience of it. The parables of the grain of Mustard-seed and of the Leaven, whereby Jesus sought to illustrate the development of the kingdom of God (Luke xiii. 18–21), are witnesses to His conception of the kingdom of God as already existing on earth. For these parables do not accord with the manner in which the kingdom of God will arrive at a state of heavenly glory in the future, since this future glorious kingdom will not gradually extend itself, but will be established in its full extent at the time of the second coming of the Messiah. But they fitly refer to the kingdom of God as it is developed in this dispensation on earth, seeing that from an insignificant beginning it has grown to unexpected greatness ; and with quiet but powerful influence stretches forward to new fields, and embraces them within its sweep.

But the view that the kingdom of God is already being realised on earth, must yet, in the sense used by Jesus, be supplemented by this other, that that kingdom is also a future and heavenly one, and that the present kingdom finds its true and perfect realisation only in the future heavenly state. On the other hand, the view that the kingdom of God has already its realisation on earth, in the present dispensation, must be clearly distinguished from the idea that it is a kingdom of an earthly kind, with earthly dominion, power, and pomp. Jesus could so decidedly declare that the kingdom already existed on earth, just because He so clearly conceived its non-worldly character. We might say that He regarded the kingdom of God, in so far as it was already being realised on earth, as one of an *ethical* kind ; nevertheless this view also requires to be more precisely defined, so as not to be misunderstood. For it would be wrong to suppose that Jesus looked upon the kingdom of God merely as an association of men bound together by common ideas of right religious and moral conduct. However essential an element in the idea of the kingdom of God was this feature of righteousness, or of the right fulfilment of the will of God on the part of its members, the full blessing which God gives its members was an equally essential element. Nor would Jesus have been able to speak of the kingdom of God as being already realised on earth, if He had not meant such an association or society under God's fatherly government as not only practised true righteousness, but continually enjoyed the true saving grace of God. But certainly Jesus has much more strongly emphasised, and in a much more inward and ethical way understood, the righteousness of the kingdom, than was done in the prevailing Pharisaic-Jewish view of the kingdom of the longed-for latter-day. In this respect He attached Himself to the earlier tradition of the prophetic period, and was conscious of the special inner connection of His own work with the Baptist's preparatory preaching of repentance. And it was just on account of the special value which He laid upon the inward righteousness belonging to the kingdom of God, that it was also possible for Him to regard the bestowal of God's saving grace as something that may be constantly experienced even in this earthly life. For He could refer this bestowal of grace to the inner quickening and strength imparted to men for the

fulfilment of the will of God and for victory over
temptations.   On the other hand, He could regard
even the outward troubles and ills of the earthly life
as equivalent to rest-giving grace bestowed by God,
in so far as He recognised in them a means of maintaining fidelity to our duty, and humble submission
to God.

It was indeed from a high idealistic standpoint that
Jesus proclaimed the kingdom of God as already in
existence, for there were no obvious external appearances to give support to the assertion.   Its truth
could not be directly proved to the natural understanding, and the value of the blessings signified by
it could not be sensibly experienced.   And yet the
idea of the existence of the kingdom was not a mere
abstract conception or something purely ideal.   He
knew that it expressed what was a reality, of which
He Himself had direct experience, and of which His
disciples could and should have a like experience as
He Himself.   This certainty that this kingdom announced by Him had a real existence, in spite of
being externally hidden, and that the saving benefits
it yielded, however these might be then misunderstood
and disregarded, were nevertheless the really valuable
and enduring blessings for men—this certainty He
gave expression to in teaching the future appearance
of the kingdom in heavenly glory and perfection,
when all earthly kingdoms should be ended, and all
earthly goods should have lost their value for men.

3. But in regard to these ideas of Jesus—as to the
nature and realisation of the kingdom of God, as to
its existence, even at that time, wherever God granted

His blissful, life-giving benefits, and men on their part fulfilled His will in inward righteousness, and as to the fact of its scope not being confined to the present time and to this earth, but having its fulfilment in heaven—we have to ask if, from the commencement of His ministry, Jesus possessed these ideas always and in the same way, and with the same clearness and thoroughness, or if He did not gradually acquire and form them in the course of His ministry? The assertion that the latter is the fact, and that an historical account of the teaching of Jesus must distinguish between different phases of His view of the nature and coming of the kingdom of God, has of late been plausibly set forth on various hands, especially since New Testament scholars have become clearly conscious of the task of historically understanding the life and teaching of Jesus. This supposition appears, indeed, to be demanded by a certain general consideration which has essential importance for every historical mode of study—this, namely, that a new system of thought, when it emerges, cannot be regarded as an isolated fact, but must be viewed as the outcome of a process of development which has been accomplished in a psychologically intelligible way in connection with the given historical conditions.

In applying this general principle to the historical emergence of the teaching of Jesus in regard to the kingdom of God, it has been deemed necessary to hold that, at the dawn of His Messianic consciousness, Jesus must have formed His view of the nature of the Messianic kingdom, at all events at first, upon the ideas handed down from the prophetic period, and upon those which were current among His Jewish countrymen in regard to that kingdom, and that He modified that view gradually until it took the spiritual form which we find it bearing at the close of His ministry. Certainly if, even at the outset, in accordance with His inner religious mode of judging, He had rejected the ordinary Jewish idea as to the establishment of God's kingdom after an earthly political manner as another world-empire, this must have been a chief result of the period of temptation which succeeded His baptism. On the other hand, it would have been impossible that the idea (which was the normal one in earlier prophecy and in the Jewish Apocalypse), viz. that God would suddenly, by a miraculous interposition, bring His kingdom into existence and to glorious manifestation, should already from the outset have been connected in His mind only with the completion of the kingdom of God in the far future, and not to the establishment of that kingdom in the present. And also it would have been psychologically inconceivable that, even from the very commencement of His public Messianic career, He would possess a clear knowledge of the external failure of His preaching among the people of Israel, and of the necessity of His suffering and death. It seems therefore justly to be supposed that, at the outset of His ministry, in accordance with the conviction which He had attained as to His Messiahship, He confidently expected that God would speedily, through a marvellous train of events, bring in the Messianic kingdom, not, indeed, as an external world-empire, but as a kingdom of heavenly benefit. The idea of this kingdom, which

was to be miraculously introduced, exactly corresponding to the later idea of Jesus regarding the
future perfection of the kingdom of God, must have
at first constituted His *whole* conception of that kingdom ; and He must have expected its realisation in
His present life on earth. But whereas this ideal
was not being fulfilled, but its realisation, which at
first seemed near at hand, was rather being pushed
ever further off, while He Himself still held fast on
His God-given course, in the consciousness of His
Messianic calling and in fulfilment of His mission ;
and whereas, alongside of the failure of His preaching
in relation to the great mass of the people of Israel,
He perceived its blissful influence upon the company
of His disciples ; He became gradually possessed of
the knowledge that, in another sense than He had at
first understood, the kingdom of God was already
being realised, namely, as a kingdom of an inward
kind existing in the hearts of those who believed
His message. Thus He attained His idea of the
development of the kingdom of God : as beginning
at that present time, gradually increasing in a hidden
form, and brought to a state of heavenly glory in
the future through a sudden interposition and manifestation of God.[1]

We must, above all, inquire how far the hypothesis,
that Jesus' idea of the nature and coming of the kingdom of God was gradually developed in the way now
stated, is supported by His own recorded utterances.

[1] These ideas have recently been expounded in essential accordance
by W. Beyschlag, *das Leben Jesu*, i. pp. 229 ff., 323 ff., ii. pp. 121 ff.,
158 ff. ; and by W. Baldensperger, *das Selbstbewusstsein Jesu*, pp. 107 ff.,
165 ff.

It may be appealed, in the first place, to the declaration which Mark indicates as the theme of the first public message of Jesus: "The time is fulfilled, and the kingdom of God is come near: repent ye, and believe the gospel" (Mark i. 15). Here, on the one hand, the words, "the time is fulfilled," may be taken as expressing His consciousness that He Himself was even then the Messiah, and that, inasmuch as the period of prophecy and of waiting had expired, the longed-for latter-day had already arrived; on the other hand, the words, "the kingdom of heaven is come near," may be held as evidence that Jesus at that time certainly regarded the kingdom of God as one in the immediate future, but as not yet realised. Just as, at a later period, when He taught His disciples to pray for the coming of the kingdom of God (Luke xi. 2), or when He set before them the kingdom of God as the true goal of their quest and of their confident expectation (Matt. vi. 33 ; Luke xii. 32), or He spoke of the conditions of entering into the kingdom of God (Matt. v. 20; vii. 21 ; Mark ix. 47 ; x. 15, 23–25), He meant the future glorious kingdom in heaven ; so, when He announced at the commencement of His ministry, not the existence, but the nearness of the kingdom of God, He may have had only the idea of the glorious future kingdom whose realisation by God He expected immediately.

Is this mode of explaining and applying the saying, Mark i. 15, really an obvious and necessary one? We may only ask what then would have been the form of Jesus' first message, if even then He had understood the kingdom of God as one which was to be developed gradually on earth, and which, without coming with miraculous heavenly display, would find its realisation in the loving bestowal of grace on the part of the heavenly Father to men, and in devout and righteous obedience to His will on men's part. Would He then have announced that this kingdom was already realised, whilst as yet only He Himself had fully received that Divine grace, and fully recognised and fulfilled that righteousness ? A kingdom is not constituted out of one member, and so long as the Messiah stood alone, the kingdom of God did not exist. It would come into existence through the fact of the Messiah assembling a society of other members of the kingdom. Rather we must say that the declaration, " The time is fulfilled, and the kingdom of God is come near," must be regarded as a thoroughly correct expression of the opening message of Jesus, in the case of His holding from the first such a view of the nature of the realisation of the kingdom of God as is implied in His later declaration that the kingdom had already come. The time was fulfilled, in that He was conscious of being even then the Messiah ; but the kingdom was only at hand, and was not yet fulfilled, inasmuch as the Messiah was only then beginning His active ministry with the object of setting up the kingdom. So soon as that ministry was successful, and in the measure of its success, could He declare that the kingdom had already begun to be realised in Himself and His disciples. Therefore this first announcement by Jesus does not enable us with certainty to infer such a view of the general nature and coming of the kingdom of God as differs from His later view, when He declared that the kingdom of God was, even at that present time, being realised.

But even those passages in which the kingdom of God is spoken of as one that was coming, and that was to be striven after, cannot be held as proving that Jesus regarded the kingdom of God only as one which was to appear in the future in heavenly glory. For even if, among the circle of His disciples, He plainly expressed the idea of a present realisation of the kingdom of God, still that kingdom, in His view, remained in a state of being developed, and therefore of coming ; partly in so far as it was yet to reach a wider circle of mankind, partly in so far as it was no permanent and complete possession to those who had already attained it, but was a blessing to be still striven after, and partly because its future perfecting in the heavenly glory was to follow its present earthly development. In all these respects Jesus could, in spite of the fact of its beginning to be realised, describe the kingdom as one that was to come and to be striven after, and could speak of the conditions of entering it. For the hypothesis that Jesus partly regarded the kingdom of God as one that was to appear only in heavenly glory, and not also as one that was to be secretly developed on earth, there has been just occasion given only in those passages discussed by us at an earlier point (p. 370), in which Jesus uses the idea of the kingdom of God exclusively in the sense of the future heavenly kingdom (Mark ix. 1, 47 ; x. 23 ; xiv. 25 ; Luke xiii. 28 f. ; xxii. 29 f.). But these passages belong collectively, not to the early period of the public ministry of Jesus, but to the later period, and in part to His very last conversations with His disciples. We would hereby be forced to the idea of a very remarkable vacillation on the part of Jesus, in the conception of this main idea of His teaching at the close of His public ministry, did we not rather judge that now and again Jesus used the idea of the kingdom of God in the special eschatological sense, whilst He quite simultaneously held the view that the kingdom of God in its general sense had been already set up. Since He was certain that the kingdom of God which was then already set up on earth, and was in process of development, would nevertheless not only attain to a future heavenly form, but only in this form would arrive at its just perfection, He could designate this perfected form of it as in a special sense the kingdom of God.

The fact has also been pointed out, that during a great part of His public career Jesus kept back from His disciples and the people the announcement of His Messiahship. Although the educational aim of Jesus may have certainly co-operated here, in order, as far as possible, to prevent the attachment of political expectations to His Messiahship, yet that motive may seem not to have been the only determining one. For was there not the same good ground also at a later period for the apprehension that His Messiahship would be understood in a perverted and political way? Would He, especially, have arranged His public Messianic entry into Jerusalem if He had anxiously desired to exclude such misunderstanding of His Messianic activity? And ought we not there-

fore to suppose that there was a personal as well as
an educational motive involved in His at first keeping
back the announcement of His Messiahship; not,
indeed, any personal uncertainty in regard to His
being the Messiah, but an uncertainty in regard to
the establishment of the kingdom which belonged to
Him as the Messiah? So long as He still retained
His original expectation, that God would intervene
with a miraculous manifestation of the kingdom in
heavenly glory, He had delayed divulging His consciousness of Messiahship. But after He had become
gradually certain that God would not yet bring in this
heavenly manifestation of His kingdom, and that He
Himself, as Messiah, must rather suffer and die on
earth; and after He had, in connection with this
certainty, attained the clear idea of the kingdom of
God as already existing in a secret spiritual form; He
could then freely proclaim His Messiahship to His
disciples, and make His public Messianic entrance into
Jerusalem.[1]

But this line of argument also rests on uncertain
grounds. If we proceed on the supposition that the
educational purpose of Jesus did not merely aim at
preventing political hopes and aspirations being
attached to His Messianic personality, but rather
at positively establishing a true comprehension of
His Messiahship, we can perfectly understand that,
merely for this educational reason, He did not at
first speak of Himself as the Messiah, and that
He suppressed the premature disclosure of that
truth by the demoniacs. At the same time He

[1] Cf. Baldensperger, *das Selbstbewusstsein Jesu*, p. 175 ff.

promulgated His teaching in regard to salvation and the righteousness of the kingdom, since the true character of that kingdom, and along with it the true foundation of His Messianic claim, were thereby made clear. We can also understand that He first welcomed the recognition of His Messiahship among the most intimate circle of His disciples, who had chiefly and most faithfully imbibed His instruction; and that, finally, when He saw the end of His earthly ministry approaching, heedless of the mistaken ideas, misconstruction, and hatred of the great mass of the people, He openly advanced His Messianic claim, in order to lead His disciples clearly to those consequences of His teaching at which He had aimed, and for which He had been preparing from the beginning. When Peter, as the spokesman of the disciples while on the way to Cæsarea Philippi, confessed his belief in Jesus as Messiah (Mark viii. 27–29), we must regard this as marking, not the close of a phase of the inner development of Jesus, but the close of a period of development on the part of the disciples. That confession which Jesus had elicited by His question, but which was nevertheless a free expression of the gradually matured conviction of the disciples, can only be rightly explained by presupposing that Jesus did not then for the first time teach, but had already continuously taught, His disciples such a view of the kingdom of God as formed the true basis for the recognition of His already existing Messiahship. In other words, He had directed their attention, not merely to the coming of a kingdom of heavenly glory, but also to a kingdom of God, which was even then being gradually unfolded upon earth; and He had indicated as its characteristic features, the continuous bestowal, on the part of the heavenly Father, of grace which tended to eternal life; and, on the other hand, the true inward righteousness on men's part. For, according to the degree in which they had personally imbibed this teaching, and in which they had recognised that Jesus was not only the teacher, but the perfect representative of this kingdom of God,—inasmuch as He stood in perfect fellowship of love with the Father, continually enjoyed the blessings of God, and fulfilled the Divine will in true filial obedience, —they could gradually acquire the conviction that He was even then the Messiah of the kingdom. Yet along with this they might easily cling to the hope that the period of earthly obscurity and humiliation of the Messiah and of His kingdom would be speedily brought to an end, by the manifestation of the heavenly glory of the kingdom; and they might find the thought of the final rejection and condemnation to death of the Messiah by the authorities still strange and offensive (Mark viii. 32). Just on that account, however, Jesus began at that very time frankly to inform them of His impending sufferings and death (Mark viii. 31 f.). After they had attained this well-grounded faith in His Messiahship, they required to be still further built up in right views as to the Messiah. They required to learn to recognise, as a necessity founded on the true nature of the Messianic kingdom and the Messiah, what, from another view of the nature of the kingdom of God, would appear to be the greatest contradiction of His Messiahship. We cannot as yet take up the question whether Jesus Himself was clearly acquainted from the commencement of His ministry with the necessity of His sufferings. We shall only assert here, that at all events the giving of His first clear intimation of His sufferings at the period when the disciples recognised His Messiahship, is only perfectly intelligible to us on the supposition that Jesus had an educational aim in view, and that we can by no means infer that Jesus Himself had then for the first time attained a knowledge of the necessity of His sufferings.

That spontaneous recognition of the Messiahship of Jesus on the part of the disciples, in spite of His not having expressly designated Himself as Messiah, is only really psychologically intelligible to us, on the supposition of their previous constant instruction by Jesus in regard to the true nature and existence of the kingdom of God as being gradually developed even then upon earth. But we have other and direct testimony for the fact that, even in the earlier period of His ministry, Jesus proclaimed the kingdom of God as already existing. Both the Gospel of Mark (vi. 7 ff.) and the Logia of Matthew (Luke x. 1 ff.) tell us that Jesus already, during the period of His own ministry, sent forth His nearest disciples to spread the tidings of the kingdom of God. This sending out of the disciples cannot belong to the later period of His ministry, when, on account of the misapprehension and enmity He met with from the great mass of the Jewish people, He withdrew from these and directed His teaching expressly to the small circle of His susceptible hearers. That commission to the disciples is only intelligible as happening in the early period of His ministry, when He felt called upon to deliver His message of the coming kingdom to as wide a circle as possible (Mark i. 38 f.; cf. Luke viii. 1), and when, in view of the greatness of the field of work, He supplemented His own limited power by the co-operation of the disciples (Luke x. 2).[1] Now, it is worthy of consideration that the message which the disciples were to convey into all districts of the country was expressed in this form: "The kingdom of God is come nigh unto you" (Luke x. 9). It was the self - same words which formed the opening message of Jesus Himself, according to Mark i. 15, only with the addition, "unto you." This addition, which makes the nearness of the kingdom refer specially to those people to whom the gospel was first preached, corresponds with the proviso that the kingdom of God is no longer in general only a near one, nowhere realised. The question how far the kingdom of God was elsewhere already in existence remains unanswered; only in reference to the present hearers it is said that the kingdom of God now is coming to them, and offering itself for realisation in them. Weightier still, however, than this point, in serving to confirm our explanation given above as to the opening message of Jesus, is the statement, according to the Logia - account, that, on the return of the disciples who were sent forth, Jesus clearly expressed

---

[1] Cf. *L. J* i. p. 33 f.

His certainty of the downfall of Satan from his position of power (Luke x. 18), of the prevalence of His disciples over all hostile and hurtful powers (ver. 19), and of the fulfilment of the hopes of the early prophets and saints before the eyes of the disciples (ver. 23 f.). That certainty He connected with a declaration of His own possession of absolute power and blissfulness, founding this declaration not only on the prospect of a future heavenly glory, nor upon a present miraculous preservation from troubles and trials, but rather upon His meek and lowly submission to the will of God. The same submission He set before all other men as the means of attaining true inner peace amid all the trials and burdens of the earthly life (Matt. xi. 28–30).[1] Here the thought of Jesus, that the kingdom of God is already being realised upon earth, and His idea on which that thought is founded,— that He and His disciples possessed a state of blessedness, not in the way of outward earthly prosperity and splendour, yet as an absolute present reality,—is most clearly expressed. The term "kingdom of God" is not used, indeed, but the reality is indicated with perfect clearness. Jesus may well have spoken those words at an hour of special inward exaltation; yet we have no right to conclude that He had here risen to an exceptional altitude of view which at other times was absent from the contents of His consciousness. We can only say that what is here recorded of that hour of rapt elevation of Jesus, affords a testimony to the loftiness and inner harmony of His idea of the

---

[1] See above, pp. 225–231 ; and cf. *Log.* § 8, *L. J.* i. p. 90 ff.

present realisation upon earth of the Divine kingdom of grace; and we must take that testimony as a direct proof that this was already the ruling one in His mind at the time of the sending out of His disciples.

We can go a step farther back, however, and declare that, from the beginning of His public Messianic career, Jesus must have held this view of the already present realisation of the kingdom upon earth, mainly in the same sense, and on the same ground, as at the later period, since the dawn and confirmation of His own Messianic consciousness is by no means intelligible to us otherwise than in connection with this view. That general historical-psychological mode of view, that Jesus first attained His idea of the kingdom of God by founding upon the traditional Jewish expectation, and that, through His own inner development, He gradually drifted apart from and abandoned the Jewish traditional view, is quite justifiable and necessary. But it is wrong to draw the conclusion that this process of founding upon and gradually abandoning the Jewish view was gone through *during* the time of His public ministry, and was the cause of a gradual change then in His teaching in regard to the nature and coming of the kingdom of God. We must rather connect this whole development with the period *before* the commencement of His public ministry, unless we are to regard the revelation which gave Him the assurance of His Messianic calling as an occurrence which happened to him in a psychologically isolated way, and which, in its significance and results, was im-

perfectly understood and thought out by Him.   I
may here direct attention again to the account
given at the beginning (Section I. chapter iii.), of
the development of Jesus' religious mode of view,
and of the special significance of His experience at
baptism.   It is evident that Jesus did not first occupy
Himself with the ideal hopes of His people as to the
promised kingdom of God only from the time of His
baptism, when His own Messiahship became certain,
but that He had previously cherished and pondered
these hopes.   *Before* His baptism these must have
been historically founded on the hopes which were
handed down from the time of the early prophets
through the Holy Scriptures, and which had present
vitality among the people in manifold forms and
degrees.   In accordance with His general religious-
ethical attitude of mind, Jesus certainly from the
first kept back the external political - national expectations current in regard to those hopes, and, in
accordance with the older prophetic idea, strongly
accented the element of inner religious fellowship
through grace between God and His righteous
people; yet He could not also have then possessed
the idea, as He afterwards taught it, of a gradual
realisation of the kingdom of God, insignificant in
external appearance, and resting on spiritual fellowship between God and His devout people.   He no
doubt expected, like the Old Testament prophets
and the Jews of His time (even John the Baptist),
that the kingdom would be visibly manifested in
glory through a sudden miraculous interposition of
God.   On the other hand, He must already, before

His baptism, have possessed the abiding consciousness of standing in a filial relation of loving fellowship
with His heavenly Father, of bearing within Him a
source of living power, of being under the continual,
blissful guidance, even on earth, of His Father's
loving hand, and of being Himself employed in
fulfilling the will of God with childlike obedience.
This consciousness which He possessed, furnished the
psychological ground of His attaining the assurance
of His Messiahship, and, along with this, of His
being able to conceive, in a new and higher manner,
the nature and coming of the kingdom of God.   But
before His baptism this inference from His filial and
spiritual fellowship with God was not yet clear.   This
was just the significance of His baptismal experience,
namely, that since He had here the revelation of His
being a Son of God in loving fellowship with His
Father, and the object of the goodwill of God, He
Himself must be the promised Messiah ; and that, in
such a blessed relationship to God as He experienced,
the true nature of the ideal hoped-for kingdom of
God found a present realisation upon earth.   These
two sides of the revelation which He received at
His baptism—the knowledge of His own Messiahship, and the knowledge of the true nature of the
kingdom of God and of its possible realisation even
then upon earth — cannot be separated from each
other, since they arise directly from the same ground,
and mutually condition each other.   If He possessed
such a vivid consciousness of the reality and preciousness of His inner fellowship with God, and of the
blessed life which He enjoyed through the love of

His heavenly Father, that He could find in that
consciousness a sure experimental proof of His
Messiahship, in spite of His being, to all external
appearance, only an ordinary humble Israelite, without the glorious characteristics and the splendid
miraculous installation which Jewish tradition connected with the character and advent of the Messiah,
—if that were indeed so, why should not the conviction of the reality and preciousness of such a
loving gracious fellowship between God and men,
appear to Him sufficient to permit of His declaring
that the kingdom of God was already being realised
on earth, in so far as men experienced the grace of
the heavenly Father and willed to walk as His
children? If it be said that Jesus had indeed
attained the certainty of His Messiahship at baptism,
but had not at that time arrived at the idea of the
realisation and development of the kingdom of God
as something which was to be established already on
the earth, though in a gradual unimposing way, and
that, on the contrary, He still clung to the idea of
a miraculous heavenly manifestation of the kingdom,
we must draw one or other of two conclusions. Either
we must suppose that He had attained the certainty
of His Messiahship without a knowledge of its peculiar
fundamental principles, and that this certainty, at least
in the early period of His Messianic career, did not
yet stand upon any solid basis; or we must judge that
He had still only half thought out the ideas on which
His Messianic assurance was founded, since He had
not perceived the necessary mutual relation between
the Messiah and the kingdom of God, and between

the nature of the Messiah and the nature of the kingdom, and had not yet attributed to these the same truth and value for other men which they had for Himself. We have no right, merely in order to save our hypothesis of the human psychological development of Jesus, to attribute to Him such a manifest inconsistency in His mode of view.

No doubt it is true that when Jesus at baptism suddenly attained assurance of His Messiahship, He did not at once clearly perceive all its consequences, and cannot directly have overcome all opposing difficulties. For such a sudden miraculous attainment were certainly not in harmony with the laws of the human mind and spirit. But here is just the significance of the period of the temptation which Jesus underwent immediately after His baptism, viz. that He did not actually enter upon His Messianic career until He had been confronted with objections and opposition to His Messiahship and His view of the kingdom of God, and until those objections, arising out of the traditional Old Testament Jewish mode of view and hopes, had, with all their plausible reasons and allurements, been clearly and definitely overcome by Him.[1] In that period of temptation, the view, which He afterwards taught, of the already present establishment of the kingdom of God on earth, had attained definite development and confirmation. If it be maintained that this view was first formed on His part during the period of His public ministry, the history would be thus independently construed without any support in the recorded

[1] Cf. above, p. 101 ff.

utterances of Jesus, or rather in opposition to what has been recorded in our best sources in regard to the decisive facts of His development before His entrance on His vocation; and, on the other hand, in regard to the contents of His preaching during His Messianic activity.

From this result, however, namely, that during the few years of the public ministry of Jesus His general idea of the nature and coming of the kingdom of God remained the same, we cannot infer that during this period the contents of that idea *in no respect* underwent development or change. And conversely, from the general consideration that His ideas did not remain rigidly uniform amid all the impressions and experiences of His ministry, and that He did not from the beginning foresee the non-success of His work among His countrymen, and the necessity of His sufferings and crucifixion, we cannot draw the conclusion that, during the course of His public ministry, He must have developed and transformed His general view of the nature and coming of the kingdom of God. Without doubt, as a consequence of His progressive experiences, and of the vivid impression which the success and non-success of His work made upon Him, His views *did* develop and expand during His Messianic career. *But this development and expansion did not affect the general principle of the nature and coming of the kingdom of God, but only the application of that general principle to the present and the foreseen future historical circumstances.* It did not affect His assurance of being already the Messiah, which He never lost

since the time of His temptation. But it affected
His knowledge of how, in view of the reception
which He actually met with, His public ministry
among the people and His private ministry among
His disciples should be shaped, so that the object of
His preaching and founding of the kingdom of God
might be attained as largely as possible; and it
affected His knowledge of how, because of His
ministry, He should be treated by men. That
development, also, did not affect His assurance that
the kingdom of God was already being set up on
earth ; but it did affect His knowledge of the extent
of and hindrances to the further development of the
kingdom of God on earth, and of the task and the
fate which lay before His disciples on earth in the
future. Certainly He entered on His mission with
high hope that His glad message as to the kingdom
of God would find comparatively rapid and great
success. He Himself would be recognised as the
anointed Messiah by the chosen people as a whole ;
and the kingdom of God as He understood it, that is,
a kingdom of ideal fellowship of grace between the
heavenly Father and men, would, with its leavening
power, pervade foreign regions and powers of the
world, and assimilate them to itself. And certainly,
at the beginning of His career, the necessity of His
death had not occurred to Him, far less the thought
of so early and so dreadful a death. As, at a later
period, in spite of His declaration that He knew not
the day nor the hour of His return at the close of the
earthly development of the kingdom of God (Mark
xiii. 32), He proceeded on the supposition that that

period was comparatively near, and that the generation of His disciples then living would see it (Mark
ix. 1); so, at the entrance of His Messianic career, we
may believe that He expected that He would Himself live upon earth at the term fixed by Divine
decree, at the close of the world's history, and, as the
Messiah, would effect the transition from the Church's
earthly to its heavenly state.   Probably He expected that, directly upon the success, speedy or more
remote, of His Messianic work upon earth, God
would sooner or later put the term to the earthly
development of the kingdom of God.   In all these
respects, His ideas, during the course of His ministry,
passed through a process of development of a highly
significant kind.   The hope that His work would
find comparatively speedy and great success in Israel
was delusive.   Through fruitless endeavours to win
the faith of the chosen people and that of the theocratic centre of Judaism, Jerusalem (Luke xiii. 34),
He learnt that it was not the many called, or the
first invited, who were destined actually to participate
in the kingdom of God (Luke xiii. 28-30; xiv. 16 ff.;
Matt. xxii. 14; Mark xii. 1-11).   With growing clearness, the first glimpse He caught of cruel suffering
and a violent death in store for Him grew upon
His vision; and out of this glimpse there arose, not
without stern inner conflict, the idea of the necessity
of His death, and its saving significance in the
purpose of God.   His experiences of hatred and
persecution from men showed Him that His disciples
would be hated and persecuted for His sake in the
future to the end by the world (Matt. x. 24 f.).   And

the expectation that He Himself would, as the
Messiah upon earth, effect the transition of the
members of the kingdom of God from the state of
earthly imperfection and progress to the state of
heavenly perfection, was transformed for Him into
the idea that He as Messiah, first raised up to the
heavenly life at God's right hand, would, at the end
of the world, return to His own on earth to convey
them to the heavenly glory.

But this whole actual process of development in the
views of Jesus in the course of His earthly activity,
which will be more particularly discussed in later
sections, is thoroughly compatible with the supposition that Jesus from the first possessed and retained
a permanent general idea of the nature and coming
of the kingdom of God on earth—beginning imper-
ceptibly, and gradually growing until it should be at
length transplanted into the state of heavenly perfection, the foundation of which would be laid even here
upon earth in the bestowal of Divine blessings, even
as the true righteousness could and should be performed already upon earth. Even if Jesus from the
outset of His ministry did not count upon any miraculously glorious installation in His present Messianic
vocation, nor any externally splendid and prosperous
manifestation and establishment of the kingdom of
God during the time of its earthly development, He
might still hope for a comparatively great and easy
success for His Messianic work, and a much more
rapid growth of the kingdom of God than it actually
experienced. And even though He was aware that
the rule in the kingdom of God on earth for the

Messiah, as for all its members, was earnest self-denial and joyful renunciation, yet He needed not to have expected at first that such a degree of humiliation was in store for the Messiah as brought Him to cruel suffering and crucifixion. In itself it was certainly quite possible that Jesus should at first have regarded the future heavenly state of perfection as the peculiar realisation of the kingdom of God, and the prior stage of it, which by His ministry He was establishing on earth, as being merely preparatory, and that in His later progress He first began to conceive this earthly preparatory stage as the gradually expanding germ of the real kingdom of God. But it is of no value to follow out such an abstract possibility, since it does not agree with the reality as attested by our sources, and since that reality is thoroughly intelligible from a psychological point of view. *Jesus possessed*, as I have said above, *in His personal piety, from the first too keen a consciousness of an already existing state of gracious fellowship with His Father in heaven, too rich an experience of the possession of Divine power and of guidance by the fatherly love of God, and too firm confidence in the accessibility of this blessed state to all other men, to lead Him to believe or to proclaim the kingdom of God to be a merely future and heavenly one, and not rather as being in essence already in course of realisation here upon earth.*

Or, finally, are we still met with the objection, that it would have been impossible for Jesus to approach His Jewish countrymen, from the first, with the spiritually deeper conception of the nature and coming of the kingdom as He proclaimed these at a later time, since the Jews clung to the prophetic idea of a miraculously sudden introduction and a glorious external appearance of the kingdom of God, and therefore possessed no preparation and no mental condition for receiving that deeper conception of the kingdom of God ?   To this it can be replied, that if, further on in the course of His ministry, Jesus could deem it possible to represent to His disciples and the Jews that gradual, outwardly imperceptible realisation of the kingdom of God as the fulfilment of the Old Testament hopes, He might have presented this view of the kingdom to them at the commencement of His ministry, and claimed their believing recognition of it. For this view which He had of the nature and coming of the kingdom of God appeared to the Jews, in rela-tion to the traditional Old Testament view, to be as novel and strange, as imperfect and as false, at the later period as at the beginning of His ministry.   But because of this novelty and strangeness of His view, Jesus did not at once present it to His countrymen in a ready formulated shape, but He sought to lead up gradually, in an educational way, to their understand-ing of it.   When He began with the message that the kingdom of God was at hand, that announcement would naturally be understood by them at first in the same sense in which they had understood the Baptist's message, that is, as the announcement of the speedy miraculous appearance of the kingdom of God in out-ward splendour.   But in the course of His continual instruction in regard to the fatherly goodwill and bene-ficence of God, in whom men could confidently trust even in this earthly life, in regard also to the true righteousness whereby God is honoured, and the gradual growth and development of the kingdom of God from small beginnings to the greatest expansion and influence, He made it possible for the susceptible to understand the real sense in which His message of the coming of the kingdom of God was to be meant. Was it, then, through unwarranted duplicity that He used the general term kingdom of God from the very first, and that He declared the imminence of its realisation, in spite of His knowledge that His hearers understood this term in a different sense than He, and in spite of His being able only through gradual instruction to lead them up to His own view? We must remember that for Jesus Himself, as well as for the Jews, the term kingdom of God indicated the state, promised by the Old Testament prophets, of perfect, blissful fellowship between God and His people in the latter - day. Now, Jesus had the un-wavering certainty that the state of fellowship between God and His people taught by Himself was the *true* realisation even of this state of blessedness promised by the prophets. Although, from an external mode of view, and in the judgment of His countrymen, the kingdom of God which He announced seemed to fall far short, as to work and glory, of that pro-phetic ideal, yet He was certain that the kingdom of God in His sense would fulfil the prophetic hopes in no incomplete or improper way, but much rather in their highest and only genuine sense. He was convinced that the Divine benefits which were to accrue from the kingdom of God, which even then was being set up, were not inferior to those promised by the prophets, but were the highest and purest realisation of the prophetic promises. They were not mere seeming, transitory, external benefits; but they were eternal benefits, constituting the only true life of man. Though, from an external mode of view, those benefits seemed imperfect, because they included no external prosperity, and excluded no external evils or suffering, yet Jesus knew that they were the perfect and enduring blessings, since they were neither hindered nor impaired, but rather sustained and furthered, through earthly evil and death (Mark viii. 35). In His certainty in regard to the relation between the kingdom of God in His sense and that of prophetic promise, lay His moral right to regard His conception and teaching on that subject as having exclusive truth. In the following chapter we will more closely consider this consciousness which Jesus had in reference to the Old Testament revelation and promises.

———

4. If the conception of the kingdom of God which Jesus held, and which we have sought to set forth according to the synoptical sources, cannot be established out of the Johannine discourses by sayings in which the idea of the kingdom of God is directly employed, the reason of this is only to be sought in the fact that, because these discourses belong to the closing period of Jesus' ministry, they do not so much bear witness to the teaching in regard to the general nature and coming of the kingdom of God, as to His special Messianic claim and mediatorial significance. Nevertheless, it is true that that idea of the general

nature and coming of the kingdom of God, as we have already viewed it in immediate and necessary mutual relation to the personal certainty of Messiah-ship on the part of Jesus, finds in the Johannine discourses an expresssion which, if indirect, is yet very clear. The saying of Jesus to the woman of Samaria, " The hour cometh, and now is, when the true worshippers shall worship the Father in spirit and in truth " (iv. 23), stands along with this other, " The hour cometh, and now is, when the dead shall hear the voice of the Son of God ; and they that hear shall live " (v. 25). As in the former passage Jesus indicates the true and perfect worship of God in the latter-day, so in the latter He indicates the eternal and blessed life of the latter-day period. But in both passages He represents what belongs to the latter-day as something future, and yet as something already existing in the present. The idea, peculiar to the Johannine discourses, of "eternal life" as not a benefit to be hoped for merely in the future, but as a present blissful possession on the part of believers,[1] stands in the clearest correspondence to Jesus' view of the kingdom of God found in the synoptical dis-courses. We can find no deeper ground for this Johannine usage of the originally purely eschatological conception of "eternal life," than the one involved in that view of Jesus in regard to the kingdom of God, viz. that the state of high blessedness, which the Jews regarded only as eschatological, and as one to be introduced by God through a miraculous change of all things and relationships, was, in His view, already

[1] Cf. p. 246 ff.

being realised in the earthly present. And, conversely, the usage of the conception of the kingdom of God in the synoptical discourses, as partly denoting the ideal state of blessing which Jesus was aware of being in large measure established even in the present life, and partly that future heavenly state in which Jesus foresaw the goal of the present development of the kingdom of God, has no more striking analogy than the Johannine usage of the idea " eternal life." This latter idea also, in part, signifies the possession of Divine blessings of which believers have inward experience on earth, and, in part, simply the future heavenly life of bliss, which has its real foundation in the present possession of Divine grace.[1] As little can we regard this Johannine usage as a contradictory one, and as little can we conclude from it that the writer of these discourses had changed and developed his view of eternal life, as we can conclude from the analogous usage of the idea of the kingdom of God in the synoptical discourses, that Jesus at different times possessed a different view of the nature of the kingdom of God. The same expression may well be used in a wider and a narrower sense.

5. In conclusion, we must refer to the fact that Paul has used the idea of the kingdom of God in the same sense as we have found employed by Jesus. The idea is not often expressed by Paul, but, remarkably enough, he uses it several times in sententious sayings, in which the apostle reminds his reader of the general principles which he regards as the

[1] Cf. the passages cited formerly at p. 248 f.

elements of the Christian doctrine communicated to them. With him the idea, in part, plainly refers to the future heavenly state of the kingdom as it is to be introduced by the second coming of Christ. When Paul "forewarned" the Galatians, as he had previously forewarned them, that they who practise the works of the flesh, fornication, impurity, etc., cannot inherit the kingdom of God (Gal. v. 21), it is clear that the latter term is understood eschatologically. The same must be the case where he reminds the Corinthians that an immoral walk excludes men from inheriting the kingdom of God: "Know ye not that the unrighteous shall not inherit the kingdom of God? Be not deceived; neither fornicators, nor idolators, etc., shall inherit the kingdom of God" (1 Cor. vi. 9 f.). The same meaning is intended by him when, in course of his discussion on the resurrection of the dead at the Parousia, and the simultaneous change on the living, he lays down the principle: "Flesh and blood shall not inherit the kingdom of God; neither doth corruption inherit incorruption" (1 Cor. xv. 50). Also when he reminds the Thessalonians how he had formerly, when present among them, testified to them that they should walk "worthily of God who calleth you to His kingdom and glory" (1 Thess. ii. 12), he indicates that future kingdom to which God at present calls Christians; just as he does in speaking to them of the kingdom of God, which they would be counted worthy to reach because of their bearing sufferings in the present (2 Thess. i. 5). But along with these passages there are others, in which the kingdom of God is even as plainly represented as one to be attained and realised at present, and consisting in the present possession of salvation on the part of Christians, and in their present exercise of righteousness. When he writes to the Corinthians, "The kingdom of God is not in word, but in power" (1 Cor. iv. 20), as the ground for declaring that when he should come to Corinth he would know, not the word, but the power of those who were puffed up in the Church (ver. 21), and also when he writes to the Romans, "The kingdom of God is not meat and drink; but righteousness, and peace, and joy in the Holy Ghost" (Rom. xiv. 17); whence he deduced the precept to show a spirit of peaceableness and of loving forbearance towards brethren who were weak in faith (ver. 19 ff.), the context makes it clear in both places that he speaks of the kingdom of God as already existing. Also in the words to the Colossians, in which it is declared of God, "He has delivered us from the power of darkness, and has set us in the kingdom of the Son of His love" (Col. i. 13), the use of the past tense of the verbs clearly shows that the kingdom was one of which Paul and the Colossians were even then members, since they had been delivered from bondage to the powers of evil, and, in union with Christ, had become objects of the love of God. This difference of meaning in the use of the idea of the kingdom by Paul, with whom that idea does not stand as the central point of his doctrine, is all the more striking because its reason is not directly apparent. But we find the historical explanation of this peculiar Pauline usage of speech in the transformation which the idea of Jesus as to the kingdom of God underwent, and in the way in which he employed this traditional idea. And, conversely, this Pauline usage in its turn attests that the view of the kingdom of God which we have seen to be that of Jesus, can very well be regarded as a unity in spite of the term being employed in different ways in different places.[1]

---

[1] The fact that the expression used by Paul is "the kingdom of God" and not "the kingdom of heaven," affords additional evidence that the former title was the older one in the Christian Church. If Paul had used the expression "kingdom of heaven," this would have been regarded as plain evidence that this was the term actually employed by Jesus, and that the expression "kingdom of God" was introduced at a later time. We must draw the conclusion analogously from Paul's usage of the expression "kingdom of God." The form "kingdom of heaven" would very well have accorded with Paul's other views, expressed in such passages as 2 Cor. v. 1 ff.; Col. i. 5; iii. 1-4; Phil iii. 20 f.

BENGEL'S GNOMON.

'Stands out among the exegetical literature not only of the eighteenth century, but of all centuries, for its masterly terseness and precision, and for its combination of spiritual insight with the best scholarship of his time.'—Professor W. Sanday, D.D., Oxford.

Gnomon of the New Testament. By John Albert Bengel. Translated into English. With Original Notes, Explanatory and Illustrative. Edited by the Rev. Andrew R. Fausset, M.A. The Original Translation was in Five Large Volumes, demy 8vo, averaging more than 550 pp. each, and the very great demand for this Edition has induced the Publishers to issue the *Five* Volumes bound in *Three*, at the Subscription Price of 24s. net. They trust by this still further to increase its usefulness.

** The Five Volume Edition may still be had at the original Subscription, Price, £1, 11s. 6d. net.

The Bishop of Gloucester and Bristol says of Bengel:—' There is one expositor so uniquely eminent in drawing from Holy Scripture its deeper spiritual meaning, that it may be well for the student always to have at hand, for the New Testament, the *Gnomon* of *Bengel*, and to acquire through the help of this most introspective expositor the aptitude of drawing from the Holy Word its full message to the soul.'

STIER'S WORDS OF THE LORD JESUS.

The Words of the Lord Jesus. By Dr. Rudolph Stier. Eight Vols. 8vo (or the Eight Vols. bound in Four), £2, 2s. net.

The Words of the Risen Saviour, 8vo, 10s. 6d.; and

The Words of the Apostles, 8vo, 10s. 6d. (Or the Ten Volumes for £2, 12s. 6d. net.)

' The whole work is a treasury of thoughtful exposition. Its measure of practical and spiritual application, with exegetical criticism, commends it to the use of those whose duty it is to preach as well as to understand the Gospel of Christ.'—*Guardian.*

LANGE'S LIFE OF CHRIST.

The Life of the Lord Jesus Christ: A Complete Critical Examination of the Origin, Contents, and Connection of the Gospels. Translated from the German of J. P. Lange, D.D., Professor of Divinity in the University of Bonn. Edited, with additional Notes, by Marcus Dods, D.D. Cheap Edition, in Four Volumes, demy 8vo, price 28s. net.

' Stands in the front rank of lives of Christ; it first presents the life of Christ as given in the four Gospels together, and then as given by each Gospel separately from its peculiar standpoint.'—Principal A. Cave, D.D.

PROFESSOR EADIE'S COMMENTARIES.

Ephesians, Philippians, Colossians. By the late Professor J. Eadie, D.D. The Three Volumes are supplied at the price of 18s. net, or in separate Volumes, at 10s. 6d. each. They have been carefully edited by the Rev. William Young, M.A., Glasgow.

THE ANTE-NICENE CHRISTIAN LIBRARY.

The Ante-Nicene Christian Library. A Collection of all the Works of the Fathers of the Christian Church prior to the Council of Nicæa. Edited by the Rev. Professor ROBERTS, D.D., and Principal JAMES DONALDSON, LL.D., St. Andrews. In Twenty-four handsome 8vo Volumes, Subscription Price £6, 6s. net; or a selection of Twelve Volumes for £3, 3s. net.

Any Volume may be had separately, price 10s. 6d.

This Series has been received with marked approval by all sections of the Christian Church in this country and in the United States, as supplying what has long been felt to be a want, and also on account of the impartiality, learning, and care with which Editors and Translators have executed a very difficult task.

The following Works are included in the Series :—

Apostolic Fathers, comprising Clement's Epistle to the Corinthians; Polycarp to the Ephesians; Martyrdom of Polycarp; Epistle of Barnabas; Epistles of Ignatius (longer and shorter, and also the Syriac Version); Martyrdom of Ignatius; Epistle to Diognetus; Pastor of Hermas: Papias; Spurious Epistles of Ignatius. One Volume. **Justin Martyr; Athenagoras.** One Volume. **Tatian; Theophilus; The Clementine Recognitions.** One Volume. **Clement of Alexandria,** comprising Exhortation to Heathen; The Instructor; and the Miscellanies. Two Volumes. **Hippolytus,** Volume First; Refutation of all Heresies, and Fragments from his Commentaries. **Irenæus,** Volume First. **Irenæus** (completion) and **Hippolytus** (completion); Fragments of Third Century. One Volume. **Tertullian against Marcion.** One Volume. **Cyprian;** The Epistles and Treatises; **Novatian; Minucius Felix.** Two Volumes. **Origen:** De Principiis; Letters; and portion of Treatise against Celsus. Two Volumes. **Tertullian:** To the Martyrs; Apology; To the Nations, etc. Three Volumes. **Methodius; Alexander of Lycopolis; Peter of Alexandria Anatolius; Clement on Virginity;** and Fragments. One Volume. **Apocryphal Gospels, Acts, and Revelations;** comprising all the very curious Apocryphal Writings of the first Three Centuries. One Volume. **Clementine Homilies; Apostolical Constitutions.** One Volume. **Arnobius.** One Volume. **Gregory Thaumaturgus; Dionysius; Archelaus; Syrian Fragments.** One Volume. **Lactantius;** together with the Testaments of the Twelve Patriarchs, and Fragments of the Second and Third Centuries. Two Volumes. **Early Liturgies and Remaining Fragments.** One Volume.

ST. AUGUSTINE'S WORKS.

The Works of Aurelius Augustine, Bishop of Hippo. Edited by MARCUS DODS, D.D. In Fifteen Volumes, demy 8vo, Subscription Price £3, 19s. net.

Any Volume may be had separately, price 10s. 6d.

The 'City of God.' Two Volumes.

Writings in connection with the Donatist Controversy. One Volume.

The Anti-Pelagian Works. Three Volumes.

Treatises against Faustus the Manichæan. One Volume.

On the Trinity. One Volume.

Commentary on John. Two Volumes.

The Harmony of the Evangelists, and the Sermon on the Mount. One Volume.

'Letters.' Two Volumes.

On Christian Doctrine, Enchiridion, on Catechising, and on Faith and the Creed. One Volume.

'Confessions.' With Copious Notes by Rev. J. G. PILKINGTON.

'For the reproduction of the "City of God" in an admirable English garb we are greatly indebted to the well-directed enterprise and energy of Messrs. Clark, and to the accuracy and scholarship of those who have undertaken the laborious task of translation.'—*Christian Observer.*

N.B.—Messrs. CLARK offer a Selection of Twelve Volumes from either or both of those Series at the Subscription Price of Three Guineas net (or a larger number at same proportion).

MEYER'S COMMENTARY ON THE NEW TESTAMENT.

'*Meyer has been long and well known to scholars as one of the very ablest of the German expositors of the New Testament. We are not sure whether we ought not to say that he is unrivalled as an interpreter of the grammatical and historical meaning of the sacred writers. The Publishers have now rendered another seasonable and important service to English students in producing this translation.*'—GUARDIAN.

Critical and Exegetical Commentary on the New Testament. By Dr. H. A. W. MEYER, Oberconsistorialrath, Hannover. Under the editorial care of Rev. Dr. DICKSON, late Professor of Divinity in the University of Glasgow. In Twenty handsome 8vo Volumes, price £5, 5s. net. Or a selection may now be made of any Eight Volumes for Two Guineas net (or a larger number at the same proportion).

Any Volume may be had separately, price 10s. 6d.

ST. MATTHEW'S GOSPEL, Two Volumes; MARK AND LUKE, Two Volumes; ST. JOHN'S GOSPEL, Two Volumes; ACTS OF THE APOSTLES, Two Volumes; ROMANS, Two Volumes; CORINTHIANS, Two Volumes; GALATIANS, One Volume; EPHESIANS AND PHILEMON, One Volume; PHILIPPIANS AND COLOSSIANS, One Volume; THESSALONIANS, One Volume; TIMOTHY AND TITUS, One Volume; HEBREWS, One Volume; JAMES AND JOHN, One Volume; PETER AND JUDE, One Volume.

The series, as written by Meyer himself, is completed by the publication of Ephesians with Philemon in one volume. But to this the Publishers have thought it right to add Thessalonians and Hebrews, by Dr. Lünemann, and the Pastoral and Catholic Epistles, by Dr. Huther.

'I need hardly add that the last edition of the accurate, perspicuous, and learned commentary of Dr. Meyer has been most carefully consulted throughout; and I must again, as in the preface to the Galatians, avow my great obligations to the acumen and scholarship of the learned editor.'—Bishop ELLICOTT in Preface to his *Commentary on Ephesians.*

'The ablest grammatical exegete of the age.'—PHILIP SCHAFF, D.D.

Works of Dr. John Owen. Edited by Rev. W. H. GOOLD, D.D., Edinburgh. In 24 Volumes, demy 8vo, price £4, 4s. net.

THE COMMENTARY ON THE EPISTLE TO THE HEBREWS, in Seven Volumes, may be had separately, price 42s.

Works of John Calvin. COMMENTARIES, Forty-five Volumes. TRACTS ON THE REFORMATION, Three Volumes.

A Selection of Six Volumes (or more at the same proportion) for 21s., with the exception of *PSALMS*, Vols. I. and V.; *HABAKKUK* and *CORINTHIANS*, 2 Vols.—which are now out of print. Any separate Volume (with the above exceptions), 6s.

THE LETTERS, Edited by Dr. BONNET, Two Volumes, 10s. 6d.

THE INSTITUTES, Two Volumes, Translated, 14s.

THE INSTITUTES, in Latin, Two Volumes, Tholuck's Edition, price 14s. net.

GRIMM'S LEXICON.

Greek-English Lexicon of the New Testament, Being Grimm's Wilke's Clavis Novi Testamenti. Translated, Revised, and Enlarged by JOSEPH HENRY THAYER, D.D., Bussey Professor of New Testament Criticism and Interpretation in the Divinity School of Harvard University. Now ready, Fourth Edition, demy 4to, price 36s.

'The best New Testament Greek Lexicon. . . It is a treasury of the results of exact scholarship.'—Bishop WESTCOTT.

'I regard it as a work of the greatest importance. . . . It seems to me a work showing the most patient diligence, and the most carefully arranged collection of useful and helpful references.'—THE BISHOP OF GLOUCESTER AND BRISTOL.

'An excellent book, the value of which for English students will, I feel sure, be best appreciated by those who use it most carefully.'—Professor F. J. A. HORT, D.D.

'This work has been eagerly looked for. . . . The result is an excellent book, which I do not doubt will be the best in the field for many years to come.'—Professor W. SANDAY, D.D., in *The Academy.*

'Undoubtedly the best of its kind. Beautifully printed and well translated, . . . it will be prized by students of the Christian Scriptures.'—*Athenœum.*

CREMER'S LEXICON.

Biblico - Theological Lexicon of New Testament Greek. By HERMANN CREMER, D.D., Professor of Theology in the University of Greifswald. Translated from the German of the Second Edition by WILLIAM URWICK, M.A. In demy 4to, Fourth Edition, with SUPPLEMENT, price 38s.

This Lexicon deals with words whose meaning in the Classics is modified or changed in Scripture, words which have become the bases and watchwords of Christian theology, tracing their history in their transference from the Classics into the LXX., and from the LXX. into the New Testament, and the gradual deepening and elevation of their meaning till they reach the fulness of New Testament thought.

'Dr. Cremer's work is highly and deservedly esteemed in Germany. It gives with care and thoroughness a complete history, as far as it goes, of each word and phrase that it deals with. . . . Dr. Cremer's explanations are most lucidly set out.'—*Guardian.*

'It is hardly possible to exaggerate the value of this work to the student of the Greek Testament. . . . The translation is accurate and idiomatic, and the additions to the later edition are considerable and important.'—*Church Bells.*

'We cannot find an important word in our Greek New Testament which is not discussed with a fulness and discrimination which leaves nothing to be desired.'—*Nonconformist.*

A Treatise on the Grammar of New Testament Greek, Regarded as a sure Basis for New Testament Exegesis. Translated from the German of Dr. G. B. WINER. Edited by Rev. W. F. MOULTON, D.D. With large additions and full Indices. In One large 8vo Volume, Ninth English Edition, price 15s.

'We need not say it is *the* Grammar of the New Testament. It is not only superior to all others, but *so* superior as to be by common consent the one work of reference on the subject. No other could be mentioned with it.'—*Literary Churchman.*

Greek and English Lexicon of the New Testament. By Professor EDWARD ROBINSON, D.D. In demy 8vo, price 9s.

'Excellent.'—Principal CAVE, D.D , Hackney College.

Abbott (T. K., B.D., D.Lit.)—EPHESIANS AND COLOSSIANS. (*International Critical Commentary.*) Post 8vo, 10s. 6d.

Adam (J., D.D.)—AN EXPOSITION OF THE EPISTLE OF JAMES. 8vo, 9s.

Adamson (Rev. T., B.D.)—STUDIES IN THE MIND OF CHRIST.

——— THE SPIRIT OF POWER.

Ahlfeld (Dr.), etc.—THE VOICE FROM THE CROSS. Cr. 8vo, price 5s.

Alcock (Deborah)—THE SEVEN CHURCHES OF ASIA. 1s.

Alexander (Prof. W. Lindsay)—BIBLICAL THEOLOGY. Two vols. 8vo, 21s.

Allen (Prof. A. V. G., D.D.)—LIFE OF JONATHAN EDWARDS. Fcap. 8vo, 5s.

——— CHRISTIAN INSTITUTIONS. (*International Theological Library.*) Post 8vo, 12s.

Ancient Faith in Modern Light, The. 8vo, 10s. 6d.

Andrews (S. J.)—THE LIFE OF OUR LORD. Large post 8vo, 9s.

Ante-Nicene Christian Library—A COLLECTION OF ALL THE WORKS OF THE FATHERS OF THE CHRISTIAN CHURCH PRIOR TO THE COUNCIL OF NICÆA. Twenty-four vols. 8vo, Subscription price, £6, 6s. *Additional Volume, containing MSS. discovered since the completion of the Series,* 12s. 6d. net.

Augustine's Works—Edited by MARCUS DODS, D.D. Fifteen vols. 8vo, Subscription price, £3, 19s. net.

Balfour (R. G., D.D.)—CENTRAL TRUTHS AND SIDE ISSUES. Crown 8vo, 3s. 6d.

Bannerman (Prof.)—THE CHURCH OF CHRIST. Two vols. 8vo, 21s.

Bannerman (D. D., D.D.)—THE DOCTRINE OF THE CHURCH. 8vo, 12s.

Baumgarten (Professor)—APOSTOLIC HISTORY. Three vols. 8vo, 27s.

Bayne (P., LL.D.)—THE FREE CHURCH OF SCOTLAND. Post 8vo, 3s. 6d.

Beck (Dr.)—OUTLINES OF BIBLICAL PSYCHOLOGY. Crown 8vo, 4s.

——— PASTORAL THEOLOGY IN THE NEW TESTAMENT. Crown 8vo, 6s.

Bengel—GNOMON OF THE NEW TESTAMENT. With Original Notes, Explanatory and Illustrative. Five vols. 8vo, Subscription price, 31s. 6d. *Cheaper Edition, the five volumes bound in three,* 24s.

Besser's CHRIST THE LIFE OF THE WORLD. Price 6s.

Beyschlag (W., D.D.)—NEW TESTAMENT THEOLOGY. Two vols. demy 8vo, 18s. net.

Bible Dictionary. Edited by JAS. HASTINGS, D.D. *See page* 16. *Special Prospectus on application.*

** Detailed Catalogue free on application.

Bible-Class Handbooks. Crown 8vo. Forty-three Volumes, 1s. 3d. to 3s. each. Edited by Prof. MARCUS DODS, D.D., and ALEX. WHYTE, D.D. *Detailed List free on application.*

Bible-Class Primers. Thirty-three now issued in the Series. Edited by Prof. S. D. F. SALMOND, D.D. Paper covers, 6d. each ; free by post, 7d. In cloth, 8d. ; free by post, 9d. *Detailed List free on application.*

Blaikie (Prof. W. G., D.D.)—THE PREACHERS OF SCOTLAND FROM THE 6TH TO THE 19TH CENTURY. Post 8vo, 7s. 6d.

Blake (Buchanan, B.D.)—HOW TO READ THE PROPHETS. Part I.— The Pre-Exilian Minor Prophets (with Joel). Second Edition, 4s. Part II. —Isaiah (ch. i.-xxxix.). Second Edition, 2s. 6d. Part III.—Jeremiah, 4s. Part IV.—Ezekiel, 4s. Part V.—Isaiah (ch. xl.-lxvi.), and the Post-Exilian Prophets. *The Series being now complete, Messrs. Clark offer the Set of Five Volumes for* 15s.

Bleek's INTRODUCTION TO THE NEW TESTAMENT. Two vols. 8vo, 21s.

Briggs (Prof. C. A., D.D.)—BIBLICAL STUDY. Fourth Edition, post 8vo, 7s. 6d.

———— AMERICAN PRESBYTERIANISM. Post 8vo, 7s. 6d.

———— MESSIANIC PROPHECY. Post 8vo, 7s. 6d.

———— THE MESSIAH OF THE APOSTLES. Post 8vo, 7s. 6d.

———— THE MESSIAH OF THE GOSPELS. Post 8vo, 6s. 6d.

———— WHITHER ? A Theological Question for the Times. Post 8vo,7s.6d.

———— THE BIBLE, THE CHURCH, AND THE REASON. Post 8vo, 6s. 6d.

———— THE HIGHER CRITICISM OF THE HEXATEUCH. 6s. 6d.

Brockelmann (C.)—LEXICON SYRIACUM. With a Preface by Professor T. NÖLDEKE. Crown 4to, 30s. net.

Bruce (Prof. A. B., D.D.)—THE TRAINING OF THE TWELVE ; exhibiting the Twelve Disciples under Discipline for the Apostleship. Fifth Edition, 8vo, 10s. 6d.

———— THE HUMILIATION OF CHRIST. 3rd Ed., 8vo, 10s. 6d.

———— THE KINGDOM OF GOD ; or, Christ's Teaching according to the Synoptical Gospels. New Edition, 7s. 6d.

———— APOLOGETICS ; OR, CHRISTIANITY DEFENSIVELY STATED. (*International Theological Library.*) Post 8vo, 10s. 6d.

———— ST. PAUL'S CONCEPTION OF CHRISTANITY. Post 8vo, 7s. 6d.

Bruce (W. S., D.D.)—THE ETHICS OF THE OLD TESTAMENT. Cr. 8vo, 4s.

Buchanan (Professor)—THE DOCTRINE OF JUSTIFICATION. 8vo, 10s. 6d.

———— ON COMFORT IN AFFLICTION. Crown 8vo, 2s. 6d.

———— ON IMPROVEMENT OF AFFLICTION. Crown 8vo, 2s. 6d.

Bungener (Felix)—ROME AND THE COUNCIL IN 19TH CENTURY. Cr.8vo,5s.

Burton (Prof. E.)—SYNTAX OF THE MOODS AND TENSES IN NEW TESTAMENT GREEK. Post 8vo, 5s. 6d. net.

Calvin's INSTITUTES OF CHRISTIAN RELIGION. (Translation.) 2vols.8vo,14s.

———— COMMENTARIES. Forty-five Vols.

Calvini Institutio Christianæ Religionis. Curavit A. THOLUCK. Two vols. 8vo, Subscription price, 14s.

Candlish (Prof. J. S., D.D.)—THE KINGDOM OF GOD, BIBLICALLY AND HISTORICALLY CONSIDERED. 8vo, 10s. 6d.

Caspari (C. E.)—A CHRONOLOGICAL AND GEOGRAPHICAL INTRODUCTION TO THE LIFE OF CHRIST. 8vo, 7s. 6d.

Caspers (A.)—THE FOOTSTEPS OF CHRIST. Crown 8vo, 7s. 6d.

Cassel (Prof.)—COMMENTARY ON ESTHER. 8vo, 10s. 6d.

Cave (Principal A., D.D.)—THE SCRIPTURAL DOCTRINE OF SACRIFICE AND ATONEMENT. Second Edition, 8vo, 10s. 6d.

———— AN INTRODUCTION TO THEOLOGY. Second Edition, 8vo, 12s.

Chapman (Principal C., LL.D.)—PRE-ORGANIC EVOLUTION AND THE BIBLICAL IDEA OF GOD. Crown 8vo, 6s.

Christlieb (Prof. T., D.D.)—MODERN DOUBT AND CHRISTIAN BELIEF. 8vo, 10s. 6d.

———— HOMILETIC: Lectures on Preaching. 7s. 6d.

Concordance to the Greek Testament—MOULTON (W. F., D.D.) and GEDEN (A. S., M.A.). Crown 4to, 26s. net.

Crawford (J. H., M.A.)—THE BROTHERHOOD OF MANKIND. Crown 8vo, 5s.

Cremer (Professor)—BIBLICO-THEOLOGICAL LEXICON OF NEW TESTAMENT GREEK. Third Edition, with Supplement, demy 4to, 38s.

Crippen (Rev. T. G.)—A POPULAR INTRODUCTION TO THE HISTORY OF CHRISTIAN DOCTRINE. 8vo, 9s.

Critical Review OF THEOLOGICAL AND PHILOSOPHICAL LITERATURE. Edited by Prof. S. D. F. SALMOND, D.D. Quarterly, 1s. 6d.

Cunningham (Principal)—HISTORICAL THEOLOGY. Two vols. 8vo, 21s.

Curtiss (Dr. S. I.)—THE LEVITICAL PRIESTS. Crown 8vo, 5s.

———— FRANZ DELITZSCH: A Memorial Tribute. *Portrait.* Cr. 8vo, 3s.

Dabney (Prof. R. L., D.D.)—THE SENSUALISTIC PHILOSOPHY OF THE NINETEENTH CENTURY CONSIDERED. Crown 8vo, 6s.

Dahle (Bishop)—LIFE AFTER DEATH. Demy 8vo, 10s. 6d.

Davidson (Prof. A.B., D.D., LL.D.)—AN INTRODUCTORY HEBREW GRAMMAR. With Progressive Exercises in Reading and Writing. 14th Edition, 8vo, 7s. 6d.

———— A SYNTAX OF THE HEBREW LANGUAGE. 2nd Ed., 8vo, 7s. 6d.

Deane (Wm., M.A.) — PSEUDEPIGRAPHA: An Account of Certain Apocryphal Writings of the Jews and Early Christians. Post 8vo, 7s. 6d.

Delitzsch (Prof.)—SYSTEM OF BIBLICAL PSYCHOLOGY, 8vo, 12s.; NEW COMMENTARY ON GENESIS, 2 vols. 8vo, 21s.; PSALMS, 3 vols., 31s. 6d.; PROVERBS, 2 vols., 21s.; SONG OF SOLOMON AND ECCLESIASTES, 10s. 6d.; ISAIAH, Fourth Edition, rewritten, 2 vols., 21s.; HEBREWS, 2 vols., 21s.

Dillmann (Prof. A., D.D.)—GENESIS: Critical and Exegetical Commentary. Two vols., 21s.

Doedes—MANUAL OF NEW TESTAMENT HERMENEUTICS. Cr. 8vo, 3s.

Döllinger (Dr.)—HIPPOLYTUS AND CALLISTUS. 8vo, 7s. 6d.

———— DECLARATIONS AND LETTERS ON THE VATICAN DECREES, 1869-1887. Authorised Translation. Crown 8vo, 3s. 6d.

Dorner (Professor)—HISTORY OF THE DEVELOPMENT OF THE DOCTRINE OF THE PERSON OF CHRIST. Five vols. 8vo, £2, 12s. 6d.

Dorner (Professor)—SYSTEM OF CHRISTIAN DOCTRINE. 4 vols. 8vo, £2, 2s.

——— SYSTEM OF CHRISTIAN ETHICS. 8vo, 14s.

Driver (Prof. S. R., D.D.)—AN INTRODUCTION TO THE LITERATURE OF THE OLD TESTAMENT. (*International Theological Library.*) Sixth Edition, post 8vo, 12s.

——— DEUTERONOMY : A Critical and Exegetical Commentary. (*International Critical Commentary.*) Post 8vo, 12s.

Du Bose (Prof. W. P., D.D.)—THE ECUMENICAL COUNCILS. (*Eras of Church History.*) 6s.

Duff (Prof. David, D.D.)—THE EARLY CHURCH. 8vo, 12s.

Dyke (Paul Van)—THE AGE OF THE RENASCENCE. With an Introduction by HENRY VAN DYKE. (*Eras of Church History.*) 6s.

Eadie (Professor)—COMMENTARIES ON ST. PAUL'S EPISTLES TO THE EPHESIANS, PHILIPPIANS, COLOSSIANS. New and Revised Editions, Edited by Rev. WM. YOUNG, M.A. Three vols. 8vo, 10s. 6d. each ; *or set,* 18s. net.

Ebrard (Dr. J. H. A.)—THE GOSPEL HISTORY. 8vo, 10s. 6d.

——— APOLOGETICS. Three vols. 8vo, 31s. 6d.

——— COMMENTARY ON THE EPISTLES OF ST. JOHN. 8vo, 10s. 6d.

Edgar (R. M'C., D.D.)—THE GOSPEL OF A RISEN SAVIOUR. Post 8vo, 7s. 6d.

Elliott—ON THE INSPIRATION OF THE HOLY SCRIPTURES. 8vo, 6s.

Eras of the Christian Church—
    Du BOSE (Prof. W. P., D.D.)—The Ecumenical Councils. 6s.
    DYKE (PAUL VAN)—The Age of the Renascence. 6s.
    LOCKE (CLINTON, D.D.)—The Age of the Great Western Schism. 6s.
    LUDLOW (J. M., D.D.)—The Age of the Crusades. 6s.
    VINCENT (Prof. M. R., D.D.)—The Age of Hildebrand. 6s.

  The following Volumes are in preparation—
    BARTLET (J. VERNON, M.A.)—The Apostolic Age.
    CLARK (Prof. W. R., LL.D., D.C.L.)—The Anglican Reformation.
    POTTER (Right Rev. H. C., D.D., LL.D.)—The Post-Apostolic Age.
    WALKER (Prof. W., Ph.D., D.D.)—The Protestant Reformation.
    WELLS (Prof. C. L.)—The Age of Charlemagne.

Ernesti—BIBLICAL INTERPRETATION OF NEW TESTAMENT. Two vols., 8s.

Ewald (Heinrich)—HEBREW SYNTAX. 8vo, 8s. 6d.

——— REVELATION : Its Nature and Record. 8vo, 10s. 6d.

——— OLD AND NEW TESTAMENT THEOLOGY. 8vo, 10s. 6d.

Expository Times. Edited by JAMES HASTINGS, D.D. Monthly, 6d.

Fairbairn (Prin.)—THE REVELATION OF LAW IN SCRIPTURE, 8vo, 10s. 6d.

——— EZEKIEL AND THE BOOK OF HIS PROPHECY. 4th Ed., 8vo, 10s. 6d.

——— PROPHECY. Second Edition, 8vo, 10s. 6d.

——— PASTORAL THEOLOGY. Crown 8vo, 6s.

Fisher (Prof. G. P., D.D., LL.D.)—HISTORY OF CHRISTIAN DOCTRINE. (*International Theological Library.*) Post 8vo, 12s.

Forbes (Prof.)—SYMMETRICAL STRUCTURE OF SCRIPTURE. 8vo, 8s. 6d.

——— ANALYTICAL COMMENTARY ON THE ROMANS. 8vo, 10s. 6d.

——— STUDIES IN THE BOOK OF PSALMS. 8vo, 7s. 6d.

——— THE SERVANT OF THE LORD IN ISAIAH XL.–LXVI. Cr. 8vo, 5s.

Foreign Theological Library—*For details see p.* 13.

Forrest (D. W., M.A.)—THE CHRIST OF HISTORY AND OF EX-PERIENCE. 10s. 6d.

Frank (Prof. F. H.)—SYSTEM OF CHRISTIAN EVIDENCE. 8vo, 10s. 6d.

Funcke (Otto)—THE WORLD OF FAITH AND THE EVERYDAY WORLD, As displayed in the Footsteps of Abraham. Post 8vo, 7s. 6d.

Gebhardt (H.)—THE DOCTRINE OF THE APOCALYPSE, AND ITS RELATION TO THE DOCTRINE OF THE GOSPEL AND EPISTLES OF JOHN. 8vo, 10s. 6d.

Gerlach—COMMENTARY ON THE PENTATEUCH. 8vo, 10s. 6d.

Gieseler (Dr. J. C. L.)—ECCLESIASTICAL HISTORY. Four vols. 8vo, £2, 2s.

Gifford (Canon)—VOICES OF THE PROPHETS. Crown 8vo, 3s. 6d.

Given (Rev. Prof. J. J.)—THE TRUTH OF SCRIPTURE IN CONNECTION WITH REVELATION, INSPIRATION, AND THE CANON. 8vo, 6s.

Glasgow (Prof.)—APOCALYPSE TRANSLATED AND EXPOUNDED. 8vo, 10/6.

Gloag (Paton J., D.D.)—THE MESSIANIC PROPHECIES. Crown 8vo, 7s. 6d.

—— INTRODUCTION TO THE PAULINE EPISTLES. 8vo, 12s.

—— INTRODUCTION TO THE CATHOLIC EPISTLES. 8vo, 10s. 6d.

—— EXEGETICAL STUDIES. Crown 8vo, 5s.

—— INTRODUCTION TO THE SYNOPTIC GOSPELS. 8vo, 7s. 6d.

—— THE PRIMEVAL WORLD. Crown 8vo, 3s.

Godet (Prof. F.)—AN INTRODUCTION TO THE NEW TESTAMENT: 'The Epistles of St. Paul.' *Authorised Translation.* 8vo, 12s. 6d. net.

—— COMMENTARY ON ST. LUKE'S GOSPEL. Two vols. 8vo, **21s.**

—— COMMENTARY ON ST. JOHN'S GOSPEL. Three vols. 8vo, 31s. 6d.

—— COMMENTARY ON EPISTLE TO THE ROMANS. Two vols. 8vo, 21s.

—— COMMENTARY ON 1ST EPISTLE TO CORINTHIANS. 2 vols. 8vo, 21s.

—— DEFENCE OF THE CHRISTIAN FAITH. Cheap Edition, crown 8vo, 4s.

Goebel (Siegfried)—THE PARABLES OF JESUS. 8vo, 10s. 6d.

Gotthold's Emblems; or, INVISIBLE THINGS UNDERSTOOD BY THINGS THAT ARE MADE. Crown 8vo, 5s.

Gould (Prof. E. P., D.D.)—ST. MARK. (*International Critical Commentary.*) Post 8vo, 10s. 6d.

Grimm's GREEK-ENGLISH LEXICON OF THE NEW TESTAMENT. Translated, Revised, and Enlarged by JOSEPH H. THAYER, D.D. Demy 4to, 36s.

Guyot (Arnold, LL.D.)—CREATION; or, The Biblical Cosmogony in the Light of Modern Science. With Illustrations. Crown 8vo, 5s. 6d.

Hagenbach (Dr. K. R.)—HISTORY OF DOCTRINES. 3 vols. 8vo, 31s. 6d.

—— HISTORY OF THE REFORMATION. 2 vols. 8vo, 21s.

Halcombe (Rev. J. J., M.A.)—WHAT THINK YE OF THE GOSPELS? A Handbook of Gospel Study. 8vo, 3s. 6d.

Hall (Newman, D.D.)—THE LORD'S PRAYER. Third Edition, crown 8vo, 4s. 6d.

—— GETHSEMANE; or, Leaves of Healing from the Garden of Grief. Second Edition, crown 8vo, 4s.

—— DIVINE BROTHERHOOD. Crown 8vo, 4s.

Hamilton (T., D.D.)—BEYOND THE STARS; or, Heaven, its Inhabitants, Occupations, and Life. Third Edition, crown 8vo, 3s. 6d.

Harless (Dr. C. A.)—SYSTEM OF CHRISTIAN ETHICS. 8vo, 10s. 6d.

Harris (S., D.D.)—GOD THE CREATOR AND LORD OF ALL. Two vols. post 8vo, 16s.

Haupt (Erich)—THE FIRST EPISTLE OF ST. JOHN. 8vo, 10s. 6d.

Hävernick (H. A. Ch.)—INTRODUCTION TO OLD TESTAMENT. 10s. 6d.

Heard (Rev. J. B., A.M.)—THE TRIPARTITE NATURE OF MAN—SPIRIT, SOUL, AND BODY. Fifth Edition, crown 8vo, 6s.

———— OLD AND NEW THEOLOGY. A Constructive Critique. Cr. 8vo, 6s.

———— ALEXANDRIAN AND CARTHAGINIAN THEOLOGY CONTRASTED. The Hulsean Lectures, 1892-93. Crown 8vo, 6s.

Hefele (Bishop)—A HISTORY OF THE COUNCILS OF THE CHURCH. Vol. I., to A.D. 325. Vol. II., A.D. 326 to 429. Vol. III., A.D. 431 to the close of the Council of Chalcedon, 451. Vol. IV., A.D. 451 to 680. Vol. V., A.D. 626 to 787. 8vo, 12s. each.

Hengstenberg (Professor)—COMMENTARY ON PSALMS, 3 vols. 8vo, 33s.; ECCLESIASTES, ETC., 8vo, 9s.; EZEKIEL, 8vo, 10s. 6d.; THE GENUINENESS OF DANIEL, ETC., 8vo, 12s.; HISTORY OF THE KINGDOM OF GOD, 2 vols. 8vo, 21s.; CHRISTOLOGY OF THE OLD TESTAMENT, 4 vols. 8vo, £2, 2s.; ST. JOHN'S GOSPEL, 2 vols. 8vo, 21s.

Herzog—ENCYCLOPÆDIA OF LIVING DIVINES, ETC., OF ALL DE-NOMINATIONS IN EUROPE AND AMERICA. (*Supplement to Herzog's Encyclopædia.*) Imp. 8vo, 8s.

Hill (Rev. J. Hamlyn, D.D.)—THE EARLIEST LIFE OF CHRIST EVER COMPILED FROM THE FOUR GOSPELS: Being 'The Diatessaron of Tatian' Literally Translated from the Arabic Version, and containing the Four Gospels woven into one Story. With an Historical and Critical Introduction, Notes, and Appendix. 8vo, 10s. 6d.

———— ST. EPHRAEM THE SYRIAN. 8vo, 7s. 6d.

Hutchison (John, D.D.)—COMMENTARY ON THESSALONIANS. 8vo, 9s.

———— COMMENTARY ON PHILIPPIANS. 8vo, 7s. 6d.

———— OUR LORD'S SIGNS IN ST. JOHN'S GOSPEL. Demy 8vo, 7s. 6d.

International Critical Commentary.
DRIVER (Prof. S. R., D.D.)—Deuteronomy. Post 8vo, 12s.
MOORE (GEORGE, D.D.)—Judges. Post 8vo, 12s.
GOULD (Prof. E. P., D.D.)—St. Mark. Post 8vo, 10s. 6d.
PLUMMER (ALFRED, D.D.)—St. Luke. Post 8vo, 12s.
SANDAY (Prof. W., D.D.) and HEADLAM (A. C., B.D.)—Romans. Post 8vo, 12s.
ABBOTT (Prof. T. K., B.D., D.Lit.)—Ephesians and Colossians. Post 8vo, 10s. 6d.
VINCENT (Prof. M. R., D.D.)—Philippians and Philemon. Post 8vo, 8s. 6d.
For List of future Volumes see p. 15.

International Theological Library.
DRIVER (Prof. S. R., D.D.)—An Introduction to the Literature of the Old Testament. Post 8vo, 12s.
SMYTH (NEWMAN, D.D.)—Christian Ethics. Post 8vo, 10s. 6d.
BRUCE (Prof. A. B., D.D.)—Apologetics. Post 8vo, 10s. 6d.
FISHER (Prof. G. P., D.D., LL.D.)—History of Christian Doctrine. Post 8vo, 12s.
ALLEN (Prof. A. V. G., D.D.)—Christian Institutions. Post 8vo, 12s.
MCGIFFERT (Prof. A. C., Ph.D.)—The Apostolic Age. Post 8vo, 12s.
For List of future Volumes see p. 14.

Janet (Paul)—FINAL CAUSES. Second Edition, demy 8vo, 12s.

────── THE THEORY OF MORALS. Demy 8vo, 10s. 6d.

Johnstone (Prof. R., D.D.)—COMMENTARY ON 1ST PETER. 8vo, 10s. 6d.

Jones (E. E. C.)—ELEMENTS OF LOGIC. 8vo, 7s. 6d.

Jouffroy—PHILOSOPHICAL ESSAYS. Fcap. 8vo, 5s.

Kaftan (Prof. J., D.D.)—THE TRUTH OF THE CHRISTIAN RELIGION. *Authorised Translation.* 2 vols. 8vo, 16s. net.

Kant—THE METAPHYSIC OF ETHICS. Crown 8vo, 6s.

────── PHILOSOPHY OF LAW. Trans. by W. HASTIE, B.D. Cr. 8vo, 5s.

────── PRINCIPLES OF POLITICS, ETC. Crown 8vo, 2s. 6d.

Keil (Prof.)—PENTATEUCH, 3 vols. 8vo, 31s. 6d. ; JOSHUA, JUDGES, AND RUTH, 8vo, 10s. 6d. ; SAMUEL, 8vo, 10s. 6d. ; KINGS, 8vo, 10s. 6d.; CHRONICLES, 8vo, 10s. 6d. ; EZRA, NEHEMIAH, ESTHER, 8vo, 10s. 6d. ; JEREMIAH, 2 vols. 8vo, 21s. ; EZEKIEL, 2 vols. 8vo, 21s. ; DANIEL, 8vo, 10s. 6d. ; MINOR PROPHETS, 2 vols. 8vo, 21s. ; INTRODUCTION TO THE CANONICAL SCRIPTURES OF THE OLD TESTAMENT, 2 vols. 8vo, 21s. ; HANDBOOK OF BIBLICAL ARCHÆOLOGY, 2 vols. 8vo, 21s.

Kennedy (H. A. A., M.A., D.Sc.)—SOURCES OF NEW TESTAMENT GREEK. Post 8vo, 5s.

Keymer (Rev. N., M.A.)—NOTES ON GENESIS. Crown 8vo, 1s. 6d.

Kidd (James, D.D.)—MORALITY AND RELIGION. 8vo, 10s. 6d.

Killen (Prof.)—THE FRAMEWORK OF THE CHURCH. 8vo, 9s.

────── THE OLD CATHOLIC CHURCH. 8vo, 9s.

────── THE IGNATIAN EPISTLES ENTIRELY SPURIOUS. Cr. 8vo, 2s. 6d.

König (Dr. F. E.)—THE RELIGIOUS HISTORY OF ISRAEL. Cr. 8vo, 3s. 6d.

Krummacher (Dr. F. W.)—THE SUFFERING SAVIOUR ; or, Meditations on the Last Days of the Sufferings of Christ. Eighth Edition, crown 8vo, 6s.

────── DAVID, THE KING OF ISRAEL. Second Edition, cr. 8vo, 6s.

────── AUTOBIOGRAPHY. Crown 8vo, 6s.

Kurtz (Prof.)—HANDBOOK OF CHURCH HISTORY (from 1517). 8vo, 7s. 6d.

────── HISTORY OF THE OLD COVENANT. Three vols. 8vo, 31s. 6d.

Ladd (Prof. G. T.)—THE DOCTRINE OF SACRED SCRIPTURE: A Critical, Historical, and Dogmatic Inquiry into the Origin and Nature of the Old and New Testaments. Two vols. 8vo, 1600 pp., 24s.

Laidlaw (Prof. J., D.D.)—THE BIBLE DOCTRINE OF MAN ; or, The Anthropology and Psychology of Scripture. New Edition Revised and Rearranged, post 8vo, 7s. 6d.

Lane (Laura M.)—LIFE OF ALEXANDER VINET. Crown 8vo, 7s. 6d.

Lange (J. P., D.D.)—THE LIFE OF OUR LORD JESUS CHRIST. Edited by MARCUS DODS, D.D. 2nd Ed., in 4 vols. 8vo, price 28s. net.

——— COMMENTARIES ON THE OLD AND NEW TESTAMENTS. Edited by PHILIP SCHAFF, D.D. OLD TESTAMENT, 14 vols. ; NEW TESTAMENT, 10 vols. ; APOCRYPHA, 1 vol. Subscription price, net, 15s. each.

——— ST. MATTHEW AND ST. MARK, 3 vols. 8vo, 31s. 6d. ; ST. LUKE, 2 vols. 8vo, 18s. ; ST. JOHN, 2 vols. 8vo, 21s.

Lechler (Prof. G. V., D.D.)—THE APOSTOLIC AND POST-APOSTOLIC TIMES. Their Diversity and Unity in Life and Doctrine. 2 vols. cr. 8vo, 16s.

Lehmann (Pastor)—SCENES FROM THE LIFE OF JESUS. Cr. 8vo, 3s. 6d.

Lewis (Tayler, LL.D.)—THE SIX DAYS OF CREATION. Cr. 8vo, 7s. 6d.

Lichtenberger (F., D.D.)—HISTORY OF GERMAN THEOLOGY IN THE 19TH CENTURY. 8vo, 14s.

Lilley (J. P., M.A.)—THE LORD'S SUPPER : Its Origin, Nature, and Use. Crown 8vo, 5s.

Lisco (F. G.)—PARABLES OF JESUS EXPLAINED. Fcap. 8vo, 5s.

Locke (Clinton, D.D.)—THE AGE OF THE GREAT WESTERN SCHISM. (*Eras of Church History.*) 6s.

Lotze (Hermann)—MICROCOSMUS : An Essay concerning Man and his relation to the World. Cheaper Edition, 2 vols. 8vo (1450 pp.), 24s.

Ludlow (J. M., D.D.)—THE AGE OF THE CRUSADES. (*Eras of Church History.*) 6s.

Luthardt, Kahnis, and Brückner—THE CHURCH. Crown 8vo, 5s.

Luthardt (Prof.)—ST. JOHN THE AUTHOR OF THE FOURTH GOSPEL. 7s.6d.

——— COMMENTARY ON ST. JOHN'S GOSPEL. 3 vols. 8vo, 31s. 6d.

——— HISTORY OF CHRISTIAN ETHICS. 8vo, 10s. 6d.

——— APOLOGETIC LECTURES ON THE FUNDAMENTAL (7 *Ed.*), SAVING (5 *Ed.*), MORAL TRUTHS OF CHRISTIANITY (4 *Ed.*). 3 vols. cr. 8vo, 6s. each.

Macdonald—INTRODUCTION TO PENTATEUCH. Two vols. 8vo, 21s.

——— THE CREATION AND FALL. 8vo, 12s.

Macgregor (Rev. Jas., D.D.) — THE APOLOGY OF THE CHRISTIAN RELIGION. 8vo, 10s. 6d.

——— THE REVELATION AND THE RECORD : Essays on Matters of Previous Question in the Proof of Christianity. 8vo, 7s. 6d.

——— STUDIES IN THE HISTORY OF NEW TESTAMENT APOLOGETICS. 8vo, 7s. 6d.

Macgregor (Rev. G. H. C., M.A.)—SO GREAT SALVATION. Crown 32mo, 1s.

Macpherson (Rev. John, M.A.)—COMMENTARY ON THE EPISTLE TO THE EPHESIANS. 8vo, 10s. 6d.

McCosh (James), Life of. 8vo, 9s.

McGiffert (Prof. A. C., Ph.D.)—HISTORY OF CHRISTIANITY IN THE APOSTOLIC AGE. (*International Theological Library.*) Post 8vo, 12s.

M'Realsham (E. D.)—ROMANS DISSECTED. A Critical Analysis of the Epistle to the Romans. Crown 8vo, 2s.

Mair (A., D.D.)—STUDIES IN THE CHRISTIAN EVIDENCES. Third Edition, Revised and Enlarged, crown 8vo, 6s.

Martensen (Bishop)—CHRISTIAN DOGMATICS. 8vo, 10s. 6d.

———— CHRISTIAN ETHICS. (GENERAL — INDIVIDUAL — SOCIAL.) Three vols. 8vo, 10s. 6d. each.

Matheson (Geo., D.D.)—GROWTH OF THE SPIRIT OF CHRISTIANITY, from the First Century to the Dawn of the Lutheran Era. Two vols. 8vo, 21s.

Meyer (Dr.) — CRITICAL AND EXEGETICAL COMMENTARIES ON THE NEW TESTAMENT. Twenty vols. 8vo. *Subscription Price*, £5, 5s. *net ; Non-Subscription Price*, 10s. 6d. each volume.
> ST. MATTHEW, 2 vols. ; MARK AND LUKE, 2 vols. ; ST. JOHN, 2 vols. ; ACTS, 2 vols. ; ROMANS, 2 vols. ; CORINTHIANS, 2 vols. ; GALATIANS, one vol. ; EPHESIANS AND PHILEMON, one vol. ; PHILIPPIANS AND COLOSSIANS, one vol.; THESSALONIANS (*Dr. Lünemann*), one vol. ; THE PASTORAL EPISTLES (*Dr. Huther*), one vol. ; HEBREWS (*Dr. Lünemann*), one vol. ; ST. JAMES AND ST. JOHN'S EPISTLES (*Huther*), one vol. ; PETER AND JUDE (*Dr. Huther*), one vol.

Michie (Charles, M.A.)—BIBLE WORDS AND PHRASES. 18mo, 1s.

Milligan (Prof. W., D.D.)—THE RESURRECTION OF THE DEAD. Second Edition, crown 8vo, 4s. 6d.

Monrad (Dr. D. G.)—THE WORLD OF PRAYER. Crown 8vo, 4s. 6d.

Moore (Prof. G., D.D.)—JUDGES. (*International Critical Commentary.*) Post 8vo, 12s.

Morgan (J., D.D.)—SCRIPTURE TESTIMONY TO THE HOLY SPIRIT. 7s. 6d.

———— EXPOSITION OF THE FIRST EPISTLE OF JOHN. 8vo, 7s. 6d.

Moulton (W. F., D.D.) and Geden (A. S., M.A.)—A CONCORDANCE TO THE GREEK TESTAMENT. Crown 4to, 26s. net, and 31s. 6d. net.

Muir (Sir W.)—MOHAMMEDAN CONTROVERSY, ETC. 8vo, 7s. 6d.

Müller (Dr. Julius)—THE CHRISTIAN DOCTRINE OF SIN. 2 vols. 8vo, 21s.

Murphy (Professor)—COMMENTARY ON THE PSALMS. 8vo, 12s.

———— A CRITICAL AND EXEGETICAL COMMENTARY ON EXODUS. 9s.

Naville (Ernest)—THE PROBLEM OF EVIL. Crown 8vo, 4s. 6d.

———— THE CHRIST. Translated by Rev. T. J. DESPRÉS. Cr. 8vo, 4s. 6d.

———— MODERN PHYSICS. Crown 8vo, 5s.

Neander (Dr.)—CHURCH HISTORY. Eight vols. 8vo, £2, 2s. net.

Nicoll (W. Robertson, M.A.., LL.D.)—THE INCARNATE SAVIOUR. Cheap Edition, price 3s. 6d.

Novalis—HYMNS AND THOUGHTS ON RELIGION. Crown 8vo, 4s.

Oehler (Prof.)—THEOLOGY OF THE OLD TESTAMENT. 2 vols. 8vo, 21s.

Olshausen (Dr. H.)—BIBLICAL COMMENTARY ON THE GOSPELS AND ACTS. Four vols. 8vo, £2, 2s. *Cheaper Edition*, four vols. crown 8vo, 24s.

———— ROMANS, one vol. 8vo, 10s. 6d. ; CORINTHIANS, one vol. 8vo, 9s. ; PHILIPPIANS, TITUS, AND FIRST TIMOTHY, one vol. 8vo, 10s. 6d.

Oosterzee (Dr. Van)—THE YEAR OF SALVATION. 2 vols. 8vo, 6s. each.

———— MOSES : A Biblical Study. Crown 8vo, 6s.

Orelli (Dr. C. von)—OLD TESTAMENT PROPHECY ; COMMENTARY ON ISAIAH ; JEREMIAH ; THE TWELVE MINOR PROPHETS. 4 vols. 8vo, 10s. 6d. each.

Owen (Dr. John)—WORKS. *Best and only Complete Edition.* Edited by Rev. Dr. GOOLD. Twenty-four vols. 8vo, Subscription price, £4, 4s. The '*Hebrews*' may be had separately, in seven vols., £2, 2s. net.

Philippi (F. A.)—COMMENTARY ON THE ROMANS. Two vols. 8vo, 21s.

Piper—LIVES OF LEADERS OF CHURCH UNIVERSAL. Two vols. 8vo, 21s.

Popular Commentary on the New Testament. Edited by PHILIP SCHAFF, D.D. With Illustrations and Maps. Vol. I.—THE SYNOPTICAL GOSPELS. Vol. II.—ST. JOHN'S GOSPEL, AND THE ACTS OF THE APOSTLES. Vol. III.—ROMANS TO PHILEMON. Vol. IV.—HEBREWS TO REVELATION. In four vols. imperial 8vo, 12s. 6d. each.

Plummer (Alfred, D.D.)—ST. LUKE. (*International Critical Commentary*). Post 8vo, 12s.

Pressensé (Edward de)—THE REDEEMER : Discourses. Crown 8vo, 6s.

Pünjer (Bernhard)—HISTORY OF THE CHRISTIAN PHILOSOPHY OF RELIGION FROM THE REFORMATION TO KANT. 8vo, 16s.

Räbiger (Prof.)—ENCYCLOPÆDIA OF THEOLOGY. Two vols. 8vo, 21s.

Rainy (Principal) — DELIVERY AND DEVELOPMENT OF CHRISTIAN DOCTRINE. 8vo, 10s. 6d.

Reusch (Prof.)—NATURE AND THE BIBLE : Lectures on the Mosaic History of Creation in Relation to Natural Science. Two vols. 8vo, 21s.

Reuss (Professor)—HISTORY OF THE SACRED SCRIPTURES OF THE NEW TESTAMENT. 640 pp. 8vo, 15s.

Riehm (Dr. E.)—MESSIANIC PROPHECY. New Edition. Post 8vo, 7s. 6d.

Ritter (Carl)—COMPARATIVE GEOGRAPHY OF PALESTINE. 4 vols. 8vo, 26s.

Robinson (Rev. S., D.D.)—DISCOURSES ON REDEMPTION. 8vo, 7s. 6d.

Robinson (E., D.D.)—GREEK AND ENG. LEXICON OF THE N. TEST. 8vo, 9s.

Rooke (T. G., B.A.)—INSPIRATION, and other Lectures. 8vo, 7s. 6d.

Ross (C.)—OUR FATHER'S KINGDOM. Crown 8vo, 2s. 6d.

Rothe (Prof.)—SERMONS FOR THE CHRISTIAN YEAR. Cr. 8vo, 4s. 6d.

Saisset—MANUAL OF MODERN PANTHEISM. Two vols. 8vo, 10s. 6d.

Salmond (Prof. S. D. F., D.D.)—THE CHRISTIAN DOCTRINE OF IMMORTALITY. 8vo, 14s.

Sanday (Prof. W., D.D.) and **Headlam (A. C., B.D.)**—ROMANS. (*International Critical Commentary.* Post 8vo, 12s.

Sartorius (Dr. E.)—DOCTRINE OF DIVINE LOVE. 8vo, 10s. 6d.

Schaff (Professor)—HISTORY OF THE CHRISTIAN CHURCH. (New Edition, thoroughly Revised and Enlarged.) Six 'Divisions,' in 2 vols. each, extra 8vo.

   1. APOSTOLIC CHRISTIANITY, A.D. 1–100, 2 vols. 21s. 2. ANTE-NICENE, A.D. 100–325, 2 vols., 21s. 3. NICENE AND POST-NICENE, A.D. 325–600, 2 vols., 21s. 4. MEDIÆVAL, A.D. 590–1073, 2 vols., 21s. (*Completion of this Period*, 1073–1517, *in preparation*). 5. THE SWISS REFORMATION, 2 vols., extra demy 8vo, 21s. 6. THE GERMAN REFORMATION, 2 vols., extra demy 8vo, 21s.

Schleiermacher's CHRISTMAS EVE. Crown 8vo, 2s.

Schmid's BIBLICAL THEOLOGY OF THE NEW TESTAMENT. 8vo, 10s. 6d.

Schubert (Prof. H. Von., D.D.)—THE GOSPEL OF ST. PETER. Synoptical Tables. With Translation and Critical Apparatus. 8vo, 1s. 6d. net.

Schultz (Hermann)—OLD TESTAMENT THEOLOGY. Two vols. 18s. net.

Schürer (Prof.)—HISTORY OF THE JEWISH PEOPLE. 5 vols. 8vo, 52/6.

Schwartzkopff (Dr. P.)—THE PROPHECIES OF JESUS CHRIST. Crown 8vo, 5s.

Scott (Jas., M.A., D.D.)—PRINCIPLES OF NEW TESTAMENT QUOTATION ESTABLISHED AND APPLIED TO BIBLICAL CRITICISM. Cr. 8vo, 2nd Edit., 4s.

Sell (K., D.D.)—THE CHURCH IN THE MIRROR OF HISTORY. Cr. 8vo, 3/6.

Shedd—HISTORY OF CHRISTIAN DOCTRINE. Two vols. 8vo, 21s.

———— SERMONS TO THE NATURAL MAN. 8vo, 7s. 6d.

———— SERMONS TO THE SPIRITUAL MAN. 8vo, 7s. 6d.

———— DOGMATIC THEOLOGY. Three vols. ex. 8vo, 12s. 6d. each.

Simon (Prof.)—THE BIBLE; An Outgrowth of Theocratic Life. Cr. 8vo, 4/6.

———— THE REDEMPTION OF MAN. 8vo, 10s. 6d.

Skene-Bickell—THE LORD'S SUPPER & THE PASSOVER RITUAL. 8vo, 5s.

Smeaton (Professor)—DOCTRINE OF THE HOLY SPIRIT. 2nd Ed., 8vo, 9s.

Smith (Professor Thos., D.D.)—MEDIÆVAL MISSIONS. Cr. 8vo, 4s. 6d.

Smyth (Newman, D.D.)—CHRISTIAN ETHICS. (*International Theological Library*). Post 8vo, 10s. 6d.

Somerville (Rev. D., M.A.)—ST. PAUL'S CONCEPTION OF CHRIST. 9s.

Stählin (Leonh.)—KANT, LOTZE, AND RITSCHL. 8vo, 9s.

Stalker (Jas., D.D.)—LIFE OF CHRIST. Large Type Ed., cr. 8vo, 3s. 6d.

———— LIFE OF ST. PAUL. Large Type Edition, crown 8vo, 3s. 6d.

Stanton (V. H., D.D.)—THE JEWISH AND THE CHRISTIAN MESSIAH. A Study in the Earliest History of Christianity. 8vo, 10s. 6d.

Stead (F. H.)—THE KINGDOM OF GOD. 1s. 6d.

Steinmeyer (Dr. F. L.)—THE MIRACLES OF OUR LORD. 8vo, 7s. 6d.

Steinmeyer (Dr. F. L.)—THE HISTORY OF THE PASSION AND RESURRECTION OF OUR LORD, considered in the Light of Modern Criticism. 8vo, 10s. 6d.

Stevenson (Mrs.)—THE SYMBOLIC PARABLES. Crown 8vo, 3s. 6d.

Steward (Rev. G.)—MEDIATORIAL SOVEREIGNTY. Two vols. 8vo, 21s.

———— THE ARGUMENT OF THE EPISTLE TO THE HEBREWS. 8vo, 10s. 6d.

Stier (Dr. Rudolph)—ON THE WORDS OF THE LORD JESUS. Eight vols. 8vo, Subscription price of £2, 2s. Separate volumes, price 10s. 6d.

———— THE WORDS OF THE RISEN SAVIOUR, AND COMMENTARY ON THE EPISTLE OF ST. JAMES. 8vo, 10s. 6d.

———— THE WORDS OF THE APOSTLES EXPOUNDED. 8vo, 10s. 6d.

Stirling (Dr. J. Hutchison)—PHILOSOPHY AND THEOLOGY. Post 8vo, 9s.

———— DARWINIANISM: Workmen and Work. Post 8vo, 10s. 6d.

Tholuck (Prof.)—THE EPISTLE TO THE ROMANS. Two vols. fcap. 8vo, 8s.

Thomson (J. E. H., B.D.)—BOOKS WHICH INFLUENCED OUR LORD AND HIS APOSTLES. 8vo, 10s. 6d.

Thomson (Rev. E. A.)—MEMORIALS OF A MINISTRY. Crown 8vo, 5s.

Tophel (Pastor G.)—THE WORK OF THE HOLY SPIRIT. Cr. 8vo, 2s. 6d.

Troup (Rev. G. Elmslie, M.A.)—WORDS TO YOUNG CHRISTIANS: Being Addresses to Young Communicants. On antique laid paper, chaste binding, fcap. 8vo, 4s. 6d.

Trumbull (H. Clay, D.D.)—THE THRESHOLD COVENANT. Post 8vo, 6s. 6d.

Uhlhorn (G.)—CHRISTIAN CHARITY IN THE ANCIENT CHURCH. Cr. 8vo, 6s.

Ullmann (Dr. Carl)—REFORMERS BEFORE THE REFORMATION, principally in Germany and the Netherlands. Two vols. 8vo, 21s.

Urwick (W., M.A.)—THE SERVANT OF JEHOVAH: A Commentary upon Isaiah lii. 13–liii. 12; with Dissertations upon Isaiah xl.–lxvi. 8vo, 3s.

Vinet (Life and Writings of). By L. M. LANE. Crown 8vo, 7s. 6d.

Vincent (Prof. M. R., D.D.)—THE AGE OF HILDEBRAND. (*Eras of Church History.*) 6s.

———— PHILIPPIANS AND PHILEMON. (*International Critical Commentary.*) Post 8vo, 8s. 6d.

Walker (J., D.D.)—THEOLOGY AND THEOLOGIANS OF SCOTLAND. New Edition, crown 8vo, 3s. 6d.

Warfield (B.B.)—THE RIGHT OF SYSTEMATIC THEOLOGY. Crown 8vo, 2s.

Watt (W. A.)—THE THEORY OF CONTRACT IN ITS SOCIAL LIGHT. 8vo, 3s.

Watts (Professor)—THE NEWER CRITICISM AND THE ANALOGY OF THE FAITH. Third Edition, crown 8vo, 5s.

———— THE REIGN OF CAUSALITY: A Vindication of the Scientific Principle of Telic Causal Efficiency. Crown 8vo, 6s.

———— THE NEW APOLOGETIC. Crown 8vo, 6s.

Weir (J. F., M.A.)—THE WAY: THE NATURE AND MEANS OF SALVATION. Ex. crown 8vo, 6s. 6d.

Weiss (Prof.)—BIBLICAL THEOLOGY OF NEW TESTAMENT. 2 vols. 8vo, 21s.

———— LIFE OF CHRIST. Three vols. 8vo, 31s. 6d.

Wendt (H. H., D.D.)—THE TEACHING OF JESUS. 2 vols. 8vo, 21s.

Wenley (R. M.)—CONTEMPORARY THEOLOGY AND THEISM. Crown 8vo, 4s. 6d.

White (Rev. M.)—SYMBOLICAL NUMBERS OF SCRIPTURE. Cr. 8vo, 4s.

Williams (E. F., D.D.)—CHRISTIAN LIFE IN GERMANY. Crown 8vo, 4s.

Winer (Dr. G. B.)—A TREATISE ON THE GRAMMAR OF NEW TESTAMENT GREEK, regarded as the Basis of New Testament Exegesis. Third Edition, edited by W. F. MOULTON, D.D. Ninth English Edition, 8vo, 15s.

———— THE DOCTRINES AND CONFESSIONS OF CHRISTENDOM. 8vo, 10s. 6d.

Witherow (Prof. T., D.D.)—THE FORM OF THE CHRISTIAN TEMPLE. 8vo, 10/6.

Woods (F. H., B.D.)—THE HOPE OF ISRAEL. Crown 8vo, 3s. 6d.

Workman (Prof. G. C.)—THE TEXT OF JEREMIAH; or, A Critical Investigation of the Greek and Hebrew, etc. Post 8vo, 9s.

Wright (C. H., D.D.)—BIBLICAL ESSAYS. Crown 8vo, 5s.

THE FOREIGN THEOLOGICAL LIBRARY.

The following are the Works from which a Selection of EIGHT VOLUMES for £2, 2s. (or more at the same ratio) may be made. (Non-subscription Price within brackets):—

Baumgarten—The History of the Church in the Apostolic Age. Three Vols   (27s.)
Bleek—Introduction to the New Testament. Two Vols. (21s.)
Cassel—Commentary on Esther. One Vol. (10s. 6d.)
Christlieb—Modern Doubt and Christian Belief. One Vol. (10s. 6d.)
Delitzsch—New Commentary on Genesis. Two Vols. (21s.)
—— Commentary on the Psalms. Three Vols. (31s. 6d.)
—— Commentary on the Proverbs of Solomon. Two Vols. (21s.)
—— Commentary on Song of Solomon and Ecclesiastes. One Vol. (10s. 6d.)
—— Commentary on the Prophecies of Isaiah. *Last Edition.* Two Vols. (21s.)
—— Commentary on Epistle to the Hebrews. Two Vols (21s.)
—— A System of Biblical Psychology. One Vol. (12s.)
Döllinger—Hippolytus and Callistus; or, The Church of Rome: A.D. 200-250. One Vol. (7s. 6d.)
Dorner—A System of Christian Doctrine. Four Vols. (42s.)
—— History of the Development of the Doctrine of the Person of Christ. Five Vols. (52s. 6d.)
Ebrard—Commentary on the Epistles of St. John. One Vol. (10s. 6d.)
—— The Gospel History. One Vol. (10s. 6d.)   Apologetics. Three Vols. (31s. 6d.)
Ewald—Revelation : Its Nature and Record. One Vol. (10s. 6d.)
—— Old and New Testament Theology. One Vol. (10s. 6d.)
Frank—System of Christian Certainty. One Vol. (10s. 6d.)
Gebhardt—Doctrine of the Apocalypse. One Vol. (10s. 6d.)
Gerlach—Commentary on the Pentateuch. One Vol. (10s. 6d.)
Gieseler—Compendium of Ecclesiastical History : A.D. 451-1409. Three Vols. (31s. 6d.)
Godet—Commentary on St. Luke's Gospel. Two Vols. (21s.)
—— Commentary on St. John's Gospel. Three Vols. (31s. 6d.)
—— Commentary on the Epistle to the Romans. Two Vols. (21s.)
—— Commentary on 1st Corinthians. Two Vols. (21s.)
Goebel—On the Parables. One Vol. (10s. 6d.)
Hagenbach—History of the Reformation. Two Vols. (21s.)
—— History of Christian Doctrines. Three Vols. (31s. 6d.)
Harless—A System of Christian Ethics. One Vol. (10s. 6d.)
Haupt—Commentary on the First Epistle of St. John. One Vol. (10s. 6d.)
Hävernick—General Introduction to the Old Testament. One Vol. (10s. 6d.)
Hengstenberg—Christology of the Old Testament. Four Vols. (42s.)
—— Commentary on the Psalms. Three Vols. (33s.)
—— On the Book of Ecclesiastes, etc. etc. One Vol. (9s.)
—— Commentary on the Gospel of St. John. Two Vols. (21s.)
—— Commentary on Ezekiel. One Vol. (10s. 6d.)
—— Dissertations on the Genuineness of Daniel, etc. One Vol. (12s.)
—— The Kingdom of God under the Old Covenant. Two Vols. (21s.)
Keil—Introduction to the Old Testament. Two Vols. (21s.)
—— Commentary on the Pentateuch. Three Vols. (31s. 6d.)
—— Commentary on Joshua, Judges, and Ruth. One Vol. (10s. 6d.)
—— Commentary on the Books of Samuel. One Vol. (10s. 6d.)
—— Commentary on the Books of Kings. One Vol. (10s. 6d.)
—— Commentary on the Books of Chronicles. One Vol. (10s. 6d.)
—— Commentary on Ezra, Nehemiah, and Esther. One Vol. (10s. 6d.)
—— Commentary on Jeremiah and Lamentations. Two Vols. (21s.)
—— Commentary on Ezekiel. Two Vols. (21s.)   Book of Daniel. One Vol. (10s. 6d.)
—— Commentary on the Minor Prophets. Two Vols. (21s.)
—— Biblical Archæology. Two Vols. (21s.)
Kurtz—History of the Old Covenant; or, Old Testament Dispensation. Three Vols. (31s. 6d.)
Lange—Commentary on the Gospels of St. Matthew and St. Mark. Three Vols. (31s. 6d.)
—— Commentary on the Gospel of St. Luke. Two Vols. (18s.)   St. John. Two Vols. (21s.)
Luthardt—Commentary on the Gospel of St. John. Three Vols. (31s. 6d.)
—— History of Christian Ethics to the Reformation. One Vol. (10s. 6d.)
Macdonald—Introduction to the Pentateuch. Two Vols. (21s.)
Martensen—Christian Dogmatics. One Vol. (10s. 6d.)
—— Christian Ethics. General—Social—Individual. Three Vols. (31s. 6d.)
Müller—The Christian Doctrine of Sin. Two Vols. (21s.)
Murphy—Commentary on the Psalms. *To count as Two Volumes.* One Vol. (12s.)
Neander—General History of the Christian Religion and Church. Vols. I. to VIII. (60s.)
Oehler—Biblical Theology of the Old Testament. Two Vols. (21s.)
Olshausen—Commentary on the Gospels and Acts. Four Vols. (42s.)
—— Commentary on Epistle to the Romans. One Vol. (10s. 6d.)   Corinthians. One Vol (9s.)
—— Commentary on Philippians, Titus, and 1st Timothy. One Vol. (10s. 6d.)
Orelli—Prophecy regarding Consummation of God's Kingdom. One Vol. (10s. 6d.)
—— Commentary on Isaiah. One Vol. (10s. 6d.)   Jeremiah. One Vol. (10s. 6d.)
Philippi—Commentary on Epistle to Romans. Two Vols. (21s.)
Räbiger—Encyclopædia of Theology. Two Vols. (21s.)
Ritter—Comparative Geography of Palestine. Four Vols. (26s.)
Sartorius—The Doctrine of Divine Love. One Vol. (10s. 6d.)
Schürer—The Jewish People in the Time of Christ. Five Vols. (10s. 6d. each.)
Shedd—History of Christian Doctrine. Two Vols. (21s.)
Steinmeyer—History of the Passion and Resurrection of our Lord. One Vol. (10s. 6d.)
—— The Miracles of our Lord in relation to Modern Criticism. One Vol (7s. 6d.)
Stier—The Words of the Lord Jesus. Eight Vols. (10s. 6d. per vol.)
—— The Words of the Risen Saviour, and Commentary on Epistle of St. James. One Vol. (10s. 6d.)
—— The Words of the Apostles Expounded. One Vol. (10s. 6d.)
Ullmann—Reformers before the Reformation. Two Vols. (21s.)
Weiss—Biblical Theology of the New Testament. 2 Vols. (21s.) The Life of Christ. 3 Vols. (31s. 6d.)
Winer—Collection of the Confessions of Christendom. One Vol. (10s. 6d.)

THE INTERNATIONAL THEOLOGICAL LIBRARY.

THE following eminent Scholars have contributed, or are engaged upon, the Volumes named :—

An Introduction to the Literature of the Old Testament.
By S. R. DRIVER, D.D., Regius Professor of Hebrew, and Canon of Christ Church, Oxford.   [*Sixth Edition.*

Christian Ethics.
By NEWMAN SMYTH, D.D., Pastor of the First Congregational Church, New Haven, Conn.   [*Third Edition.*

Apologetics.
By A. B. BRUCE, D.D., Professor of New Testament Exegesis, Free Church College, Glasgow.   [*Third Edition.*

History of Christian Doctrine.
By G. P. FISHER, D.D., LL.D., Professor of Ecclesiastical History, Yale University, New Haven, Conn.   [*Second Edition.*

A History of Christianity in the Apostolic Age.
By ARTHUR CUSHMAN McGIFFERT, Ph.D., D.D., Professor of Church History, Union Theological Seminary, New York.   [*Just published.*

Christian Institutions.
By A. V. G. ALLEN, D.D., Professor of Ecclesiastical History, Episcopal Theological School, Cambridge, Mass.   [*Just published.*

Theology of the Old Testament.
By A. B. DAVIDSON, D.D., LL.D., Professor of Hebrew, New College, Edinburgh.

An Introduction to the Literature of the New Testament.
By S. D. F. SALMOND, D.D. Professor of Systematic Theology and New Testament Exegesis, Free Church College, Aberdeen.

Old Testament History.
By H. P. SMITH, D.D., late Professor of Hebrew, Lane Theological Seminary, Cincinnati, Ohio.

Theology of the New Testament.
By GEORGE B. STEVENS, Ph.D., D.D., Professor of New Testament Criticism and Interpretation in Yale University, U.S.A.

The Christian Pastor.
By WASHINGTON GLADDEN, D.D., Pastor of Congregational Church, Columbus, Ohio.

Canon and Text of the New Testament.
By CASPAR RENÉ GREGORY, Ph.D., Professor in the University of Leipzig.

The Latin Church.
By ARCHIBALD ROBERTSON, D.D., Principal of King's College, London.

The Ancient Catholic Church.
By ROBERT RAINY, D.D., Principal of the New College, Edinburgh.

Encyclopædia.
By C. A. BRIGGS, D.D., Professor of Biblical Theology, Union Theological Seminary, New York.

Contemporary History of the Old Testament.
By FRANCIS BROWN, D.D., Professor of Hebrew and Cognate Languages, Union Theological Seminary, New York.

Contemporary History of the New Testament.
By FRANK C. PORTER, Ph.D., Yale University, New Haven, Conn.

Philosophy of Religion.
By ROBERT FLINT, D.D., LL.D., Professor of Divinity in the University of Edinburgh.

The Study of the Old Testament.
By HERBERT E. RYLE, D.D., President of Queens' College, Cambridge.

Rabbinical Literature.
By S. SCHECHTER, M.A., Reader in Talmudic in the University of Cambridge.

The Life of Christ.
By WILLIAM SANDAY, D.D., LL.D., Lady Margaret Professor of Divinity, and Canon of Christ Church, Oxford.

EDINBURGH: T. & T. CLARK, 38 GEORGE STREET.

THE INTERNATIONAL CRITICAL COMMENTARY.

SEVEN VOLUMES NOW READY, VIZ.:—

Deuteronomy, Judges, S. Mark, S. Luke, Romans, Ephesians and Colossians, Philippians and Philemon.

THE following other Volumes are in course of preparation:—

THE OLD TESTAMENT.

Genesis.	T. K. CHEYNE, D.D., Oriel Professor of the Interpretation of Holy Scripture, Oxford.
Exodus.	A. R. S. KENNEDY, D.D., Professor of Hebrew, University of Edinburgh.
Leviticus.	Rev. H. A. WHITE, M.A., Fellow of New College, Oxford, and Theological Tutor in the University of Durham.
Numbers.	G. BUCHANAN GRAY, M.A., Lecturer in Hebrew, Mansfield College, Oxford.
Joshua.	GEORGE ADAM SMITH, D.D., Professor of Hebrew, Free Church College, Glasgow.
Samuel.	H. P. SMITH, D.D., late Professor of Hebrew, Lane Theological Seminary, Cincinnati, Ohio.
Kings.	FRANCIS BROWN, D.D., Professor of Hebrew and Cognate Languages, Union Theological Seminary, New York.
Isaiah.	A. B. DAVIDSON, D.D., LL.D., Professor of Hebrew, Free Church College, Edinburgh.
Jeremiah.	A. F. KIRKPATRICK, D.D., Regius Professor of Hebrew, and Fellow of Trinity College, Cambridge.
Minor Prophets.	W. R. HARPER, Ph.D., President of Chicago University.
Psalms.	C. A. BRIGGS, D.D., Edward Robinson Professor of Biblical Theology, Union Theological Seminary, New York.
Proverbs.	C. H. TOY, D.D., Professor of Hebrew, Harvard University, Cambridge, Massachusetts.
Job.	S. R. DRIVER, D.D., Regius Professor of Hebrew, Oxford.
Daniel.	Rev. JOHN P. PETERS, Ph.D., late Professor of Hebrew, P. E. Divinity School, Philadelphia, now Rector of St. Michael's Church, New York City.
Ezra and Nehemiah.	Rev. L. W. BATTEN, Ph.D., Professor of Hebrew, P. E. Divinity School, Philadelphia.
Chronicles.	EDWARD L. CURTIS, D.D., Professor of Hebrew, Yale University, New Haven, Conn.

THE NEW TESTAMENT.

Acts.	FREDERICK H. CHASE, D.D., Christ's College, Cambridge.
Corinthians.	ARCH. ROBERTSON, D.D., Principal of King's College, London.
Galatians.	Rev. ERNEST D. BURTON, A.B., Professor of New Testament Literature, University of Chicago.
The Pastoral Epistles.	Rev. WALTER LOCK, M.A., Dean Ireland's Professor of Exegesis, Oxford.
Hebrews.	T. C. EDWARDS, D.D., Principal of the Theological College, Bala; late Principal of University College of Wales, Aberystwyth.
James.	Rev. JAMES H. ROPES, A.B., Instructor in New Testament Criticism in Harvard University.
Peter and Jude.	CHARLES BIGG, D.D., Rector of Fenny Compton, Leamington; Bampton Lecturer, 1886.
Revelation.	Rev. ROBERT H. CHARLES, M.A., Trinity College, Dublin, and Exeter College, Oxford.

Other engagements will be announced shortly.

EDINBURGH: T. & T. CLARK, 38 GEORGE STREET.

LONDON: SIMPKIN, MARSHALL, HAMILTON, KENT, & CO. LTD

THE NEW
DICTIONARY OF THE BIBLE.

EDITED BY

Rev. JAMES HASTINGS, M.A., D.D.,

EDITOR OF 'THE EXPOSITORY TIMES.'

Messrs. T. & T. CLARK have pleasure in announcing this important Work. The need of a comprehensive Dictionary, recording the results of present-day scholarship, is keenly felt. The new Dictionary will seek to cover the whole range of Bible knowledge, including Biblical Theology. The Editor is being assisted by Specialists in the oversight of the various departments.

The Contributors include the following well-known scholars:— Professors S. R. DRIVER, W. SANDAY, G. A. SMITH, A. B. DAVIDSON, F. BROWN, J. A. ROBINSON, W. LOCK, G. G. FINDLAY, W. T. DAVISON, A. B. BRUCE, W. H. BENNETT, R. FLINT, D. S. MARGOLIOUTH, H. E. RYLE, S. D. F. SALMOND, W. MAX MÜLLER, FLINDERS PETRIE, W. M. RAMSAY, H. M. GWATKIN, MARCUS DODS, RENDEL HARRIS, V. H. STANTON, J. DENNEY, A. MACALISTER, J. T. MARSHALL, J. ORR, FR. HOMMEL, W. G. H. NOWACK, K. BUDDE, H. STRACK, W. W. BAUDISSIN, J. H. THAYER, B. B. WARFIELD, O. C. WHITEHOUSE, A. STEWART, H. B. SWETE, A. H. SAYCE, Sir CHARLES WARREN, Sir C. W. WILSON, Lt.-Col. CONDER, Dr. GEORGE E. POST, Mr. T. G. PINCHES, The Very Rev. Dean FARRAR, Principal OTTLEY, Principal CHASE, Dr. MOULTON, and others.

It is expected that the Work will be completed in Four Volumes of about 900 pp. each. The First Volume is now in type, and Messrs. CLARK hope to issue it in February 1898. Full particulars, together with a Prospectus of the Work, will be sent to all who desire information about the Dictionary.

EDINBURGH: T. & T. CLARK, 38 GEORGE STREET.